8/2023
STRAND PRICE
$5.00

DI064175

Third Force Psychology and the Study of Literature

Third Force Psychology and the Study of Literature

Edited and with an introduction
by *Bernard J. Paris*

Rutherford • Madison • Teaneck
Fairleigh Dickinson University Press
London and Toronto: Associated University Presses

Associated University Presses
440 Forsgate Drive
Cranbury, NJ 08512

Associated University Presses
25 Sicilian Avenue
London WC1A 2QH, England

Associated University Presses
2133 Royal Windsor Drive
Unit 1
Mississauga, Ontario
Canada L5J 1K5

The paper used in this publication meets the requirements of the American National Standard for Permanence of Paper for Printed Library Materials Z39.48-1984.

Library of Congress Cataloging-in-Publication Data
Main entry under title:

Third force psychology and the study of literature.

Bibliography: p.
Includes index.
1. Literature and psychology—Addresses, essays, lectures. 2. English literature—History and criticism—Addresses, essays, lectures. 3. American fiction—20th century—History and criticism—Addresses, essays, lectures. 4. Maslow, Abraham Harold—Influence—Addresses, essays, lectures. 5. Horney, Karen, 1885–1952—Influence—Addresses, essays, lectures. 6. Characters and characteristics in literature—Addresses, essays, lectures. 7. Social psychology in literature—Addresses, essays, lectures. I. Paris, Bernard J.

PR408.P83T48 1986 801′.95 85-47629
ISBN 0-8386-3263-7 (alk. paper)

Printed in the United States of America

For Alan Hollingsworth

Contents

Acknowledgments

This collection began as a special issue of *The Literary Review* (vol. 24, no. 2) devoted to Third Force psychology and the study of literature. I wish to thank Harry Keyishian for inviting me to guest edit that issue and for his support of this volume at every stage. I also wish to thank the Division of Sponsored Research of the University of Florida for grants that have speeded the completion of this volume and Catherine Lewis for her excellent research assistance and careful preparation of the index. Her contribution to this project has been a major one. My gratitude to Alan Hollingsworth for his unfailing encouragement over the past eighteen years is expressed by the dedication.

Copyrighted material has been quoted from the following works:

Saul Bellow, *Herzog*, copyright 1961, 1963, 1964, by Saul Bellow. The Viking Press. Reprinted by permission of the publisher.

Robert Bolt, *A Man for All Seasons*, copyright 1960, 1962, by Robert Bolt. Random House. Reprinted by permission of the publisher.

Karen Horney, *Neurosis and Human Growth*, copyright 1950, by W. W. Norton and Company, Inc. Reprinted by permission of the publisher.

Karen Horney, *Our Inner Conflicts*, copyright 1945, by W. W. Norton and Company, Inc. Reprinted by permission of the publisher.

Abraham Maslow, *Toward a Psychology of Being*, copyright 1962, by D. Van Nostrand Company, Inc.

Bernard J. Paris, *A Psychological Approach to Fiction*, copyright 1974, Indiana University Press, 1983, Bernard J. Paris. Indiana University Press. Reprinted by permission of the author.

The following essays in this volume were originally published in *The Literary Review* 24 (1981), and are reprinted here, in revised form, with the kind permission of the editors of that journal:

Karen Ann Butery, "Jane Eyre's Flights from Decision."

Patricia R. Eldredge, "The Lost Self of Esther Summerson: A Horneyan Interpretation of *Bleak House*."

Marjorie B. Haselswerdt, "I'd Rather Be Ratliff: A Maslovian Study of Faulkner's *Snopes*."

Bernard J. Paris, "Third Force Psychology and the Study of Literature, Biography, Criticism, and Culture." The present version of the above essay contains an analysis of *Herzog* most of which originally appeared in "Herzog the

Man: An Analytic View of a Literary Figure," *American Journal of Psychoanalysis* 36 (1976), and which is reprinted here with the kind permission of the editors of that journal.

Norman Friedman's essay, "Psychology and Literary Form: Toward a Unified Approach," first appeared in *The Psychocultural Review* 2 (1978), and is reprinted here, in revised form, with the kind permission of the publishers of that journal.

Introduction

Bernard J. Paris

For many readers, the title of this book may raise the questions, what is Third Force psychology and why should it be used in the study of literature? These questions are answered at length in the essays that comprise this volume; but for purposes of orientation, I shall provide some brief answers here.

The term "Third Force" was introduced by Abraham Maslow in 1962 in the preface of *Toward a Psychology of Being:* "The two comprehensive theories of human nature most influencing psychology until recently have been the Freudian and the experimental-positivistic-behavioristic. All other theories were less comprehensive and their adherents formed many splinter groups. In the last few years, however, these various groups have rapidly been coalescing into a third, increasingly comprehensive theory of human nature, into what might be called a 'Third Force.'"[1] Maslow includes these groups in the Third Force: Adlerians; Rankians; Jungians; neo-Freudians; such post-Freudians as Wheelis, Marmor, Szasz, and Schachtel; Kurt Goldstein; Gestalt therapists; such personality psychologists as Allport, Murphy, Moreno, and Murray; Self-psychologists; phenomenological psychologists; growth-psychologists; Rogerian psychologists; and humanistic psychologists. Indeed, the term "humanistic psychology" is often used interchangeably with "Third Force."

Third Force psychology is, then, a group of theories that offers a comprehensive view of human nature distinct from that of Freudians and behaviorists. It builds upon "the available *data* of experimental psychology and psychoanalysis," accepting "the empirical and experimental spirit of the one, and the unmasking and depth-probing of the other"; but it rejects "the *images* of man which they generated."[2] It presents "a different philosophy of human nature" (p. x). The difference in philosophy has been defined in a number of ways—greater optimism, a more holistic approach to human behavior, a richer array of inherent needs and values; but the crucial difference, it seems to me, is the contention that man is not simply a tension-reducing or a conditioned animal, but that there is present in him a third force, an "evolutionary constructive" force, which urges "him to realize his given potentialities."[3] Each person has an intrinsic nature that it is his object in life to fulfill. The "single ultimate value for mankind," the "far goal toward which all men strive," has been "called variously by different authors self-actualization, self-realization, integration, psychological health, individuation, autonomy, creativity," and "productivity" (*PB*, p. 145). Though they use different terms, all Third Force psychologists agree that the highest value for a human being is to realize his potentialities, to become "fully human," everything he "*can* become" (*PB*, p. 145).

It is Abraham Maslow, more than any other Third Force psychologist, who has attempted to determine what human beings require if they are to actualize their potentialities—or, to use the term he borrowed from Karen Horney, their "real selves." We have, according to Maslow, a number of basic needs, arranged in a hierarchy of prepotency, which must be gratified if we are to achieve full psychological development. These are, in order of decreasing strength, physiological, safety, love and belonging, and esteem needs, and, at the top of the hierarchy, the need for self-actualization, for the fulfillment of our unique potentialities. Maslow includes aesthetic needs and needs for knowledge and understanding among our basic requirements, but he does not integrate them into his hierarchy. If our basic needs are reasonably well gratified, we remain in touch with our real thoughts, feelings, and interests, and we find our own course. If they are frustrated, we develop various defensive strategies that are designed to compensate for our deprivation, and we are motivated by them rather than by our genuine desires. According to Third Force psychology, then, human beings develop in either a self-actualizing or a self-alienated way, or in some combination of both, depending upon the degree to which their basic needs are gratified.

Maslow includes a great many theorists within the Third Force group, but so far only a few have proved to be of value in the study of literature. The most useful theories have been those of Horney and Maslow. It is Maslow who offers the best study of psychological growth and healthy values and Horney who provides the most comprehensive account of the defensive strategies that arise in the course of self-alienated development. Since fictional characters and their creators are more frequently self-alienated than self-actualizing, it is Horney's theory that is most useful for the study of literature. Maslow is important, however. He has synthesized the findings of many other workers, and he is the leading spokesman for Third Force psychology as a whole. In the opening essay of this volume, I shall present its basic ideas about human nature, human values, and the human condition largely through his vocabulary. In the essays that follow, Horney is used by Paris, Butery, Eldredge, Lewis, Smalley, Haselswerdt, Straub, and Huffman; and Maslow is used by Paris, Smalley, Straub, and Haselswerdt. Other Third Force psychologists are employed as well. Erich Fromm is used by Straub and Nelson, Carl Rogers and R. D. Laing by Smalley, Fritz Perls by Friedman, and Marvin Daniels by Gordon. The theories of Fromm, Perls, and Daniels are expounded in the essays that employ them, while those using Horney and Maslow rely, in part at least, upon the exposition of their theories in the opening essay.

Having identified Third Force psychology, I have still to explain why it should be used in the study of literature. The simplest answer, I suppose, is that it explains some things, for some people, better than any other theory. I do not feel that this or any other psychology can explain all things to all people. Theories appeal to us because they are congruent at once with the phenomena we are trying to understand and our own premises, temperaments, and modes of explanation. Different psychological theories focus upon different kinds of phenomena and appeal to different kinds of people. There are some literary phenomena that seem especially suited to Third Force analysis, while others are best approached from other perspectives. Each theory is better at explaining some things than others and is best used by those who have a genuine feeling for it in the study of phenomena with which it is highly congruent.

Those of us who have contributed to this volume use Third Force psychology because it talks about things that interest us in ways that make sense to us, and our essays will have their strongest appeal to those who share our interests and premises. I hope that they will also interest readers who favor other perspectives. It is possible to use the insights that an empirically based theory can yield even when we do not subscribe to all of its premises or its metapsychological speculations. There is a special value, moreover, in perspectives that are different from our own. As John Stuart Mill observes in his essay on Bentham, we all have our "peculiar biasses—[our] peculiar faculties for perceiving some things, and for missing or forgetting others."[4] Because of this, we need "to fortify the weak side" of our intellect by studying "the modes of thought most opposite to our own"; for "it is there that [we] will find the experiences denied to [ourselves]; the remainder of the truth of which [we see] but half."

There are a number of literary phenomena that a Third Force perspective can help us to understand. One of these is realistic characterization. Not all literary characters are appropriate objects of psychological analysis. Many must be understood primarily in terms of their formal and thematic functions in the artistic whole of which they are a part. Some are so highly individualized, however, that they have an internal motivational system. These "round" or "mimetic" characters are described by E. M. Forster as "creations inside a creation."[5] They have their functions within the larger creation, but they are inwardly intelligible as well, and their behavior can be understood in psychological terms. The study of such characters is one of the least developed areas of literary criticism, in large part because we have lacked a conceptual system that would permit us to see and to talk about them in detail. For many characters, Karen Horney's theory supplies this deficiency. Her theory helps us to make sense of the often unusual behavior of these characters and to see them, however remote their period or culture, as human beings who are very much like ourselves. It enhances our appreciation of the authors' achievements, since it permits us to recover their psychological intuitions and to do justice, perhaps for the first time, to their genius in mimetic characterization.

The most commonly used theory for character study has been Freudian psychoanalysis, but this theory, as some of its leading practitioners have argued, is ill-suited for the study of mimetic characterization. The chief weakness of psychoanalytic studies of character has been their use of a diachronic mode of analysis that explains the present in terms of the past. Because of their reliance upon infantile experience to account for the behavior of the adult, they must often posit events in the character's early life that are not depicted in the text. This results in the generation of crucial explanatory material out of the premises of the theory, with no corroborating literary evidence except the supposed results of the invented experiences, which were inferred from these results to begin with. This procedure has resulted in a justifiable distrust of the psychological study of character. Because of its emphasis upon infantile origins, psychoanalysis has, ironically, made literary characters seem less accessible to motivational analysis than they did in pre-Freudian days.

Meredith Skura argues, indeed, that because psychoanalysis "locates a source for behavior in something besides current experience," "we have no basis for psychoanalyzing" literary characters.[6] The poet and the analyst both ask about "a character's unacknowledged motives," but "unlike the poet, [the analyst] traces these back to other thoughts, other experiences, other contexts, which give rise to the motives and give them their only meaning" (p. 39). Since these other thoughts, experiences, and contexts are not present in the literary work, they cannot be evoked to explain the character's current behavior. The "reality" of a literary character "does not include the kind of unconscious experience on which an analysis is based" (p. 38). If we presuppose or invent such unconscious experience in order to make analysis possible, we are no longer constrained by the text: "If purely unconscious motives *are* there, they are hard to locate: Is Brutus unconsciously killing his father when he kills Caesar? There is no room for these motives in the fully explained world of the play; or, rather, there is room for too many of them" (p. 40). If we are psychoanalyzing a real person, we have ways of determining which of a whole range of possible unconscious motives are actually involved in his behavior; but there is no way of doing this with a literary character. "It is only in the psychoanalytic process," says Skura, "that characters, and people, can be psychoanalyzed" (p. 38); and since characters cannot enter into that process, they cannot be analyzed.

I think that Skura has made a powerful case against the use of the Freudian paradigm for analyzing literary characters; but I do not conclude with her that characters cannot, therefore, be understood in motivational terms. She is driven to this conclusion because her "conventions for analyzing behavior in life" (p. 41) are not applicable to literary characters, but hers are not the only conventions. Although Horney, like Freud, sees psychological problems as beginning in early childhood, she does not see the adult as simply repeating earlier patterns; and she does not explain his behavior through analogies with childhood experience. Once the child begins to adopt defensive strategies, his particular system develops under the influence of external factors, which encourage some strategies and discourage others, and of internal necessities, whereby each defensive move requires others in order to maintain its viability.

The character structure of the adult has its origins in early childhood, but it is also the product of a complicated evolutionary history, and it can be understood in terms of the present constellation of defenses. Horney's theory has, then, a diachronic component; but it is primarily a synchronic theory that enables us to understand the present structure of the psyche as an inwardly intelligible system and to explain behavior in terms of its function within that system. Skura's conventions for analyzing behavior involve tracing motives "back to other thoughts, other experiences, other contexts, which give rise to the motives and give them their only meaning" (p. 39). This approach supplies one kind of meaning, but by no means the only kind. An individual's motives are meaningful also when we understand them synchronically, in terms of their function within his present system of defense. Such an approach is highly suitable for the analysis of literary characters, since we are often supplied with ample information about their existing personality structures. It permits us to account for the characters' thoughts, feelings, and actions on the basis of what has actually been given in the text. If childhood material is present it can be used, but if it is absent it need not be invented.

In the essays that follow, there is an extensive array of character analyses, most of which are conducted from a Horneyan perspective. These include analyses of Jane Eyre (Butery), Esther Summerson (Eldredge), Guido Franceschini (Lewis), Dollie Urquhart (Smalley), Joe Christmas (Haselswerdt), Moses Herzog (Paris), Nat Turner (Huffman), and the priest in Greene's *The Power and the Glory* (Straub). Bolt's Sir Thomas More (Paris) and Faulkner's V. K. Ratliff (Haselswerdt) are discussed in terms of Maslovian theory, the narrator of "Locksley Hall" is analyzed from the perspective of Fritz Perls (Friedman), and a number of Kosinski's protagonists are examined with the aid of Marvin Daniels' essay, "Pathological Vindictiveness and the Vindictive Character" (Gordon). In addition, there are reflections on the Third Force approach to characterization in Robert de Beaugrande's "Third Force Analysis and the Literary Experience."

When we analyze mimetic characters from a psychological point of view, we often become aware of a disparity between interpretation and representation, between the author's view of his character and the character whom he has actually presented. Mimetic characters tend to escape the categories by which the author tries to understand them and to undermine his evaluations of their life-styles and solutions. The great psychological realists have the capacity to see far more than they can understand. Their grasp of inner dynamics and of interpersonal relations is so subtle and profound that concrete representation is the only mode of discourse that can do it justice. When they analyze what they have represented or assign their characters illustrative roles, they are limited by the inadequacy both of abstractions generally and of the conceptual systems of their day. Their judgments, moreover, are often a product of their defensive needs. As Robert de Beaugrande observes, the literary "imagination invents what it wants to understand, yet cannot definitively understand what it has invented." Psychological analysis helps us to see the character that the author has actually created, rather than the one he thinks he has created, and to appreciate his genius in characterization despite his deficiencies in analysis and judgment. It provides us with a sophisticated method for evaluating the author's judgments of his characters and the adequacy for life of the solutions that he affirms. Works in which the author's judgments are confused become intelligible when we see his inconsistencies as part of a structure of inner conflicts.

The disparity between representation and interpretation is explored in the essays by Paris, Butery, Eldredge, Haselswerdt, Straub, and Friedman; and it is further analyzed in de Beaugrande's concluding essay. In my discussion of George Eliot, I try to show how the novelist glorifies the self-destructive behavior of such characters as Dorothea Brooke, whose compulsions are similar to her own. Karen Butery explores the way in which Charlotte Brontë creates the illusion that Jane Eyre has resolved her inner conflicts by manipulating the world of the novel to conform to Jane's needs, and Patricia Eldredge similarly shows how Dickens celebrates Esther Summerson's compulsive self-effacement and "manipulates fate to reward Esther's suffering and to allow her an innocent revenge." Commenting on the disparity between representation and interpretation in *Bleak House,* Eldredge observes that "the text both knows and does not know; it tells us the truth about Esther, but it lies about her as well." In her study of *Light in August,* Marjorie Haselswerdt helps us to appreciate the subtlety of Faulkner's mimetic portrait of Joe Christmas, but she also points out how Faulkner romanticizes Joe at the end of the novel: "Joe's soaring departure is made possible not by the realities of his characterization, but by the tendency of Joe's creator to mistake Joe's idealized self for reality, and to manipulate his fictional world to honor Joe's neurotic bargains with fate." Joe Straub makes a similar point about Graham Greene's treatment of the priest in *The Power and the Glory.* Greene celebrates the priest's sacrifice of his real self in the name of a neurotic search for glory that is sanctioned—indeed, encouraged—by his church. Finally, in his analysis of "Locksley Hall," Norman Friedman examines the "disparity between the evident *structure* of the poem and its inner *emotional* process." The poem gives an impression of resolution in which we cannot believe if we have understood the psychology of the speaker. As de Beaugrande observes, "the author can no longer control or prescribe what the facts which he or she has invented must mean for everyone else"; "we've agreed to let him make up the plot, but we reserve the right to contest what it demonstrates."

A disparity between representation and interpretation is one kind of inconsistency that is illuminated by a Third Force approach. Another is inconsistency within the interpretation itself. The author's attitudes toward his characters are often self-contradictory as a result of his inner conflicts. One virtue of Third Force psychology, and especially of Karen Horney's theory, is that it enables us to recognize inconsistencies and to make sense of them without resorting to the sort of rationalization that is common in literary criticism. Many critics have the temperament, as well as the training, of theologians; their object is to preserve the glory of the author by demonstrating the perfection of his creation, no matter what the difficulties. The most recent trend, of course, is toward the opposite extreme; as de Beaugrande says, the deconstructionists "enjoy subverting unification." I take an agnostic position: the work may or may not hang together. Beginning with pious hopes, I do my best to find an internal organizing principle; but I am open to the possibility that the work is not, in fact, a coherent teleological system; and after my best effort, I am willing to give up. I still wish to comprehend it, however, if not in its own terms, then in some other; and I find Horney's theory a powerful tool for making sense of inner contradictions. "This critical movement in which the psychological analysis first deconstructs and then restores literary values is highly characteristic," de Beaugrande finds, of Third Force criticism. The Third Force approach has some things in common with deconstructionism, but its "readings leave the story intact and affirm its readability, whereas the deconstructionists' readings disseminate the story and assert its 'unreadability.' "

We have a tendency to attribute to the author, too, a higher degree of integration than he actually possesses; we want him to have a greater wisdom and a more coherent set of values than most people have been able to attain. Whatever his gifts, however, the artist is subject to the same inconsistencies that plague the rest of us, the same waverings, uncertainties, and self-contradictions. Horney's theory at once sharpens our awareness of these inconsistencies and helps us to understand them as part of a system of inner conflicts. It leads us to dethrone the author as a source of wisdom and guidance, to uncouple "the greatness and insight of the work . . . from a vision of the author as a universal sage and interpreter" (de Beaugrande). But it restores the author to us as a complex and fascinating human being whose problems are similar to our own, and it focuses our attention upon his real rather than his imaginary achievements.

Of the essays in this collection, those by Eldredge *(Bleak House)*, Haselswerdt *(Light in August)*, and Paris *(Wuthering Heights)* explore conflicting authorial attitudes. "Caught in his own conflict between compliance and aggression," observes Eldredge, Dickens "is divided and paralyzed." Haselswerdt finds *Light in August* to be "primarily an aggressive novel which seeks to compensate for its tendency to 'move against' humanity by martyring its aggressive protagonist, and by making various mostly halfhearted and unsuccessful attempts to affirm the value of life and love." As Norman Friedman observes, with the help of a psychological approach, we can "mak[e] . . . sense out of formal anomalies." This will not "unify a disunified" text, but it will "tell us why it is disunified." Texts are often disunified because the author has inner conflicts, but authorial conflict does not necessarily produce formal anomalies. In my discussion of *Wuthering Heights* I argue that Emily Brontë's inner conflicts are successfully managed by her elaborate narrative technique, which gives expression to all of her conflicting trends but avoids thematic confusion by dramatizing interpretation.

The technique of *Wuthering Heights* avoids problems that would almost certainly have been created by omniscient narration, but it creates a problem of narrative reliability. We do not know where in the novel's system of conflicting values the author stands, and we do not know how far to trust the interpretations and judgments, indeed, even the accounts of character and event, of the dramatized narrators. Catherine Lewis deals with a similar problem in her analysis of Browning's Guido. Our information about Guido comes primarily from Guido himself, and Guido's accounts of himself are full of lies, distortions, and inconsistencies. "How, then," asks Lewis, "is Guido's true identity to be known?" As Lewis observes, Karen Horney's theory "is well equipped to deal with the epistemological problems raised by a character like Guido" because Horney "accounts for the process of self-fictionalization as characteristic of neurotic development, in which the imagination plays a crucial role." Given the number of works in eighteenth-, nineteenth-, and twentieth-century literature that are narrated by unreliable characters, a method of dealing with the epistemological problems this creates is a major contribution to literary criticism.

Third Force psychology is useful, then, for the analysis of realistic characters, of the relation between rhetoric and mimesis, of conflicting authorial attitudes, and of unreliable narration. As some of these uses suggest, it can help us to understand the psyche of the implied author, that is, of the author who can be inferred from the literary text. The essays by Paris, Butery, Eldredge, Straub, Haselswerdt, Huffman, Gordon, and Nelson all attempt to characterize the implied authors of the works that they discuss. The Third Force approach tends to demythify the author, to point out his obsessions, inconsistencies, and blind spots. At the same time, it seeks to recover his psychological intuitions and to enhance our appreciation of his mimetic achievement. Even as it insists upon the destructiveness of the solutions that he glorifies, it celebrates his capacity to give us a phenomenological grasp of what it is like to live by those solutions. While his rhetoric romanticizes his favored strategies of defense, his mimetic portrayal of experience *shows* us their unsatisfactoriness. As Andrew Gordon observes, we sense beneath the "vindictiveness and cool detachment" of Kosinski's characters "the terrible price they pay in incompleteness and loneliness." Though Kosinski seems to share his protagonists' neuroses, his "novels allow us access into the inner world of the pathologically vindictive character; in that sense, we are . . . the beneficiaries of his psychological intuition and his fiercely controlled imagination."

The Third Force approach can help us to talk not only about the implied authors of individual works, but also about the authorial personality that can be inferred from more than one work and, indeed, the writer as a person. The essays by Gordon (Kosinski), Nelson (O'Brien), and Paris (Shakespeare) all explore the relationship between the works and the psychology of the author. The most overtly biographical essay is the one by Andrew Gordon. It employs a diachronic model, derived from Marvin Daniels, to discuss the relationship between Kosinski's traumatic childhood and the obsessive nature of his artistic activity.

There are several other uses of Third Force psychology that are illustrated in this collection. In my essay on "Third Force Psychology and the Study of Literature, Biography, Criticism, and Culture," I discuss the psychology of critical response by analyzing some of the differences between my current view of George Eliot and the view contained in *Experiments in Life,* my earlier book on that novelist. I try to provide, as de Beaugrande has seen, "a way to view literary responses in terms of the reader's own interactive strategies." Such a step is "vital," he feels, "for helping literary criticism to develop an explicit epistemology that includes its own activities as part of an interactive process of discovering and reporting on literary works." In that essay I also try to suggest the usefulness of Third Force psychology in the study of influence, religion, philosophy, and culture, using Victorian culture as my primary example. Joe Straub's essay on *The Power and the Glory* also examines the psychology of religion; and James Huffman ventures into social psychology by analyzing the impact, on both blacks and whites, of the institution of slavery. In her study of Tim O'Brien's Vietnam trilogy, Marie Nelson explores the relationship between psychology and ethics with the help of Erich Fromm's distinction between the authoritarian and the humanistic conscience. The trilogy begins, she says, "with the question of whether a man who wants to be good can follow the demands of his authoritarian conscience. It ends with a demonstration that a man can learn to listen to the inner voice of his humanistic conscience." In his analysis of Graham Greene's priest, Joe Straub also employs Fromm's distinction. In the concluding essay, Robert de Beaugrande places the Third Force approach in its context of aesthetic and critical theories and offers a series of rich reflections on the relations of literary art to health and neurosis.

The essays collected here are on nineteenth- and twentieth-century English and American literature, but it should not be assumed that the approach is confined to literature of these periods or countries. It has been used in published studies of such writers as Shakespeare, Richardson, Stendhal, Flaubert, Balzac, Ibsen, and Dostoevsky; and I have used it to teach such writers as Aeschylus, Sophocles, Euripides, Milton, Cervantes, Goethe, Tolstoy, and Hesse. Third Force psychology works very well with a great deal of Western literature (and Western philosophy and theology, too) from the Bible to the present day.

A frequent objection to psychological criticism is that it is reductive, that it turns great works of literature into case histories, puts labels on characters, and equates them with their neuroses. All criticism is reductive in some degree; there is no approach that can do justice to literature's strangeness and power, and to its complexity. Properly used, the Third Force approach is one of the least reductive ways of talking about mimetic characterization. It gives us a much fuller sense of a character's individuality than does any kind of functional analysis; and it does not reduce adult behavior to infantile origins, as do most forms of psychoanalytic criticism. As de Beaugrande observes, "whereas a Freudian interpretation becomes a new story in place of the author's, a Third Force interpretation enters the old story at certain points with explanations that not only leave the story intact, but demonstate that it is more motivated and coherent than we may have imagined. In consequence, the author can appear more skillful than he or she was judged by conventional criticism." The approach does employ psychological categories in terms of which it selects and organizes data, but this is the price of conceptual clarity. In an unmediated experience of the text we are confronted by a mass of details the relationships of which we can perceive but dimly. The use of psychological categories helps us to see these details as parts of larger patterns within which their relationships become intelligible. There is some simplification, to be sure, and an inevitable thinning out of experience, but less, I believe, than with most other approaches.

In minimizing reductiveness, the important thing is not to avoid using analytic categories, but to avoid using them in a mechanical way, as a substitute for real thought and feeling. Psychological categories can have a considerable heuristic value; they can help us to see things that we could not have seen at all, or so clearly, without them. But our interpretations should not be just the result of the application of a theory to a text. We should approach each character with empathy and a concern for the particularities of his or her situation. We should try to enter imaginatively into the inner world of character and author by drawing upon the elements in our own personality and experience that parallel theirs. Our interpretation should be the result of an interaction between theory, the text, and ourselves.

A major source of reductiveness is the privileging of a conceptual scheme over the literary experience, so that we give the impression that what the text is *really* about is the generalizations of the critic. I believe that Third Force psychology has much to contribute to our understanding of literature, that it permits a conceptual clarity that cannot be derived from literature alone. Literary texts have a contribution of at least equal importance to make to the theories that help us to understand them. In discussing an aspect of vindictiveness, Horney observed that "great writers have intuitively grasped [this phenomenon] and have presented it in more impressive forms than a psychiatrist can hope to do" (*NHG*, p. 198). This is true of a large number of the phenomena that psychology describes. Psychological theory is quite thin and abstract compared to the concrete portrayals of experience in literature. There is a reciprocal relation, I propose, between psychological theory and the literary presentation of the phenomena it describes. The theory provides categories of understanding that help us to recover the intuitions of the great writers about the workings of the human psyche. These intuitions, once recovered, become part of our conceptual understanding of life. Just as the good analyst learns something about his theory from every patient, so the student of literature finds himself understanding certain aspects of human nature in a fuller way because of the richness of artistic presentation.

Literature has more to offer the student of human nature than an enrichment of psychological theory. It is the product of a different mental process than that which produces analytic systems, and it makes available a different kind of knowledge. Psychology gives us truths *about* human behavior, whereas literature gives us truth *to* experiences of life. The psychologist and the literary artist often deal with the same phenomena, but the artist's grasp of psychological process is of a more concrete and intuitive sort, deriving, as it often does, from his gift for imitation. His genius is in embodying and structuring his observations, rather than in analyzing them. Literature operates below the level of changing conceptualizations, including those of the artist himself. This is one of the things that makes it universal and enduring.

Because of its concrete, dramatic quality, literature enables us not only to observe people other than ourselves, but also to enter into their experience of life, to discover what it feels like to *be* these people and to be confronted with their destiny. We can gain in this way a phenomenological grasp of experience that cannot be derived from theories alone, and not from case histories either, unless they are also works of art. It is because it provides this kind of knowledge that literature has a potentially liberalizing effect; it offers us an opportunity to amplify our experience, to escape the limitations of our time and culture, as no other form of discourse can do.

The kind of empathic understanding of which I am speaking can be gained only through a total immersion in the literary work. One form of the charge of reductiveness is that criticism interferes with such an immersion and thereby distorts the literary experience. This is certainly a danger, but it is one which it is up to the reader to avoid. Most forms of criticism interfere with immediate response by putting the reader into an analytical frame of mind and placing him at too great a distance from the text. The reader should not stop with the critic's formulations, however, but should use them to help him re-experience the work with a heightened sensitivity. As I observed in *A Psychological Approach to Fiction,* "the movement away from empathy which is inseparable from analysis must be counterbalanced by a return to the phenomenological grasp of experience which literature affords. . . . psychology helps us to talk about what the [artist] knows, but [literature] helps us to know what the psychologist is talking about. The marriage of these two ways of apprehending experience is essential if we are to have both empathy and insight" (p. 286).

NOTES

1. *Toward a Psychology of Being* (New York: Van Nostrand, 1968), p. vi. Hereafter cited in the text as *PB.*

2. Abraham Maslow, *Motivation and Personality,* 2d ed. (New York: Harper and Row, 1970), pp. ix–x.

3. Karen Horney, *Neurosis and Human Growth* (New York: Norton, 1950), p. 15. Hereafter cited in the text as *NHG.*

4. *The Philosophy of John Stuart Mill,* ed. Marshall Cohen (New York: Modern Library, 1961), p. 21.

5. *Aspects of the Novel* (London: Edward Arnold, 1927), chap. 4. The term "mimetic characters" is taken from Robert Scholes and Robert Kellogg, *The Nature of Narrative* (New York: Oxford University Press, 1966). For a fuller rationale for the psychological analysis of mimetic characters, see Bernard J. Paris, *A Psychological Approach to Fiction* (Bloomington: Indiana University Press, 1974), chap. 1.

6. *The Literary Use of the Psychoanalytic Process* (New Haven: Yale University Press, 1981), p. 38. Hereafter cited in the text.

Third Force Psychology and the Study of Literature

1
Horney, Maslow, and the Third Force

Bernard J. Paris

The most fundamental concept of Third Force psychology is that we have an intrinsic nature, a "real self," which it is our purpose in life to fulfill. Healthy growth is a process of actualizing this self and neurotic development is a process of becoming alienated from it. Of all the Third Force psychologists, Abraham Maslow is the greatest student of self-actualization, and Karen Horney offers the most systematic account of self-alienation. I shall present my account of Third Force psychology largely through their theories, though I shall draw at times upon the contributions of other members of the group.

It is not my purpose here to enter into a defense of Third Force psychology, to trace its history, or to compare it systematically with other leading theories. My object is to expound its central ideas, stressing those which I have found to be of value in the study of literature, but giving, at the same time, an accurate account of the overall structure of the theory. Hence, though I have found Horney's ideas to be more applicable to the study of literature than those of any other Third Force psychologist, I have given a good deal of space to Maslow, whose ideas are entirely compatible with hers and are needed to provide a comprehensive theory of human nature.

The exposition of Third Force psychology that follows will be divided into three parts: first, I shall examine its conceptions of human nature, the human condition, and human values; next, its treatment of self-actualization; and, finally, its analysis of self-alienation. Since these concerns are overlapping and conceptually interdependent, no strict division will be possible. Some ideas that are introduced early may not become entirely clear until they are developed more fully in later sections.

1. HUMAN NATURE, THE HUMAN CONDITION, AND HUMAN VALUES

It is its view of human nature, more than any other part of its theory, that unifies Third Force psychology as a movement and distinguishes it from the other two major forces (Freudianism and behaviorism) in modern psychology. This psychology contends, in essence, that the human being is not simply a tension-reducing or a conditioned animal, but that there is present in him a third force, an "evolutionary constructive" force, "which urge[s] him to realize his given potentialities."[1] Each person has "an essential biologically based inner nature" which is "good or neutral rather than bad" and which should be brought out and encouraged rather than suppressed. If this inner nature "is permitted to guide our life, we grow healthy, fruitful, and happy." If it is "denied or suppressed," we get "sick sometimes in obvious ways, sometimes in subtle ways, sometimes immediately, sometimes later." This inner nature "is weak and delicate and subtle and easily overcome by habit, cultural pressure, and wrong attitudes toward it"; but, "even though weak, it rarely disappears. . . . Even though denied, it persists underground forever pressing for actualization."[2]

This view of human nature is based on the Third Force psychologists' experience with psychotherapy and on their study of exceptionally healthy people. Psychotherapy has shown that there is a drive toward self-realization, however weak, which makes change possible; that cure involves helping the individual first to get in touch with and then to live from his essential inner nature; and that this inner nature, when uncovered, turns out to be a source of spontaneous virtues and intrinsic values rather than a thing to be feared and repressed. The study of exceptionally healthy people has shown that the views of human nature that we find in most philosophies, theologies, and psychologies are based on the observation of imperfectly developed people (who constitute the vast majority) and that they do not characterize the essential nature of humanity. In attempting to describe human nature, the Third Force psychologists have asked not only what are most people like but also what is the essential nature of the species as it is represented by its most fully developed individuals?

One of the most interesting Third Force contributions to our understanding of the essential nature of the species is Abraham Maslow's theory of the hierarchy of basic needs. According to this theory, all people have needs for physiological satisfaction, for safety, for love and belonging, for esteem, and for self-actualization. These needs are not always experienced consciously; indeed, they tend to be more unconscious than conscious. The needs are hierarchical in that they exist in an order of prepotency; the physiological needs are the most powerful, and so on. The needs at the upper end of the hierarchy (higher needs) are much weaker than the lower needs, though they are no less basic.[3] The needs are basic in the sense that they are built into the nature of all people as a function of their biological structure, and they must be gratified if the organism is to develop in a healthy way. Though the particular form in which they are expressed and the possibility of their satisfaction depend upon the surrounding culture, they exist prior to culture as part of the hereditary nature of the individual.

Because they are biologically based, Maslow calls the basic needs instinctoid.

They are not like the instincts of animals—"powerful, strong, unmodifiable, uncontrollable, unsuppressible" (*MP,* p. 81); they are weak, especially the higher ones, and are "easily repressed, suppressed, . . . masked or modified . . . by habits, suggestions, by cultural pressures, by guilt, and so on" (*MP,* p. 82). Though weak, they are in a sense also very strong; for they are "inconceivably stubborn and recalcitrant. . . . Consciously or unconsciously they are craved and sought forever. They behave always like stubborn, irreducible, final, unanalyzable facts that must be taken as given or as starting points not to be questioned" (*MP,* pp. 78–79).

Each individual presses by nature for the fulfillment of all of these needs, but at any given time his motivational life will be centered around the fulfillment of one of the basic needs. Since a higher need emerges strongly only when the needs below it have been sufficiently met, the individual tends to be occupied with the basic needs in the order of their prepotency. When he is at a given stage in the hierarchy, the needs that have already been met tend to cease functioning as motivators and the needs that are higher in the hierarchy are felt only weakly. The person living in an environment favorable to growth will move steadily up the hierarchy until he is free to devote most of his energies to self-actualization, which is the full and satisfying use of his capacities in a calling suitable to his nature. The higher needs tend to emerge not only with the fulfillment of the lower needs but also with the maturing of the organism.

The hierarchy of basic needs, then, establishes the pattern of psychological evolution. If the individual is not adequately fulfilled in his lower needs, he may become fixated at an early stage of development; or, if he passes beyond that stage, he may be subject to frequent regressions. Frustration of a basic need intensifies the need and ensures its persistence; gratification diminishes its strength as a motivating force. People who have been very well satisfied in their lower needs early in life may develop a "frustration tolerance" that permits them to experience later deprivation without regressing. The more fully evolved person may regress, however, if he is deprived of a lower need in a severe way or for an extended period of time.

Maslow cautions us against understanding the dynamics of the hierarchy of basic needs in too crude or mechanical a way. Most behavior is multimotivated; in any given instance there may be several or all of the basic needs at work, though they will not all be equally powerful. Most members of our society are partially satisfied and partially unsatisfied in all of their basic needs at the same time. There are decreasing percentages of satisfaction, however, as we move up the hierarchy of prepotency. Under especially favorable conditions we may have episodes of higher need motivation, and under particularly unfavorable conditions we may regress to a lower level of needing. Behavior is not solely determined by inner needs; the cultural setting and the immediate situation are also important determinants. The hierarchy of prepotency will determine what we want, but not necessarily how we will act.

Movement from one stage of psychological evolution to another has the following profound effects upon our attitudes toward the basic needs and their satisfiers. These include

> Independence of and a certain disdain for the old satisfiers and goal objects, with a new dependence on satisfiers and goal objects that hitherto have been overlooked, not wanted, or only casually wanted. . . . Thus there are changes in interests. That is, certain phenomena become interesting for the first time and old phenomena become boring, or even repulsive. This is the same as saying that there are changes in human values. In general, there tend to be: (1) overestimation of the satisfiers of the most powerful of the ungratified needs; (2) underestimation of the satisfiers of the less powerful of the ungratified needs (and of the strength of these needs); and (3) underestimation and even devaluation of the satisfiers of the needs already gratified (and of the strength of these needs). This shift in values involves, as a dependent phenomenon, reconstruction in philosophy of the future, of the Utopia, of the heaven and hell, of the good life, and of the unconscious wish-fulfillment state of the individual in a crudely predictable direction. (*MP*, pp. 60–61)

These observations are extraordinarily useful in helping us to understand conflicts and changes in values and differences among the various psychological theories.

People at different stages of psychological evolution are bound to have different philosophies of life and to emphasize different values. Those at the lower stages of the evolutionary process will be unable to understand the values of those at the higher stages, while those at the higher stages are likely to underemphasize the importance of some of the lower needs. Those who are still growing psychologically will inevitably change their philosophic orientation and will realize, on the basis of past experiences of change, that their present position is most likely incomplete. People who are fixated at a certain stage of growth will tend to interpret everything in terms of the values appropriate to that stage and to believe that all other values are illusory. Values come from human needs; when they are felt in a healthy way, all of the basic needs are sources of legitimate values. Any value system based on only one or a few needs, however, is bound to be incomplete and to involve a distortion of human nature. An adequate conception of human nature and human values can be derived only from the perspective of the most fully evolved people, though, as we have seen, this perspective is likely to underemphasize the importance of the lower needs. Perhaps there is no one perspective that does not involve some distortion.

Each of the major psychological theories tends to focus on some part of the hierarchy of needs rather than upon the whole hierarchy. Jungian and Maslovian psychology focus on the upper end of the hierarchy and are scanty in their treatment of the lower needs. Freudian id psychology and behaviorist psychology are strong in their treatment of the lower needs but weak in their handling of the higher needs. Horney, Fromm, Rogers, the Freudian ego psychologists, and the existential psychologists focus on the middle of the hierarchy. Horney is mainly concerned with the neurotic processes that occur as a result of the frustration of the needs for safety, love, and esteem.

An awareness of the partial nature of most psychologies helps us to assess both their achievements and limitations and puts us on guard against the problems to which such incompleteness may lead. A psychology devoted to the observation and explanation of certain aspects of human nature may provide excellent insight into the phenomena it studies; but it is liable to serious error and distortion if it attempts to account for higher or lower needs mainly in terms of the needs on which it is focused. Many psychologies are weak in their picture of human nature because they attempt to derive the whole of man from the part which they know or which they feel can be studied best. The most frequent error, of course, is reductionism in which only the lower needs are seen as inherent motivators and the higher strivings are seen as derived from and therefore reducible to the lower ones. One of the most significant features of Third Force psychology is that it recognizes the higher needs to be just as much a part of our nature as the lower ones. It gives them an autonomous status and permits us to understand them and the values arising from them in their own terms.

As the preceding discussion indicates, Maslow's conception of the hierarchy of basic needs and of its dynamics has a number of important implications for our understanding of human nature, the human condition, and human values. As Maslow sees it, psychological evolution is determined mainly by two factors: the structure of needs inherent in the human organism and the degree to which these needs are satisfied. Gratification of the basic needs produces health; it permits the individual to continue on his way toward self-actualization. The basic needs can be fulfilled only by intrinsically appropriate gratifiers, and their fulfillment is conducive to a sound development only when they are felt in a healthy way. The gratification of neurotic needs is not health producing.

Frustration of the basic needs produces pathology; it arrests the individual's development, alienates him from his real self, and leads him to develop neurotic strategies for making up his deficiencies. The frustration of nonbasic needs is not harmful; the person who is fairly well gratified in his basic needs can handle considerable frustration in other areas. Only frustration of basic needs is truly threatening. Destructiveness, aggression, and a need to be omnipotent are not part of man's essential nature; they are defensive reactions to basic threat. They are potentialities of his essential nature, however; for man is so constituted that he will sicken if his basic needs are not met, and he will then seek fulfillment in ways harmful to himself and to others. There are valuable as well as harmful frustrations. The individual must discover not only his potentialities, but also the limitations imposed by his nature, his place in the cosmos, and the social character of his existence.

There is no reason for frustrating any of the basic needs, for they are not, when experienced in the course of a healthy development, in conflict with civilization and our higher values. The interests of the individual and of society are in conflict only under bad conditions; they are synergic under good conditions. The function of society should be to fulfill rather than to repress our spontaneous wants. The traditional distinctions between reason and impulse, spirit and body, our higher and lower natures are based upon false dichotomies. The higher and lower needs are in conflict only when there is deprivation; in the most fully evolved people they are in harmony. Both impulse and rationality are part of our essential nature; in healthy people they "are synergic, and strongly tend to come to similar conclusions rather than contrasting ones" (*MP,* p. 3). "In these people, desires are in excellent accord with reason. St. Augustine's 'Love God and do as you will' can easily be translated, 'Be healthy and then you may trust your impulses' " (*MP,* p. 179).

The Third Force psychologists seem optimistic (when compared, say, with Freud) in that they believe in the possibility of health and find the healthy person to be a relatively happy, harmonious, and creative being. It must be pointed out, however, that Maslow's self-actualizing people comprise no more than 1 percent of the population, and perhaps less. Because the instinctoid needs (especially the higher ones) are so weak and the voice of the real self is so faint, it is extremely difficult for human beings to be impulse aware, to know how they really feel and what they really want. They are by nature easily self-alienated; they are sensitive plants who require such special and complex conditions for healthy growth that they rarely achieve a sound maturity. Raising a child to health is an extraordinarily difficult task, and the creation of a healthy society is incomparably more difficult.

It is difficult for humans to know what they want and difficult for them to get what they need. When they get what they need, they will not be satisfied, for needing never ceases: "the human being is never satisfied except in a relative or one-step-along-the-path fashion" (*MP,* p. 25). Satisfaction of any one need produces no more than a momentary tranquillity; other and higher needs soon emerge and striving is renewed. The satisfaction of the lower needs does not result in stagnation, as many seem to fear. Rather it "elevate[s]" the individual "to the point where he is civilized enough to feel frustrated about the larger personal, social, and intellectual issues" (*MP,* p. 70).

The more highly evolved individual, though always basically engaged in a process of becoming, will frequently have end (or "peak") experiences. These are experiences of being that are self-sufficient and intrinsically valuable. They are not means to other ends but are the ends to which all other forms of gratification are the means. They are moments of complete fulfillment from which no higher strivings will emerge.[4] The highly evolved individual will have such experiences frequently; but they will not free him more than momentarily from the condition of wanting, for having had them will make him want them again.

Though suffering and limitation are the fate of all human beings, people at different stages of psychological evolution will, to some extent, experience different kinds of frustration and have different views of the human condition. We will be able to see this more clearly if we divide human problems into three kinds: personal, historical, and existential.[5] Personal problems are rooted in the life history of the individual; they are symptomatic of the interferences with his psychological evolution that have been produced by the frustration of his basic needs. Historical problems arise from the social, cultural, and economic development of a particular community. They are shared by all members of the community, but not all communities have the same problems. Personal problems are partly the result of historical problems; but temperament and the immediate family situation also play large roles in individual development. Not all members of the community are affected by their common environment in the same way. Historical problems are partly the result of individual problems, and they are perpetuated by the neuroses they help to foster. Both personal and historical problems are accidental, variable, and, theoretically at least, remediable. Existential problems arise out of the disparity between our natural wants (for such things as life, health, and control of our destiny) and the unalterable cosmic and historical conditions of our existence. They are shared by all human beings, and they are irremediable.

The Third Force psychologists do not feel that our existential problems are such as to prevent healthy development and a reasonably satisfactory existence. The historical problems of our society make a high degree of psychological evolution impossible for most people. Even our most mature people are significantly hampered by historical problems and have achieved considerably less than full humanness. Even so, the freedom, tolerance, prosperity, and diversity of our society, combined with our rapidly developing psychological insight and the emergence of effective psychotherapies, make our environment more favorable to self-actualization than most others that humans have experienced.

Self-actualizing people are by no means free of conflict and suffering, but they suffer mainly from historical and existential rather than from personal problems. Their relative freedom from personal problems makes them more accurately aware of historical and existential problems than are most self-alienated people. They tend to work in a patient, realistic way for the alleviation of historical problems and to approach existential problems with a combination of resignation and humor. Their positive experiences are so numerous and so rewarding that they feel generally accepting toward the human condition, without being at all blind to its tragedies. That their lives are so full of possibilities leads them at times to feel the limitations of time, age, death, and the gap between aspiration and opportunity with special poignancy. Their awareness of the impoverished quality of most human lives fills them with an unmitigable sadness.

Self-alienated people usually see the possibilities for fulfillment as fewer and the frustrations of the human lot as greater than do self-actualizing people. In forming an estimate of the human condition they tend to generalize from their own experience, in which end experiences are rare and suffering is frequent. Because of their insecurities and their compensatory strategies, they over-react to historical and existential problems. They then judge the magnitude of the problems by the intensity of their response. Because of their limited experience, their need to externalize, and their desire to avoid feelings of uncertainty, isolation, and inferiority, they tend to see their personal problems not as belonging to themselves, but as historical or existential in nature. They confuse neurotic anxiety with existential *Angst* and neurotic despair with a philosophic sense of the absurdity of human existence.

An individual's view of the human condition, then, like his view of human nature and human values, will depend upon the stage of psychological evolution he has attained. The self-alienated person's view of the human situation is not very reliable; it is egocentric, it lacks proportion, and it is often characterized by distortion, projection, and externalization. The perspective of the self-actualizing person gives us a far more just conception of the possibilities and limitations of human existence.

We have already seen some of the implications of Third Force psychology for our understanding of human values. Values are derived from human nature and its needs. Those things are good that gratify basic needs and are thus conducive to healthy development; those things are bad that arrest or distort our psychological evolution. What an individual values most will be largely determined by the most powerful of his ungratified needs: "So far as he is concerned, *the* absolute, ultimate value, synonymous with life itself, is whichever need in the hierarchy he is dominated by during a particular period" (*PB*, pp. 153–54). Just as there are higher and lower needs, there are also higher and lower values. An individual who has been gratified in both will place a greater value upon a higher need than upon a lower one. The "basic needs or basic values . . . may be treated *both* as ends and as steps toward a single end-goal. It is true that there is a single, ultimate value or end of life and *also* . . . that we have a hierarchical and developmental system of values, complexly interrelated" (*PB*, p. 154).

Maslow's account of the relation of values to the stages of psychological evolution applies mainly to the healthy components of an individual's development. As we shall see when we discuss Horney, the self-alienated person's values are determined not only by his ungratified basic needs but also by his defensive strategies. Neurotic needs result from the frustration of basic needs, but they are not the same as basic needs. The self-alienated person tends to value not so much what he needs in order to grow as what he needs in order to maintain his system of defense. Insofar as his defensive strategies are necessary to his survival, his values have a certain functional legitimacy and must be respected. They are, however, in no way normative, as are the values deriving from the needs that are part of his essential nature.

Though they use different terms, all Third Force psychologists agree that the highest value for a human being is to realize his potentialities, to become "fully human, everything that [he] *can* become" (*PB*, p. 153). This is the highest good, the *summum bonum*, for all people, whether they realize it or not. This does not mean that all self-actualizing people will want the same things or have exactly the same values. Each person has a different self to actualize, and these constitutional differences generate differences in values. People are most like each other in their lower needs and most idiosyncratic in their self-actualizing activities. This means that some values are species-wide (though they take different forms in different cultures), and that some values are unique to the individual or are shared only by individuals with similar capacities and temperaments. Self-actualization, the fulfillment of both our species-wide and our unique natures, takes many different forms; but it is the *raison d'être* of all people. It is the reason for being also of our various social institutions, and the worth of these institutions is to be measured by their success or failure in fostering individual growth.

It should be evident by now that the Third Force psychologists reject many of the relativisms characteristic of our time. Some of them, like Maslow, feel that they have the solution to the modern crisis in values.[6] The values they propose are, of course, relative to human beings; but for human beings they are absolute.

The cultural anthropologists did a great service, they feel, by alerting us to our ethnocentricity; but cultural relativism goes too far when it derives all values from culture and proclaims itself unable to distinguish between good and bad cultures. "In general," says Maslow, "the paths by which the main goals in life are achieved are . . . determined by the nature of the particular culture. . . . We win the love of other people and express our affections for them through culturally approved channels" (*MP*, p. 314). But the goals themselves are not culturally determined. "The fundamental or ultimate desires of all human beings," Maslow observes, "do not differ nearly as much as do their conscious every day desires" (*MP*, p. 22). The former are determined by essential human nature, the latter by the mores, patterns, and opportunities of the surrounding culture.

Cultures, too, operate according to the hierarchy of needs.[7] They are organized around the lower needs first, and only when these are adequately met can they respond to the higher needs of their members. A highly evolved individual can be produced only by a highly evolved culture. Those individuals who, through especially fortunate circumstances or contact with a higher civilization, have evolved beyond their immediate culture often become progressive forces within their society. Individuals who are products of a culture at an early stage of evolution will not be able to feel the higher needs very strongly, but the needs will continue to exist and will exert an upward pressure.

Being, for the most part, therapists, the Third Force psychologists recognize the importance of understanding each individual in his own terms and of accepting the fact that each individual's value system has a certain logic and validity, for him. They do feel, however, that there is a way of choosing between differing value systems and ways of being in the world. Though they employ a phenomenological perspective, they do not confine themselves to it. To understand all is not necessarily to abandon judgment. Some values are healthy and some are not; some are conducive to a fuller realization of human potentialities and some result in a stunting of human growth. Frustration of the basic needs so alienates the individual from his essential nature and so disturbs the course of his development that he is no longer aware of his own best interests or able to pursue them. "Only the choices and tastes and judgments of healthy human beings," says Maslow, "will tell us much about what is good for the human species in the long run. The choices of neurotic people can tell us mostly what is good for keeping a neurosis stabilized" (*PB*, p. 151).

The value theory that Maslow proposes is essentially a hedonism that differs from past hedonisms in its more complete understanding of humanity's essential nature and in its more sophisticated approach to the problems of distinguishing between higher and lower values, healthy and sick pleasures. "No [value] theory will be adequate," Maslow argues, "that rests simply on the statistical description of the choices of unselected human beings. To average the choices of good and bad choosers, of healthy and sick people is useless" (*PB*, p. 151). The values of healthy individuals hold for all people, whether they believe in them or not; for "good choosers can choose better than bad choosers what is better for the bad choosers themselves" (*PB*, p. 151). Many people have had no opportunity to choose higher over lower, healthy over sick pleasures. If both their natures and their cultures were highly enough evolved to give them the opportunity for choice, they would choose the pleasures of self-actualization over all else. One evidence for this is that people undergoing psychotherapy tend to change their values in a predictable direction. Maslow feels that a naturalistic value system can be arrived at by observing what "our best specimens choose, and then assuming that these are the highest values for all mankind" (*PB*, p. 169).

Maslow contends, in effect, that there is an essential human nature, that we can identify the people in whom this nature has achieved its fullest growth, and that we can derive from the observation of these individuals an idea of what would be good (growth-fostering) for all people and of what all people would want if they were fully evolved. There are a number of difficulties in this argument. It is impossible to establish conclusively that there is an essential human nature; all value systems based on this premise begin with a leap of faith. It is impossible to demonstrate that one has actually identified the best specimens. Maslow derives his scientifically based, naturalistic value system from the observation of good choosers; but, as he himself recognizes, the good choosers must be chosen, and there is no way of establishing the credentials of the original choosers. The possibilities of projection are great; one may just be choosing those whose personalities and value systems are parallel to one's own or are the embodiment of a neurotic ideal. Just when we think that we have escaped from relativism, we realize that there is no way of validating, for those who are not already convinced, the criteria of psychological health, the criteria by which the good choosers are chosen. This, I think, is an existential problem.

2. SELF-ACTUALIZATION

According to Maslow, "healthy people have sufficiently gratified their basic needs for safety, belongingness, love, respect and self-esteem so that they are motivated primarily by trends to self-actualization." Maslow defines self-actualization as the "ongoing actualization of potentials, capacities and talents, as fulfillment of mission (or call, fate, destiny, or vocation)." It involves "a fuller knowledge of, and acceptance of, the person's own intrinsic nature" and "an unceasing trend toward unity, integration or synergy within the person" (*PB*, p. 25).

This definition, which embodies the conception of self-actualization we have developed so far, presents self-actualization as a process that occurs in the later stages of psychological evolution. Maslow's total conception of self-actualization is much broader than this, however. His study of peak experiences has led him to see that in such experiences "any person . . . takes on temporarily many of the characteristics" of "self-actualizing individuals" (*PB*, p. 97). Self-actualization can be defined, then, "as an episode, or a spurt in which the powers of the person come together in a particularly efficient and intensely enjoyable way. . . . He becomes in these episodes more truly himself, more perfectly actualizing his potentialities, closer to the core of his Being" (*PB*, p. 97). All people, then, can have experiences of self-actualization. What distinguishes "self-actualizing people . . . is that in them these episodes seem to come far more frequently, and intensely and perfectly than in average people" (*PB*, p. 97). Self-actualization, then, is "a matter of degree and of frequency rather than an all-or-none affair" (*PB*, p. 97).

Self-actualization involves more than the actualization of "potentials, capacities and talents"; it involves the actualization of the real self at every point in the process of psychological evolution. Its opposite is self-alienation, which means alienation not only from one's capacities but also from one's spontaneous feelings and individual life rhythms. Frustration of the basic needs is not the only source of pathology; illness is produced also by the frustration of self-expression "and of the tendency of the person to grow in his own style and at his own pace" (*PB*, pp. 193–94). One of the requirements for health is that the individual be free to have his own feelings, to make his own choices, and to pursue his basic needs in his own way.

This discussion of self-actualization will not deal with all aspects of this complicated phenomenon; it will focus mainly upon the real self and upon some of the chief characteristics of self-actualizing people. Since all people may be self-actualizing at times, perhaps it would be more accurate to say that we shall discuss not simply self-actualizing people, but the ways in which all people relate to self, to others, and to the world when they are functioning in a self-actualizing fashion.

It was not until her last book, *Neurosis and Human Growth,* that Karen Horney introduced the concept of the real self as a foundation stone of her system. Her "theoretical and therapeutic approach" had always rested upon "the belief in an inherent urge to grow" (*NHG,* p. 38); now she identified the real self as "the 'original' force toward individual growth and fulfillment, with which we may again achieve full identification when freed of the crippling shackles of neurosis" (*NHG,* p. 158). It is the real self for which we are looking "when we say that we want to find ourselves" (*NHG,* p. 158).

In the course of his development the child is much influenced by the things he learns—such as skills, coping behaviors, social roles, and reward and punishment associations. "But there are also forces in him," says Horney, "which he cannot acquire or even develop by learning. You need not, and in fact cannot, teach an acorn to grow into an oak tree, but when given a chance, its intrinsic potentialities will develop. Similarly, the human individual, given a chance, tends to develop his particular human potentialities" (*NHG,* p. 17).

Under favorable conditions, the individual "will develop . . . the unique alive forces of his real self: the clarity and depth of his own feelings, thoughts, wishes, interests; the ability to tap his own resources, the strength of his will power; the special capacities or gifts he may have; the faculty to express himself, and to relate himself to others with his spontaneous feelings. All this will in time enable him to find his set of values and his aims in life" (*NHG,* p. 17). Such a development, says Horney, "is far from uniform." It will be influenced by "his particular temperament, faculties, propensities, and the conditions of his earlier and later life. . . . But wherever his course takes him, it will be *his* given potentialities which he develops" (*NHG,* p. 13).

Under unfavorable conditions, when the people around him are prevented by their own needs from relating to him with love and respect, the child develops a "feeling of being isolated and helpless in a world conceived as potentially hostile" (*NHG,* p. 18). This feeling of "basic anxiety" makes the child fearful of spontaneity, and, forsaking his real self, he develops strategies for coping with his environment. The real self, though abandoned or suppressed, remains alive, however; and it is possible, with the help of therapy or other favorable conditions, for the individual to get back to it and to grow from it again. The real self remains a possibility, a "possible self" (*NHG,* p. 158).

The preceding paragraphs contain the best of Horney's relatively few direct statements about the real self. There is much that we can infer about it from her analysis of self-alienation, of course; and our later discussion of her theories will deepen our understanding of her conception of the real self. To clarify our notion of the real self we can also draw upon the work of Abraham Maslow, who has adopted Horney's term and whose theories are in many ways an extension of her concept.

"One's personal biology," says Maslow, "is beyond question a *sine qua non* component of the 'Real Self.' Being oneself, being natural or spontaneous, being authentic, expressing one's identity, all these are also biological statements since they imply the acceptance of one's constitutional, temperamental, anatomical, neurological, hormonal, and instinctoid-motivational nature."[8] Each person's real self "has some characteristics which all other selves have . . . and some which are unique to the person" (*PB*, p. 191). All persons, except those who are extraordinarily stunted, have the basic needs for physiological gratification, safety, love and belonging, self-esteem, self-actualization, beauty, knowledge, and understanding. Each person has his own talents, capacities, tastes, temperamental predispositions, physiological peculiarities, and so forth.

As we have seen, Maslow holds that the choices or values of self-actualizing people (or of all people in their moments of self-actualization) are normative for the species as a whole. He calls these values Being-values (or B-values) and lists them as follows: truth, goodness, beauty, wholeness, dichotomy-transcendence, aliveness, uniqueness, perfection, necessity, completion, justice, order, simplicity, richness, effortlessness, playfulness, self-sufficiency.[9] Maslow feels that the B-values are part of the real self; that is, all human beings by their nature have a potentiality for experiencing these as the highest values, they must have their desire for these values satisfied if they are to achieve full humanness, and they cannot violate these values without damage to themselves. The B-values are not arranged in a species-wide hierarchy of prepotency; rather "each individual seems to have his own priorities . . . in accordance with his own talents, temperament, skills, capacities, etc." The "spiritual life," then, "is part of the Real Self, of one's identity, of one's inner core, of one's specieshood, of full-humanness. To the extent that pure expressing of oneself, or pure spontaneity is possible, to that extent," says Maslow, will the B-values "also be expressed."[10]

Following Horney and Fromm, Maslow affirms the existence of an "intrinsic conscience" which generates "intrinsic guilt" and which is also part of the real self. "The serious thing for each person to recognize vividly and poignantly, each for himself, is that every falling away from species-virtue, every crime against one's own nature, every evil act, *every one without exception records itself* in our unconscious and makes us despise ourselves" (*PB*, p. 5). Our intrinsic conscience, which has nothing to do with local customs or the Freudian super-ego, generates appropriate feelings of guilt whenever we violate the B-values or betray any aspect of our real selves: "It insists that we be true to our inner nature and that we do not deny it out of weakness or for advantage or for any other reason" (*PB*, p. 7). We are not always consciously aware of our self-betrayals, but every destructive act is "registered," to use Horney's term,[11] by the unconscious.

The components of the real self, says Maslow, "are potentialities, not final actualizations. Therefore they have a life history and must be seen developmentally. They are actualized, shaped or stifled mostly (but not altogether) by extra-psychic determinants (culture, family, environment, learning, etc.)" (*PB*, pp. 190–91). The real self is actualized only as a self-in-the-world; the way in which it is actualized and the degree to which it is actualized are determined largely by the nature of its world.

The actualization of the real self requires a culture that offers a course of activity congruent with the individual's inner bent and that permits him to realize his capacities. It requires, even more, a set of significant adults who are interested in the child as a being for himself and who will allow him to have his own feelings, tastes, interests, and values. Whenever possible, the child must be allowed to make his own choices. The alternative to choosing according to "the subjective experiences of delight and boredom" is "making the choice in terms of the wish of another person. The Self is lost when this happens" (*PB*, p. 58).

The child is a weak and dependent being whose needs for safety, protection, and acceptance are so strong that he will sacrifice himself, if necessary, in order to get these things. If the child is "faced with a . . . choice between his own delight experiences and the . . . approval [of] others, [he] must generally choose approval from others, and then handle his delight by repression or letting it die, or not noticing it or controlling it by will-power. In general, along with this will develop a disapproval of the delight experience, or shame and embarrassment and secretiveness about it, with finally, the inability even to experience it" (*PB*, p. 51). "The primal choice," says Maslow, "is between others' and one's self. If the only way to maintain the self is to lose others, then the ordinary child will give up the self" (*PB*, p. 52).

The person who is able to develop in accordance with his real self possesses a number of characteristics that distinguish him from the self-alienated person. The child who is not permitted to be himself and who does not live in a safe, relatively transparent world develops a defensiveness that cuts him off both from himself and from external reality. Defensiveness, says Carl Rogers, is "the organism's response to experiences which are perceived or anticipated as threatening. . . . These threatening experiences are temporarily rendered harmless by being distorted in awareness, or being denied to awareness."[12] The opposite of defensiveness is "openness to experience," and the self-actualizing person is characterized above all by his openness to his own inner being and to the world around him.

The self-actualizing person's openness to himself is manifested in his greater congruence, his greater transparence, and his greater spontaneity. A person is congruent, says Rogers, when whatever feeling or attitude he is experiencing is matched by his awareness of that attitude (*BP*, p. 51). A congruent person knows what he wants, feels, thinks, and values. In Maslow's terms, he is impulse aware; his "inner signals" are relatively loud and clear. He is not self-deceived or torn by unconscious conflicts. He may not have a direct intellectual cognition of his inner depths, but there is no significant disparity between his conscious and unconscious selves.

A person is transparent when his acts, words, and gestures are an accurate indicator of what is going on inside of him. Transparency is synonymous with honesty, lack of pose, and genuineness. A person must be congruent before he can be transparent; an incongruent person invariably transmits confusing or misleading signals. Transparency requires self-acceptance and a confidence that one's real self will be accepted by other people or that one can handle rejection. It requires great strength and courage.

Spontaneity involves both congruence and transparence; it involves an absence of inhibition both in experiencing and in expressing the real self. Healthy spontaneity should not be confused with the acting out of neurotic compulsions that often goes on in its name. Such behavior does not flow freely from the real self but is a product of defensiveness and involves a breaking through rather than a freedom from inhibitions. Spontaneity cannot exist without a profound self-trust, and it is only the psychologically healthy person who can have such trust in himself.

There is no serious conflict between spontaneity and morality, for people cannot be truly spontaneous unless they are self-actualizing, and insofar as they are self-actualizing they are spontaneously constructive. The self-actualizing person "is so constructed that he presses toward . . . what most people would call good values, toward serenity, kindness, courage, honesty, love, unselfishness, and goodness" (*PB*, p. 155). Such people "spontaneously tend to do right because that is what they *want* to do, what they *need* to do, what they enjoy" (*PB*, p. 159). Most Third Force psychologists would agree with Horney that the way to become good is to become healthy and that our "prime moral obligation" is not to control ourselves, but "to work at ourselves" (*NHG*, p. 15).

The self-actualizing person is a superior ethical being partly because he is living from his inner core, which is good, and partly because he is extraordinarily open to others and to the total situation in which he is acting. By a process of partly conscious and partly unconscious calculation, he seeks that course of action which permits the maximum fulfillment of all his needs, which offers the highest degree both of self-realization and of social good possible under the circumstances. Rogers describes this process in its ideal form in his picture of the fully functioning person:

> The person who is fully open to his experience would have access to all of the available data in the situation, on which to base his behavior; the social demands, his own complex and possibly conflicting needs, his memories of similar situations, his perception of the uniqueness of this situation, etc., etc. The data would be very complex indeed. But he could permit his total

> organism, his consciousness participating, to consider each stimulus, need, and demand, its relative intensity and importance, and out of this complex weighing and balancing, discover that course of action which would come closest to satisfying all his needs in the situation. (*BP,* p. 190)

The world-openness of the self-actualizing person is manifested in his ways of perceiving and of relating himself to external reality. Ernest Schachtel observes that "only thought which is sufficiently free from the pressure of urgent needs or fears can contemplate its object fully and recognize it in relative independence from the thinker's needs and fears—that is, as something objective."[13] When they are self-actualizing, people are relatively free of urgent needs and fears, and they have, therefore, an unusual ability to attend to the external world and to perceive it objectively. In Schachtel's terms, defensive people tend to be autocentric (subject-centered) in their perceptions, while self-actualizing people tend to be allocentric (object-centered) in their approach to reality.

In the autocentric mode of perception "there is little or no objectification; the emphasis is on how and what the person feels; there is a close relation, amounting to a fusion, between sensory quality and pleasure or unpleasure feelings, and the perceiver reacts primarily to something impinging on him" (*M,* p. 83). The world is divided into "objects-of-use" and "objects-to-be-avoided." Things and people are seen in terms of "how they will serve a certain *need* of the perceiver, or how they can be *used* by him for some purpose, or how they have to be *avoided* in order to prevent pain, displeasure, injury, or discomfort" (*M,* p. 167). The perceiver focuses not upon "the object in its own right, but [upon] those of its aspects which relate to" his own purposes, needs, and fears (*M,* p. 167). Autocentric perception corresponds closely to what Maslow calls D-cognition, that is, "cognition organized by the deficiency needs of the individual" (*PB,* p. 73).

In the allocentric mode of perception (which corresponds to Maslow's Being or B-cognition) "there is objectification; the emphasis is on what the object is like; there is . . . a less pronounced . . . relation between perceived sensory qualities and pleasure-unpleasure feelings . . . ; the perceiver usually approaches the object actively and in doing so either opens himself toward it receptively or . . . takes hold of it, tries to 'grasp' it" (*M,* p. 83). In allocentric perception "the object is perceived in its suchness, without any labeling, naming, classifying, thinking of possible similarities, relations to other objects, etc." (*M,* p. 179). The perceiver exposes himself to the object with relatively few preconceptions and protective devices. The "allocentric attitude" is "one of profound interest in the object, and complete openness and receptivity toward it, a full turning toward the object which makes possible the direct encounter with it and not merely a quick registration of its familiar features according to ready labels" (*M,* pp. 220–21). Interest is in the whole object and the perceiver turns toward it with the whole of his being.

Allocentric perception provides a far richer and more accurate picture of the world than does the more usual autocentric mode. It is alive to the wonder of the familiar, which, because it is nonthreatening, has receded into the background for most people. It is more ideographic than conceptual and hence restores to awareness those aspects of reality that our systematic knowledge has ignored. It gives us "the real, concrete world" rather than the "system of rubrics, motives, expectations, and abstractions which we have projected onto" it (*PB*, p. 41). It "breaks through and transcends the confines of the labeled, the familiar, and establishes a relation in which a direct encounter with the object itself . . . takes place" (*M*, p. 177). It permits us to see other people as they are in and for themselves, holistically, "as complicated, unique individuals" (*PB*, p. 36). "Because self-actualizing people ordinarily do not have to abstract need-gratifying qualities nor see the person as a tool," observes Maslow, "it is much more possible for them to take a non-valuing, non-judging, non-interfering, non-condemning attitude toward others. . . . This permits much clearer . . . perception . . . of what is there" (*PB*, pp. 40–41).

There is a close connection between allocentric perception and what Maslow calls Being-love.[14] Those who see all human relationships as I-it relationships, in which people use each other as objects and in which the subjectivity of the other is threatening and must be denied, are describing as inherent in the general human condition relationships as they exist between deficiency-motivated, autocentrically oriented people. In the Being-love relationship the other person is seen allocentrically, as he is in and for himself, and he is loved for what he is and because he is understood rather than for what he can give to the lover. The B-love relationship is a nonclinging relationship in which there is respect for the other's dignity and autonomy and a desire for the other's growth. B-love is not confined to one partner but is extended to all persons who are seen allocentrically; it is the central feature of all the relationships that Carl Rogers characterizes as "helping relationships." Being-love is what all people need, more than anything else, in order to grow (see *PB*, p. 43). One of our profoundest cravings is to be allocentrically perceived by another: "We all want to be recognized and accepted for what we are in our fulness, richness and complexity. If such an acceptor cannot be found among human beings, then the very strong tendency appears to project and create a god-like figure, sometimes a human one, sometimes supernatural" (*PB*, p. 93).

Allocentric perception has an "enriching, refreshing, vitalizing" effect upon the perceiver (*M*, p. 177). But it is also a frightening experience, a venture into the unknown, which requires unusual inner strength and autonomy. The "immediate and live contact with the ineffable objects of reality," says Schachtel, "is dreadful and wonderful at the same time. It can be frightening, as though it were death itself" (*M*, p. 193). It is so fearsome because it threatens our defenses and disturbs our embeddedness.

Schachtel sees human development as, in part, a conflict between our tendencies toward embeddedness and our tendencies toward openness and growth. There is in everyone's psychic evolution a conflict between the wish to remain embedded in the womb or in the mother's care, eventually in the accustomed, the fear of separation from such embeddedness, and the wish to encounter the world and to develop and realize, in this encounter, the human capacities" (*M*, p. 151).

Schachtel's concept of embeddedness provides the best bridge between Freudian and Third Force psychologies, since it allows him to "incorporate what is valid in Freud's law of the pleasure principle" (*M*, p. 60), while indicating at the same time its incompleteness. There are states that seem to be governed by the pleasure principle, "and others . . . where we find a desire for, and enjoyment of, stimulation and activity rather than the wish to get rid of it" (*M*, p. 56). Schachtel would replace the pleasure principle with the "law of embeddedness," which holds that an increase of stimulation is not always unpleasure, "but that the more nearly complete the state of embeddedness of the organism, the more strongly negative is [its] reaction . . . to any change . . . and the less does [it] want to stir from a state of quiescent equilibrium" (*M*, p. 60). Freud's concept of the pleasure principle accurately describes a certain portion of our experience, but it leaves out "the phenomena, so striking in the growing infant and child, of the pleasure and fulfillment found in the encounter with an expanding reality and in the development, exercise, and realization of his growing capacities, skills, and powers" (*M*, p. 9).

Schachtel revises Freud's theory of affect accordingly, distinguishing between embeddedness- and activity-affect. The former "is characterized by helpless distress" and the latter "by active coping. . . . They represent two different ways of dealing with the separation from the intrauterine situation of continuous supply and shelter. One implies basically the wish for the return to this stage or the frustration, anger, impatience that such a return is not possible; the other represents the adaptation to the new, separate forms of existence" (*M*, p. 29). The function of embeddedness-affect is to "activate the care of the mothering one, . . . to induce the environment to do something about the organism's needs" (*M*, p. 31). The function of activity-affect is "to establish an effective emotional link between the separate organism and the environment, so that the organism will be able to engage in those activities which will satisfy his needs, develop his capacities, and further his life" (*M*, p. 31). Instead of seeking the reduction of tension, as do embeddedness-affects, activity-affects "have energetic, zestful, interested feeling tones and . . . are characterized by a positive tension feeling; they lend impetus to the ongoing activity and are felt to energize, activate, and sustain it" (*M*, p. 32).

In the course of healthy development "the embeddedness principle yields to the transcendence principle of openness toward the world and of self-realization which takes place in the encounter with the world" (*M*, p. 157). Under unfavorable conditions, such as "anxiety arousing early experiences in the child-parent relationship, the embeddedness principle may remain pathologically strong, with the result that the encounter with the world is experienced in an autocentric way as an unwelcome impinging of disturbing stimuli" (*M*, pp. 157–58). When this happens, the individual fears and avoids "everything new or strange that might disturb the . . . embeddedness in a closed pattern or routine, which may be the pattern of a particular culture, a particular social group, a personal routine pattern of life, or, usually, a combination of all these" (*M*, p. 167). Embeddedness and openness are always matters of degree; the conflict between them is never finally resolved: "Man always lives somewhere between these two poles of clinging to a rigid attitude with its closed world and of leaping into the stream of life with his senses open toward the inexhaustible, changing, infinite world" (*M*, pp. 199–200).

The self-actualizing person is distinguished, then, not only by his courage to be himself, but also by his courage to be in the world. "All rubricizing," says Maslow, "is, in effect, an attempt to 'freeze the world'" (*MP*, p. 212). The anxious person is "afraid that without the support of his accustomed attitudes, perspectives, and labels he will fall into an abyss or founder in the pathless" (*M*, p. 195). He tries to "'freeze or staticize or stop the motion of a moving, changing process world in order to be able to handle it'" (*MP*, p. 213). The self-actualizing person is able to recognize and live with the fact that "the world is a perpetual flux and all things are in process" (*MP*, p. 212). He trusts his real self enough to follow its promptings without knowing exactly where they will lead, and he trusts his ability to sustain his encounters with the world enough to be open to an authentic experience of the out there. "I find I am at my best," says Rogers, "when I can let the flow of my experience carry me, in a direction which appears to be forward, toward goals of which I am but dimly aware. . . . When I am thus able to be in process, it is clear that there can be no closed system of beliefs, no unchanging set of principles which I hold. Life is guided by a changing understanding of . . . my experience. It is always in process of becoming" (*BP*, p. 27).

3. SELF-ALIENATION

According to Third Force psychology, self-alienation occurs when the individual's basic needs are not met. He loses touch with his real feelings, becomes fixated on his lowest unmet need, and develops elaborate strategies of defense. Of all the Third Force psychologists, Karen Horney has described these strategies most brilliantly. She is concerned, in particular, with what happens to people when they are deprived of their needs for safety, love and belonging, and esteem, the middle needs on the Maslovian hierarchy. One of the things that happens is that they cease to experience these needs in a healthy way. Instead of being gratifiable through the appropriate sources of supply, the needs become insatiable and never go away. People who have been severely deprived of love, for example, come to feel unlovable and cannot believe they are being loved, even when such is the case. The defensive strategies they develop will be attempts to compensate for the frustration not merely of their basic needs but of the neurotic needs that have taken their place.

Though the concept of the real self did not become central in Horney's thinking until her last book, she began quite early to conceive of neurosis as a process of self-alienation and of therapy as a process of giving the individual "the courage to be himself."[15] In order to "restore the individual to himself, to help him regain his spontaneity and find his center of gravity in himself," therapy must "lessen his anxiety to such an extent that he can dispense with his 'neurotic trends'" (*NW*, p. 11). As Horney sees it, adverse conditions in his environment produce in the individual a feeling of "basic anxiety," which he seeks to overcome by developing certain neurotic trends, certain interpersonal and intrapsychic strategies of defense. His strategies of defense, however, by virtue of the inner conflicts they generate and the increased self-alienation they entail, tend to create new problems and to exacerbate the conditions they were devised to remedy. Neurotic development is characterized by a number of "vicious circles" in which the individual's efforts to protect himself lead to self-betrayal and a kind of psychic death.[16] We shall trace here the process by which the self is lost and a false-self system is formed.[17]

According to Horney, neurosis begins as a defense against basic anxiety.[18] Basic anxiety is a "profound insecurity and vague apprehensiveness" (*NHG*, p. 18), which is produced by what Maslow calls "basic threat," that is, by the frustration of basic needs. It involves a dread of the environment as a whole, which is "felt to be unreliable, mendacious, unappreciative, unfair, . . . begrudging and merciless" (*NW*, p. 75). As a result of this dread, the child develops self-protective strategies, which in time become compulsive. His "attempts to relate himself to others are determined not by his real feelings but by strategic necessities. He cannot simply like or dislike, trust or distrust, express his wishes or protest against those of others, but has automatically to devise ways to cope with people and to manipulate them with minimum damage to himself."[19] He abandons himself in order to protect himself, but as the real self becomes weaker the environment becomes more threatening. Environmental threat weakens the self, the weakness of the self increases the sense of threat, and a basic anxiety takes the place of basic trust in self and in the world.

Basic anxiety involves a fear not only of the environment but also of the self. A threatening environment is bound to produce in the child both an intense hostility and a profound dependency that makes him terrified of expressing his hostility and compels him to repress it. Because he "registers within himself the existence of a highly explosive affect" (*NP*, p. 8), he is extremely fearful of himself, afraid that he will let out his rage and thus bring the anger of others down upon him. The child's hostility is generated not only by the unfairness of his treatment, but also by his knowledge, at some level, that he is being forced to abandon his real self and, with it, his chance for a meaningful life. He hates those who are compelling him to the sacrifice, and he hates himself, as well, for his weakness.

The repression of hostility has very bad consequences. It reinforces the child's feeling of defenselessness; it leads him to blame himself for the situation about which he is angry and to "feel unworthy of love" (*NP*, p. 84); and it makes him extremely fearful of spontaneity. It may lead to the development of a retaliation fear, a fear that others will do to him what he wants (unconsciously) to do to them. Since the child needs to get rid of the hostility that is so dangerous to him, he often projects his hostile impulses onto the outside world, in which case he feels himself in the hands of malign powers. This, of course, increases his fear of the world and leads to an intensification of both anxiety and hostility.

Basic anxiety affects the individual's attitudes toward both himself and others. He feels himself to be impotent, unlovable, of little value to the world. Because of his sense of weakness he wants to rely on others, to be protected and cared for, but he cannot risk himself with others because of his hostility and deep distrust. The invariable consequence of his basic anxiety "is that he has to put the greatest part of his energies into securing reassurance" (*NP*, p. 96). He seeks reassurance in his relation to others by developing the interpersonal strategies of defense that we shall examine next, and he seeks to compensate for his feelings of worthlessness and inadequacy by an intrapsychic process of self-glorification. These strategies constitute his effort to fulfill his now insatiable needs for safety, love and belonging, and self-esteem. They are also designed to reduce his anxiety and to provide a safe outlet for his hostility. They are usually self-defeating. They cut the individual off from both himself and others; and, as a consequence, they reinforce the feelings of isolation, helplessness, fear, and rage that they were designed to assuage. In addition, they create inner divisions that threaten the person's sense of wholeness and identity, and thus they create new problems, which must be resolved by additional self-defeating measures.

There are three main ways in which the child, and later the adult, can move in his effort to overcome his feelings of helplessness and isolation and to establish himself safely in a threatening world. He can adopt a compliant or self-effacing solution and move *toward* people; he can develop an aggressive or expansive solution and move *against* people; or he can become detached or resigned and move *away from* people. The healthy person moves flexibly in all three directions. The self-alienated person, however, "is not flexible; he is driven to comply, to fight, to be aloof, regardless of whether the move is appropriate in the particular circumstance, and he is thrown into a panic if he behaves otherwise" (*OIC*, p. 202). Each of these solutions carries with it "certain needs, qualities, sensitivities, inhibitions, anxieties, and . . . values" (*OIC*, p. 49). Each solution involves also a view of human nature, a sense of the world order, and a bargain with fate in which certain qualities, attitudes, and behaviors are supposed to be rewarded.

In each of the defensive moves "one of the elements involved in basic anxiety is overemphasized": helplessness in the compliant solution, hostility in the aggressive solution, and isolation in the solution of detachment. Since under the conditions that produce neurosis all of these feelings are bound to arise, the individual will come to make all three of the defensive moves compulsively.

The three moves involve incompatible value systems and character structures, however; and a person cannot move in all three directions without feeling terribly confused and divided. In order to gain some sense of wholeness and ability to function, he will emphasize one move more than the others and will become predominantly compliant, aggressive, or detached. Which move he emphasizes will depend upon the particular combination of temperamental and environmental factors at work in his situation.

The other trends will continue to exist quite powerfully, but they will operate unconsciously and will manifest themselves in devious and disguised ways. The "basic conflict" will not have been resolved, but will simply have gone underground. When the submerged trends are for some reason brought closer to the surface, the individual will experience severe inner turmoil, and he may be paralyzed, unable to move in any direction at all. Under the impetus of some powerful influence or of the dramatic failure of his predominant solution, the individual may embrace one of the repressed attitudes. He will experience this as conversion or education, but it will be merely the substitution of one defensive strategy for another.

As we discuss the three interpersonal moves and the character types to which they give rise, let us keep in mind that we will find neither characters in literature nor people in life who correspond exactly to Horney's descriptions. As Horney herself observes, "although people tending toward the same main solution have characteristic similarities they may differ widely with regard to the level of human qualities, gifts, or achievements involved."

> Moreover, what we regard as "types" are actually cross sections of personalities in which the neurotic process has led to rather extreme developments with pronounced characteristics. But there is always an indeterminate range of intermediate structures deriding any precise classification. These complexities are further enhanced by the fact that, owing to the process of psychic fragmentation, even in extreme instances there is often more than one main solution. "Most cases are mixed cases," says William James, "and we should not treat our classifications with too much respect." Perhaps it would be more nearly correct to speak of directions of development than of types. (*NHG*, p. 191)

If we keep these qualifications in mind, we shall find Horney's analysis of the process of self-alienated development and of the kinds of character structures to which it gives rise to be of great value for the appreciation of literature. If we forget them, we are liable to focus on identifying neurotic types, rather than upon grasping the complexity and the phenomenological reality of individual characters and implied authors, and our analysis will be nothing more than a reductive labeling.

The person in whom compliant trends are dominant tries to overcome his basic anxiety by gaining affection and approval and by controlling others through his need of them. He needs to feel himself part of something larger and more powerful than himself, a need which often manifests itself as religious devotion, identification with a group or cause, or morbid dependency in a love relationship. *"His salvation lies in others"* (*NHG*, p. 226). As a result, "his need for people . . . often attains a frantic character" (*NHG*, p. 226). His "self-esteem rises and falls" with the approval or disapproval of others, with "their affection or lack of it" (*OIC*, p. 54).

In order to gain the love, approval, acceptance, and support he needs, the basically compliant person develops certain qualities, inhibitions, and ways of relating. He seeks to attach others to him by being good, loving, self-effacing, and weak. He tries to live up to the expectations of others, "often to the extent of losing sight of his own feelings" (*OIC*, p. 51). "He becomes 'unselfish,' self-sacrificing, undemanding—except for his unbounded desire for affection. He becomes . . . overconsiderate . . . over-appreciative, over-grateful, generous" (*OIC*, pp. 51–52). He is appeasing and conciliatory and tends to blame himself and to feel guilty whenever he quarrels with another, feels disappointed, or is criticized. Regarding himself as worthless or guilty makes him feel more secure, for then others cannot regard him as a threat. For similar reasons, "he tends to subordinate himself, takes second place, leaving the limelight to others" (*OIC*, p. 52). Because "any wish, any striving, any reaching out for more feels to him like a dangerous or reckless challenging of fate," he is severely inhibited in his self-assertive and self-protective activities and has powerful taboos against "all that is presumptuous, selfish, and aggressive" (*NHG*, pp. 218, 219). Through weakness and suffering he at once controls others and justifies himself. His motto is: "You must love me, protect me, forgive me, not desert me, *because* I am so weak and helpless" (*OIC*, p. 53).

The compliant defense brings with it not only certain ways of feeling and behaving, but also a special set of values and beliefs. "They lie in the direction of goodness, sympathy, love, generosity, unselfishness, humility; while egotism, ambition, callousness, unscrupulousness, wielding of power are abhorred—though these attributes may at the same time be secretly admired because they represent 'strength' " (*OIC*, pp. 54–55). Citing their possible neurotic origin does not necessarily mean, of course, that these values are no good or that they are always held for neurotic reasons. The compliant person, however, does not hold them as genuine ideals but because they are necessary to his defense system. He must believe in turning the other cheek, and he must see the world as displaying a providential order in which virtue is rewarded. His bargain is that if he is a good, loving, noble person who shuns pride and does not seek his private gain or glory, he will be well treated by fate and by other people. If his bargain is not honored, he may despair of divine justice, he may conclude that he is the guilty party, or he may have recourse to belief in a higher justice that transcends human understanding. He needs to believe not only in the fairness of the world order, but also in the goodness of human nature. In this area, too, he is vulnerable to disappointment. As a result, there is a "curious ambivalence" in his attitude toward his fellows: "a surface prevalence of 'naive' optimistic trust and an undercurrent of just as indiscriminate suspiciousness and resentment" (*NHG,* p. 233). This ambivalence characterizes his attitude toward life in general.

In the compliant person, says Horney, there is "a variety of aggressive tendencies strongly repressed." These aggressive tendencies are repressed because feeling them or acting them out would clash violently with the compliant person's need to feel that he is loving and unselfish and would radically endanger his strategy for gaining love and approval. It would also endanger his bargain with fate, since the essence of such a bargain is that the person must live up to the dictates of his solution if his claims upon life are to be honored. The compliant person's strategies tend to increase rather than to diminish his basic hostility, for "self-effacement and 'goodness' invite being stepped on," and "dependence upon others makes for exceptional vulnerability" (*OIC,* pp. 55–56). But his inner rage threatens his self-image, his philosophy of life, and his safety; and he must repress, disguise, or justify his anger in order to avoid arousing self-hate and the hostility of others.

The meaning of life for the compliant person usually lies in the love relation. Love appears "as the ticket to paradise, where all woe ends: no more feeling lost, guilty, and unworthy; no more responsibility for self; no more struggle with a harsh world for which he feels hopelessly unequipped" (*NHG,* p. 240). If he finds a partner "whose neurosis fits in with his own, his suffering may be considerably lessened and he may find a moderate amount of happiness" (*OIC,* p. 62). As a rule, however, "the relationship from which he expects heaven on earth only plunges him into deeper misery. He is all too likely to carry his conflicts into the relationship and thereby destroy it" (*OIC,* p. 26). Because of his need for surrender and for a safe expression of his aggressive tendencies, the compliant person is frequently attracted to his opposite, the masterful, expansive person: "To love a proud person, to merge with him, to live vicariously through him would allow him to participate in the mastery of life without having to own it to himself" (*NHG,* p. 244). This kind of relationship generally develops into a "morbid dependency," in which "the dependent partner is in danger of destroying himself, slowly and painfully" (*NHG,* p. 243).[20] When the love relation fails him, the compliant person will be terribly disillusioned and will feel either that he did not find the right person or that nothing is worth having.

The person in whom aggressive tendencies are predominant has goals, traits, and values that are quite the opposite of those of the compliant person. Since he seeks safety through conquest, "he needs to excel, to achieve success, prestige, or recognition" (*OIC,* p. 65). What appeals to him most is not love, but mastery. He abhors helplessness and is ashamed of suffering. He seeks to cultivate in himself "the efficiency and resourcefulness" necessary to his solution (*OIC,* p. 167). There are three aggressive types: the narcissistic, the perfectionistic, and the arrogant-vindictive. They all "aim at mastering life. This is their way of conquering fears and anxieties; this gives meaning to their lives and gives them a certain zest for living" (*NHG*, p. 212).

The narcissistic person seeks to master life "by self-admiration and the exercise of charm" (*NHG*, p. 212). He has an "unquestioned belief in his greatness and uniqueness," which gives him a "buoyancy and perennial youthfulness" (*NHG*, p. 194). "He has (consciously) no doubts; he *is* the anointed, the man of destiny, the prophet, the great giver, the benefactor of mankind" (*NHG*, p. 194). His insecurity is manifested in the fact that he "may speak incessantly of his exploits or of his wonderful qualities and needs endless confirmation of his estimate of himself in the form of admiration and devotion" (*NHG*, p. 194). He frequently gets into trouble because he "does not reckon with limitations" and he "over-rates his capacities" (*NHG*, 195). On the surface he is "rather optimistic" and "turns outward toward life," but "there are undercurrents of despondency and pessimism" (*NHG*, p. 196). He sees the world as a fostering parent and expects continual good fortune in the form of good luck and the fulfillment of his wishes by fate and by other people. His bargain is that if he holds onto his dreams and to his exaggerated claims for himself, life is bound to give him what he wants. Since life can never match his expectations, he feels, in his weaker moments, that it is full of tragic contradictions.

The perfectionistic person "feels superior because of his high standards, moral and intellectual, and on this basis looks down on others" (*NHG*, p. 196). He needs "to attain the highest degree of excellence"; and because of the difficulties which this entails, he tends "to equate in his mind standards and actualities—*knowing* about moral values and *being* a good person" (*NHG*, p. 196). While he in this way deceives himself, he may insist that others live up to "his standards of perfection and despise them for failing to do so. His own self-condemnation is thus externalized" (*NHG*, p. 196). The imposition of his standards on others leads to admiration for a select few and a critical or condescending attitude toward the majority of mankind. The perfectionistic person has a legalistic conception of the world order. Through the height of his standards, he compels fate:

> His claims are based less on a "naive" belief in his greatness than . . . on a "deal" he has secretly made with life. Because he is fair, just, dutiful, he is entitled to fair treatment by others and by life in general. This conviction of an infallible justice operating in life gives him a feeling of mastery. His own perfection therefore is not only a means to superiority but also one to control life. His own success, prosperity, or good health is . . . less something to be enjoyed than a proof of his virtue. (*NHG*, p. 197)

Ill fortune shakes him "to the foundations of his psychic existence. It invalidates his whole accounting system and conjures up the ghastly prospect of helplessness." "His recognition of an error or failure of his own making" also "pulls the ground away from under him. . . . Self-effacing trends and undiluted self-hate, kept in check successfully hitherto, then may come to the fore" (*NHG*, p. 197).

The arrogant-vindictive person is motivated chiefly by a need for vindictive triumphs. Whereas the narcissistic person received early admiration, and the perfectionistic person "grew up under the pressure of rigid standards," the arrogant-vindictive person was "harshly treated" (*NHG*, p. 221). He has a need to retaliate for all injuries and to prove his superiority to all rivals. He is extremely competitive: "he cannot tolerate anybody who knows or achieves more than he does, wields more power, or in any way questions his superiority. Compulsively he has to drag his rival down or defeat him" (*NHG*, p. 198). In his relations with others he is at once ruthless and cynical. He seeks to "exploit others, to outsmart them, to make them of use to himself" (*OIC*, p. 167). He trusts no one and is out to get others before they get him. He avoids emotional involvement and dependency and uses the relations of friendship and marriage as a means by which he can possess the desirable qualities of others and so enhance his own position. He wants to be hard and tough, and he regards all manifestation of feeling as sloppy sentimentality. Since it is important for a person "as isolated and as hostile" as he is not to need people, he "develops a pronounced pride in a godlike self-sufficiency" (*NHG*, p. 204).

The philosophy of the arrogant-vindictive type tends to be that of an Iago or a Nietzsche. He feels "that the world is an arena where, in the Darwinian sense, only the fittest survive and the strong annihilate the weak. . . . [A] callous pursuit of self-interest is the paramount law" (*OIC*, p. 64). Considerateness, compassion, loyalty, self-sacrifice are all scorned as signs of weakness; those who value such qualities are fools whom it is no crime to take advantage of, since they are just asking for it. The only moral law inherent in the order of things is that might makes right.

Just as the compliant person must repress his hostile impulses in order to make his solution work, so for the aggressive person "any feeling of sympathy, or obligation to be 'good,' or attitude of compliance would be incompatible with the whole structure of living he has built up and would shake its foundations" (*OIC*, p. 70). It is because his own softer feelings are such a threat to him that he must deny them so completely. He despises the Christian ethic and is "likely to feel nauseated at the sight of affectionate behavior in others" (*OIC*, p. 69). His reaction is so extreme because "it is prompted by his need to fight all softer feelings in himself. Nietzsche gives us a good illustration of these dynamics when he has his superman see any form of sympathy as a sort of fifth column, an enemy operating from within" (*OIC*, pp. 69–70). He fears the emergence of his own compliant trends because they would make him vulnerable in an evil world, would confront him with self-hate, and would threaten his bargain, which is essentially with himself. He does not count on the world to give him anything, but he is convinced that he can reach his ambitious goals if he remains true to his vision of life as a battle and does not allow himself to be seduced by his softer feelings or the traditional morality. If his expansive solution collapses, self-effacing trends may emerge quite powerfully.

The basically detached person worships freedom and strives to be independent of both outer and inner demands. He pursues neither love nor mastery; he wants, rather, to be left alone, to have nothing expected of him and to be subject to no restrictions. He has a "*hypersensitivity to influence, pressure, coercion* or *ties* of any kind" (*NHG*, p. 266). He may react with anxiety to physical pressure from clothing, closed in spaces, long-term obligations, and inexorability of time and the laws of cause and effect, traditional values and rules of behavior, or, indeed, anything that interferes with his absolute freedom. He wants to do what he pleases, when he pleases; but, since he is alienated from his spontaneous desires, his freedom is rather empty. It is a *freedom from* what he feels as coercion rather than a *freedom to* fulfill himself. His desire for freedom may take the form of a craving for serenity, which "means for him simply the absence of all troubles, irritations, or upsets" (*NHG*, p. 263).

The detached person handles a threatening world by removing himself from its power and by shutting others out of his inner life. He disdains the pursuit of worldly success and has a profound aversion to effort. He has a very strong need for superiority and usually looks upon his fellows with condescension; but he realizes his ambition in imagination rather than through actual accomplishments. He feels "that the treasures within him should be recognized without any effort on his part; his hidden greatness should be felt without his having to make a move" (*OIC*, p. 80). He makes himself invulnerable by being self-sufficient. This involves not only living in imagination but also restricting his desires. In order to avoid being dependent on the environment, he tries to subdue his inner cravings and to be content with little. He cultivates a "don't care" attitude and protects himself against frustration by believing that "nothing matters." He seeks privacy, shrouds himself "in a veil of secrecy" (*OIC*, p. 76), and, in his personal relations, draws around himself "a kind of magic circle which no one may penetrate" (*OIC*, p. 75). He may feel an "intolerable strain in associating with people" (*OIC*, p. 73), and he "may very readily go to pieces" (*OIC*, p. 90) if his magic circle is entered and he is thrown into intimate contact with others. His panic is so great because "he has no technique for dealing with life. . . . He is as defenseless as an animal that has only one means of coping with danger—that is, to escape and hide" (*OIC*, p. 92).

The detached person withdraws from himself as well as from others. "There is a general tendency to suppress all feeling, even to deny its existence" (*OIC*, p. 82). His resignation from active living gives him an "onlooker" attitude toward both himself and others and often permits him to be an excellent observer of his own inner processes. His psychological insight is divorced from feeling; he looks at himself "with a kind of objective interest, as one would look at a work of art" (*OIC*, p. 74). The detached person's withdrawal from himself is in part an effort to resolve his basic conflict. In the detached person, compliant and aggressive trends are not deeply repressed; both are visible to the trained observer and are rather easily brought to awareness. The detached person tries to resolve the conflict between his aggressive and compliant trends not by excluding one or the other of them, but by immobilizing both of them. This solution through evasion is "the most radical and most effective" of the defenses erected against the major conflicts; but "it is no true solution because the compulsive cravings for closeness as well as for aggressive domination, exploitation, and excelling remain, and they keep harassing if not paralyzing their carrier" (*OIC*, p. 95).

The detached person is more likely than the other two types to entertain the attitudes and to display the moves of the subordinated solutions. As a result, "in contrast to the clearly defined values of the other two types, his sets of values are most contradictory" (*OIC*, p. 94). He has a "permanent high evaluation of what he regards as freedom and independence" (*OIC*, p. 94); and he cultivates individuality, self-reliance, and an indifference to fate. But "he may at some time . . . express an extreme appreciation for human goodness, sympathy, generosity, self-effacing sacrifice, and at another time swing to a complete jungle philosophy of callous self-interest" (*OIC*, p. 94). In order to reduce his vulnerability, he believes, "consciously or unconsciously, that it is *better* not to wish or expect anything. Sometimes this goes with a conscious pessimistic outlook on life, a sense of its being futile anyhow and of nothing being sufficiently desirable to make an effort for it" (*NHG*, p. 263). He does not usually rail against life, however, but resigns himself to things as they are and accepts his fate with ironic humor or stoical dignity. He tries to escape suffering by being independent of external forces, by feeling that nothing matters, and by concerning himself only with those things that are within his power. His bargain is that if he asks nothing of others, they will not bother him; that if he tries for nothing, he will not fail; and that if he expects little of life, he will not be disappointed.

An individual's defensive strategies for coping with other people are designed to reduce his anxiety by giving him a feeling of safety and belonging, but in reality they are destructive to him, and this for several reasons. His compulsive behavior makes his human relations more rather than less disturbed. His self-protective moves create a basic inner conflict that threatens to tear him apart. His choice of safety over spontaneous growth leads to greater and greater self-alienation, for his artificial strategies create a system of neurotic feelings that has little to do with the feelings of his real self. Finally, his self-alienation intensifies his original feeling of weakness, and his self-betrayal intensifies his feeling of worthlessness, for every time he chooses against the interests of his real self he incurs self-hatred.

While interpersonal difficulties are creating the movements toward, against, and away from people, and the basic conflict, the concomitant intrapsychic problems are producing their own self-defeating defensive strategies. The destructive attitudes of others, his alienation from his real self, and his self-hatred make the individual feel terribly weak and worthless. To compensate for this he creates, with the aid of his imagination, an "idealized image" of himself: "In this process he endows himself with unlimited powers and with exalted faculties; he becomes a hero, a genius, a supreme lover, a saint, a god" (*NHG*, p. 22). The idealized image serves also to provide inner unity and a sense of identity; it is "a kind of artistic creation in which opposites appear reconciled or in which, at any rate, they no longer appear as conflicts to the individual himself" (*OIC*, p. 104).

The nature of the idealized image depends upon the individual's "own special experiences, his earlier fantasies, his particular needs, and . . . his given faculties" (*NHG*, p. 22). Its content is determined particularly by the individual's predominant solution to his basic conflict; it contains all the attributes that are exalted by the compliant, aggressive, or detached moves. The submerged trends may be glorified, too; but they remain in the background, are isolated through compartmentalization, or are seen, somehow, as "compatible aspects of a rich personality" (*NHG*, p. 23). In the course of neurotic development, the idealized image assumes more and more reality. It becomes the individual's "idealized self"; it represents to him "what he 'really' is, or potentially is—what he could be, and should be" (*NHG*, p. 23).

The idealized image is designed to enhance the individual's feeling of worth and to provide a sense of identity, but it rather quickly leads to increased self-contempt and additional inner conflicts. The qualities with which the individual invests himself are dictated by his predominant interpersonal strategy, each of which glorifies, as we have seen, a different set of traits. The repressed solutions are also represented, however; and, as a result, the idealized image has contradictory aspects, all of which the individual must try to live up to. Since he can feel worthwhile only if he *is* his idealized image, everything that falls short is deemed worthless; and there develops a "despised image" that is just as unrealistic as its idealized counterpart. "He wavers then between self-adoration and self-contempt, between his idealized image and his despised image, with no solid middle ground to fall back on" (*OIC*, p. 112).

There are now four selves competing for his allegiance: the real (or possible) self; the idealized (or impossible) self; the despised self; and the actual self, which is what he realistically is at the moment. The more self-actualizing a person is, the greater will be the congruence between the real self and the actual self and the less likelihood will there be that he will harbor idealized and despised selves. The more self-alienated a person is, the greater will be the distance between the real self and the actual self, the actual self and the idealized self, and the idealized self and the despised self.

The increased self-hate and inner conflict produced by the formation of the idealized image lead to further self-glorification (with its concomitant of intensified self-contempt) and to compulsive efforts to realize the idealized image, either in action or in imagination. Thus begins the "search for glory," as "the energies driving toward self-realization are shifted to the aim of actualizing the idealized self" (*NHG*, p. 24). The search for glory often takes the form of a quest of the absolute: "All the drives for glory have in common the reaching out for greater knowledge, wisdom, virtue, or powers than are given to human beings. . . . Nothing short of absolute fearlessness, mastery, or saintliness has any appeal. . . . The needs for the *absolute* and the *ultimate* are so stringent that they override the checks which usually prevent our imagination from detaching itself from actuality" (*NHG*, pp. 34–35). Imagination is put into the service of neurosis not only in the creation of the idealized self and the formation of lofty dreams but also in the continual falsification of reality that is necessary to protect the precious illusions.

Horney does not see the search for glory, the quest of the absolute, the need to be God as an essential ingredient of human nature. Because he has the ability to imagine and to plan, the human being is always reaching beyond himself; but the healthy individual reaches for the possible (he dreams a possible dream) and he works to achieve his goals within the context of human and cosmic limitations. He is able to take satisfaction in his achievements and to sustain his frustrations without rage, self-hate, or despair. The self-alienated individual, however, is either all or he is nothing. Indeed, it is because he feels himself to be nothing that he must claim to be all. He who can be a man does not need to be God.

For the self-alienated individual, the search for glory is often the most important thing in his life. It gives him the sense of meaning and the feeling of superiority that he so desperately craves. He fiercely resists all encroachments upon his illusory grandeur and may prefer death to the shattering of his dream. He pays a heavy price, however, for his sense of exaltation, a price that is symbolized, Horney feels, by the story of the devil's pact: "The devil, or some other personification of evil, tempts a person who is perplexed by spiritual or material trouble with the offer of unlimited powers. But he can obtain these powers only on the condition of selling his soul or going to hell" (*NHG*, p. 39). Some people sacrifice their lives to preserve their idealized selves; all who engage in the search for glory condemn themselves to a kind of psychic damnation: "the easy way to infinite glory is inevitably also the way to an inner hell of self-contempt and self-torment. By taking this road, the individual is in fact losing his soul—his real self" (*NHG*, p. 39).

The creation of the idealized image produces not only the search for glory but a whole structure of neurotic strategies that Horney calls "the pride system." The idealized image leads the individual to make both exaggerated *claims for* himself and excessive *demands upon* himself. He takes an intense pride in the attributes of his idealized self, and on the basis of this pride he makes "neurotic claims" upon others. At the same time he feels that he *should* perform in a way commensurate with his idealized attributes.

The over-all function of neurotic claims is to perpetuate the individual's "illusions about himself, and to shift responsibility to factors outside himself"

(*NHG*, p. 63). "As long as his personal aggrandizement is too indispensable to be touched, he can but conclude that there is something wrong with the world. It ought to be different. And so, instead of tackling his illusions, he presents a claim to the outside world. He is entitled to be treated by others, or by fate, in accord with his grandiose notions about himself" (*NHG*, p. 41). Neurotic claims are extremely tenacious, partly because they are necessary to the preservation of the idealized image and partly because their failure threatens the individual with intense self-hate. Failures are rationalized away. The discovery "that others do not accede to his claims, that laws do apply to him, that he is not above common troubles and failures—all of this is no evidence against his unlimited possibilities. It merely proves that, *as yet*, he has had an unfair deal. But if only he upholds his claims, some day they will come true. *The claims are his guaranty for future glory*" (*NHG*, p. 62).

The general characteristics of neurotic claims are that they are unrealistic, they are egocentric, they demand results without effort, they are vindictive, they are based on an assumption of specialness or superiority, they deny the world of cause and effect, and they are "pervaded by expectations of magic" (*NHG*, p. 62). The effects of neurotic claims are "a diffuse sense of frustration," a "chronic discontent," and intensification of the burdensomeness of any hardship, an attitude of envy and insensibility toward others, an uncertainty about rights, and a feeling of inertia (*NHG*, p. 57). Because they increase his vulnerability and "prevent him from squaring himself with his difficulties" (*NHG*, p. 63), neurotic claims perpetuate rather than alleviate the individual's difficulties.

The individual's need to actualize his idealized image leads him not only to make excessive claims upon others, but also to impose stringent demands and taboos upon himself ("the tyranny of the should"). The function of the shoulds is "to make oneself over into one's idealized self: *the premise on which they operate is that nothing should be, or is, impossible for oneself*" (*NHG*, p. 68). Since the idealized self is for the most part a glorification of the compliant, aggressive, or detached solutions, the individual's shoulds are determined largely by the character traits and values associated with his predominant trend. The shoulds are impossible to live up to, partly because they demand perfection and partly because they reflect the individual's inner conflicts and are often contradictory.

People with different solutions not only have different (predominant) shoulds, but they also have different attitudes toward the inner dictates. The aggressive person tends to identify with his shoulds, to accept their validity, and to try "to actualize them in one way or another" (*NHG*, p. 76). He covers over his shortcomings with imaginative reconstruction of reality, with arrogance, or with arbitrary rightness. The compliant person also feels "that his shoulds constitute a law not to be questioned" (*NHG*, p. 76); but, though he tries desperately to measure up to them, "he feels most of the time that he falls pitiably short of fulfilling them. The foremost element in his conscious experience is therefore self-criticism, a feeling of guilt for *not* being the supreme being" (*NHG*, p. 77). The detached person, with his ideal of freedom and his hypersensitivity to coercion, tends to rebel against his shoulds, especially those of the aggressive and the compliant attitudes, which in him are rather close to the surface. He may rebel passively, in which case "everything that he feels he should do arouses conscious or unconscious resentment, and in consequence makes him listless" (*NHG*, p. 77). Or he may rebel actively and behave in ways that defy his inner dictates and violate his taboos.

Characteristics of the shoulds are their coerciveness, their disregard for feasibility, their imperviousness to psychic laws, and their reliance on will-power for fulfillment and on imagination for the denial of failure. The individual's bargain with fate is that if he lives up to his shoulds, his claims will be honored. There is a good deal of externalization connected with the shoulds. The individual feels his shoulds as the expectations of others, his self-hate as their rejection, and his self-criticism as their unfair judgment. He expects others to live up to his shoulds and displaces onto others his rage at his own failure to live up to his standards. The chief effects of the shoulds are a pervasive feeling of strain, hypersensitivity to criticism, impairment of spontaneity, and emotional deadness. The shoulds are a defense against self-loathing, but, like the other defenses, they aggravate the condition they are employed to cure. Not only do they increase self-alienation, but they also intensify self-hate, for they are impossible to live up to. The penalty for failure is the most severe feeling of worthlessness and self-contempt. This is why they have such a tyrannical power. "It is the threat of a punitive self-hate that lurks behind them, that truly makes them a regime of terror" (*NHG*, p. 85).

Neurotic pride is "the climax and consolidation of the process initiated with the search for glory" (*NHG*, p. 109). It substitutes for realistic self-confidence and self-esteem a pride in the attributes of the idealized self, in the successful assertion of claims, and in the "loftiness and severity" (*NHG*, p. 92) of the inner dictates. What the individual takes pride in will be determined largely by his predominant solution; anything can become a source of pride. There is commonly a great pride in the mental processes of imagination, reason, and will: "The infinite powers the neurotic ascribes to himself are, after all, powers of the mind. . . . Incessant work of intellect and imagination . . . goes into maintaining the private fictitious world through rationalizations, justifications, externalizations, reconciling irreconcilables—in short, through finding ways to make things appear different from what they are. The more a person is alienated from himself, the more his mind becomes supreme reality" (*NHG*, p. 91).

Pride is vitally important to the individual; but, since it is based on illusion and self-deception, it makes him extremely vulnerable. Threats to it produce anxiety and hostility; its collapse results in self-contempt. The individual is especially subject to feelings of shame (when he violates his own pride) and humiliation (when his pride is violated by others). He reacts to shame with self-hate and to humiliation with a vindictive hostility ranging "from irritability, to anger, to a blind murderous rage" (*NHG*, p. 99).

There are various devices for restoring pride. They include retaliation, which reestablishes the superiority of the humiliated person, and loss of interest in that which is threatening or damaging. They include also various forms of distortion, such as forgetting humiliating episodes, denying responsibility, blaming others, and embellishing. Sometimes "humor is used to take the sting out of an otherwise unbearable shame" (*NHG*, p. 106). There is an effort to protect pride by a system of avoidances. This includes not trying, restricting wishes and activities, and remaining detached, at a safe distance from involvement. "It is safer to renounce, to withdraw, or to resign than to take the risk of exposing one's pride to injury" (*NHG*, p. 108). This process, if it is widespread, "can actually cripple a person's life. He does not embark on any serious pursuits commensurate with his gifts lest he fail to be a brilliant success" (*NHG*, p. 107).

The pride system is in large measure a defense against self-hate; but, as we have seen, it cannot work and only intensifies the problem it is designed to solve. Self-hate is a neurotic phenomenon that must not be confused with intrinsic guilt or healthy self-criticism. The self-actualizing person will not always like himself, but he will not hate himself. He will handle feelings of guilt and inadequacy in a basically self-accepting and constructive way by recognizing his limitations as a human being and by doing everything he can to repair damage and to avoid future error. He will work at himself patiently, realistically, and without expecting miracles. The self-alienated person will resort to the strategies of self-glorification, neurotic claims, tyrannical shoulds, and neurotic pride in order to blot out his deficiencies and to maintain his self-esteem. It is these strategies, ironically, that are the major source of self-hate; for the individual's loathing for himself is generated not so much by impaired functioning or by intrinsic guilt as by the disparity between what his pride system compels him to be and what he can be. "We do not hate ourselves because we are worthless," says Horney, "but because we are driven to reach beyond ourselves" (*NHG*, p. 114).

Self-hate is essentially the rage that the idealized self feels toward the actual self for not being what it "should" be. The actual self "is such an embarrassing sight when viewed from the perspective of a godlike perfection" that the individual "cannot help but despise it" (*NHG*, p. 110). Since "the human being which he actually is keeps interfering—significantly—with his flight to glory," he "is bound to hate it, to hate himself" (*NHG*, p. 110). As the real self emerges in the course of favorable development, there occurs what Horney calls the "central inner conflict"—between the real self and the pride system—and "self-hate now is not so much directed against the limitations and shortcomings of the actual self as against the emerging constructive forces of the real self" (*NHG*, p. 112). Living from the real self involves accepting a world of uncertainty, process, and limitation. It means giving up the search for glory and settling for a less exalted existence. The proud self therefore senses the real self as a threat to its very existence and turns upon it with scorn. Though it occurs at a rather late stage in the development from self-alienation to self-actualization, the central inner conflict is a fierce one. The person who has centered his life for a long time on dreams of glory may never be able fully to free himself from his idealized image, with its concomitants of pride, claims, shoulds, and self-hate.

Self-hate is for the most part an unconscious process, since "there is a survival interest in *not* being aware of its impact" (*NHG*, p. 115). The chief defense against awareness is externalization, which may be either active or passive: "The former is an attempt to direct self-hate outward, against life, fate, institutions, or people. In the latter the hate remains directed against the self but is perceived or experienced as coming from the outside" (*NHG*, p. 115). Self-hate operates in six ways, through "relentless demands on self, merciless self-accusation, self-contempt, self-frustrations, self-tormenting, and self-destruction" (*NHG*, p. 117). There is often a pride in self-hate that serves to maintain self-glorification: "The very condemnation of imperfection confirms the godlike standards with which the person identifies himself" (*NHG*, pp. 114–15).

Self-hate is the end result of the pride system. Horney sees it as "perhaps the greatest tragedy of the human mind. Man in reaching out for the Infinite and Absolute also starts destroying himself. When he makes a pact with the devil, who promises him glory, he has to go to hell—to the hell within himself" (*NHG*, p. 154). Only when self-hate abates can "unconstructive self-pity turn into a constructive sympathy with self" (*NHG*, p. 153). In order for this to happen the individual must have "a beginning feeling for his real self and a beginning wish for inner salvation" (*NHG*, p. 153).

Karen Horney is often thought of as a social-psychological theorist or as a member of the "cultural school," but she is more properly understood as part of Third Force psychology. Maslow included her within this group; and, had she lived longer, she would, I think, have identified herself with it. Since the phenomena that Horney describes occur frequently in literature, biography, criticism, and culture, hers is, for my purposes, the most useful of the Third Force theories. She had less philosophic breadth than Freud, Jung, or Erikson; but there are many phenomena for which she has provided the most powerful explanation; and if we combine her theory with Maslow's, the two taken together provide a comprehensive model of human nature.

I have contended that Maslow and Horney operate from the same premises and that their theories are entirely compatible, but it might be argued that Maslow's is a biologically based theory that seeks to describe our essential nature while Horney's is a culturally oriented theory that seeks to describe the neurotic personality of our time. Horney, indeed, is often denied her proper importance because she is perceived as having described the neurotic personality of upper-middle class New Yorkers in the 1930s and 1940s. This view of

Horney derives, I believe, from an overemphasis upon her early work and a misreading of her mature theory. Horney was in the beginning a member of the "cultural school"; but as her theory evolved, it lost its sociological focus. As I have shown through my use of her theory in the study of literature, Horney has described interpersonal and intrapsychic strategies of defense that are present in a wide variety of periods and cultures. The strategies take somewhat different forms in different cultures, and different cultures favor different strategies and foster different patterns of inner conflict; but, like Maslow's basic needs, the movements toward, away from, and against others seem to be part of human nature rather than culturally derived. To my knowledge, Horney never made the point; but any student of animal behavior should recognize her strategies as complex human versions of the basic mechanisms of defense: fight, flight, and submission. Along with our basic needs, our defensive strategies may be instinctoid; and this may be one of the reasons for the wide applicability of Karen Horney's theory.

NOTES

1. Karen Horney, *Neurosis and Human Growth* (New York: Norton, 1950), p. 15. Hereafter cited in the text as *NHG.*
2. Abraham Maslow, *Toward a Psychology of Being,* 2d ed. (New York: Van Nostrand, 1968), pp. 3–4. Hereafter cited in the text as *PB.*
3. There are two other needs which Maslow defines as basic, but which he does not integrate into his hierarchy of prepotency. They are the needs to know and understand and the aesthetic needs. For a fuller discussion of each of the basic needs, see Maslow, *Motivation and Personality,* 2d ed. (New York: Harper and Row, 1970), chap. 4. Hereafter cited in the text as *MP.*
4. For a fuller discussion of peak experiences, see Maslow, *Psychology of Being,* chaps. 6 and 7.
5. I am indebted here to Erich Fromm's discussion of "The Existential and Historical Dichotomies in Man," in *Man for Himself* (New York: Holt, Rinehart and Winston, 1947), pp. 40–50.
6. For a valuable collection of essays on the relation between psychological theory and value theory, see *New Knowledge in Human Values,* ed. Abraham Maslow (New York: Harper and Row, 1959).
7. For an application of Maslow's hierarchy to the study of culture, see Joel Aronoff, *Psychological Needs and Cultural Systems* (Princeton: Van Nostrand, 1967).
8. "A Theory of Metamotivation: The Biological Rooting of the Value Life," in *The Farther Reaches of Human Nature* (New York: Viking, 1971), p. 338.
9. For a discussion of B-values, see *Religions, Values, and Peak Experiences* (Columbus: Ohio State University Press, 1964), Appendix G, and "A Theory of Metamotivation."
10. "A Theory of Metamotivation," p. 325.
11. For a discussion of this concept, see Karen Horney, *The Neurotic Personality of Our Time* (New York: Norton, 1936), p. 69. Hereafter cited in the text as *NP.*
12. Carl Rogers, *On Becoming a Person* (Boston: Houghton Mifflin, 1961), p. 187. Hereafter cited in the text as *BP.*
13. *Metamorphosis* (New York: Basic Books, 1959), p. 273. Hereafter cited in the text as *M.*
14. See ibid., p. 226, for a discussion of the relation between allocentric interest and love. See also Erich Fromm, *The Art of Loving* (New York: Harper and Row, 1956).

15. *New Ways in Psychoanalysis* (New York: Norton, 1939), p. 305. Hereafter cited in the text as *NW.*

16. This process is vividly described in a letter from a patient that Horney published in *The American Journal of Psychoanalysis* 9 (1949): 4–7. I shall quote some relevant excerpts:

> From ten thousand miles away I saw it as a blinding light: the importance, the necessity of a Self! One's own single self. My original life—*what had happened to it?* . . . Instantly I knew in my bones, and by grief itself, that I had discovered the very core and essence of neurosis—my neurosis and perhaps every neurosis. The secret of wretchedness was SELFLESSNESS! Deep and hidden, the fact and the fear of not having a self. Not being a self. Not-being. And at the end—actual chaos. . . .
>
> How is it possible to lose a self? The treachery, unknown and unthinkable, begins with our secret psychic death in childhood—if and when we are not loved and are cut off from our spontaneous wishes. (Think: What is left?) But wait—it is not just this simple murder of a psyche. That might be written off, the tiny victim might even "outgrow" it—but it is a perfect double crime in which he himself also gradually and unwittingly takes part. He has not been accepted for himself, as he is.
>
> Oh, they "love" him, but they want him or force him or expect him to be different! Therefore he must be unacceptable. He himself learns to believe it and at last even takes it for granted. He has truly given himself up. No matter now whether he obeys them, whether he clings, rebels or withdraws—his behavior, his performance is all that matters. His center of gravity is in "them," not in himself—yet if he so much as noticed it he'd think it natural enough. And the whole thing is entirely plausible; all invisible, automatic, and anonymous!
>
> This is the perfect paradox. Everything looks normal; no crime was intended; there is no corpse, no guilt. All we can see is the sun rising and setting as usual. But what has happened? He has been rejected, not only by them, but by himself. (He is actually without a self.) What has he lost? Just the one true and vital part of himself: his own yes-feeling, which is his very capacity for growth, his root system. But alas, he is not dead. "Life" goes on, and so must he. From the moment he gives himself up, and to the extent that he does so, all unknowingly he sets about to create and maintain a pseudo-self. But this is an expediency—a "self" without wishes. This one shall be loved (or feared) where he is despised, strong where he is weak; it shall go through the motions (Oh, but they are caricatures!) not for fun or joy but for survival; not simply because it wants to move but because it has to obey. This necessity is not life—not his life—it is a defense mechanism against death. It is also the machine of death. From now on he will be torn apart by compulsive (unconscious) *needs* or ground by (unconscious) conflicts into paralysis, every motion and every instant canceling out his being, his integrity; and all the while he is disguised as a normal person and expected to behave like one!
>
> In a word, I saw that we *become* neurotic seeking or defending a pseudo-self, a self-system; and we *are* neurotic to the extent that we are self-less.

17. The term "false-self system" (which Horney's patient almost formulates) is used by R. D. Laing in *The Divided Self* (Baltimore: Penguin, 1965). Though Laing is an existential-phenomenological analyst who seems unaware of Horney and Maslow, his findings, and even sometimes his language, are amazingly close to theirs. In Laing I find the best description of how defense systems such as those that Horney analyzes operate in psychosis.

18. Horney's conception of basic anxiety is very close to and can be enriched by Laing's notion of "ontological insecurity." See *The Divided Self,* chap. 3.

19. *Our Inner Conflicts* (New York: Norton, 1945), p. 219. Hereafter cited in the text as *OIC.*

20. For a description of the typical course of such a relationship, see Horney, *Neurosis and Human Growth*, pp. 247–58.

2
Third Force Psychology and the Study of Literature, Biography, Criticism, and Culture

Bernard J. Paris

Third Force psychology is a powerful tool of critical, biographical, and cultural analysis, the usefulness of which is just beginning to be properly appreciated. In literary criticism, it has been employed so far in three major ways: to analyze literary characters in motivational terms; to analyze the implied authors of individual works, showing their inner conflicts and blind spots; and to analyze the personality of the author as it can be inferred from all of his works. It has also been used to examine the influence of the reader's personality upon his critical response. The theory has many possible uses in the study of intellectual and cultural history, but these have been largely unexplored.

In this essay, I shall illustrate these uses of Third Force psychology through analyses of *A Man for All Seasons, Herzog, Wuthering Heights,* Shakespeare, my own earlier criticism of George Eliot, and Victorian culture. I shall consider Bolt's Sir Thomas More from a Maslovian perspective, as a fictional representation of a self-actualizing person. Moses Herzog is one of the greatest mimetic characters in twentieth-century fiction; I shall analyze him from a Horneyan point of view, showing how his psychological conflicts generate his intellectual confusion and emotional paralysis. In my discussion of *Wuthering Heights,* I shall argue that the novel's complex narrative structure is the means by which the implied author reveals, conceals, and manages her psychological conflicts. My brief examination of Shakespeare will suggest the kind of insight into his personality that can be generated by a Horneyan analysis of his works, and I shall consider the role that the psychology of the critic plays in literary criticism by examining the influence of my own defensive needs upon my early work on George Eliot. I shall conclude by suggesting the usefulness of Third Force psychology in the study of influence, religion, philosophy, and culture, using Victorian culture as my primary example.

1

Maslow had hoped to illustrate his description of the self-actualizing person with some examples from literature, but he and his students were unable to find any. My students and I have found only two. In "I'd Rather Be Ratliff,"

Marjorie Haselswerdt makes a convincing case that the sewing machine salesman in Faulkner's Snopes trilogy possesses many of the attributes that the Third Force psychologists associate with healthy human development; and I believe that Sir Thomas More as he is depicted in *A Man for All Seasons* is a self-actualizing person. Most characters in literature who choose death, as Sir Thomas does, do so for reasons that I cannot admire. The meaning of life for the self-alienated person lies in the actualization not of his real self, but of an idealized image of himself that he creates, with the aid of his imagination, in order to compensate for feelings of worthlessness and inadequacy. Such a person is often driven to sacrifice his life, in a compulsive way, in order to realize a dream of glory. Sir Thomas More, on the other hand, does everything that he possibly can to avoid martyrdom; but he is finally forced to choose death because he will not give up his real self.

There is a widespread feeling that health is uninteresting and that this accounts for the absence of self-actualizing people in literature. What Robert Bolt has perceived is that it is extremely difficult for a person to resist all of the pressures upon him to abandon his real self, especially under oppressive social or political conditions, and that the struggle to remain true to one's self can generate intense conflict and be highly dramatic. What Sir Thomas suffers from is not a psychological, but a historical problem, the nature of which he defines in one of his last speeches to Cromwell: "What you have hunted me for is not my actions, but the thoughts of my heart. It is a long road you have opened. For first men will disclaim their hearts and presently they will have no hearts. God help the people whose Statesmen walk your road."[1] When people are forced to conceal or repress their true thoughts, they will lose touch with their own inner reality. It is the threat to his self which Sir Thomas is determined, above all, to resist.

As the play opens, Richard Rich proclaims his belief that "every man has his price," and Sir Thomas replies, "No no no" (p. 4). More is above all a man who has the courage to say no, despite ever increasing pressures to comply, when saying yes means betraying his values, his sense of reality, and his feeling of selfhood. He refuses to assist Rich in getting a position, partly because he knows that Rich's ambition will make him corrupt, but also partly because he would prefer to see Rich engage in the vocation to which his abilities ought to be calling him: "You'd be a fine teacher," he tells Rich, "perhaps even a great one"; but there is not enough glory here to satisfy Richard's ambition. "Who would know it?" he asks (p. 6). Rich is the chief foil to Sir Thomas: he loses his self (a process that is climaxed by his swearing a false oath), while Sir Thomas preserves his.

Unlike Richard Rich, Sir Thomas is not driven by ambition, which is always subordinate, for him, to the values of self-actualization. He says that he himself has been "commanded into office" (p. 6), though Rich cannot believe it. He is later willing to serve as Lord Chancellor to keep the unscrupulous Cromwell from getting the office and to keep the state from being worse than it is; but he does not seem to hunger after power, he has a shrewd and humorous sense of realities, and he knows that he cannot remake the world. He remains cheerful in poverty—"at the worst, we could be beggars, and still keep company, and be merry together" (p. 64)—and even the hardships of prison do not break his spirit or sour his temper. He has a firm hold on what is important in life; and, above all, he remains at peace with himself. As Sir Thomas's fortunes decline, those of Richard Rich rise. He is appointed Attorney-General for Wales as a reward for his perjury, and he eventually becomes Lord Chancellor. Bolt leaves no doubt, however, as to which man has made the better choice.

Sir Thomas's downfall is the fault not of his character but of his historical situation. He maneuvers realistically in a very dangerous world and bends as much as he can without abandoning his principles, but he always says no when that is the only way in which he can maintain his personal integrity. He resists Wolsey's demand that he compromise his conscience for the sake of policy; and, though he is loathe to displease the king, he will do so if he must. "You've crossed him," complains his wife, Alice. "I couldn't find the other way," replies Sir Thomas. "Be ruled!" his wife begs. "There's a little . . . little area," Sir Thomas responds, "where I must rule myself" (pp. 33–34). He will not give in to the entreaties of Alice and Norfolk that he stay on as Lord Chancellor after the church submits to the king; and he insists that his resignation was not a "noble gesture": "I was not *able* to continue" (p. 54). He hopes that if he remains quiet, he will be left alone; but after the king charges him with ingratitude, he has a clear sense of his danger. Even then, he resists Norfolk's well-meant plea that he submit: "I will not give in because I oppose it—I do—not my pride, not my spleen, nor any other of my appetites, but *I* do—*I!* . . . Is there no single sinew in the midst of this that serves no appetite of Norfolk's but is just Norfolk? There is! Give *that* some exercise, my lord!" (pp. 71–72). Even though Norfolk is a weak, self-alienated man, like almost everyone else who surrounds him, Sir Thomas is not really scornful of him, but is loving and compassionate. He even provokes a quarrel with him in order to ease the conscience of his friend.

As his conversation with Norfolk makes clear, it is not his beliefs but his self that Sir Thomas is defending. "Does this make sense?" asks Norfolk; "You'll forfeit all you've got—which includes the respect of your country—for a theory?" "What matters to me," Sir Thomas replies, "is not whether it's true or not but that I believe it to be true, or rather, not that I *believe* it, but that *I* believe it" (p. 53). Sir Thomas does not insist that he is right or that anyone else agree with him, but he feels that no one else has the right to ask him to give up his version of reality. "In matters of conscience," he tells Cromwell, "the loyal subject is more bounden to be loyal to his conscience than to any other thing" (p. 89). "And so provide a noble motive," Cromwell replies, "for his frivolous self-conceit!"

> MORE: *(Earnestly)* It is not so, Master Cromwell—very and pure necessity for respect of my own soul.
> CROMWELL: Your own self, you mean!
> MORE: Yes, a man's soul is his self! (p. 89)

It is his soul, then, or his self, for which Sir Thomas is prepared to sacrifice everything else.

Sir Thomas resists not only political pressures but pressures from his family as well. As much as he loves his daughter Margaret, he will not consent to her marriage to Roper as long as Will is a heretic. He maintains his position toward Roper, as he has maintained his position toward Richard Rich, without defensiveness or hostility, and even with affection. He is deeply concerned by his wife's anxieties, but he will not be ruled by them. He feels that his safety lies in silence, and he will not reveal his position to his family, even though they interpret this as a lack of love and trust. He manages here, as elsewhere, however, to reassure them of his love even while he frustrates their desires.

The most moving scene between Sir Thomas and his family occurs in prison, when they are allowed to visit him in order to persuade him to swear to the Act of Succession, and thus to return home. "Say the words of the oath," pleads Margaret, "and in your heart think otherwise."

> When a man takes an oath [Sir Thomas replies], he's holding his own self in his own hands. Like water. *(He cups his hands)* And if he opens his fingers *then*—he needn't hope to find himself again. Some men aren't capable of this, but I'd be loathe to think your father one of them. (p. 81)

The hostility of Alice is almost more than Sir Thomas can bear. He needs her to love him and to understand what he is doing. She does not understand, and she is afraid that she will hate him after he is dead: "well, you mustn't, Alice, that's all" (p. 83). This brings about the reconciliation that permits him to die at peace not only with himself but also with his loved ones.

It may be argued that what motivates Sir Thomas is not the desire to preserve his real self at all, but his belief in God and in the sacredness of an oath and his desire to save his immortal soul. I had developed my own interpretation of Sir Thomas before I read Robert Bolt's preface to *A Man for All Seasons,* and I was pleased to discover that the playwright saw his character exactly as I do.

> At any rate, Thomas More, as I wrote about him, became for me a man with an adamantine sense of his own self. He knew where he began and left off, what area of himself he could yield to the encroachments of his enemies, and what to the encroachments of those he loved. It was a substantial area in both cases, for he had a proper sense of fear, and was a busy lover. Since he was a clever man and a great lawyer he was able to retire from those areas in wonderfully good order, but at length he was asked to retreat from that final area where he located his self. And there this supple, humorous, unassuming

and sophisticated person set like metal, was overtaken by an absolutely primitive rigor, and could no more be budged than a cliff.

This account of him developed as I wrote: what first attracted me was a person who could not be accused of any incapacity for life, who indeed seized life in great variety and almost greedy quantities, who nevertheless found something in himself without which life was valueless and when that was denied him was able to grasp his death. For there can be no doubt, given the circumstances, that he did it himself. . . .

This brings me to something which I feel the need to explain, perhaps apologize for. More was a very orthodox Catholic and for him an oath was something perfectly specific; it was an invitation to God, an invitation God would not refuse, to act as a witness, and to judge; the consequence of perjury was damnation, for More another perfectly specific concept. So for More the issue was simple (though remembering the outcome it can hardly have been easy). But I am not a Catholic nor even in the meaningful sense of the word a Christian. So by what right do I appropriate a Christian saint to my purposes? Or to put it the other way, why do I take as my hero a man who brings about his own death because he can't put his hand on an old black book and tell an ordinary lie?

For this reason: A man takes an oath only when he wants to commit himself quite exceptionally to the statement, when he wants to make an identity between the truth of it and his own virtue; he offers himself as a guarantee. And it works. There is a special kind of shrug for a perjurer; we feel that the man has no self to commit, no guarantee to offer. . . . though few of us have anything in ourselves like an immortal soul which we regard as absolutely inviolable, yet most of us still feel something which we should prefer, on the whole, not to violate. . . . It may be that a clear sense of the self can *only* crystallize round something transcendental, in which case our prospects look poor, for we are rightly committed to the rational. I think the paramount gift our thinkers, artists, and for all I know, our men of science should labor to get for us is a sense of selfhood without resort to magic. (pp. xi–xiii)

This is, among other things, what Third Force psychology has to offer us: a sense of selfhood without magic.

By saying that I have found only two self-actualizing characters in literature, I do not mean to imply that literature is devoid of healthy experience or healthy perspectives. Many writers have been aware of the phenomenon of self-alienation and of the need to overcome it. It is the real self from which Matthew Arnold feels separated in "The Buried Life" and which many of Hesse's heroes are attempting to recover. D. H. Lawrence's psychological theories are harmonious in many ways with Third Force psychology. His "pristine unconscious" is, in some respects at least, a metaphor for the real self. Lawrence diagnoses the sickness of modern man as self-alienation; and in *Women in Love* he shows Birkin struggling to reverse this process and to establish contact once again with his authentic center of being. The novel ends, however, with Ursula and Birkin being reborn as infants, so that it provides no picture of adult health. The healthiest component of literature is not to be found in its images of man or in its thematic affirmations, but in its allocentric perceptions, in its expressions of what Maslow calls Being-love and Being-cognition. Much romantic poetry tries to express what it is like to have peak experiences or to lose the capacity to have them. Many great artists have had the ability to rise above their autocentricity and to see the world in remarkably fresh and vivid ways. This is one of the things that we mean by an aesthetic perspective, that is, a free, contemplative, nonneeding mode of perception. As I tried to show in *A Psychological Approach to Fiction*, the great character creations in realistic novels are a product of the artist's ability to transcend his own defenses and to see others as they really are, rather than as he needs or fears them to be. Iris Murdoch equates this with love, and I agree.[2]

2

Herzog is so full of ideas—of speculations on the nature of man, the modern plight, the human condition—that it seems to invite a primarily thematic reading. The ideas belong, however, not to Saul Bellow, the implied author, but to Moses Herzog, the central character. The novel is almost wholly confined to Herzog's point of view, and there is little reason to suppose that he is a reliable narrator whose attitudes are sanctioned by the author. He is capable of considerable objectivity, but only for brief moments. Most of the time his thinking is a reflection of his inner turmoil. When he does "momentarily" join "the objective world," he looks down on himself with an amused contempt.[3] In his moments of greatest lucidity he sees the compulsiveness of his behavior and the defensiveness of his thinking. There is little to suggest that Bellow sees Herzog, even at the end, as a healthy man with a balanced view of the world. At best he is a damaged man who must "*play the instrument* [he's] *got,*" but who even "*on these terms*" can "*apprehend certain things*" (p. 330). Bellow's chief object, however, is neither to classify Herzog as healthy or sick, nor to present through him a world view of his own. It is to render Herzog from the inside, to give us an immediate experience of his emotional life and his sense of the world. "After smiling," Herzog "must return to his own Self and see the thing through": "But there still remained the fact. *I* am Herzog. I have to *be* that man" (p. 67). What the novel says to us is, this is what it is like to *be* that man.

The central achievement of *Herzog,* then, is its mimetic portrait of Moses. From this point of view, the book is a masterpiece, for Moses Elkanah Herzog is one of the great characters in literature. The chief thing needful for a proper appreciation of this portrait is a psychological understanding of Herzog the man. The author himself says little or nothing about his character; he depicts him. Herzog says much about himself, but most of what he says is revelation rather than reliable analysis. Given his problems, Herzog cannot be expected to have more than fragmentary and fleeting insights into his own psychology.

The novel's technique induces us to experience Herzog in his own terms. If we are to understand him, we need a standpoint in the objective world from which to view him. The theories of Karen Horney are extraordinarily useful in helping us to understand Herzog the man. They are highly congruent with his character, and they permit us to comprehend from an objective standpoint what Bellow has enabled us to experience from within.

In Horneyan terms, Herzog is a basically compliant person who hopes to gain safety, love, worth, and glory by moving toward people, by being good, loving, sensitive, long-suffering, helpless, and full of high ideals. At the same time he has many expansive drives and longs to be masterful, a triumphant scholar, a man who knows the world for what it is and is able to vindicate himself and defeat his enemies. These two sides of Moses generate different values, different personality traits, different internal shoulds and external claims, and different conceptions of human nature and the human condition.

As he himself recognizes, Herzog belongs to "a class of people secretly convinced they [have] an arrangement with fate; in return for docility or ingenuous good will they [are] to be shielded from the worst brutalities of life" (p. 154). Herzog's bargain, his "psychic offer" (p. 154), is succinctly expressed in his favorite Mother Goose rhyme:

> *I love little pussy, her coat is so warm*
> *And if I don't hurt her, she'll do me no harm.*
> *I'll sit by the fire and give her some food,*
> *And pussy will love me because I am good.*
> (p. 118)

If he is good, gentle, loving, childishly weak and naive, people will love him and do him no harm: "Having discovered that everyone must be indulgent with bungling child-men, pure hearts in the burlap of innocence . . . , he had set himself up with his emotional goodies—truth, friendship, devotion to children . . . , and potato love" (p. 266).

Herzog hopes to control both the universe as a whole (fate) and other people through his self-effacing strategies. His weakness, his dependency, his "trick of appealing for sympathy" (p. 12) compel others to give way, to take care of him. When Madeleine rejects him, he does not "stand his ground," or fight back, but hopes to win "by the appeal of passivity, of personality, win on the ground of being, after all . . . Moses Elkanah Herzog—a good man, and Madeleine's particular benefactor. He had done everything for her—everything!" (p. 10). As Ramona puts it, he hopes "to win by sacrificing" himself (p. 195). He accepts blows (p. 57), he is a patient Griselda (p. 64), in the belief that his suffering will ultimately bring him glory (*"Hitch your agony to a star"*—p. 16) and prove him to be a superior being, capable of "higher emotions" (p. 57).

Both Herzog's values and his life goals are deeply influenced by his self-effacing solution. He is the carrier of the Old World ideals of "Love" and "Filial Emotion" (p. 281) that are scorned by the crass aggressiveness of contemporary society. He believes that "'Man liveth not by Self alone but in his brother's face'" (p. 272) and rejects Nietzsche's contention "'that Jesus made the whole world sick, infected it with his slave morality'" (p. 54). He wants to revise "the old Western, Faustian ideology," to overturn "the romantic errors about the uniqueness of the Self," and to show "how life could be lived by renewing universal connections" (p. 39). He feels that the meaning of life lies not in the realization of the unique self, but in living for others, in a merging of the self with something great outside of it. Herzog wants to lead a moral, useful, active life, to "make his sacrifice to truth, to order, peace" (p. 308). He wants to be a good son, a good parent, a good husband, a good friend. He idealizes the life of personal relations and seeks his glory there. In his high school graduation speech he quotes Emerson: *"The main enterprise of the world, for splendor . . . is the upbuilding of a man. The private life of one man shall be a more illustrious monarchy . . . than any kingdom in history"* (p. 160). He is not a "power-lover" (p. 125); he is going to do "the work of the future," to show men how to live: "the revolutions of the twentieth century, the liberation of the masses by production, created a private life but gave nothing to fill it with. This was where such as he came in. The progress of civilization—indeed, the survival of civilization—depended on the success of Moses E. Herzog" (p. 125).

Herzog's self-effacing trends are at the bottom not only of his world view, his values, and his life goals, but also of his need to have a favorable conception of human nature. The self-effacing person must believe that people are basically good. If they are not, his strategies will not work; his "emotional goodies" will not impress them, and his dependency will only make him vulnerable. Equally important, since he prides himself on his own goodness, dim views of human nature are directly threatening to his idealized image. The modern philosophies that proclaim the death of God must be resisted because they confront Herzog with an amoral cosmic order in which goodness has no power. Those that proclaim the death of the old, exalted conception of man must be resisted because they confront him with a sordid human nature in which there is no goodness, not even his own.

Herzog must resist the "post-Renaissance, post-humanistic, post-Cartesian dissolution" not only with his learning and intelligence but also with the quality of his life. "Predictably bucking such trends," he tries "to be a *marvelous* Herzog" whose personal triumph will prove the existence of "faithfulness," "generosity," a "sacred quality" in human nature (p. 93). At the time of the action Herzog recognizes clearly enough his failure to actualize his idealized image, but he clings desperately to a belief in the reality of his goodness: "what about all the good I have in my heart!—doesn't it mean anything? Is it simply a joke? A false hope that makes a man feel the illusion of worth? But this good is no phony. I know it isn't. I swear it" (p. 207).

In addition to his self-effacing trends, Moses has powerful aggressive drives that are quite close to the surface. He alternately glorifies and scorns his idealism, his suffering, his lack of worldliness. His expansive trends emerge most powerfully when his compliant solution is failing. At such times he looks with contempt on "foolish, feeling, suffering Herzog" (p. 58), with his propensity for "potato love." He sees that "the more individuals are destroyed . . . the worse their yearning for collectivity" (p. 176). He despises his humble self, scorns the career of personal relations, and is disgusted with his weakness and dependency. He takes pride in his anger and likes to see himself as "a difficult, aggressive man" (p. 188): *"I have a wild spirit in me though I look meek and mild"* (p. 16). In his letters "he communicates with the mighty of this world, or speaks words of understanding and prophecy" (p. 166). He dreams of intellectual conquest; he replaces the illusion of mastery through moral superiority with "the delusion of total *explanations*" (p. 166).

Both Moses' self-effacing and his expansive trends have been profoundly influenced by his Jewish culture, with its glorification of suffering on the one hand and of achievement on the other. The most important transmitter of this culture was his mother. She encouraged his dependency and his trick of appealing for sympathy by her indulgence; and, at the same time, by her self-sacrifice she provided a model of what he was supposed to be. You are " 'a good man,' " says Nachman, " 'a good heart. Like your mother. A gentle spirit. You got it from her' " (p. 134). He also got from her, however, his ambition, his need to be great, "the caste madness of *yichus*" (p. 141). She didn't " 'want the children to be common' " (p. 142); she wanted "them to be lawyers, gentlemen, rabbis, or performers . . . No life so barren and subordinate that it didn't have imaginary dignities, honors to come" (p. 141).

His mother is only one of a number of influences, of course, that lead Moses to grow up under a very strong pressure to distinguish himself by some outstanding achievement. Since his gifts are intellectual, he invests his pride in his intelligence and pursues an academic career. He will become a world famous scholar, the Lovejoy of his generation. He will prove his superiority to all other intellectuals: "He was going . . . to wrap the subject up, to pull the carpet from under all other scholars, show them what was what, stun them, expose their triviality once and for all" (p. 119). His ambition becomes truly grandiose. He believes that the modern world is in deep trouble because it believes in the wrong ideas and that mankind depends on him "for certain intellectual work, to change history, to influence the development of civilization" (p. 105). Alternating with his dream of saving the world by becoming an exemplar of the private life is this vision of achieving world historical importance through his intellectual gifts. It should be noted, however, that he makes this expansive dream of glory compatible with his compliant solution: his intellectual powers are to be used to vindicate the self-effacing world view.

There are times, however, when disillusionment sets in and Moses accepts the expansive view as truth.

> The vision of mankind as a lot of cannibals, running in packs, gibbering, bewailing its own murders, pressing out the living world as dead excrement.

> Do not deceive yourself, dear Moses Elkanah, with childish jingles and Mother Goose. Hearts quaking with cheap and feeble charity or oozing potato love have not written history . . . Fountains of human blood that squirted from fresh graves! Limitless massacre! I never understood it! (p. 77)

Moses feels that he must choose between Mother Goose and this nightmare vision of men as monsters. He wants the world to be one in which the self-effacing solution works; but the exploitation of his own goodness, combined with his awareness of his own murderous impulses, drives him to see nothing but evil in the world and to conclude that " 'history is the history of cruelty, not love, as soft men think' " (p. 290). When he is in this frame of mind, he scorns his idealism, his naiveté, his childish belief, and becomes a "snarling" realist: "Get smart, sucker!" (p. 291).

The conflict between his compliant and aggressive trends produces much of Moses' emotional and intellectual turmoil, drives him into inconsistent behavior, and generates intense anxiety and self-hate. Moses is caught in a crossfire of conflicting shoulds. He takes great pride in his self-effacing qualities and feels that they mark him as a superior person. At the same time, however, his expansive side has intense scorn for his self-effacing attitudes; and he sees himself as a "suffering joker," a victim, a fool, a "dumb prick." His expansive side wants him "to hate, to be in a position to do something about it. Hatred is self-respect" (p. 289). He longs to be violent, to hit back, to inspire fear; and he takes great pride in his aggressive behavior. But whenever he begins to act out his rage, or even to imagine doing it, he feels very guilty and hates himself for his violation of his self-effacing shoulds. Whether he is aggressive or compliant, then, Moses is bound to violate his own inner dictates and to hate himself intensely. Toward the end of the novel he defends himself against his inner conflict by adopting the strategy of detachment.

Herzog dramatizes a crisis in Moses' mental history. As the novel opens, Moses feels that he is "going to pieces," "breaking up" (p. 7), disintegrating. The crisis is precipitated by a series of blows to his pride that shatter his defenses, exacerbate his inner conflicts, and fill him with "horrible rage" (p. 155) and self-hate. He dwells obsessively upon "how he was swindled, conned, manipulated . . . driven into debt, his trust betrayed by wife, friend, physician" (p. 156). He is "*bursting with the wrongs*" (p. 30) that Madeleine and others have done to him and craves a violent revenge: " 'Let their names be blotted out! They prepared a net for my steps. They digged a pit before me. Break their teeth, O God, in their mouth!' " (p. 203). His self-hatred is almost equally intense. He feels like a "hopeless fool," a "sucker," a "stupid prick!" " 'Oneself is simply grotesque!' " (p. 219).

Herzog is disturbed about many things, but most of all about Madeleine's rejection and Gersbach's betrayal. He has done a great deal for both of them, and he expects to be rewarded by their loyalty, gratitude, and devotion. The failure of his bargain calls his whole strategy for living into question: it undermines his belief in the power of goodness and the reality of love, friendship, and justice. The frustration of his claims intensifies his feeling of vulnerability, heightens his anxiety, and pushes him in the direction of expansive attitudes and values. He feels betrayed also by the other "sharpies"—his lawyer and his psychiatrist—who, together with Madeleine and Valentine, have administered a "primitive cure" (p. 93), teaching him that men cannot be trusted, that idealists are fools, and that the world has not been accurately described by Mother Goose.

As is often the case with self-effacing people, Herzog has a "weakness for grandeur" (p. 61) and is drawn to self-assured, expansive people who will take over his life and allow him to participate in their glory. Daisy is a good but commonplace woman with whom he leads the ordinary life of an assistant professor. Dissatisfied with this, he leaves her and becomes involved with Sono, a glamorous, exotic woman who feeds his pride by her extravagant respect for his intellectual attainments: "She rated him higher than kings and presidents" (p. 172). Sono, however, is "not *serious* enough" (p. 103); her esteem means little because she is so much his inferior. Herzog craves a brilliant, domineering partner who will at once humble and exalt him.

Madeleine is just the woman he is looking for. "Her decisiveness fascinate[s] him" (p. 111); he "relie[s] completely on her intellectual judgments" (p. 72). "Everyone close to Madeleine, everyone drawn into the drama of her life," becomes "exceptional, deeply gifted, brilliant. It . . . happened also to him" (p. 38). His ability to attract such a woman gives him a sense of great power and worth. Initially, at least, she believes in his dream of intellectual conquest and wants him to be an ambitious Herzog. His relation with her permits him to satisfy both his self-effacing and his expansive drives. He will cure her neurosis by supplying the love she never had, thus proving his goodness. He gives over the direction of his life to her, thus satisfying his needs for fusion and dependency. And he will be great for her sake, thus satisfying his expansive needs for glory without violating his self-effacing taboos against personal aggrandizement. Herzog's idealized image contains a composite of expansive and self-effacing goals, qualities, and values. In the initial phase of his relationship with Madeleine he comes closer than he ever had to feeling that he *is* his idealized self.

Madeleine's rejection deals Herzog a devastating blow. His intimacy with her had given his life an aura of glamour, of grandeur, of glory. Now he is "sent back into the darkness" (p. 38). His project of being a marvelous Herzog is in ruins: he has failed again as husband and father and he has lost the ability to work. Madeleine is now the rising scholar. His pride is crushed. He has glorified Madeleine, transferred his pride to her, made her the measure of his worth. As a result, he has very little defense against her adverse judgment. When she stops loving him, he becomes his despised self and is flooded with guilt, self-hate, and a sense of total failure.

At the point at which the novel opens, Herzog has been "overcome by the need to explain, to have it out, to justify, to put in perspective, to clarify, to make amends" (p. 2). As he lies on the sofa "taking stock," he concludes that he has "mismanaged everything" and that his life is "ruined" (p. 3). Both his expansive and his self-effacing projects have failed. He has always prided himself on being smart, but instead of becoming "a clever character," he chose "to be dreamy . . . , and the sharpies cleaned him out" (p. 3). His career got off to "a brilliant start," but his "ambitious projects" have dried up (p. 4). He has lost the ability to concentrate, and he is moving more and more to the fringes of academia.

His intellect would have been more effective, he feels, "if he had had an aggressive, paranoid character, eager for power" (p. 4). Instead, he is "depressive," "masochistic," an "anachronistic" believer in love, goodness, and high ideals. But he is not more successful at being good than he is at being great: "he admitted that he had been a bad husband—twice. . . . To his son and daughter he was a loving but bad father. To his own parents he had been an ungrateful child. To his country an indifferent citizen. To his brothers and sisters, affectionate but remote. With his friends, an egotist. With love, lazy" (pp. 4–5).

Herzog is obsessed not only with his failures but also with his wrongs. He tells himself that since his life "had not been much to begin with, there was not much to grieve about" (p. 3); but he feels deep down that he is a great man who has been ruined by others; and he is full of rage and self-pity. His stock taking leads him to the climactic scene with Madeleine, in which "her pride [is] so fully satisfied" and he is "beaten . . . so badly" (p. 9). He recognizes the futility of his self-effacing response, which only invites her abuse and leaves him completely vulnerable; and he wonders what would have happened if he had fought back: "What if he had knocked her down, clutched her hair, dragged her screaming and fighting around the room, flogged her until her buttocks bled. What if he had! He should have torn her clothes, ripped off her necklace, brought his fists down on her head" (p. 10). He rejects this "mental violence" because it is in conflict with his self-effacing shoulds; but he recognizes that he is "really given in secret to this sort of brutality"; and he is looking, through most of the novel, for a way to act out his rage.

We are now in a position to understand Herzog's behavior during his crisis. He is desperately struggling to restore his pride, to expiate his guilt, and to satisfy his rage through vindictive triumphs. His letters serve all of these purposes. They show him to be a concerned citizen, they display his learning and intelligence, they conciliate those whom he had injured, triumph over his competitors, and strike down those who have injured him. They "explain," they "justify," they "make amends." Since it is Madeleine and Gersbach who have most severely injured his pride, he must villify them in every possible way, he must expose them, he must have his revenge. He feels abused, humiliated, spat upon; he must prove that he is a man to be feared and respected, not a weakling and a fool. He must show everyone (including the dead) that he is living up to his shoulds—that he is a good, sensitive, and loving man on the one hand, and a brilliant, powerful, aggressive man on the other.

As we have seen, his relationship with Madeleine permitted Moses to satisfy both his self-effacing and his expansive drives. The breakdown of this relationship and, with it, of his predominant solution, exposes him to terrible inner conflicts. He oscillates between expansive and self-effacing views of himself, of human nature, and of the world order. His intellectualizing is in part a form of display, a pride restoring device; but it is also a defense against disintegration. He throws himself into "elaborate abstract intellectual work . . . as if it were the struggle for survival" and has a fear that he will "die when thinking stop[s]" (p. 265). His intellectualizing is a desperate effort to hold himself and his world together by arriving at a coherent view of reality. His problems, of course, are emotional in nature and cannot be solved by intellectual means. His philosophical vacillations and confusions are a reflection of his inner conflicts; he will never arrive at clear ideas as long as his personality remains unintegrated.

One of Herzog's most severe problems is the management of his anger. His "rage" toward Madeleine and Gersbach "is so great and deep, so murderous, bloody, positively rapturous, that his arms and fingers ache to strangle them" (p. 220). In an early letter to Zelda, he thinks of the revolver his father left in his desk: *"It's still there. But I'm no criminal, don't have it in me; frightful to myself instead"* (p. 41). On the one hand, he is proud of not being a criminal. On the other hand, he scorns his softness as unmanly and feels that you have to be able to take revenge "if you want to hold your head up among people" (p. 289). He is under a terrible pressure to vindicate himself by an act of violence; but he knows that he could not live with himself after such a violation of self-effacing taboos. He manages his rage by turning it on himself *("frightful to myself instead"),* by displacing it onto a variety of other, safer objects, and by ventilating it harmlessly in his letters. These measures, however, give only temporary relief.

Herzog's crisis reaches a critical point when he identifies both himself and his daughter with the child who has been murdered by its mother. His rage had been gathering force; his experience in the courtroom releases it. Incensed by the letter from Geraldine Portnoy that describes Junie crying in the Lincoln Continental and reinforced by Ramona's response to the recital of his wrongs, he had called Simpkin that morning to discuss measures for getting his daughter back. When Simpkin sympathetically observes that " 'in a manner of speaking' " Madeleine and Gersbach had tried " 'to murder *you*,' " Herzog realizes that he actually feels "capable of murdering them both," without "horror" or "guilt" (p. 214). At the least, he would like to put them "on the stand under oath, torture them, hold a blow torch to their feet" (p. 220). As he dresses to go downtown, his craving for justice, so out of keeping with contemporary views of reality, rises to the surface: "But Moses E. Herzog, at the top of his lungs, bellowing with pain and anger, has to have justice. It's his *quid pro quo,* in return for all he has suppressed, his right as an Innocent Party" (p. 220). It is

Madeleine and Gersbach, of course, who have denied him his *quid pro quo*, thus destroying his solution and confronting him with the absurd. He feels toward them a "deep . . . murderous, bloody" rage (p. 220).

Before he witnesses the trial, Herzog's indignation alternates with self-accusation. Remembering such things as his treatment of his mother, he does not feel so innocent. When he hears the story of the girl who brutally beat her child to death while her lover was "lying on the bed smoking" (p. 239), he becomes once again the "Innocent Party." He feels "the terror of the child," identifies himself and Junie with the victim, Madeleine and Gersbach with the defendants, and sets out to revenge himself and his daughter upon their tormentors. He is released from his taboos against violence and feels free to murder.

There are several reasons for this. One is that the martyrdom of the child deals the *coup de grace* to his belief in justice. Trying with " 'all his might,' " he can "get nothing for the buried boy." The collapse of his dream of justice leaves him feeling, like Ivan Karamazov, that everything is permitted. Why restrain oneself when there is no God in the heavens, when the self-effacing bargain is so obviously ineffectual. Another reason for Herzog's new sense of the freedom to kill is that his mind is now operating at the primitive level of the talion principle. *He* has been killed, and *they* have done it; therefore, he has a right to kill them in turn, "with a clear conscience": "They had opened the way to justifiable murder. They deserved to die. . . . In spirit she was his murderess, and therefore he was turned loose, could shoot or choke without remorse" (pp. 254–55). Finally, insofar as it is June as well as himself who is the victim, he has a father's right to avenge his daughter—or, at least, to save her from her potential destroyers.

Herzog has an opportunity to kill Gersbach when he sees him bathing June, but he does not shoot: "The hated traits were all there. But see how he was with June, scooping the water on her playfully, kindly" (p. 257). Gersbach's gentleness with June breaks down Moses' identification of him with the murderers of the buried boy, and his habitual defenses resume operation. He realizes that to shoot Gersbach would be a confession of weakness, a revelation of how deeply he had been hurt: "He was not ready to make such a complete fool of himself. Only self-hatred could lead him to ruin himself because his heart was 'broken.' How could it be broken by such a pair?" (p. 258). For him to shoot Gersbach would demonstrate Valentine's potency, not his own. He feeds his pride and releases his aggression by seeing Gersbach as contemptible, a buffoon, unworthy of his revenge. Herzog, moreover, is above such behavior. He recalls "with inexpressible relish" that *"Tante Zipporah told Papa he could never use a gun on anyone, never keep up with teamsters, butchers, sluggers, hooligans, razboiniks"* (p. 258).

With the abatement of his murderous rage, Herzog's inner conflicts resume. He sees himself once again as an anachronistic man, infected with Old World feelings like love and filial emotion (p. 281). He longs once more for "brotherhood," for an "Eternal Father," for a "true employment" by "other human beings" (pp. 272–73). He reaches a solution to the problem of evil from the self-effacing point of view. His own lust for violence has shown him that it is not God but man who is responsible for evil: " 'Our own murdering imagination turns out to be the great power, our human imagination which starts by accusing God of murder. At the bottom of the whole disaster lies the human being's sense of a grievance, and with this I want nothing more to do. It's easier not to exist altogether than accuse God' " (p. 290). We can have God, we can have divine justice, if we accept our guilt, abase ourselves, and stop feeling aggrieved. His Ivan-like indictment of God has received Father Zossima's answer.

At the same time, Moses continues to display aggressive attitudes. He gratifies his pride through June: "he thought how she would inherit this world of great instruments, principles of physics and applied science. She has the brains for it. He was already intoxicated with pride, seeing another Madame Curie in her" (p. 277). He rejects "weakness, or sickness, with which he had copped a plea all his life" as a modus operandi: "He seemed to have come to the end of *that*" (p. 285). He is determined to be a realist, to give up his childish credo from Mother Goose, to stop being a sucker, a fool, a "stumbling, ingenuous burlap Moses, a heart without guile, in need of protection" (p. 307).

Though it has done nothing to resolve his basic conflict, Herzog's encounter with Gersbach does contribute toward the resolution of his crisis. He has been obsessed with his wrongs, eaten up with anger, bursting with a lust for violence toward Madeleine and her lover. As he looks at him through the bathroom window, he has Valentine in his power. He can kill him if he likes. He handles his decision not to pull the trigger in a way that feeds his own pride and humiliates Gersbach. He has had a vindictive triumph, and from this point on he is no longer obsessed by Gersbach.

His confrontation with Madeleine at the police station enables him to get free of her also. Madeleine is her usual masterful self; and when he attacks Edvig, Herzog makes another of his Ikey-Fishbones errors: "The other team is scoring—clearing all bases. She was making brilliant use of [his] error" (p. 300). The tide begins to turn, however, when Madeleine stridently demands protection from violence and the sergeant begins to look at her suspiciously. Then Herzog has the vindictive triumph he has been waiting for:

> Madeleine now spoke to Herzog for the first time, pointing a rigid finger to the two bullets and looking him in the eyes. "One of those was for me, wasn't it!"
>
> "You think so? I wonder where you get such ideas? And who was the other one for?" He was quite cool as he said this, his tone was level. He was doing all he could to bring out the hidden Madeleine, the Madeleine he knew. As she stared at him her color receded and her nose began to move very slightly. She seemed to realize that she must control her tic and the

> violence of her stare. But by noticeable degrees her face became very white, her eyes smaller, stony. He believed he could interpret them. They expressed a total will that he should die. This was infinitely more than ordinary hatred. It was a vote for his nonexistence, he thought. He wondered whether the sergeant was able to see this. "Well, who do you think that second imaginary shot was for?"
>
> She said no more to him, only continued to stare in the same way.
>
> "That'll be all now, lady. You can take your child and go." (p. 301)

Moses has won a tremendous victory. Madeleine had hoped to humiliate him, to get him into deeper trouble; but she loses her composure, exposes her own weaknesses, and is dismissed. She is the crazy one, not he. Herzog has remained cool; he has stood up to Madeleine at last and reduced her to silence. His gun and his bullets, symbols of his manhood, have frightened her. Her hatred does not unman him; he is able, in the face of it, to repeat his devastating question. Madeleine's wish for his death is immensely gratifying; it shows that he has gotten to her. Now it is she who must carry the burden of impotent rage. Madeleine's fear and hatred make Moses feel potent, restore his pride, and free him from his obsession with his injuries.

As he calls his brother from the police station, Herzog feels "rather free" (p. 302). He believes that he has done well and is "temporarily lighthearted, even gay" (p. 302). No longer obsessed by his anger, his indignation, his lacerated pride, he turns his attention to rebuilding his defenses, to pulling himself together. He adopts more and more the strategy of detachment, withdrawal, resignation.

He had tried this strategy earlier, but without success. He ran from the city in order "to be sane, and to live": "He was getting away from all burdens, practical questions, away also from Ramona. There were times when you wanted to creep into hiding, like an animal" (p. 27). But he could not get away from the pressure of his emotions, from himself; and he left Martha's Vineyard within a few hours of his arrival. On a later occasion he found himself "quivering": "And why? Because he let the entire world press upon him" (p. 201). He thought of Nietzsche's advice—"Strong natures . . . forget what they [can] not master" (p. 201)—but he was not yet ready for this solution. After the encounter with Gersbach, withdrawal becomes a real possibility: "Count me out. Except in what concerns June. But for the rest, I withdraw from the whole scene as soon as I can. Good-by to all" (p. 299). After the confrontation with Madeleine, it becomes a fixed determination: "he'd leave Chicago immediately. . . . No more of this hectic, heart-rent, theatrical window-peering; no more collision, fainting, you-fight-'m-'e-cry encounters, confrontations" (p. 303). What he wants now is "peace—peace and clarity" (p. 314).

Moses holds onto his sanity and gains some peace and clarity by moving away from other people and from his own feelings. He is tired of struggling, of striving, of suffering. He wants to stop grappling with the nightmares of personal and historical existence. He wants to follow Nietzsche's "grand advice": he wants to be "strong," to "forget what [he] can't bear," to "shut out history" (p. 289). He stops contending against evil and fighting for personal growth. He resigns himself to unalterable realities: *"Myself is thus and so, and will continue thus and so. And why fight it? My balance comes from instability. Not organization, or courage, as with other people. It's tough, but that's how it is. . . . Must play the instrument I've got"* (p. 330).

Moses' journey to the edge of ruin has frightened him, and he tries to build a defense system that will protect him from both internal compulsions and external threats. He is afraid of life, and he does not trust himself. He protects himself by renouncing his desires and expectations so that he can't be disappointed and by keeping himself independent, out of the clutches of both Will and Ramona. He knows that he has been self-destructive and that his insight has been of no help: " 'I think, I figure things out. I see exactly what I should avoid. Then, all of a sudden, I'm in bed with that very thing and making love to it' " (pp. 333–34). His solution is to stay out of all beds, to avoid everything.

Earlier Moses had felt, "better the void than the torment and boredom of an incorrigible character, doing always the same stunts, repeating the same disgraces" (p. 182). Now, in order to avoid doing the same stunts and disgracing himself again, Moses chooses, in a sense, the void. He refuses to enact any longer "the peculiarities of life" (p. 340). He gives up the project of being a marvelous Herzog:

> *Oh, that's a plague, the life that exhibits itself, a real plague! There comes a time when every ridiculous son of Adam wishes to arise before the rest, with all his quirks and twitches and tics, all the glory of his self-adored ugliness, his grinning teeth, his sharp nose, his madly twisted reason, saying to the rest—in an overflow of narcissism which he interprets as benevolence—"I am here to witness. I am come to be your exemplar." Poor dizzy spook!* (p. 324)

This solution is not without its satisfactions. Not only does it protect him against the self-hate he incurs whenever he does something foolish but it also feeds his pride. But for his refusal to exhibit himself, he would be one of those ridiculous sons of Adam, as he has been in the past. As it is, he can look down from a position of superiority on all those poor dizzy spooks who have not yet learned to see their own absurdity. Herzog has finally found a use for his intelligence; the detached individual takes great pride in his insight.

Has Moses made any real progress? Yes and no. He has survived his crisis. The danger of psychological disintegration and a descent into criminal violence has passed. He has gotten Madeleine and Gersbach out of his system and is free of his obsessions. "The spell" is really "passing" (p. 341). The "murky fire" (p. 27) has gone out. He is better defended at the end of the novel than he has been during most of his adult life. His solution, however, is neither a healthy nor a permanent one. Like many detached people, he is open to the beauty of nature and is capable of intense aesthetic experience; but in other respects he is afraid of life and is closed to its possibilities. He is still driven by neurotic pride and the tyranny of his shoulds. His pride system is now that of the detached solution. This solution is working for him at the moment; but how long can he isolate himself from the life outside, and how long can he repress his inner conflicts? We leave him inert, stretched upon his sofa, with "no message for anyone. Nothing. Not a single word" (p. 341). We cannot help feeling that with any significant word, movement, or intrusion his peace will be shattered. He will violate the taboos of his detached solution and will be subject to self-hate and renewed inner turmoil. As he himself knows, he has not changed in any fundamental way: *"you can't teach old dogs"* (p. 330). He has achieved only a temporary respite, an unstable equilibrium: "The bitter cup would come round again, by and by" (p. 326).

3

The Horneyan approach to character that is illustrated in my discussion of *Herzog* works very well with a great deal of literature from Shakespeare to the present day. As I have tried to show elsewhere, one text that can be analyzed from this perspective is *Wuthering Heights.*[4] Heathcliff displays all of the Horneyan tendencies: he is self-effacing toward Cathy, vindictive toward Hindley and the Lintons, and detached from everyone else. He and Cathy are basically aggressive people who suffer from ontological insecurity and cling to each other in a mutual morbid dependency.

Wuthering Heights is fascinating not only for its portrayal of character but also for its narrative technique, which makes it extremely difficult to interpret thematically. It seems to be one of those novels about which Wayne Booth complains in which the author has disappeared. The story is told largely by Nelly, through Lockwood, and there is little agreement about Emily Brontë's relation to her narrators. There is clearly a system of contrasts in the novel involving Heathcliff, Cathy, and the Heights on the one hand and the Lintons, Nelly, and the Grange on the other; but what exactly is it that is being contrasted? According to Mark Schorer, Brontë is presenting through Heathcliff and Cathy "a devastating spectacle of human waste,"[5] but many other critics feel that theirs is the story of a splendid passion, the grandeur of which is emphasized by the contrast with ordinary experience. What *is* Emily Brontë's attitude toward Heathcliff and Cathy, Nelly and the Lintons, the Heights and the Grange? Why does she tell her story of extreme love and extreme hate through the medium of Nelly and Lockwood, never speaking in her own voice? These questions can be examined from a variety of perspectives. I shall try to show what light can be thrown on them by our psychological approach.

From a Horneyan perspective, the Heights represents extreme forms of both aggressive and self-effacing behavior (there is extreme withdrawal, too), whereas the Grange represents a moderate form of self-effacing behavior combined with a moderate withdrawal. Heathcliff, Cathy, and Hindley are all highly vindictive people, while the Lintons represent a more charitable attitude. They turn vindictive when they are persecuted, but for them this is a passing phase rather than a fixed trait of character. In the second generation, the characteristics associated with both Heights and Grange are combined and softened. The novel's system of contrasts is developed not only through the juxtaposition of Heights and Grange but also through its narrative technique. The story of extreme love and extreme hate is told by the moderate and predominantly self-effacing Nelly to the detached Lockwood, who tells it to us. All three of the Horneyan trends are present in the novel in varying degrees of intensity and in various combinations.

Where does Emily Brontë stand in this system of contrasts? If, as Mark Schorer says, it is Nelly's voice which endures at the end, Brontë would seem to be favoring the moderate self-effacing position. A good case can be made for this. Nelly represents the standard compliant values of her culture. She is the voice of the community and perhaps also of the author. She stands for forgiveness as opposed to the arrogant-vindictive emphasis on revenge. " 'It is for God to punish wicked people,' " she admonishes Heathcliff when he swears to even the score with Hindley; " 'we should learn to forgive.' "[6] She later urges Isabella to " 'be more charitable' " toward Heathcliff (p. 143) and scolds her for her vindictiveness: " 'One might suppose you have never opened a Bible in your life' " (p. 148). She disapproves of Cathy's vanity and arrogance and hopes that they will be "chastened" (p. 62). Of Heathcliff she thinks, " 'Your pride cannot blind God! You tempt Him to wring [your heart and nerves], till He forces a cry of humiliation' " (p. 139). When Heathcliff is near death, she urges him to send for a minister—" 'you have lived a selfish, unchristian life' " (p. 262)— and is "shocked at his godless indifference" (p. 263). She sides with Edgar against Cathy, "for he was kind, and trustful, and honourable," whereas she has "little faith" in Cathy's "principles, and still less sympathy for her feelings" (p. 93). She compares Hindley's moral deterioration after the death of his wife to Edgar's pious resignation: "Linton . . . displayed the true courage of a loyal and faithful soul: he trusted God, and God comforted him. One hoped, and the other despaired" (p. 152). The novel is full of Nelly's pious reflections. If she does not speak for all of Emily Brontë, she is certainly the voice of the curate's daughter.

One of Nelly's dicta is that " 'people who do their duty are always finally rewarded' " (p. 206); and this, with its corollary, that the wicked are punished, is borne out by the novel. Heathcliff and Cathy are, as Schorer says, "a devastating spectacle of human waste: ashes" (p. xi). They are miserable and self-destructive. Edgar suffers from the loss of his wife, but he is "too good to be thoroughly unhappy long" (p. 151). The novel ends, of course, with the good people triumphant. Brontë seems to be trying to provide through Cathy II and Hareton a more desirable alternative to the personalities and actions of Cathy and Heathcliff. In Cathy II, her mother's spirit and rebelliousness are present, but much softened, and are combined with her father's moderate compliant traits: "her anger was never furious; her love never fierce; it was deep and tender" (p. 155). She seems to combine the best of the Heights and the Grange. It is Cathy who breaks the cycle of injury and revenge by her movement toward Hareton, after she has treated him scornfully. She is prompted to this by Nelly (" 'Were you not naughty?' " [p. 246]) and by her conscience, which makes her feel guilty for having put an end to his efforts at self-improvement. The marriage of Hareton and Cathy represents the triumph of love and forgiveness over hatred and revenge, and it is " 'the crown' " of Nelly's wishes: " 'I shall envy no one on their wedding-day—there won't be a happier woman than myself in England!' " (p. 250). The fact that Cathy and Hareton are going to move to the Grange seems to be a final endorsement of the values for which it stands.

Plausible as the preceding interpretation is, it is not the dominant view of the novel, which tends, rather, to see it as celebrating the intensity of Cathy and Heathcliff's love for each other and justifying, to some extent at least, Heathcliff's revenge. Nelly surrounds Cathy and Heathcliff's story with a haze of disapproval, but their glamour somehow shines through her moralizing and makes her and the people she favors seem dull and commonplace by comparison. As many critics have pointed out, Emily Brontë makes it quite evident that Nelly is frequently obtuse in her dealings with Cathy and sometimes drives her into frenzies of self-destructive behavior because of her mistakes. It is not difficult to make a case that Nelly is an object of satire in the novel and the source of much of the mischief.[7] Although self-effacing traits and values are often glorified in the novel, they are also mocked and scorned, especially by Cathy and Heathcliff. Cathy has contempt for Edgar's "weak nature" (p. 99) and Heathcliff for his "puny being" (p. 126). Edgar's attendance on Catherine during her illness is scoffed at by Heathcliff: " 'that insipid, paltry creature attending her from *duty* and *humanity!* From *pity* and *charity!*' " (p. 129). These are feeble motives compared to Heathcliff's all-consuming passion. Heathcliff has enormous contempt for Isabella's "sighing and wheedling" (p. 127). Though she talks of her vindictive impulses to Nelly, when she has the chance, Isabella is incapable of taking revenge. Hindley tries to enlist her as an ally—" 'Are you as soft as your brother?' " (p. 145); but when Heathcliff appears Isabella does her " 'duty' " (p. 146) and warns him that Hindley intends to shoot him. When Hindley abuses her for her "base spirit" (p. 146), we tend to agree and to sympathize with his contention that " 'treachery and violence are a just return for treachery and violence!' " (p. 145). Many critics have argued that Heathcliff's victims are getting what they deserve. There are things in the novel that make vindictiveness seem justified.

There are also things, in addition to the scorn of Cathy and Heathcliff, that make humane or compliant behavior seem weak or foolish. The kindhearted Mr. Earnshaw harbors Heathcliff " 'to his bane' " (p. 260), and Edgar's parents die as a result of caring for the sick Catherine. Edgar is caught when Cathy strikes him and then threatens to cry herself sick if he leaves. Nelly tries to encourage him to depart:

> "Miss is dreadfully wayward, sir!" I called out. "As bad as any marred child—you'd better be riding home, or else she will be sick, only to grieve us."
>
> The soft thing looked askance through the window: he possessed the power to depart, as much as a cat possesses the power to leave a mouse half killed, or a bird half eaten.
>
> Ah, I thought, there will be no saving him—He's doomed, and flies to his fate! (p. 66)

A blow to the pride is often what precipitates love in a self-effacing person, and a display of suffering usually has coercive power upon him. Cathy, like Heathcliff, understands the weaknesses of those she wishes to manipulate and very skillfully exploits them. The scorn for Edgar comes here from Nelly, who stands up to aggressive people but is herself a soft touch for self-effacing ones. She urges Edgar to confront Heathcliff after his return: " 'There's harm in being too soft' " (p. 98); but a good deal of mischief is caused by her inability to be firm with Cathy II. When Heathcliff puts pressure on Cathy to come to see Linton despite her father's prohibition, Nelly gives in: " 'I couldn't bear to witness her sorrow' " (p. 190). Cathy is likewise compelled by Linton's sufferings. Her "indulgent tenderness" (p. 212) toward that repulsive young man puts her in his power, and in Heathcliff's. It is an unsavory spectacle that does not win admiration for self-effacing behavior. Nelly and Cathy are happy in the end, of course, as their virtue is rewarded; but so is Heathcliff, who dies in a state of exultation. God never forces a cry of humiliation from him; he remains entirely unrepentant.

Miriam Allott argues that *Wuthering Heights* "is an effort to explore and, *if possible,* to reconcile conflicting 'attractions'; it is sufficiently clear . . . that Emily Brontë was drawn . . . by different parts of her nature . . . towards both storm and calm."[8] I would say that she was drawn by different parts of her nature toward the arrogant-vindictive and the self-effacing solutions and that our inability to determine where she stands in the system of contrasts results from the fact that her inner conflict is expressed but not resolved by the novel. She is attracted to both solutions and at the same time sees their destructiveness. She sees each not only from within but also from the perspective of the other, and she feels for each the scorn generated by the opposing set of shoulds. She manages to give coherent expression to her very mixed and complicated attitudes by means of her narrative technique. She allows the aggressive side of her nature to be expressed through the story of Cathy and Heathcliff, but she combines with it a continuous commentary from the self-effacing point of view. This covers her tracks with the readers and makes it impossible for us to accuse her of approving these monsters. Her scorn for her self-effacing side is expressed through Cathy and Heathcliff, and in other ways as well, while having Nelly tell the story permits her to pass moral judgment and to satisfy her self-effacing shoulds.

There is another side of Emily Brontë that gets expressed through her narrative technique, and that is her detachment. Lockwood is usually seen as the representative of civilization; but it is more interesting and appropriate, I think, to see him as a representative of detachment. He comes to the region in order to get away from his fellows and finds it "a perfect misanthrope's heaven" (p. 13). He tells us a great deal about himself in his reaction to Heathcliff's reserve. At first he attributes Heathcliff's moroseness to "an aversion to showy displays of feeling," but he then realizes that he may be bestowing his "own attributes over-liberally on him" (p. 15). Lockwood despises himself for his own detachment: "Let me hope my constitution is almost peculiar: my dear mother used to say I should never have a comfortable home, and only last summer I proved myself perfectly unworthy of one" (p. 15). He was attracted to "a most fascinating creature" until she showed signs of reciprocating his interest, and he then "shrunk icily into [himself], like a snail" (p. 15). Lockwood longs for human companionship, but he is terrified of emotional involvement. He visits Heathcliff a second time because Heathcliff's own greater reserve makes him safe to be with. After his painful experience, however, he curses himself for his social impulse and reminds himself that "a sensible man ought to find sufficient company in himself" (p. 32). He seeks Nelly's company despite his determination to hold himself "independent of all social intercourse" (p. 35) and then feels himself to be a "weak wretch" (p. 36) for doing so. The outermost frame of the novel is Lockwood's flirtation with the idea of a romance with Cathy II, but he is very much afraid of "the fascination that lurks" in her eyes (p. 130) and does not want to "venture [his] tranquillity by running into temptation" (p. 205). When he returns to find Cathy engaged to Hareton, however, he bites his lip "in spite, at having thrown away [his] chance" (p. 243). It seems clear at the end that Lockwood will never be able to form a loving relationship and have "a comfortable home."

Nelly's narrative enables Lockwood to engage in a characteristically detached way of experiencing life, that is, through other people's passions. Lockwood is afraid of his feelings and is constantly defending himself against them. The result of his detachment, however, is boredom, a sense of the emptiness of life. Nelly's story is of people who are acting out their impulses all the time, in an intense, uninhibited way. Cathy and Heathcliff are not emotionally dead, the way Lockwood is; and through them he gets a vicarious sense of being alive: "'I could fancy a love for life here almost possible'" (p. 58). What makes Cathy and Heathcliff appealing to the reader is, in part, their juxtaposition with Lockwood. They have the vitality and intensity that he lacks. Their grand passion is self-consuming, but his tepid little romance never gets off the ground, and he goes away with nothing. By contrast with them, his life is sterile. The detached side of Emily Brontë is attracted by the intensity of Cathy and Heathcliff, just as Lockwood is; but, like him, she is also frightened by it. Cathy and Heathcliff are fascinating creatures; but they confirm Lockwood's worst fears, that if you lose control of your emotions, especially in relation to the opposite sex, you will be destroyed. Their fate reinforces his detached solution, just as it does Nelly's self-effacing one, at the very same time that it challenges its validity. Detachment is treated with the same ambivalence as are the aggressive and compliant solutions.

Given Emily Brontë's inner conflicts, it is amazing that *Wuthering Heights* is not thematically confused as is, say, a novel like *Vanity Fair.* The difference lies in the narrative technique. By having the story told by Nelly and Lockwood, with much internal quotation from Cathy and Heathcliff, Emily Brontë can give expression to all of her trends, and to the crossfire of conflicting shoulds that they generate, without having any one position emerge as normative, and therefore as inadequate to the novel's ambivalence. Each set of trends can be at once expressed, justified, and criticized from the point of view of the others. Thackeray's inner conflicts wreak havoc in a novel that employs omniscient narration; but *Wuthering Heights* is an impressionistic novel, like *Lord Jim,* in which interpretation is dramatized.[9] All of the value judgments and attitudes belong to the characters and are appropriate to their personalities. This creates a problem of narrative reliability in the sense that we do not know where in the novel's system of conflicting values the author stands, but it avoids the problems that would have resulted from the establishment of a moral norm. Brontë's narrative technique serves the needs of her detachment by preserving her privacy, by enabling her to disappear. She does not want us to know where she stands. It is a way of managing her inner conflicts that does much to produce the novel's richness and complexity, its elusiveness and its never-ending fascination.

4

When we use the name of the author, we may be referring to the implied author of one of his works, to the authorial personality that can be inferred from several or all of his works, or to the historical person who, among other things, wrote the books that bear his name. I have been speaking mainly of the Emily Brontë that I can infer from an analysis of *Wuthering Heights,* but I believe that this description of the implied author of the novel tells us much about Brontë the person. We must be very careful, of course, when we try to infer the historical person from his artistic creations. We must recognize that the historical person has a life independent of his works, that many of his attitudes and attributes may never appear in his fictions, and that those that do appear may have been disguised or transformed by the process of artistic creation. We allow, moreover, for artistic motivations, for generic requirements, and for the inner logic of the individual work. It is possible, nonetheless, to tell a good deal about the author from his works when we examine such things as his recurring preoccupations, the personal element in his fantasies, the kinds of characters he habitually creates, and his rhetorical stance. In this delicate biographical enterprise, Horney's theory is again very helpful.

Horneyan psychology can help us to illuminate the author through his works because in the course of artistic creation the author's defensive strategies tend to express themselves in a variety of ways. His works are, among other things, efforts to reinforce his predominant solution and to resolve his inner conflicts by showing himself, as well as others, the good and evil consequences of the various trends that are warring within him. He will tend to glorify characters whose strategies are similar to his own and to satirize those who embody his repressed solutions. His rhetoric will affirm the values, attitudes, and traits of character that are demanded by his dominant solution, while rejecting those forbidden by it. His plots will often be fantasies in which his claims are honored in a magical way, while his repressed strategies are shown to bring misery and retribution. Because he cannot help expressing his subordinate trends also, however, his works will frequently manifest his inner conflicts. His attitudes, values, and beliefs will often be inconsistent or self-contradictory. His conflicting trends will lead him to criticize each solution from the point of view of the others and to have toward his characters the mixed feelings that he has toward the aspects of himself that they embody. The relationships among his solutions may vary, moreover, in the course of his life; and this will be reflected in changes in the kinds of characters he portrays, in his rhetoric, and in his dominant fantasies. I have shown how all of this works in an analysis of Jane Austen.[10] For purposes of illustration here, I give a brief account of a basic conflict in Shakespeare's personality that can be inferred from a study of his works.

From *1 Henry VI* to *The Tempest,* a frequent concern of Shakespeare's plays is how to cope with wrongs, how to remain good in an evil world. In the histories and the tragedies, the tendency of the main characters is to respond to wrongs by taking revenge; but this contaminates the revenger and eventually results in his own destruction. In Horney's terms, the aggressive solution, with its emphasis upon retaliation and vindictive triumph, does not work. But the self-effacing solution does not work in these plays either, as many innocent, well-intentioned, but weak characters perish. Hamlet's problem, as I see it, is how to take revenge and remain innocent. The problem is insoluble and nearly drives him mad. In a number of the comedies and romances, Shakespeare explores a different response to being wronged—namely, mercy and forgiveness. Because of the conventions of these genres, with their providential universe and miraculous conversions, wronged characters do not have to take revenge: either fate does it for them or they forgive their enemies, who are then permanently transformed. In these plays, the self-effacing solution, with its accompanying bargain, works very well, but only because the plays are unrealistic.

What I infer about Shakespeare from his plays is that he has strong vindictive impulses, but even stronger taboos against those impulses and a fear of the guilt and punishment to which he would be exposed if he acted them out. He does act them out imaginatively in the histories and tragedies and is purged of them through the destruction of his surrogate aggressors. He also has a fear of his self-effacing side, however; and he shows both himself and us through characters like Henry VI, Hamlet, Desdemona, and Timon that people who are too good and trusting cannot cope and will be destroyed. In the tragedies he portrays the inadequacy of both solutions. In some of the comedies and in the romances he fantasizes the triumph of good people and avoids guilt either by glorifying forgiveness or leaving revenge to the gods. In *The Tempest,* through Prospero's magic, he imagines a solution to Hamlet's problem; for Prospero is at once vindictive and noble, vengeful and innocent. He takes his revenge through his magic, by raising a tempest and inflicting various psychological torments; but he does not really hurt anybody; and when he has had his vindictive triumph, he gives up his magic and forgives everyone. Many critics have been uncomfortable with his forgiveness of Antonio, who shows no sign of repentance; and they have, I think, good reason; for it is the product of Prospero's compulsions and is inappropriate to the practical and moral realities of the situation. Like the Duke in *Measure for Measure* and many other of Shakespeare's self-effacing characters, Prospero cannot, in the final analysis, place blame where it belongs and effectively deal with the guilty. The unworkability of the solution that Shakespeare has embodied in *The Tempest* begins to be felt when we imagine the return to Italy.

From a psychological point of view, one of Shakespeare's major projects was to find a way of giving expression to the hostile, vindictive, aggressive side of his personality without violating his stronger need to be noble, loving, and innocent. Recognizing this helps us to understand many of his plays and also, I believe, a number of the sonnets. *The Tempest* is perhaps the most brilliant solution that he ever imagined to this essentially insoluble problem, and it is not surprising that it was his last great play. In *Henry VIII,* which followed, the self-effacing side of Shakespeare is overwhelmingly predominant, and we no longer feel ourselves to be in the presence of a complex and fascinating personality. Shakespeare's inner conflicts have much to do, I suspect, with the richness and ambiguity of his greatest art.[11]

5

Shakespeare's inner conflicts have much to do also with a number of the major controversies among critics, some of whom respond to one side of Shakespeare's personality and some to another. For example, those who offer the orthodox Christian readings of Shakespeare are responding to that side of Shakespeare which believes that right makes might and that virtue is rewarded, while those who claim that his portrayal of reality is closer to the modern absurdist position are more sensitive to that side of him which sees through the self-effacing bargain. Each group is partially right, for both perspectives are present in the plays. Norman Rabkin and Bernard McElroy invoke the principle of complementarity to account for the coexistence of opposite points of view in Shakespeare,[12] but it makes more sense to me to explain it in terms of his inner conflicts.

A similar state of affairs exists in Jane Austen criticism. There are strong elements of aggressiveness, compliance, and detachment in Jane Austen's personality, all of which get expressed in her fiction. Some critics emphasize the aggressive, satirical component of her art; some stress her gentleness and conservatism; and some focus upon the detached, ironic quality of her vision. Each group over-emphasizes something that is there. An analysis of Jane Austen's personality shows how these diverse components of her nature are related to each other in a structure of inner conflicts.

Considerable attention has been focused of late upon the reading process, which is coming to be seen more and more as a transaction in which the reader's personality plays an important part. Horneyan psychology can help us to be aware of the influence that the reader's defensive strategies have upon his critical perceptions. To begin with, as I explain in *A Psychological Approach to Fiction,*

> it can identify the conflicts, solutions, and values to which the audience is responding. Then, it can account for partial, biased, or conflicting responses. If a character or a work embodies an aggressive, a detached, or a self-effacing solution, or a particular structure of inner conflicts, readers will respond in terms of their own predominant solution or their own structure of conflicts. Criticism often tells us as much about the critic as it does about the work of art. It would be extremely interesting to analyze the whole body of criticism on a work from a psychological point of view. Not only would we learn much about the work and about the dynamics of literary response, but we would also gain insight into the subjectivity of perception and the inevitability of conflicting interpretations. (pp. 288–89)

In *Vanity Fair,* Amelia and Dobbin are self-effacing and Becky is aggressive. Most critics feel that Amelia and Dobbin are presented in a favorable light and that Becky is portrayed as a monster all along. An important minority feels, however, that Thackeray has contempt for Amelia and Dobbin, that he admires Becky, and that he is inconsistent toward the end when he characterizes Becky as a monster. According to my analysis, Thackeray has a personality in which self-effacing trends are predominant but in which there are also powerful aggressive drives that get themselves expressed in indirect or disguised ways.[13] The self-effacing side of him exalts Amelia and Dobbin and condemns Becky, while his aggressive side delights in Becky's triumphs and scorns Amelia as a parasite and Dobbin as a spooney. Each set of critics sees something that is there, but each also ignores something else that is also present; and what these critics see and ignore is largely determined, I suspect, by their own personalities. The same thing holds true for the critics of Shakespeare and Austen referred to above.

It is a very risky business, of course, to psychoanalyze one's fellow critics on the basis of their criticism. There is rarely enough information to warrant more than a guess, and there is considerable danger of giving offense. Perhaps the best way to illustrate the influence of the psychology of the critic upon his criticism is through an analysis of one's own work, especially of earlier work from which the necessary distance has been attained. I have engaged in this sort of analysis in "Experiences of Thomas Hardy," in which I was invited to describe my own shifting relationship to this author. I illustrate my point here with a consideration of some of the ways in which my personal psychology influenced my critical perceptions in my book on George Eliot[14] and of how my psychological development has affected my more recent perceptions both of Eliot and of my critical reactions to her.

Experiments in Life examines George Eliot's ideas in relation to her time and her art in relation to her ideas. In her novels, which she called "experiments in life," George Eliot explored the moral implications of science and positivistic philosophy in an effort to discover enduring truths that would ennoble human existence and replace the outmoded beliefs and institutions of the past. She was profoundly influenced by the teachings of Feuerbach, Comte, Mill, Spencer, and Lewes; but, because of her distrust of "shifting theory" and her reluctance to "adopt any formula which does not get itself clothed . . . in some human figure and individual experience,"[15] art was the only means she could confidently employ to verify and communicate her values. Her protagonists arrive, through a varied course of experiences, at some version of the Religion of Humanity, in which living for others, for something beyond the self, gives meaning and value to their lives.

Experiments in Life was originally my doctoral dissertation. While I was writing it, I identified completely with George Eliot's point of view. I not only expounded, but I also believed in her theory of fiction and her Religion of Humanity. I was convinced that she had solved the value problems of modern man living in a universe without God, and I expected my book to have an important effect upon the way in which enlightened men henceforth thought and lived. When my dissertation director, Hillis Miller, posed marginal questions about why George Eliot believed as she did, I felt that it was silly of him to ask why someone believed the truth.

A strange thing happened after I completed my dissertation. When I was given the chance to teach George Eliot at last, I found that my enthusiasm had disappeared, that her beliefs had lost their magic. I remained convinced that I had understood her correctly, but I was no longer sure of my own relation to her ideas. I was mournful at my loss of fervor and quite bewildered about what had happened.

It was at this point that I first read Karen Horney. Her description of how our value systems are often a function of our defensive strategies seemed directly applicable to me and, by extension, to George Eliot. Miller's questions began to make sense. I came to see that my relationship to George Eliot had been profoundly influenced by a shaky performance on my doctoral oral, which had hurt my pride, undermined my confidence, and made me turn to my dissertation as the means by which I would show everybody how good I really was. Since the dissertation had to be so good, it became almost impossible to write; and there were long periods when I despaired of ever finishing. My dreams of a glorious academic career were in ruins, and I needed to find a new meaning for my life. It was while I was in this state of mind that I found George Eliot's philosophy absolutely convincing. The way to glory, she proclaimed, is not through personal ambition and triumph, but through goodness, self-sacrifice, and living for others, whose need of us gives indubitable meaning to our lives. Even if I did not become a great critic and scholar, I could be a wonderful husband, father, and friend; and I convinced myself that I was these things, though in truth I was not. The stories of Maggie Tulliver and Dorothea Brooke appealed to me as glorifications of gifted young people, much like myself, who attained a kind of moral grandeur, even though they failed to achieve an epic life. In short, my difficulty in writing my dissertation led me to abandon my expansive ambitions, which I now saw no way of fulfilling, and to embrace the self-effacing solution that I found so powerfully set forth by George Eliot.

The successful completion of my dissertation and its warm reception changed my relationship to George Eliot. Finishing the work in which I had articulated my defense against failure did away with my need for that defense and made it lose its appeal. I was once again focused on personal achievement, and living for others was no longer necessary. Hence my lack of enthusiasm when I had the chance to teach George Eliot. I had been looking forward to having the opportunity to preach her Religion of Humanity, but I found myself strangely indifferent to her ideas.

Looking back on my experience after the passage of twenty-five years, it seems to me that my personal identification with Eliot's ideas produced a combination of blindness and insight. It enabled me to understand them from within and to give them a full, accurate, and sympathetic exposition. I still believe that I interpreted Eliot's novels correctly in their own terms, that I saw her characters as she meant them to be seen, and that I gave their experience the meaning she intended it to have. I was totally responsive to her rhetoric.

That very responsiveness blinded me, however, to a number of things that I think I see more clearly now that I no longer share all of George Eliot's beliefs. Because I was so intent upon understanding her characters as illustrations of her ideas, I failed to see them as imagined human beings who are fascinating in their own right and who are not always in harmony with their formal and thematic functions. I paid no attention to George Eliot's mimetic achievement, and I had very little sense of the brilliance and complexity of her psychological insights. I did not see the necessity to distinguish between her *representation* of a character, which is usually complex, accurate, and enduring, and her *interpretation,* which is often misleading, over-simple, and confused.

I had little sense also of the unrealistic elements in her fiction. Because of my need to believe in her consistency and in the viability of her solution, I could not see that she frequently celebrated a magic bargain in which one achieves glory by being humble, good, and loving, by living for others, and, above all, by submitting oneself to a larger power outside of oneself that will provide protection and justice. In order to make this bargain work, she often created a universe that was much closer to that of her earlier Christian theology than it was to that of positive science, a universe in which aggressive qualities are punished and self-effacing ones are rewarded.

My most striking blindness, I think, was to the destructiveness of the solutions at which her characters arrive as a result of their "education." George Eliot shared with many other nineteenth-century novelists the illusion that suffering, frustration, and bad social conditions can make one, somehow, into a noble person. She depicts for us very vividly all the conditions in Dorothea Brooke's environment which thwart her healthy development, but she does not see that these conditions have actually hurt Dorothea instead of making her a superior being. She shows Dorothea making a series of terrible mistakes as a result of her compensatory search for glory, but she treats these mistakes as the product of Dorothea's "spiritual grandeur," which is "ill-matched with the meanness of opportunity."[16] As a great realistic novelist, George Eliot shows us the destructiveness of the self-effacing solution that Dorothea had adopted in response to her pathogenic environment; but since she shares this solution herself, her rhetoric glorifies it as a sign of moral nobility and places the blame for Dorothea's mistakes on external factors. Since I also shared this solution when I was writing *Experiments in Life,* I presented it with complete, though tacit, approval.

As I now see it, one of the most serious deficiencies of George Eliot's philosophy is her emphasis upon living for others as the means by which we give value to our lives and her failure to recognize the importance of self-actualization. Since our life has the meaning that other people give to it, we may be driven to satisfy their needs at all costs, regardless of our own, or to live up to their values. There is no way in George Eliot's thinking by which we can discriminate between the legitimate needs of others and their neurotic claims. Her characters can rarely defend themselves when other people make irrational demands upon them, and she tends to glorify their compulsively self-sacrificial behavior.

A prime example of this is Dorothea's decision to give in to Casaubon's demand that she complete his book if he should die prematurely. Dorothea feels that she is "going to say 'Yes' to her own doom" but she is "too full of dread at the thought of inflicting a keen-edged blow on her husband, to do anything but submit completely" (p. 353). Dorothea's situation is an extremely difficult one. A refusal would be a terrible blow to Casaubon, but to agree might bind her to a lifetime of labor on a project in which she no longer believes. What neither Dorothea nor George Eliot can grasp clearly is that Casaubon has no right to make such a demand and that Dorothea has every right to preserve herself. Eliot's rhetoric exalts Dorothea's decision as a form of moral heroism: "Neither law nor the world's opinion compelled her to this—only her husband's nature and her own compassion, only the ideal and not the real yoke of marriage. She saw clearly enough the whole situation, yet she was fettered: she could not smite the stricken soul that entreated hers. If that were weakness, Dorothea was weak" (p. 353). George Eliot seems to have an intimation that Dorothea is, indeed, acting out of weakness, but she tries to dismiss it through a rhetorical device. Dorothea is motivated not only by her compassion for Casaubon and the ideals of marriage, but also by her self-effacing shoulds, by a dread of the self-hate she would feel if she failed to live up to her idealized image of herself as a loving, devoted, self-disregarding person. As a result, she cannot assert her legitimate rights but must submit completely to Casaubon's demands. George Eliot at once rewards Dorothea's projected self-sacrifice and obscures the destructiveness of her decision by having Casaubon die just before Dorothea goes out to give her promise. She does not allow Lydgate, it might be noted, to escape the disastrous consequences of his own foolish marriage because most of his mistakes are of an expansive rather than of a self-effacing sort.

There are psychological reasons, of course, for my present view of George Eliot, just as there were for my earlier one, though I am not likely to have as clear an understanding of them. My shift from George Eliot's values to those of Horney and Maslow is a reflection of my psychological evolution, as well as of new intellectual influences, and of a change in my vision of human possibilities. I seem to be bothered by precisely those things in George Eliot to which I was attracted before. In being critical of them, I am criticizing my earlier self and am trying to exorcise the self-effacing trends which remain within me and which get in the way of my self-actualization. If I were less threatened by self-effacing tendencies in myself, I would have less need to insist upon their destructiveness in others. The expansive side of me is embarrassed, no doubt, by my former enthusiasm for compliant values; and my detached side derives pleasure from seeing through all kinds of defenses—I take great pride in my psychological insight. For these, and probably for some other reasons as well, it has given me considerable satisfaction to expose the weaknesses of George Eliot's philosophy and to analyze my previous commitment to it.

6

I have tried to show so far how Third Force psychology can be used in the study of literature, biography, and criticism. I should like to conclude by suggesting some of its applications to the study of influence, religion, philosophy, and culture. As I indicated at the outset, the power of this theory is just beginning to be understood. The present account should be taken, therefore, as exploratory and speculative.[17]

We tend to analyze influence by pointing to external factors, whether they be books, movements, people, or features of the cultural milieu. What we often ignore or underestimate is the importance of receptivity. We are all exposed to a multitude of potential influences, but we are deeply affected by only a few. We are psychologically predisposed to be highly receptive to some external stimuli and not at all to others. Influence is always the result of an *interaction* between external factors and individual psychology. My earlier receptivity to George Eliot's philosophy is a case in point. Eliot herself was deeply influenced by Feuerbach. In order to explain this we must try to understand what psychological needs Feuerbach served and why his ideas were so congenial to her. If the study of influence is to be at all sophisticated, it must address itself not only to external but also to psychological factors, to the role of receptivity. Since Horney's theory offers many insights into the relationship between belief systems and strategies of defense, it can be of great help in this undertaking.

As I see it, religious beliefs are generated and held by human beings in order to satisfy their psychological needs. In the terms of Horney's theory, most religions try to get their followers to live up to an idealized image, which varies from theology to theology, promising them rewards if they succeed and threatening them with punishments if they fail. Sometimes there are even built-in defenses against failure, which is recognized as inevitable. Most religions embody a search for glory, with its accompanying shoulds, claims, pride, and self-hate, and its bargain with fate in which certain beliefs, acts, gestures, rituals, traits of character, and so on are supposed to be rewarded. Much of the Old Testament celebrates a perfectionistic bargain in which people are driven to conform to an elaborate set of rituals and commands through a constant bombardment of threats and promises. In the New Testament, the predominant bargain changes; it is no longer obedience to the law but compliant attitudes, such as forgiveness, faith, and humility, which bring the rewards. I believe that each set of religious beliefs can be analyzed in psychological terms and that the history of religion will become more meaningful to nonbelievers if we try to understand the human needs expressed by doctrines and rituals. Understanding the needs that religion serves would help us to grasp the anguish that human beings have felt when their beliefs have been threatened and the plight of many moderns who, deprived of the communal illusion system that religion affords, must forge private solutions for which there is little consensual validation. It would also help us to discriminate between healthy and unhealthy religions, between those which foster and those which inhibit self-actualization.

Philosophic systems are also appropriate objects of psychological analysis; for they, too, are expressions of human needs and defenses. Such philosophers as Schopenhauer, Kierkegaard, and Nietzsche, for example, are fascinating to study from a Horneyan perspective. The first seems to be predominantly detached, the second self-effacing, and the third expansive; and we can see in each of them the kind of elaboration that these defenses can undergo in the hands of genius. Understanding the psychological orientation of philosophic systems can help us to see not only where these systems came from, but also the nature of their influence and appeal. It can also help us to make sense of their inconsistencies, which are often an expression of the inner conflicts of the philosopher.

A psychological perspective has the effect of bringing past systems of belief closer to us by leading us to see them as expressions of the same needs and defenses that exist in us today. It generates in this way a feeling of kinship with those who believed in them. The same thing happens in the study of past cultures. The applicability of Third Force psychology to works from a wide variety of periods and places convinces me that human beings have remained much the same. Each culture, however, has its own ways of responding to basic human needs. It has also its characteristic attitudes toward the various defense systems, its own formulations of and variations upon them, and its own particular structure of conflicts. At first glance, we are most struck by the differences between our culture and those of the past. Victorian attitudes and values, for example, seem quaint, outmoded, remote from the temper of our time. When we see them as expressions of basic needs and defenses, however, we recognize that the psychological phenomena out of which they arose have not disappeared. The preferred solution of our time is different from that of the Victorian age, as can be seen by the growing incidence of detached rather than self-effacing characters as the protagonists of our fiction; but our detachment is in large part a defense against the conflict between aggressive and compliant attitudes that was so blatant in the Victorians and that is still present in many of us.

In his brilliant study of the Victorian consciousness, Walter Houghton finds it to be full of contradictions.[18] There is little that a social, intellectual, or cultural historian can do with these contradictions except to note them. A psychological perspective enables us to make sense of these contradictions, however, by seeing them as part of a system of inner conflicts that exists within both the culture and the individuals who constitute it. The aggressive solution is visible in many of the phenomena that Houghton associates with Victorian industrialism and imperialism. These include the commercial spirit, the marriage market, the worship of success, laissez faire economics, the worship of forces, social Darwinism, and chauvinism. The compliant solution is evident in many of the phenomena associated with that other great movement of the Victorian age, Evangelicism. These include moral earnestness, the insistence on duty, the demand for moral perfection, the ethic of service, enthusiasm, idealism, and the emphasis upon sympathy and benevolence. It is also manifested in hero worship and the exaltation of home, women, and love. It is difficult to say which of these solutions was dominant in the culture; they were both very powerful. Whichever trend dominated in any individual or cultural movement, the other was present, more or less repressed. It is this inner conflict that was a major cause of Victorian hypocrisy, as people tried to reconcile aggressive behavior with self-effacing values. George Eliot's Bulstrode is a marvelous example of this.

The expansive solution tended to dominate in males and to determine the Victorian conception of manliness, while the self-effacing solution tended to dominate in women and to provide an idealized conception of femininity. The male cultivated in himself the qualities necessary to succeed in the social jungle. He had, however, a suppressed compliant side, which he fulfilled through love, home, and woman worship. This eased the discomfort caused by the violation of his self-effacing shoulds. But he rejected the feminine virtues for himself as unmanly; they violated his aggressive shoulds and were difficult to incorporate into his idealized image, though he often did this through a process of compartmentalization. The typical woman took pride in her purity, lovingness, self-sacrifice, and depth of feeling. She mastered the world through her weakness and dependency. She rejected the sexual coarseness and competitiveness associated with the male world; but, at the same time, she fulfilled her suppressed expansive drives through her identification with a domineering, adventurous, or successful man. There were numerous exceptions to these roles, however. Horneyan theory does not talk about masculine and feminine psychology, but about character traits and defensive strategies that are present, in varying degrees, in both men and women. We have in Victorian fiction such compliant men as William Dobbin, Edgar Linton, Mr. Harding, and Joe Gargery, and such aggressive women as Becky Sharp, Beatrix Esmond, Cathy Earnshaw, and Mrs. Joe. We have, above all, both men and women who are torn by inner conflicts.

I have suggested that, for those who share its premises, Third Force psychology provides a sophisticated method for evaluating an author's judgments of his characters and the healthy or unhealthy tendencies of religious beliefs. It can serve a similar function in the evaluation of cultures. Having seen through the ethnocentricity that has characterized most human societies, we have swung to the opposite extreme and have become afraid to judge cultures at all. Third Force psychology does not see values as culture-bound, but rather as generated by the nature of the species, which remains essentially the same despite the number and range of cultural variations. It permits us to evaluate cultures, therefore, in terms of a universal norm of psychological health that has nothing to do with the quite possibly misguided values of individual societies. Those things are good in a culture that satisfy the basic needs of its members and foster their full human growth, while those things are bad that frustrate the basic needs and induce self-alienation.

Despite its very great achievements, the Victorian age constituted, in many ways, a pathogenic environment that made the healthy unfolding of the human capacities extremely difficult. It was by no means, however, the worst of times. Indeed, some of the phenomena Houghton describes were signs of a growing rebellion against destructive repressions and of a freeing of the human faculties. These include the liberation from the burden of the past, the rise of the critical spirit, the rejection of dogma and authority, the attacks on hypocrisy and convention, and the battle for open-mindedness and self-development. The most eloquent spokesman for many of these positive tendencies of the age was John Stuart Mill, who had a strong sense of what was wrong with his culture and a clear vision of some of the essential requirements of human well-being. "Human nature is not a machine," Mill proclaimed, "to be built after a model, and set to do exactly the work prescribed for it, but a tree, which requires to grow and develop itself on all sides, according to the tendency of the inward forces which make it a living thing."[19] This sounds very much like Third Force psychology. We have inherited, no doubt, many of the mental ailments of the Victorian age; but we should not forget that we have also been the beneficiaries of its struggles for growth and of its highest conceptions of human development.

NOTES

1. *A Man for All Seasons* (New York: Vintage, n.d.), p. 91. Hereafter cited in the text.
2. *A Psychological Approach to Fiction: Studies in Thackeray, Stendahl, George Eliot, Dostoevsky, and Conrad* (Bloomington: Indiana University Press, 1974), pp. 280–81.
3. *Herzog* (New York: Viking Press, 1964), p. 67. Hereafter cited in the text.
4. See " 'Hush, hush! He's a human being': A Psychological Approach to Heathcliff," *Women and Literature,* n.s. 2 (1982): 101–17.
5. Introduction to *Wuthering Heights,* Rinehart edition (New York: Rinehart, 1950), p. xi.
6. I am using the Norton Critical Edition of *Wuthering Heights,* ed. William M. Sale, Jr. (New York: Norton, 1963). Hereafter cited in the text.
7. See John K. Mathison, "Nelly Dean and the Power of *Wuthering Heights,*" *Nineteenth Century Fiction* 11 (1956): 106–29 and James Hafley, "The Villain in *Wuthering Heights,*" *Nineteenth Century Fiction* 13 (1958): 199–215.
8. "*Wuthering Heights:* The Rejection of Heathcliff?" *Essays in Criticism* 8 (1958): 29.
9. See my chapters on *Vanity Fair* and *Lord Jim* in *A Psychological Approach to Fiction.*
10. *Character and Conflict in Jane Austen's Novels: A Psychological Approach* (Detroit: Wayne State University Press, 1978), chap. 6. There is a brief analysis of Hardy's personality in "Experiences of Thomas Hardy," in *The Victorian Experience,* ed. Richard A. Levine (Athens: Ohio University Press, 1976), pp. 233–36.
11. There will be an extended analysis of Shakespeare's personality in the book I am currently writing—*Bargains with Fate: A Psychological Approach to Shakespeare.*
12. Norman Rabkin, *Shakespeare and the Common Understanding* (New York: Free Press, 1967) and Bernard McElroy, *Shakespeare's Mature Tragedies* (Princeton: Princeton University Press, 1973).
13. See *A Psychological Approach to Fiction,* chap. 3.
14. *Experiments in Life: George Eliot's Quest for Values* (Detroit: Wayne State University Press, 1965).
15. *The George Eliot Letters,* ed. Gordon S. Haight (New Haven: Yale University Press, 1954–55), 4: 216–17.
16. *Middlemarch,* ed. Gordon Haight (Boston: Houghton Mifflin, 1956), Prelude.
17. Other possible applications of the theory are discussed in *A Psychological Approach to Fiction,* pp. 287–90.
18. *The Victorian Frame of Mind* (New Haven: Yale University Press, 1957).
19. *On Liberty,* chap. 3.

3

Psychology and Literary Form: Toward a Unified Approach

Norman Friedman

1

In Tennyson's "Locksley Hall," a young man reminisces about his youth, about his childhood dreams of history and progress, and about his early love for his cousin Amy. This love, however, was betrayed when she yielded to parental pressure and married a wealthier man. Remembering this, our hero is swept away on the tides of bitterness and frustration, and he curses society for forcing conventional and materialistic forms upon the vitality of the young. Now, in a whirl of ambivalence, he accuses himself of blustering, while at the same time tearing himself apart between love and hate, and he desperately looks for comfort, for escape from his pain.

He searches for some means of action in society as a way out of despair, but again he can merely see the corruption of money standing in his path. The only outlet he can imagine is to return to his young dreams, calling to the Age as his mother—whom he never knew (and his father died early on)—to hide him from his pain. Even though Amy's betrayal left him disillusioned with society, he still believes in it. But his mood continues to be unstable, and he scorns women and society altogether, yearning to live in a tropical paradise, take some savage woman, and rear a dusky race. Once again reversing himself, however, he realizes that this is all a foolish fancy and that primitive peoples are lower than the Christian child. Finally, he regards the far horizon and commits himself at last to progress, calling upon his Mother-Age to help him, as before, and saying goodbye to Locksley Hall, as a storm rises toward the sea.

Now, on the face of it, this seems to be a fairly well-constructed poem. The young man has a problem, explores it with a certain amount of self-awareness, considers alternative solutions, comes to a resolution which appears to relieve him of the problem, says goodbye to his past, and moves on to meet his destiny. Looking a bit more deeply, however, we may begin to wonder about

First delivered as a talk, in an earlier version, at Haverford College, under the sponsorship of the English Department, November 10, 1976.

the exact nature of that resolution and about its relationship to what went before. For I take it as a basic principle of literary structure—at least of those kinds of structures that aim at unity, wholeness, and completeness—that a resolution should be prepared for, should flow from the original givens of the work, should grow out of the terms of the conflict rather than contradict them, or be brought in arbitrarily from outside the work. As Aristotle would say, the ending should follow, in terms of human probability or necessity, from what went before.[1]

The question I have, then, is that the speaker's final commitment to the march of civilization seems to contradict the original formulation he himself made of the problem: that society, with its conventionalism and materialism, defeated his young love. How can he commit himself to the same society at the end that thwarted him at the beginning? It is true that he accuses himself of blustering as he rails at society, but this doesn't alter the fact that Amy did bow to societal pressures, nor does it prevent him from continuing to see society as corrupt as he looks about for something to do. Yet he accepts it as transcendentally valuable in terms of human fulfillment and progress, ignoring the fact that he has just condemned it for its antihuman materialism. He has not resolved his original problems by these means, neither that of materialism nor that of erotic frustration; he has merely shifted the terms from the personal to the historical level without accounting for that shift. Either his original distress was not in fact caused by societal pressures, or some way of incorporating its alleviation into the solution must be found. He has not so much solved his problem as escaped from solving it.

But let us look more closely. A boy full of vaulting dreams but with insufficient funds, he anticipates in interesting ways Dickens's Pip in *Great Expectations* and Fitzgerald's Gatsby. The specific nature of his dreams is that the flow of history has a meaning, life has a purpose, and things arrange themselves hierarchically according to that purpose. As with Pip and Gatsby, his vision becomes incarnate in the image of the girl he loves, and again as with these other young men, his vision shatters when she betrays that love. Our speaker has become angry, bitter, and disillusioned as a result, and he has a double dilemma: how to deal with his pain, and how to find a purpose in life once again.

He considers and rejects four alternatives before he comes to rest on a fifth—and this turns out, in effect, to be the same as the third, which is where the key to the puzzle of the poem's structure lies. His first attempt to find comfort is in the hope that he'll be able to think of her as she was before her betrayal, but this only makes things worse, for the contrast of past and present does but increase his pain. And indeed, the poem does alternate between past and present, and much of the speaker's associative flow turns on contrasts—as is characteristic of a mind imbued with the hierarchical habit. His second attempt is to avoid despair by finding something to do in the world, but here his lack of money stands in his way (as it stood between him and Amy). His third is simply to recover his youthful vision, and here he picks up where he left off and goes on to the famous "Parliament of man" passage. But then he tells how Amy's betrayal spoiled all this for him and left him with "the jaundiced eye; / Eye, to which all order festers, all things here are out of joint." The point is, we discover now, that he realizes how he's projecting his own inner state upon the world. Thus his previous and present criticisms of society are not meant to be taken as objective but rather as a sign of his own distress. This is why he can say, in the midst of his disillusionment, "Yet I doubt not thro' the ages one increasing purpose runs," and this is why he criticizes *himself* at three different points in the poem. And that is also why, as we shall see, he can conclude by accepting the very society he has been rejecting.

His fourth and most desperate maneuver is to imagine an escape from civilization and its discontents altogether into some form of non-Western existence, but paradoxically it is just this fantasy that brings him back to Western values. A life that is simple, sensuous, and passionate now strikes him as "lower" than a life of study, care, and striving—just as Amy's relationship with her loutish (but rich) husband is "lower" than that with the speaker. By contrast—by imagining an alternative existence without hierarchical values and noble purposes—he prompts himself back into his prebetrayal frame of mind: no matter how much Western culture costs, it's better than Eastern civilization. This in part, of course, rationalizes away his previous antisociety criticisms further. Thus he recovers his earlier dream, feels disillusionment and the need to project it no longer, and can once again look out on the world as offering purpose, progress, and promise: He has solved his problem, in other words, by exorcising the despair that caused him to see the world as offering no outlets: since he sees that the world's apparent hopelessness comes from within, he also sees that he can solve it from within.

This interpretation, you will recognize, is already beginning to sound somewhat psychological, and yet it has stayed withal as close to the poem as any strictly literary critic could wish. We have used only what is clearly there and to some degree clearly present in the speaker's own words. We are still left, however, with something of a structural anomaly. Exorcising despair is still not the same as working it through: the resolution, instead of bringing him to a more complex awareness of the meaning of his despair, seems now—if not self-contradictory—merely a return to the status quo ante. The problem of love and sexual fulfillment being subordinated to materialistic values still remains unresolved, and we can regard the approaching storm at the end as a substitute or symbolic orgasmic release, "sublimating" sexual need through historical energy. The speaker's personal problem of lack of money also remains unresolved. The criticism of society, however much involved in projection, remains cogent—and unanswered. The strong tradition of attacks by eminent Victorians—Carlyle, for example—on Victorian culture is something Tennyson was knowledgeable about and sympathetic with. Indeed, it is just possible that his hierarchical vision is as much a projection as his disillusioned view, and it is clear that he is not capable of realizing this. And finally, it is evident that his resolution, however we may be able to reason it through, is nevertheless regressive. It's not so much the *forward* march of the Age he's committing himself to as the *backward* march of his mind to his earlier visions of the world as a substitute for the mother he never had (he was raised, as he says, as "a selfish uncle's ward"). Certain materials remain unassimilated, then, by the poem's structure. There remains this disparity between the evident *structure* of the poem and its inner *emotional process:* the latter does not deliver what the former calls for.

Having gone as far as we can see as strictly literary critics at this point, we may still feel somewhat dissatisfied. Although we have been able to infer some of the psychological dynamic here, we still don't know exactly what the speaker really needs, nor why he cannot fulfill it. We want to know more about his emotional system, the nature of his pain and of the need that drives him back to the mother, and the structure of his obsessing and of his compulsive regression. We also want to know, if what he does is not actually a true resolution, what a true resolution might look like, in order to grasp by contrast what is going on here. We need, in other words, some psychological scheme to help us fill in the possibilities and sharpen our analysis and assessment of the poem's emotional structure. What this scheme will do for us is not to unify a disunified poem but rather to tell us why it is disunified. That it also makes sense for more successful poems will emerge as the discussion proceeds.

2

But using a psychological scheme does not necessarily mean, as is sometimes thought, that we are bringing in extraliterary material and thereby failing to read the poem as a poem. A psychological scheme may indeed *come* from someplace outside of literary studies but its *use* can remain strictly within the framework of literary form. We need not, in other words, be concerned with psychoanalyzing writers, or regard art as a neurotic symptom, or assume that fictional characters are "real," and so on, in order to make profitable use of psychology. It seems to me that if we regard it as a way of enlarging and deepening—conceptualizing, if you will—our already considerable knowledge of human emotions and motivations, then we will appreciate the possibilities of combining psychology and criticism in a unified approach.

For make no mistake: just as we cannot *understand the meaning* of literary works without an extensive knowledge of human emotions and motivations, so we cannot *analyze their artistic forms* without such knowledge. There is no distinction between form and content, at least not when form is seen in Aristotelian terms.[2] Form, that is, is not simply a matter of patterns, designs, structures, images, tensions, balances, recurrences, variations, techniques, stylistic devices, and so on—things that are abstractable and discussable apart from any given work in which they appear. It is more a matter of human characters responding to situations in certain ways, and of such actions being calculated to arouse in us certain feelings. And they respond to their situations in terms that are humanly necessary or probable, which for Aristotle provide the basis of literary structure.

The principles of probability and necessity mean that a response or sequence of responses to a situation arises out of its givens: a certain type of person will respond to a certain situation, and under certain conditions, in such a way as is consistent with what we know of human experience. Thus a knowledge of human experience is essential to formal analysis and not just to interpreting literary content. It is not for the writer simply a matter, that is, of preparing for what is to come and of making what follows grow out of what went before; it is more, within these principles, a matter of developing such an organic sequence in a way that is humanly probable or necessary, that is, in terms of what is likely under the circumstances, or inevitable.

Now, in order to know what is likely or inevitable in human life, we have to draw upon a fund of generalizations about people's emotions and motivations that we have built up from experience, introspection, observation, experimentation, study, reading, and so on. Everyone depends on such a fund in order simply to get through the day, much less to analyze literary forms. These generalizations may be more accurate or less, and they may be—indeed *should* be—subject to constant adjustment and modifications, but they provide us with a set of expectations and assumptions that we need to make our way through life and through literature. We have, in other words, to be able to make inferences from signs, to infer motive from behavior.

Thus, if a knowledge of human experience is essential for the analysis of literary form, and if psychology provides a way of conceptualizing our knowledge of emotions and motivations, then psychology offers a useful means of extending and deepening our analysis of form. We do not want to psychoanalyze authors and their characters. What we want to do is what we usually do—interpret feelings on the basis of actions. Only now we will have an organized body of knowledge to add to our natural store in making such inferences and, in particular, certain assumptions about the less obvious and visible emotions and motives.

But, of course, there is no one body of psychological knowledge. There are many psychologies, and each offers its own conceptualization of human emotions and motives, and each, therefore, will provide us with a somewhat different mode. Our interpretations of literature will vary, then, as our psychologies vary. Is there any way out of this bewildering relativism? I think there is.

In the first place, many of these psychologies, despite their important differences, do indeed overlap at significant points, and the pictures of human emotional systems they draw are essentially similar in their basic outlines. Most psychologies—with the significant exception of behaviorism—agree that all behavior is meaningful, whether we are aware of its causes or not; that undesired emotions cannot be gotten rid of but rather remain present below the level of consciousness; that such repression causes inner conflict as the rejected emotions push back; that this conflict causes us to seek inappropriate outlets rather than face and resolve the repressed feelings; that neurotic conflict tends to polarize our inner and outer lives so that extremes meet (excessive striving for power, for example, may reflect an excessive sense of powerlessness); that neurosis encourages us to project onto the world the structure of our conflict; that we employ intricate and repetitive systems of defenses to protect ourselves against the repressed feelings and to preserve the neurosis; that these systems and the conflicts that produce them are enormous consumers of our energies; that they usually derive from interruptions of the developmental cycle in early childhood; and so on.

I hope these statements sound like truisms, not to say platitudes, for then they will seem all the more readily acceptable as basic generalizations in terms of which to conceptualize human experience. And the second answer to relativism is that the value of any psychological scheme, like that of any conceptualization we choose to apply to literature, will be a function of the usefulness of the results it yields us. Where we have insufficient bases for choosing one scheme over another in terms of its truth-value, we should choose heuristically that model we feel most comfortable with and which seems to us the most illuminating in terms of its explanatory value, its usefulness in providing a framework for analysis and interpretation.

For my purposes I have found the model of inner conflict developed by Fritz Perls, the founder of Gestalt Therapy, to be the most comfortable and illuminating in analyzing and interpreting literature. Gestalt Therapy has become widely used and loosely spoken of, and it has, therefore, become something of a catchall. For Perls himself, however, it evolved into a specific theory and a definable therapeutic approach. What these are, exactly, will emerge as we sketch out its central conception and technique.

The best way to explain Perls's model, I find, is to begin with his conception of the human organism and to trace the process through which it develops, layer by layer, into a neurotic person. Then we will work backward in tracing the stages of the therapeutic process as it peels away these layers in an attempt to reestablish contact with the original organismic being.[3]

The original human organism is born with certain irreducible psychobiological needs, the natural fulfillment of which is essential to its healthy functioning. Perls crystallizes these needs around four basic emotions: grief, anger, joy, and orgasm. Optimally, when a need seeks fulfillment in relation to the person's ongoing experience, it finds some means of satisfaction, is discharged, and the person returns to a state of equilibrium—until the next stimulus arises from within or impinges from without. This process is structured, then, according to *Gestalten:* a stimulus emerges, the appropriate response is mobilized, and closure is experienced.

When, however, closure is *not* experienced, one of two things can happen: either the organism will redirect its energies toward an alternative way of discharging its need or it will carry this unfinished need around inside, where it will begin distorting its experience to conform to this frustration. Because the human organism and its developmental process are so delicate and complex, and because its period of dependency is so lengthy, it is difficult to imagine *anyone* growing up without some unfinished business to carry around. This is the human condition, and Gestalt Therapy, in being influenced by existentialism (among other things), does not see unremitting bliss at the end of the therapeutic rainbow. The fitting of human needs to a world that is other than human requires a never-ending process of adjustment.

But there are degrees of fitting, and certain societies and certain family systems are less damaging than others, over and above the inevitable problems of the human condition. In this context, the organism has two basic and potentially competing requirements: to be nurtured and supported by its environment, and to grow in tune with its own needs. Optimally, these requirements are not in competition, and the child is so nurtured as to develop a sense of trust in his own natural responses and to make the gradual shift from environmental to self-support. When this nurturance is not so optimal, however—and it is bound to be less optimal the further removed he is from genuine parenting—he develops instead a feeling that what he in fact experiences is suspect and must be altered to conform to the demands of the environment. (This in no way suggests that he should learn to cultivate the illusion that the environment should conform to *his* demands; it suggests, rather, that he can deal effectively with the environment only if he can learn to deal effectively with himself.) So overmastering is the requirement of environmental support, acceptance, and approval, that the child will choose against himself, when parental demands conflict with his own inner needs, in order to survive at all. He feels he must give up himself to gain the world. Thus he learns that he must not cry, even if he is experiencing grief; that he must not show anger, even if he is frustrated; that he must not seem too joyful, even if he is feeling good; and that he must not play with his genitals, even if it releases erotic tension. He feels that, if he dares to be himself, he will either destroy his parents or he will be destroyed himself—in other words, that some terrible catastrophe or annihilation will result.

What he learns, in place of being himself, is to manipulate the environment to get what he wants indirectly, only what he wants now is some semblance of support and acceptance in place of fulfillment of any inner organismic needs. He learns that the environment will tell him what to be. He cannot, therefore, successfully make the shift from environmental to self-support, and no matter how proficient in certain respects he may become as an adult, he still carries around inside himself this nagging sense that he isn't quite making it, that he still has to prove himself. But the fulfillment of the need for support can never satisfy the need for expressing oneself; they are simply different requirements, and one cannot take the place of the other; and no amount of societal success can fill the inner hollowness. We recognize the feeling of self-alienation here, of course, and in a terrible paradox he has had to deaden certain aspects of himself to be able to live. He is phobic about expressing authentic emotion because he has made this secret bargain to give up feeling in order to have parents, and he is expert in certain manipulations which take the place of authentic emotion and which give a semblance of meaning to his life.[4]

Images of self-alienation are not hard to find in literature, of course, and especially in modern literature, and a handy example that comes readily to mind is Randall Jarrell's poem about a woman who feels she is an eland, entitled "Seele Im Raum." I also think of Matthew Arnold's earlier and more discursive poem, "The Buried Life," in this connection. One's daily life is not real life, then, for it doesn't have real meaning; all is distorted to fit the secret bargain, and one lives out his mature life in the shadow of his unfinished childhood experience. He has not been allowed to mature by going through the natural growth process; he is incomplete, unsatisfied, not himself. So he comes to the therapist. When Fritz Perls confronts this person, he sees the structure of neurosis basically in terms of four layers of levels,[5] which he then tries to have the person work through—a cumulative process which normally takes more than a few months, which does not march progressively in a straight line from one through four, and during which more than one level may be present at any given time.

The first is *the games layer,* where the person plays out the roles and scripts assigned to him from childhood, as described by Eric Berne: the Good Girl, the Bully, the Tragedy Queen, the Cry Baby, the Strong Silent Man, the Joker, the Ironist, Humble Pie, and so on. Here he has the image of himself he feels he has to live up to, plus the sense of the impossibility of ever living up to it well enough, and so he splits up into two parts and polarizes them: the topdog or victimizer, and the underdog or victim. Usually, the person identifies with one part and tries to disown the other (hence the roles and scripts mentioned above), projecting it onto the environment and feeling "they" are doing this to him. Thus he defends against facing the feelings underneath and continues the endless and repetitive game of manipulating the world for support. He lives obsessed by ever-retreating goals, worries about time, habitually postpones gratification, is caught up in striving and insatiability—as in Thomas Wolfe, for example—or in their opposites, apathy and satiety—as in the early Swinburne, for example—and is divorced from the experience of his body and his feelings (of course, a person in the games layer can have *feelings,* but they will be less in response to the present situation than to his projection of past situations onto the present). No better instance of this level can be found than in chapter five of John Stuart Mill's *Autobiography,* where he describes how he felt before having his nervous breakdown.

The working-through of this layer involves basically encouraging the person, within the controlled therapeutic situation, to reclaim the parts of himself he has discarded or projected onto the environment, no matter how repugnant or foreign they may seem to him. And Perls's method is not verbal, with explanation, analysis, and interpretation; it is, rather, experiential, with a literal role-playing by the person of his various selves, under the guidance of the therapist, as these selves confront one another. This is quite in tune, I find, with modern literary theory and practice: to emphasize the concrete and distrust abstract statement and paraphrase. Perls finds that talking, explaining, associating, and having insights are often simply another mode of defense against the necessary task of reclaiming the organism's capacity to experience its own basic needs. And this technique, it seems to me, is quite consonant with certain common literary genres, such as the debate, the dialogue of the owl and the nightingale, the interior monologue, the confrontation of the self with its double, and so on. Think, for example, of *The Picture of Dorian Gray, Dr. Jekyll and Mr. Hyde,* "The Secret Sharer," Yeats's "Dialogue of Self and Soul," Lionel Johnson's "Dark Angel," Albee's *The Zoo Story,* and so on. Nevertheless, whatever the literary structure, the problem of the human heart in conflict with itself (as Faulkner said) is a basic literary subject and is implicitly an essential element of most literary forms.

The ultimate aim of the working-through at this level, and I do not want to give any false impression that it is quick or easy, is to help the person become *aware* of his discarded selves and then to *accept* them, to get back the energy invested in rejection and projection—which is the paradoxical but essential precondition of integration, often the hardest thing to accomplish. We naturally turn phobic at the prospect of taking responsibility for our own sadistic impulses, for example, and yet there is no other way of getting through them. On the other hand, if the person's anti-self emerges compulsively and without control, at the expense of the other self—as in *The Heart of Darkness,* for example, or in *Death in Venice, The Immoralist, Madame Bovary,* or in the classic German movie, *The Blue Angel*—it can lead to a destructive acting-out and *dis*integration that is no more liberating than remaining with the original games. The point is to take in and use the rejected energy, not to be used by it. Liberation involves integrating one's selves and not destroying one in favor of the other, however lawless and "free" the repressed other may seem. And yet there *is* a potential here for productive change, albeit a dangerous one, since getting in touch with one's anti-self *can* shake up the system and call for further self-exploration.

Then, if awareness and acceptance of one's various selves have been to some degree accomplished, and some of their energy has been reclaimed, the next and even more difficult question is whether the person can give up the games altogether. At this point something crucial happens, and we come to Perls's second layer—*the impasse.* One feels lost without the games on the one hand, and afraid to call upon one's organismic self on the other, and so experiences a blankness, confusion, dizziness, numbness; he becomes resistant and indecisive, and goes stupid, forgets, plays helpless. This is the sick point, the stuck point, and Perls prided himself in discovering a way of dealing with it therapeutically, a problem he felt most other therapies shied away from. The working through at this level is for the therapist to encourage the person to stay *with* his blankness, confusion, and so on, while at the same time refraining scrupulously from giving him support, advice, interpretations, and the like. He is fighting for self-support, and he must not be defeated by being given "help." It is the turning point not only for the person but also for the therapist—who must have sufficient trust in himself, the person, and the process to allow his patient to stay with this experience. On the other hand, he must have sufficient training and skill to be able to do this properly.

In the course of his struggle with the impasse, the person will become more deeply phobic, he will experience the profound fear of breaking his secret bargain and of losing his supports, and he will become desperate and uncomfortable. He will have a sense of catastrophe at violating the prohibition or injunction against being for himself and having his own feelings. He will not want to lose control of himself and the world for anything, for he is imagining he will break down and go mad if he does. No matter how badly he may *want* to get through this, no amount of rational persuasion and appeals to willpower or criticisms of weakness can get him through, for one cannot will to change. He must simply endure this pain and discomfort, which is naturally a most difficult thing to do. The world will become destructured for him and, stripped of its illusions (the games), will appear hideous and cruel, and he will feel nausea, boredom, bitterness, anxiety, and revulsion. Here again, of course, modern literature offers many examples of such imagery, from Baudelaire to Eliot and from Eliot to Fitzgerald: "He must have looked up at an unfamiliar sky through frightening leaves and shivered as he found what a grotesque thing a rose is and how raw the sunlight upon the scarcely created grass," as Nick says of Gatsby, who is waiting for the call from Daisy that never comes, and the bullet from Wilson, that does.

At this point several developments are possible. Most commonly, the person will avoid and deny this pain by returning to the status quo ante and taking up his polarized games again. That is why Gatsby insists that you *can* repeat the past. However dysfunctional, the games are familiar and, despite the evidence to the contrary, seem to promise the illusion of fulfillment. This is what Prufrock does in his quiet way; it is what Ahab does in his violent way; it is what Lord Jim and Gatsby do in their determined way; and it is what Magwitch and Miss Havisham do in their obsessive way. Another direction is to return to the games level but on the opposite side: to experience a "conversion"[6] in which the sinner becomes the saint or the saint becomes the sinner, and so on, which is what happens to Swinburne, for example, as he shifts from his early depravity to his later love of children.

Or, it is possible simply to remain stuck in the impasse and, without accepting it or going into it, be caught there indefinitely. Here, one is aware of the pain and in touch with the meaninglessness of life but still wishes it *had* meaning, and is thus unable either to get through it or return to the games level. This is the experience portrayed in "The Hollow Men," for example, *Notes from Underground, Waiting for Godot,* some of Chekhov's plays, much of

Kafka, and the films of Antonioni, and it is also characteristic of certain facets of Hemingway's work, as well as some of the more recent confessional poets. In Hemingway, and in his predecessors in pessimism, Hardy and Housman, there is such an intense feeling of the unsatisfactoriness of life that it can only have come from the necessary frustration of the overly high demands originally placed upon life. As many critics have suggested, Hemingway is so realistic because he is so idealistic, and his obsessive need to prove himself against death and danger is perhaps an avoidance of some painful self-confrontation. Hence you may feel the terrors at night, but in the morning you must be cheerful, strong, and tight-lipped.

On the other hand, getting in touch with one's rage at having given up the self, and one's grief at losing the comforting illusion of environmental support, although necessary stages of working through the impasse, can become sticking-points as well. Unlike Hemingway, others such as Plath, Sexton, and Berryman manage positively to dwell on self-confrontation, upon what is unpleasant and painful, but again without acceptance or relief. In Plath's poem, "Daddy," for example, there is rage aplenty, but there is also still an unacknowledged sense of the need to *have* the father, and so when the speaker says she is through, she continues to call him a bastard. She remains angry, that is, and has yet to give up her need for him altogether and start again from within herself. *Dwelling* on the hurt is mistaken for *dealing* with it; merely reenacting one's sickness, contrary to certain fashionable critical ideas, does not necessarily enable one to master and control it. And the danger of suicide points up once again the difficulty of going into this process without proper guidance and control.

To get through the impasse, then, one must deal with it, accept it, and claim responsibility for it: I have to do this to myself because I am afraid to break the secret agreement and get in touch with my organismic self, afraid to give up the struggle for environmental supports. Yet as we have seen, a neurotic pattern may be dysfunctional, but it cannot be given up without a fight for three reasons: one is that suffering affords a certain distorted sense of drama, pleasure, and importance; another is that it simply seems better to have a bad pattern than none at all, or a familiar than a strange one; and a third is that one often *can* control others through neurotic manipulations—especially when one's pattern meshes neurotically with someone else's. In other words, there is "profit" in neurosis, what psychologists refer to as primary and secondary gains,[7] and the person, no matter how well motivated for change, will fight like a tiger to hold on to his games, often surprising himself by his own irrational tenacity. Since going against the resistance will only strengthen it, what the therapist does here is to respect the fear and encourage the person to express it openly—you cannot go through something without at first accepting it. This is to claim responsibility, which also involves saying, "it's not the universe that's doing this to me, nor is it any longer even my parents. It's now up to me," as the speaker realizes, for example, in Frost's "Desert Places." And there is nothing either mystical or moralistic about it; it is simply a matter of getting your energy back from where you have thrown it away.

When such awareness can be attained, one may feel a sense of relief: "I don't have to do this to myself any more." One may also feel a sudden upsurge of grief: "all those wasted years, what have I done to myself?" Then the real abyss must be faced: "I'll never get what I want; I am finally alone and without external supports." And the third of Perls's levels is reached, what he calls *the implosive* or *death layer.* Here one confronts the nothingness left by giving up the games, which have afforded him—however tortuously—his apparent sense of identity, and feels as if he is going to be annihilated. He contracts in upon himself and experiences a paralysis of opposing forces, a void, a kind of deadness. He may experience embarrassment, fear of rejection, hopelessness, despair, desolation, devastation, and deep mourning as he gives up his attachment to parental demands and approval, and as he encounters his own slain self. He may even touch upon some psychotic material and dissociate, hallucinate, and experience hysteria. He is finishing the unfinished business: having given up the self to gain the world, he is now giving up the world to gain the self. In reality, it is the games that are dying and all the years of self he has invested in them. Examples are found in *The Waste Land,* in Fitzgerald's *The Crack-Up,* in Hopkins's later sonnets, and in Rimbaud.

Having mentioned psychosis, I must clarify and emphasize a crucial point here. I have been tracing Perls's model of *neurosis,* and what I am saying applies to that state. It does not apply, at least as I am presenting it, to *psychosis.* The basic difference between the two may be explained in terms of ego strength. In neurosis the person has a relatively more intact ego, and this can be drawn upon and strengthened in order that he may endure the experience of the impasse and the death layer. In psychosis there is, by definition, some severe ego impairment, and ego repair must therefore be the primary therapeutic objective.[8] However, it still can be said that, as with neurotic games, psychotic states are essentially systems of defense against the inner devastation except that, as the devastation is more profound, the systems must be all the more drastic. Thus, just as the neurotic may be in the impasse and yet not be able to accept it, so too the psychotic is in the death level while at the same time he is struggling to deny it—he detaches, he withdraws, he splits, he hallucinates, he manufactures delusions, he acts out against himself, and so on. Psychotic symptoms, then, do not reflect the devastation itself so much as the flight from devastation. Ultimately, assuming that the difficult work of ego repair has been gotten under way, psychosis too can be alleviated by staying with and going through the death layer.

The problem of working through at this point is not to interfere, if the person remains intact while struggling with this experience, or to provide structure and comfort if he shows signs of getting stuck there. Clearly, this is a disturbing matter and is precisely why the person wants to avoid it—it is exactly what he has been afraid of and defending against. This is what Arnold is telling us in his 1853 preface when he calls the dialogue of the mind with itself "morbid," and in his 1858 letter to his sister where he says he cannot risk going into himself for fear of tearing himself to pieces. And it is in terms of Arnold's assessment that Yeats analyzes the tragedy of his friends of the 1890s, seeing them as having taken that risk and paid the consequences.[9]

And yet here are one's real feelings and, if one can endure the fright of the journey, he will find he has been wrestling with an angel after all, emerging into Perls's fourth and final layer, what he calls *the explosive layer* or the level of authentic and organismic functioning, where the slain self can be reborn, the person can feel his body and emotions in the present, and can literally *see* the world with open eyes. The distortions are gone, and he can respond appropriately to present situations without the accumulated baggage of past frustrations, and he will be able to experience and discharge grief, anger, joy, and orgasm as they arise and are dealt with functionally. One achieves an integration, which is somewhat like the New Critics' balance and reconciliation of opposites, but which is also a good deal more—it is a *transcendence* of the polarities into a new state where the opposites are abolished, transformed, and incorporated into the self for productive use. This is what Mill felt after he recovered from his breakdown with the help of reading the Romantic poets; it is what Blake is getting at in *The Marriage of Heaven and Hell;* it is what Yeats is saying at the end of "Dialogue of Self and Soul" and Stevens at the end of "Sunday Morning"; it is how the stranger lives in Camus's novel before his trial; and it is where the heroine of Bergman's 1975 movie, *Face to Face,* emerges, after having gone through the entire four-level process during the course of the film.

3

I realize that, as literary critics, we did not need Perls to instruct us in the archetype of death and rebirth. What have we gained, then, after all this? What we do get, it seems to me, is an explanation of how and why this process works in psychological terms, of its stages, of the significance of each and their interconnections. And this explanation in turn allows us to focus more closely, in those terms, on where any given work is in that process and what is going on. I find it an extraordinarily dramatic technique, which lends itself beautifully to an examination of the drama which is central to literary form. Returning to "Locksley Hall" will help demonstrate what this model can do for us and how it can do it.

We left Tennyson's young man seeking his solution through joining society's march of progress, unaware of some of the unresolved problems involved. Let us see if we can answer more clearly now the questions remaining after our previous analyses: Why is he so afraid of his feelings? What is the need whose unfulfillment is causing him all this distress and which he has such difficulty in acknowledging and coming to grips with? Why, despite his awareness of projecting, can he only return to his earlier visions? What keeps drawing him compulsively back to the hierarchical view? What prevents him from becoming aware of the inconsistencies involved and coming to a truer resolution? It is clear that he has landed himself in the impasse; confronting the key frustration of his life, he becomes angry, spiteful, envious, ambivalent, and finally lost. He is baffled by this failure of his need to control the world, to organize it in terms of contrasts, and he doesn't know where to turn. His societal games have failed, and he turns phobic. Having just mentally scorned Amy, who has learned to suppress *her* feelings, he pretends he doesn't care. Then, apparently facing a host of feelings he *himself* is unable or unwilling to bear, he exclaims: "I myself must mix with action, lest I wither by despair."

Needing to avoid the pain of the impasse, unable to stay with it and go into his deep sorrow and fear of rejection, he goes back up to the games level and looks desperately about for "solutions." He thinks of pursuing larger societal goals, asking "thou wondrous Mother-Age" to "hide me from my deep emotion," but then becomes sick of the whole idea of society—and here is the context of the impasse imagery already cited: "my passion sweeping thro' me left me dry, / Left me with the palsied heart, and left me with the jaundiced eye; / Eye, to which all order festers, all things here are out of joint." And he yearns for an escape into a primitive paradise, where one can live simply, passionately, and without thought. He recognizes this as a foolish fantasy but can only conclude by going back once again to larger societal goals.

The point is that his consciousness is still working in terms of polarities. His disillusioned view of Western civilization is that of an ordered world failing to live up to its orderliness: disorder is the opposite of order. When he tries to imagine a true alternative, an organismic world of optimal human functioning (which is presented quite convincingly in the poem, by the way), and of transcendence of the polarities, he only succeeds in imposing the hierarchical game on it and converting it to *its* opposite—a mindless, bestial existence. And so, in turn, this becomes merely an opposite of the hierarchical world: a world without "higher" values and purposes cannot be meaningful (compare Tennyson's "Palace of Art" and "The Lotus-Eaters"). In such a game, he can only keep rounding the same bases and is locked into a closed system. Thus the speaker must revert to his original vision.

I think this interpretation clarifies Western man's perennial ambivalence toward tropical paradises: exhausted by the puritanical alienation of his own culture, he yearns for a fuller life of the body, but this then seems to him to be a life without "goals," and he can only go back home to his puritanism. It rarely occurs to him that an organismic life can have goals—as a flower or tree has goals—or that goals are better striven for, as Mill came to realize, when they need not be won. Renunciation of the *fruits* of action is not necessarily the renunciation of *action.*[10] I think this also helps explain Western man's attitudes toward "work," "recreation," "vacations," and the like: he works in order to "earn" his relaxation, and when he relaxes he must escape from his work, thereby emptying both of full human content.[11]

Thus, because our speaker cannot remain in the impasse and thereby reach the death layer, he cannot imagine any other way. However problematic it is for him to join the very society he has just been blaming for taking his girl away, it makes perfect sense, given his psychological state, and he must finally rationalize his choice to make it seem acceptable. Since the expression of the self is still forbidden, he cannot find a personal resolution and so must shift to finding one in societal terms.

But in a way, as we have seen, it *does* follow from what went before, in that he has identified his feelings about progress with his need for a mother to comfort and protect him from his pain. Only now we can see that this is not simply an instance of regressive behavior, of an attempt to find a substitute for the parenting he never had (except for that selfish uncle), but also is a part of predictable impasse behavior. That is, he is afraid to give up his need for parents—a need which never was fulfilled for him (difficult enough even when one *does* have parents) and which he has been projecting onto his vision of society and identifying with Amy—because he is desperate for environmental supports and unable to give up that image of himself he wants the environment to reflect back to him: if the world makes sense, *I'll* make sense; if society can be justified, *I'll* be justified, because, not having had parents, I need to feel I have a right to exist.

The irrationality of his decision, chosen despite its contradictions, is caused by his fear of becoming lost in his despair and of being unable to function if he breaks that secret bargain. He is motivated by all the continuing urgencies of this unfinished business and cannot see his way clear to finishing it—inside, where it belongs, rather than outside, where it distorts and frustrates, unfinishable. As we have suggested, if he can see that his disillusion is a projection, he cannot see that his vision itself is also a projection. Thus, even though he blames society for hurting him, his phobic reaction to the impasse demands that he rescind his criticism, return to the status quo ante, and rationalize a rededication to that very same society. He has no other choice, and, as Tennyson's poetic development shows, he will continue in repetitive cycles of willed resolution and inadvertent despair throughout his life.

But, it might be objected, how could we expect a Victorian poet to be so knowledgeable about modern psychology as to have resolved his poem in a more consistent fashion? I have already cited Mill and Arnold several times, and the additional examples of Hopkins, Meredith, and Dickens, also Victorian writers, albeit somewhat later, will help reply to this objection. My favorite counterbalancing quote to "I myself must mix with action, lest I wither by despair" comes from Hopkins's "No Worst, There Is None." Also in the impasse, the speaker feels desperate, looking in vain for comfort. But, instead of persisting in the search for "solutions" no matter what, he stays where he is:

> O the mind, mind has mountains; cliffs of fall
> Frightful, sheer, no-man-fathomed. Hold them cheap

May who ne'er hung there. Nor does long our small
Durance deal with that steep or deep.

There is no other solution, no looking for purpose, no need to go back up to the games level and pursue goals—the despair is simply accepted:

Here! creep,
Wretch, under a comfort serves in a whirlwind: all
Life death does end and each day dies with sleep.

Pain cannot last forever; in the organismic cycle, sleep comes, as death comes, and the creature rests.

Although there is no "solution" to the emotional problem enacted in the poem, the structure is resolved; the question raised at the outset is answered. The comfort called for at the beginning is found at the end, and the fact that it is a poor comfort makes it no less formally unified and complete, where the end follows from what went before. The basic difference between this poem and "Locksley Hall" is that Hopkins appears to understand the psychological problem and is able to incorporate it into his aesthetic structure, whereas Tennyson does not. Tennyson does not seem to grasp the principle, either on a psychological or a formal level, that a negative ending, where there is no answer, could be truer, more profound, and more consistent than his constant obsession with higher purpose. Or at least that a positive ending, if one can honestly arrive at one, can really only be won by going through the impasse and into the death layer—which reminds us of the doctrine of tension and conflict and "earning" the resolution so dear to the hearts of the New Critics. When Hopkins can write, also in his later sonnets, that God's smile "lights a lovely mile," there are also signs that he has been experiencing the void itself—"I wake and feel the fell of dark"—and gaining a sense of self-acceptance—"My own heart let me have more pity on."

Another favorite quotation comes from the climactic point of Meredith's *Modern Love,* where the husband-narrator finally sees himself as he really is. Amidst an aura of death imagery, he says:

I see no sin:
The wrong is mixed. In tragic life, God wot,
No villain need be! Passions spin the plot:
We are betrayed by what is false within.

He is aware, that is, of the futility of polarization, and is in touch with the need of acceptance. He is taking back his projection and claiming it for himself, where it belongs, no matter how painful it may be.

And certainly the way Dickens handles Pip's problem is also psychologically and formally more profound than Tennyson's way here. Pip gains immeasurably in self-awareness as he goes through the painful process of disillusionment, discovering that Miss Havisham is not his benefactor, that Estella was not meant for him, and that the life of privilege is a shallow game. He sees he is as much self-deceived as deceived, and his experience in the death layer is symbolized by his nearly losing his life in being threatened by Orlick and in rescuing Magwitch. When he returns to Joe and the forge on his penitential journey, he is not regressing to an earlier illusion that made up for his lost parents; he is rather returning to an honest, sane, and humble acceptance of life as it is. And he matures as a result, having grown up in the process. (Not to mention Fitzgerald's twentieth-century handling of Gatsby, also self-orphaned, who is indeed shattered when his illusion of Daisy is shattered; it is Nick, however, who goes through the purgative realization of the hollowness of the destructive game of wealth and illusion, and decides to make a pilgrimage to *his* healthier origins.)

We are not asking Tennyson to have had knowledge unavailable to him, then, when we ask what would have happened had he been able to see his speaker through the impasse. Would this have made for a more viable poetic structure, one which would be both psychologically more authentic and formally more consistent? Either the young man should have stayed with his despair instead of mixing with action, and let the poem end there, or he should have gotten to his positive ending by going through the impasse into the death layer. Naturally, had he done the latter, the ending would have been quite different, for he would have felt that his problem was more within himself and less in the environment than he had suspected, and that he had to learn to let the hierarchical games go. (I have said that an organismic view is not necessarily quietistic. Taking back the projection in no way implies that society doesn't need improving, therefore, but rather that one will be better able to improve society when he is less bound up in inner conflict. Thus we needn't choose between "Freud" or "Marx," for this is simply another disjunctive polarity. Naturally, society and the individual reflect one another, and a change in one will help effect a change in the other. But not automatically, and work must approach the problem from both ends.) And our speaker would have learned that his sense of self no longer could depend on wresting from the environment this or that desired object, that he now could function in terms of his inner sense of self—much as Meredith's, Hopkins's, and Dickens's characters were on their way to discovering.

Or, Tennyson could have designed the poem to show a man caught in his own psychological trap, as Eliot did, for example, in "Prufrock," and hence would have constructed the ending to be taken ironically. Which, as things now stand, I don't think we can. Tennyson seems clearly to have intended the ending to be taken positively. Not that irony would be un-Victorian either, as the examples of Browning, and Clough in his *Amours de Voyage* (which has many Prufrockian elements), evidence, but it certainly was not a characteristic Tennysonian mode. The speaker in "Locksley Hall" is aware of the foolishness of his *protests* against conventionality, whereas Browning, Clough, and Eliot are aware of the weakness of *accepting* conventionality. Tennyson's irony, in other words, proceeds toward but falls short of a more complex self-awareness.

4

What we are after, then, is an analysis of the degree of coherence that obtains between the structure of the action and the process of its inner emotional dynamic. We want to ask how well the author's grasp of human probabilities and necessities has served him in developing and resolving his structural sequence. That this can involve psychological knowledge need not surprise or distress us, for it is a perfectly normal part of formal analysis—a part that leads us, incidentally, into a natural and logical consideration of the author's vision and the period concept within formal terms. In the case of works where the fit is not close, we can locate the point where the poem gets stuck and hypothesize as to why it got stuck there, thus making psychological sense out of formal anomalies. But in the case of works where the fit is good, where inner conflict is transcended, psychology is still useful, for we can show how and why the form is perfected, and that is no small accomplishment in itself. For these tasks I hope I have shown how a marriage of psychology and formal criticism can assist.

NOTES

1. And, as I have shown elsewhere, this principle is pretty much the same as Eliot's "objective correlative" concept, put forth in the "Hamlet and His Problems" essay of 1919. That the emotion should not be in excess of its object is already, as Eliot himself suggests, a psychological as well as a formal principle—"doubtless," he says, "a subject of study for pathologists"—and a very good basis for defining neurosis (a disproportionate or inappropriate reaction to a stimulus).

2. Cf. R. S. Crane, *The Languages of Criticism and the Structure of Poetry* (Toronto: University of Toronto Press, 1953), pp. 189–90.

3. See Frederick S. Perls, *Gestalt Therapy Verbatim* (1969; reprint, New York: Bantam, 1971). For his discussion of the layers of neurosis, upon which my own analysis is based, see esp. pp. 59ff. See also Perls, "Four Lectures," lecture 2, in *Gestalt Therapy Now,* ed. Joen Fagan and Irma Lee Shepherd (Palo Alto, Calif.: Science and Behavior Books, 1970), pp. 19–26. Other useful references are Perls's earlier *Gestalt Therapy* (1951; reprint, New York: Dell, 1965), written in collaboration with Ralph E. Hefferline and Paul Goodman, and his later *The Gestalt Approach and Eye Witness to Therapy* (Ben Lomond, Calif.: Science and Behavior Books, 1973). Much has been written on Gestalt Therapy in recent years, and a good number of books have appeared, but I am concentrating, for the present purpose, on Perls himself.

4. I want to thank the staff of the Gestalt Center for Psychotherapy and Training in New York for helping me grasp such points here and throughout more clearly, especially Marilyn B. Rosannes-Berrett, Ph.D.; Sal Fusaro, M.D.; and Gerald Abraham, M.D.

5. Perls actually speaks of five levels, but I find that the essential structure of his model comes through more clearly in terms of four. His first layer, which I have omitted, is what he calls the

cliché layer and concerns the forms of petty social rituals. I am not sure these have anything to do with neurosis, nor does Perls make very much of them himself.

6. An interesting discussion of this phenomenon in literature, from a somewhat different theoretical base, is found in Bernard J. Paris, *A Psychological Approach to Fiction* (Bloomington: Indiana University Press, 1974).

7. The primary gain is to defend against an even more painful emotion—fear of abandonment, e.g.—which defense is the *raison d'être* of the neurosis, and which fear is the cause of hanging on so tightly to an otherwise irrational and frustrating pattern. It is this fear which must be dealt with in working through the impasse and (see below) death layer. Secondary gains refer to environmental benefits which one's neurosis may elicit—others may worry about one, e.g., and try to bring comforts, etc.

8. Although Eric Shelley's monograph, "Gestalt Therapy with Severely Disturbed Patients," is as yet unpublished, I would like to acknowledge my indebtedness to it. Mr. Shelley is also associated with the Gestalt Center.

9. In his *Autobiography,* "The Trembling of the Veil" (1922), bk. 4, "The Tragic Generation," sec. 9.

10. As we learn, e.g., from the *Bhagavad Gita.*

11. Cf. Octavio Paz, chap. 3, "The Day of the Dead," in *The Labyrinth of Solitude,* trans. Lysander Kemp (1950; rev. ed. 1959; reprint, New York: Grove Press, 1961), pp. 47–64.

4
Jane Eyre's Flights from Decision

Karen Ann Butery

Since its publication, *Jane Eyre* has generated critical controversy. Critics of the novel have been divided into two camps: some have been intent on pointing out the contradictions in Jane's character and the novel's lack of unity while others have been intent on denying these weaknesses.[1] The current trend reflects a considerable shift in the balance of forces to the defense of the novel's aesthetic unity. A great many critics argue that Brontë was in control by proving harmony where disharmony is apparent. Representative of this approach is Charles Burkhart's assertion that "the kind of harmony that Charlotte Brontë achieves in her best novels is a union of what at first appear to be opposites. The energy of her ability to reconcile and to transform is unique."[2]

Because most critics concur that the "real triumph of *Jane Eyre*" is "the character of Jane,"[3] many critics build a case for the novel's unity by maintaining that its apparent disharmony reflects Jane's inner conflict and, therefore, that Jane's resolution of her conflict also resolves the novel's aesthetic problems. Most critics also agree that Jane's conflict is between a personal system of values and the traditional system of religious and social values.

This is where critical agreement ends, for critics part company with regard to how Jane resolves her conflict. Some see her as achieving a Jungian balance between the opposing systems of values.[4] Others maintain that Jane ultimately chooses between these systems and that her choice represents the novel's theme. Those who concur in supporting the second thesis disagree, however, on which value system Jane chooses. One group maintains that she undergoes a Christian conversion at the novel's end while the opposing group contends that she defies the values of a patriarchal world over which she triumphs.[5] Another point on which critics are divided is whether Jane's final choice represents her maturation or whether Jane is "inflexibly right from the beginning."[6]

The attempt to save the novel's wholeness by proving that Jane has resolved her conflict has resulted not only in this critical confusion but also in the reduction of Jane's character to an illustration of a theme. Helene Moglen's conclusion that Jane's growth follows an "allegorical movement of self-discovery" indicates the danger of this approach, for it can strip Jane of vitality and, thus, impair the powerful impact of the novel, which largely depends on the intensity of her character.[7]

An analysis of Jane's conflict through the use of Karen Horney's psychology can at once clear up the critical confusion and preserve the richness of her characterization. Through this approach, I shall show what Jane's conflicts are, where they come from, and why they are not resolved. When we understand Jane's conflicts fully, we shall see that all three critical viewpoints—that Jane submits to traditional norms, that she asserts her independence from them, and that she arrives at an ideal balance between submission and independence—are partly right and partly wrong. I shall show that Jane neither matures nor proves herself right from the beginning but that, ultimately, her conflicting needs are all fulfilled through Brontë's manipulation of the plot. Thus, her conflict is evaded but never resolved. There is much more to Jane's conflict than an opposition between two sets of values, and I shall demonstrate that its unresolvability gives rise to the novel's structural tensions and thematic confusion.

A Horneyan analysis cannot save the novel; for it is, in fact, confused. What it can do is to show what makes the novel great in spite of its structural and thematic weaknesses; for although the novel is confused, its characterization is not. By analyzing in a precise way the richness, complexity, and intensity for which Jane's character has always been celebrated, a Horneyan approach can provide a deeper appreciation of the novel's greatest accomplishment.

1

According to Horneyan psychology, if a child is not given the love and security he needs to develop self-confidence and to grow in psychologically healthy ways, he will suffer from "basic anxiety" or a "feeling of being isolated and helpless in a world conceived as potentially hostile."[8] Instead of channeling his energies toward growth, the child must unconsciously marshal his forces for setting up defenses to allay anxiety. He seeks safety, love, belonging, and self-esteem in three ways—by moving toward others, against others, and away from others. In the first instance, he is compliant and strives to please others to obtain their approval. In the second case, he rebels and attempts to gain control of his situation through mastery. In the third move, he struggles to become self-sufficient and to avoid disappointment by detaching himself and minimizing his needs and expectations of others. Eventually, these "moves" become fixed so that all three are made automatically regardless of circumstances. Moreover, each move generates an elaborate system of defense mechanisms that constitutes a "solution" or a means of coping with life. Since the self-effacing, expansive, and resigned solutions are incompatible, the individual attempts to achieve an inner harmony by making one solution predominant and repressing the others. When circumstances bring the repressed solutions to the surface, however, conflict is inevitable.

To cope with the hostile environment at Gateshead Manor, Jane develops a complex network of defenses that corresponds closely to the particulars of her situation. Because of her temperament and because she has been carefully instructed to be " 'humble,' " " 'agreeable,' " " 'useful and pleasant,' "[9] Jane's primary solution is self-effacement. Her other strategies are subsidiary to it and come into play when it does not work. Because the novel opens upon the breakdown of Jane's self-effacing solution, we can see clearly the operations of all three moves. Jane's nine years of "habitua[l] obedien[ce]" have failed to prevent John's habitual cruelty and her unjust punishment. Indeed, her humility invites the Reeds' redoubled abuse. In response to Jane's pleas for " 'pity,' " " 'forgive[ness],' " and " 'mercy' " (pp. 14, 31), Mrs. Reed "abruptly thrust[s]" her back into the Red Room "and lock[s] . . . [her] in, without farther parley" (p. 15).

It is out of sheer desperation that Jane finally rebels and learns that by fighting back, she can gain respect and sometimes even affection. When she threatens to bloody John's nose, he quickly retreats; and Mrs. Reed becomes conciliatory after Jane's vehement verbal attack brought on by the despair of having her future poisoned by being labeled a liar. Finally, Bessie reinforces this lesson in self-assertion when she responds affectionately to Jane's "frank and fearless" behavior, and tells Jane that people will like her better if she is " 'bolder' " (p. 33). Thus, as a result of hard experience, Jane learns to resort to aggression when compliance fails; and she lays the groundwork for a pattern of "absolute submission" and "determined revolt" that accounts for many of her inconsistencies throughout the novel (p. 352).

Jane also learns that resignation prevents disappointment and that detachment protects her from hostility. Since the Reeds have excluded her "from every enjoyment" of family life (p. 23), Jane develops a strong tendency to shun society, withdraw from conflict, and diminish her expectations of others. She makes a virtue of necessity and compensates for this reduction of wishes and withdrawal from the real world by cultivating an imaginary world of romance and adventure. Her favorite spot is the "double retirement" of a windowseat where a heavy drape hides her from the Reeds, and the window glass both protects her from the outside and allows her to view its open vistas (p. 5). Safe from hostility, Jane can people these vistas with daring heroes and can indulge her expansive yearning for their charmed lives. She has discovered that both safety and adventure can be had by living vicariously through fantasy, history, fairy tales, and ballads.

In short, the violation of Jane's primary needs has resulted in these defensive moves toward, against, and away from others. One of the most important functions of the solutions that grow out of these moves is to compensate for an absence of self-esteem by creating an idealized self-image in which one can take pride. All her life Jane has seen herself through the Reeds' eyes as "a heterogeneous thing," "a useless thing," and "a noxious thing" who is "not worthy of notice" (pp. 12, 22); and she needs desperately to prove that this image of her is wrong. She replaces this degraded image with an idealized image that compensates point for point for the deficiencies the Reeds have assigned her. Specifically, Jane has been made to feel inferior because she is plain, dependent, morose, unfeeling, and bad.

That she is not pretty like Georgiana will always be a sensitive spot for Jane, who is taught to equate a lack of beauty with a lack of self-worth by such heartless remarks as Miss Abbot's: " 'If she were a nice, pretty child, one might compassionate her forlornness; but one really cannot care for such a little toad as that' " (p. 21). Jane can never be a beauty or the cynosure of society, but she determines to shine in another sphere. She has heard Bessie talk so often about the great "accomplishments" attained by girls at school that her "spirit . . . is moved to emulation" (p. 21). She will prove that she is clever and talented and that her accomplishments are more worthy of praise than beauty.

Moreover, by her intellectual endeavors, Jane will make her own living; for it is her economic dependence that has allowed the Reeds to victimize her. From her "very first recollections of existence," Jane has been so persistently taunted about her indigence that the "reproach of . . . [her] dependence [has] become a vague singsong in . . . [her] ear" which she unconsciously determines to silence (p. 10). By becoming self-sufficient, she will never again be forced to listen helplessly to insulting jibes that she is " 'less than a servant' " (p. 10); and she will never again be trapped in a situation in which she must either submit to arbitrary demands or " 'go a begging' " (p. 20). Through her accomplishments, therefore, Jane will both prove her superiority and achieve her independence.

The Reeds' accusation that Jane has a lachrymose, unsociable nature causes Jane a great deal of distress because it jeopardizes her primary means of coping with the world by pleasing others. Jane tries to conciliate others not only to avoid being hurt but also to gain love. Her self-effacing solution incorporates its own scales of justice by which Jane's attempts to please others should be balanced by their reciprocal love. If she is perceived as lachrymose and unsocial, however, she has no basis for her claims. The Reeds' accusation is especially tormenting to Jane because deep down she knows that her behavior has warranted it. According to her scales of justice, she would deserve loneliness if the accusation were true; and she would hate herself for having frustrated the fulfillment of her own needs. For the rest of her life, therefore, Jane will strive to please others so that she can justify the tacit "claims" she makes on them to love her. She will take pride in the capacity for love, empathy, helpfulness, and self-sacrifice on which her emotional security depends.

The fulfillment of Jane's need for love is also jeopardized by the Reeds' refusal to recognize her deep feelings. They have created an almost inhuman image of her, calling her a " 'bad animal,' " a " 'rat,' " a " 'toad,' " a " 'fury,' " and a " 'mad cat' " (pp. 7, 8, 21, 9). Adopting Mrs. Reed's portrait of Jane, Brocklehurst admonishes her to " 'pray to God . . . to take away your heart of stone and give you a heart of flesh' " (p. 28). Jane feels sorely threatened by this inhuman image of her because her inordinate craving for love is, in her mind, a basis for her belief that she deserves to be treated with affection. Horney explains that one's "*need*" actually "*turns into a claim*" (*NHG*, p. 42). Jane's "claim" is denied by Mrs. Reed's treating her as if she has " 'no feeling' " and " 'can do without one bit of love or kindness' " (p. 31). Jane vehemently protests that she " 'cannot live so' "; for perhaps more than any other imputation, she must disprove that she has a " 'heart of stone.' " By proving that she has deep feelings, she will make certain that no one ever again has just cause for treating her as if she were insensitive.

Finally, Jane chafes bitterly under the stigma of being incorrigibly bad. In their eyes, the Reeds have "proved beyond a doubt that [she is] the most wicked and abandoned child ever reared under a roof" (p. 23). Specifically, Jane needs to disprove her alleged deceitfulness—the terrible calumny with which Mrs. Reed has poisoned her future. Again, Jane feels severely threatened by this imputation both because her self-effacing solution requires that she be good and because she has, indeed, been deceitful; for all along she has been concealing her hostility. The violence of Jane's protest against being called a liar measures the intensity of her need to prove it unjust. It is in a "*savage* high voice" that she "crie[s] out," " 'deceit is not my fault!' " (p. 32, my emphasis). In the future, Jane will pride herself on her absolute candor, integrity, and morality. She has always needed to be good, but the accusation of being bad intensifies this need so strongly that she is driven to strive for nothing short of moral perfection.

Jane's idealized image glorifies resignation, self-assertion, intellectual accomplishments, independence, self-sacrifice, deep feelings, and moral perfection. In each of these points, it is not enough for Jane to prove her superiority. She must be perfect. Because her chances to develop a healthy self-esteem have been thwarted, Jane will reach for an unhealthy glory based on false pride.

This pride depends upon Jane's living up to the attributes of her idealized image. She has made a "bargain with fate" by which all her needs will be fulfilled and her pride reinforced if she actualizes her glorified self. The obverse side of this pride, however, is self-hate. The attributes of an idealized image are not simply goals but "shoulds." Jane would not only like to be perfect, she *should* be. Anything less than perfection is considered failure and results in self-contempt; for if she is not her idealized image, she is the despised image created by the Reeds. Her pride, therefore, is extremely vulnerable.

The vulnerability of Jane's pride is compounded because her bargain with fate is a composite one and her idealized image is the multi-faceted creation of three solutions each of which has a unique world view and a corresponding system of values, needs, and taboos. Although Jane's self-effacing solution is predominant, the others lie very close to the surface, resulting in Jane's need to be all at once self-effacing, expansive, and resigned. To live up to the superhuman standards of any one solution is impossible, but Jane's turmoil will be greatly magnified when she is confronted with her inability to choose between the conflicting demands of all three solutions.

The difficulty of actualizing her idealized image, the vulnerability of her pride, and the possibilities for conflict are all increased by Jane's giving to others a tremendous degree of power over her. Because she lacks a healthy self-esteem, her feelings of self-value have been transferred outside herself. She will soon tell Helen Burns that self-approval " 'is not enough: if others don't love me, I would rather die than live' " (p. 60). Indeed, Jane *cannot* think well of herself unless others do. Because it is of paramount importance that she be her glorified self in the eyes of the world, she will be victimized not only by her own conflicting needs but also by the conflicting needs of others. Thus, her conflict will arise on an interpersonal as well as on an intrapsychic level.

2

Jane plans to actualize her idealized image at Lowood, and significantly, its realization depends largely on others: "She mean[s] to be so good, and to do so much . . . to make so many friends, to earn respect, and win affection" (p. 59). She is successful, for she excels as both student and teacher; and she receives the love and approval she needs from Helen Burns and Miss Temple, who help her to prove that the Reeds' and Brocklehurst's image of her is wrong. That she has realized her goals is indicated by Bessie's admiration of her accomplishments, which she declares far surpass those of the Miss Reeds. Her exclamation that Jane is " 'quite a lady' " diametrically opposes the image of a "noxious thing" held up to Jane as a child and gives Jane exactly the brand of glory she wants (p. 80).

However, Jane cannot be satisfied with having reached her goals. Her pride needs continual reinforcement by a superior. What Jane says in reference to Diana Rivers can be applied to all her close relationships: "It was my nature to feel pleasure in yielding to an authority supported like hers; and to bend, where my conscience and self-respect permitted, to an active will" (p. 302). Such a relationship in which she is guided, loved, and approved by a superior is essential to Jane. Her accomplishments at Lowood provide no gratification in themselves but are valued only so far as they elicit Miss Temple's praise. Thus, from the day Miss Temple leaves, Jane's life is again empty as it was at Gateshead; and, as previously, Jane yearns for the compensatory life of adventure.

> Now I remembered that the real world was wide, and that a varied field of hopes and fears, of sensations and excitements, awaited those who had courage to go forth into its expanse, to seek real knowledge of life amidst its perils. . . . My eye passed all other objects to rest on those most remote, the blue peaks: it was those I longed to surmount. (p. 74)

Significantly, however, no sooner does Jane express her desires than she retracts them.

> I desired liberty; for liberty I uttered a prayer; it seemed scattered on the wind then faintly blowing. I abandoned it and framed a humbler supplication; for change, stimulus: that petition, too, seemed swept off into vague space. "Then," I cried, half desperate, "grant me at least a new servitude!" (p. 74)

Jane's expansive, self-effacing, and resigned needs are in conflict; and she demonstrates the rigidity of her childhood defense mechanisms, which operate regardless of reality. Since happiness was really out of Jane's reach at Gateshead, her resignation was at least an effective defense, even though it was self-alienating; now, however, the possibilities have changed for Jane. But in spite of her belief that adventure awaits those who have the "courage" to pursue it, her courage is dried up by her compulsive resignation before it can begin to take root.[10] Moreover, Jane's pride in always making the right decision is so vulnerable that she can afford no risk of failure, and her best means for preventing it is to destroy her chances for success. Thus, Jane automatically gives up all hope for liberty and unconsciously disguises her expansive desires in a supplication for a "new servitude." Since servitude "does not sound too sweet," it does not violate Jane's resigned bargain with fate that if she does not ask for much, she will not be disappointed (p. 75). Regardless of Bessie's advice at Gateshead, Jane is still a victim of the fear that to be " 'bolder' " invites " 'more knocks' " (p. 33).

Like her need for resignation, all of Jane's needs are compulsive and bear no relation to reality. The same kind of conflict that has just occurred is sure to arise again when circumstances bring her contradictory needs into play. Just as Jane needs adventure but cannot pursue it, she needs independence but cannot live on her own. She must have an all-encompassing relationship with a superior who will love her, guide her, reinforce her pride, take responsibility for her, and assure her success; but who, at the same time, does not threaten her freedom. It would require an almost impossible combination of circumstances to satisfy all Jane's needs and to prevent their coming into opposition.

3

Fortune, indeed, seems to favor Jane; for her relationship with Rochester at first provides the exact combination she needs. For a short while, Jane will experience complete happiness with Rochester. But his proposal will upset the precarious balance of her needs and set them against one another. Ultimately, when it becomes necessary for Jane to choose between opposing needs after the aborted wedding, she is forced to flee, not Rochester, but her own inner conflict, which threatens to tear her apart.

When Rochester rides out of the dusk into Jane's life, it is as if all her dreams have come true. Here is the powerful superior to whom Jane can transfer her pride and through whom she can live. "Dark, strong, and stern" with the "granite-hewn features" of a "fierce falcon," he is "all energy, decision, [and] will"; and his powerful demeanor is enhanced by "pungent" "sarcasm" and "harshness," "like keen condiments in a choice dish" (pp. 101, 115, 167, 153–154). Above all, Rochester supplies the adventure for which Jane has always yearned. "While . . . [she] ha[s] lived quietly with one set of people in one house," Rochester has "battled through a varied experience with many men of many nations, and roamed over half the globe" (p. 117). His very being has an aura of peril and excitement as he confesses to Jane that " 'to live, for me . . . is to stand on a crater-crust which may crack and spue fire any day' " (p. 190). Through him, Jane can also experience the thrill of standing on a crater-crust without the fear of falling into the volcanic fires. Like the window-glass at Gateshead that protected Jane from the outside world while allowing her to view its open vistas, Rochester's powerful person protects her while allowing her to experience all the excitement of his exploits. Thus, she can fulfill her expansive needs without violating her self-effacing and resigned needs. Horney points out that it is desirable for a self-effacing person "to love a proud person, to merge with him, to live vicariously through him" because it allows a "participat[ion] in the mastery of life without having to own it to [one]self" (*NHG*, p. 244).

Rochester is everything that Jane has ever wanted to be and has done everything that she has dreamed of; she could ask for nothing more than that a hero so grand should single her out as his preferred companion. Because he is "proud, sardonic, [and] harsh to inferiority of every description," Jane is assured by his "great kindness" to her that he regards her as superior in every way (p. 129). Indeed, Rochester reinforces Jane's pride in her idealized image in every way possible. He recognizes her intellectual attributes, her deep feelings, her moral probity, her helpfulness, and her independent spirit. He praises her " 'unique' " mind and makes her the confidante with whom he shares his intimate feelings (p. 126). He sees her as " 'stainless' " and treats her as a moral superior to whom he confesses his sins and from whom he asks advice (p. 119). He calls her a " 'ministrant spirit' " to whom he owes his life after the fire episode and on whom he relies during the harrowing events of Richard Mason's stay (p. 179). He makes her his social equal by assuming the role of a "relation" rather than a "master" (p. 129); and at the same time that he encourages her independence, he satisfies her need to be submissive. He insists that Jane accept his commanding habits, but he makes her acceptance unthreatening by combining his command with a conciliatory request: " 'Leaving superiority out of the question, you must still agree to receive my orders now and then without being piqued or hurt by the tone of command—will you?" (p. 118).

In short, Rochester fulfills all at once Jane's expansive, resigned, and self-effacing needs; and he reinforces her pride in her intellectual, emotional, and moral superiority. Through him Jane proves that the Reeds are wrong and that she is her idealized image. Because Rochester makes this possible, Jane idolizes him and transfers her pride to him. "The blanks of existence," Jane says, are "filled up" by Rochester (p. 129).

But such a precarious balance of contradictory needs cannot last. The very fact that Jane's relationship with Rochester is a dream come true threatens her resignation. As soon as she allows herself to hope for Rochester's proposal after the fire episode, she is thrown into conflict. Just as at Lowood she had imagined her chances for liberty "scattered on the wind," she now dreams of herself destined for Beulah on an "unquiet sea" where "now and then a freshening gale wakened by hope, bore my spirit triumphantly towards the bourne; but I could not reach it, even in fancy—a counteracting breeze blew off land, and continually drove me back" (p. 133).

Seemingly, fate punishes Jane for her "brighter hopes" because Rochester leaves the next day and returns with Blanche Ingram (p. 137). Actually, Rochester has his own inner conflict which reinforces Jane's. Because he intends to marry Jane yet feels guilty for contemplating a bigamy which could hurt her, he cannot propose until Jane first declares her love. He could then justify bigamy by convincing himself that Jane would be desperate without him.[11] Thus, his courtship of Blanche is intended to make Jane so jealous that she will be forced to avow her love. His scheme backfires, however, for it seems to fulfill the prophecy of Jane's dream and, as far as Jane is concerned, proves that Rochester is inexorably lost to her.

It is of no consequence to Jane that Rochester misled her or that circumstances are beyond her control; she puts all the blame on herself, for she *should* not have violated her resignation by hoping for Rochester's proposal. The severity of her self-hate can be measured by the bitter mockery with which she dubs herself a "fantastic idiot," a "stupid dupe," and the "great[est] fool" who ever "breathed the breath of life" (p. 140). Jane's self-hate during Rochester's courtship of Blanche is so great that she attempts to prevent its increase by punishing herself in advance to guard against ever again violating her resignation. To kill any chance for a rebirth of hope, she blinds herself to Rochester's obvious intimations of love and convinces herself that her own love "would be despised" by him (p. 142). She restores her pride by viewing this self-punishment as evidence of her "wholesome [self] discipline," "sense[,] and resolution" (p. 141).

In addition to restoring her pride, Jane manages to satisfy her needs both for resignation and for love. By continuing to torture herself with the conviction that her love for Rochester is hopeless, she satisfies her need for resignation and frees herself to fantasize. But even in fantasy, she is careful not to dare fate by enjoying a pleasure that is "too sweet." She can indulge in the "precious, yet poignant pleasure . . . [of] pure gold" her fantasy affords *only because* she mars it with a "steely point of agony" by reminding herself that she is, in fact, only fantasizing (p. 153). However, on one level Jane really does know that Rochester loves her; and although her need for resignation forces her to deny this knowledge, her need for love demands that she be aware of it. Jane fulfills these conflicting demands by becoming a shuttlecock to her inner dictates, continuously alternating between contradictory views of her situation. At one time she is convinced that Rochester loves the "noble," "accomplished" Blanche in comparison to whom she is "plain" and "insignificant," while at another time she is certain that Rochester loves her and that Blanche is "a mark beneath jealousy," indeed, "too inferior to excite the feeling" (pp. 141, 163).

Jane manages to keep hope alive by declaring it dead, to balance agony with ecstasy, and to alternate between opposing views of her situation so that her contradictory needs are being met and she is as happy as these needs allow her to be. She is so content that she has transformed England into a "splendid" dream world (p. 217). It is not surprising, then, that when she smells the cigar smoke of the flesh and blood prince whose reality threatens to dispel the dream, she instinctively knows, "I must flee" (p. 218). Rochester's proposal throws a wrench into the perfect balance of Jane's contradictory needs.

The prospect of becoming Rochester's wife sets almost all Jane's needs into opposition. Marriage would satisfy her need for love but violate her resignation; it would enable her to merge with a superior but at the cost of her independence; and it would realize her expansive desire to travel around the world but at the risk of exposing her deficiencies in grace and elegance in an unfamiliar social milieu.[12]

Again, Jane's dreams manifest her inner turmoil. Like her dream of being driven by counteracting breezes alternately toward and away from Beulah, she now dreams of struggling to climb the crumbling walls of Thornfield, which collapse the moment she reaches their summit. Moreover, her progress is impeded by a wailing infant who almost strangles her and causes her to lose sight of Rochester, who rides off in the distance as the child finally causes her downfall. The child, of course, is Jane as Mrs. Rochester whose role Jane fears she cannot play and whose birth she fears will be the death of Jane Eyre.[13]

Jane's conflict is also demonstrated by her distorted view of Rochester, her attraction toward and repulsion to exactly the same characteristics in him, and her contradictory behavior toward him. Jane reacts more strongly to Rochester's mastery than to any of his other characteristics. Of course, Rochester is domineering, but Jane needs to exaggerate this tendency. It makes him her "dread, but adored" master who is "captivating" and "irresistible" but also as fearsome as a Grand Turk who would enslave her in a harem (pp. 252, 163).[14] Because she is magnetically pulled to Rochester's mastery, Jane makes him her "whole world," her "hope of heaven," and even an "idol" who comes "between [her] and . . . God" (p. 241); yet, because she fears her own desire to be subsumed by Rochester, she refuses to go alone with him on a carriage ride, to allow his caresses, or even to dine with him "till I can't help it" (p. 237). To make matters worse, Jane's conflict is exacerbated by Rochester's contradictory behavior. Because he needs for Jane to be both independent and submissive as much as she needs to be both, he instigates her spirited defiance and saucy repartee while at the same time he reinforces her fears by compulsively trying to subdue her.

4

The blow that fells Jane's "most glorious dreams" at the very point of their realization seems like the retribution Jane has feared for daring fate (p. 261). Jane's self-hate is doubly severe because she should not have allowed herself to hope for happiness, especially after having been taught a lesson in resignation once before when her hopes for Rochester's proposal were punished by his courtship of Blanche Ingram. That she has *chosen* to violate her resignation and independence for the sake of love is bad enough; that she has done so futilely is inexcusable. The impossibility of her having foreseen the unforeseeable is irrelevant because idealized images do not make allowances for human limitations. *All* Jane's needs have been violated, and she alone is to blame. Thus, "the torrent" of self-hate "pour[s] over" her in a "full, heavy swing" (p. 261). She tortures herself mercilessly by telling herself, in spite of all evidence to the contrary, that Rochester has never had any "real affection" for her but only a "fitful passion"; and now that it is "balked," her "view must be hateful to him" (p. 260). She makes her guilty feelings as agonizing as possible and gloats over the exquisite pain she inflicts on herself: "Conscience, turned tyrant, held passion by the throat, told her tauntingly she had yet but dipped her dainty foot in the slough, and swore that with that arm of iron he would thrust her down to unsounded depths of agony" (p. 261).

Because this tremendous self-hate is the result of Jane's having chosen between conflicting needs, the necessity to make another choice between the same needs paralyzes her. A choice between leaving Rochester or staying as his mistress is made even more difficult because it threatens Jane's need to be morally perfect. She is compelled to leave to prove that she is good; but by doing so, she will be the cause of Rochester's headlong plunge into dissipation. Jane is caught in a crossfire of contradictory needs in which to resist Rochester is "cruel: to yield . . . is out of the question" (p. 268). No matter what Jane does, she will hate herself.

It is absolutely impossible for Jane to make a decision; yet, because she prides herself on doing the right thing, it is absolutely necessary that she decide. In an attempt to choose, Jane builds a case first for one side and then for the other. Like her inner dictates, these cases are contradictory. She justifies staying with Rochester by glorifying her role as his "comforter—his pride; his redeemer from misery; perhaps from ruin" (p. 283). On the other hand, she convinces herself that she must leave because she has "always believed" in the "worth" of traditional moral law; because "the more solitary," "friendless," and "unsustained" she becomes by sacrificing love for duty, "the more" she will "respect" herself; and because Rochester would soon despise her if she stayed as he does his past mistresses (p. 279).

Because many critics view Jane's reasons for leaving Rochester as evidence of her ratiocination instead of her rationalization, it must be emphasized that her reasoning is not based on reality but on the need to produce a logical basis for fulfilling her inner dictates. Although Jane says that she has "always believed" in the "worth" of God's commandments, she has proven the opposite by feeling no remorse for having made Rochester her idol. She has shown that what is important to her is to discredit the hateful image created by the Reeds by always acting *en règle* in the eyes of the world. Significantly, she has no qualms about private idolatry, but she is horrified by the idea of public adultery. Second, Jane says that she can live without love by taking comfort in a "solitary" self-respect, but she has demonstrated her inability to do so when her agony over being ostracized at Lowood was in no way relieved by her knowledge of her own innocence. As we have seen, she told Helen Burns, " 'I know I should think well of myself; but that is not enough: if others don't love me, I would rather die than live—I cannot bear to be solitary and hated' " (p. 60). Finally, Jane says that as the "successor" to Rochester's past mistresses, she would eventually share the contempt he feels for them (p. 274); but Jane has demonstrated a pride that would never allow her to admit a resemblance between herself and these mistresses by really believing that Rochester could ever feel about her as he does about them. The real basis for her belief that Rochester would despise her is evidenced by her determination to hold this "conviction" in reserve "to *serve me as aid* in the time of trial" (p. 275, my emphasis).

Again, Rochester's contradictory needs reinforce Jane's dilemma. He needs Jane to stay because she can reform him. But the proof of her goodness lies in her leaving. She could not reform him if she were persuaded by his situational ethics to step down from her saintly pedestal to his level of morality. Because of his conflicting needs, Rochester tries to convince Jane to stay even though he has already invalidated his own arguments by having assured her that he would expect her to be "immutable as a fixed star" should he ever ask her to do wrong (p. 191). Although Jane is persuaded that his arguments are "true," Rochester has made it impossible for her to be swayed by them (p. 279).

Jane is boxed in from all sides. Because her contradictory needs are equally compulsive, because her rationalizations invalidate each other, and because Rochester's conflict reinforces her own, Jane is trapped in a position in which choice is imperative but impossible. Her flight is a desperate attempt to escape this trap. Of course, since Jane's needs for resignation and independence were violated by her engagement to Rochester and since her need to appear *en règle* in the eyes of the world is put in immediate jeopardy by the prospect of adultery, these needs have become momentarily more urgent than her needs to have love and to save Rochester. Moreover, although Rochester comes before God, even he must be sacrificed to Jane's idealized image—the real idol in her life whose dictates are enforced by the threat of self-hate. On one level, therefore, Jane's flight represents an unconscious drive to prevent a public defacement of her moral image and to avoid further violation of her resignation and independence. Nonetheless, it is of paramount importance to Jane that she make no conscious choice whatsoever, for any choice would trigger immense self-hate. On the broadest level, her running away is a flight from decision. But because Jane cannot even deliberately choose not to choose without hating herself, she attempts to escape responsibility for her flight by projecting it onto a moon goddess and onto God. By seeing herself as led by a supernatural agent, Jane need not make a choice while at the same time she can believe she is doing the right thing.

Because she can avoid self-hate only by avoiding responsibility for her actions, Jane goes to a great deal of trouble to convince herself that her flight is involuntary. She draws attention to the fact that she is "*driven* to utter extremity," and that she acts "instinctively," "involuntarily," and "mechanically" (p. 268, my emphasis). Since she allows herself "no reflection" either backwards or forwards; since her "own will" and "conscience" have been "trampled" and "stifled" by "impassioned grief"; and since she is "delirious," "frantic," "blind, deaf, and distracted," she cannot be held responsible for her flight. Even on the second day of her journey, Jane still makes a point of noticing that when the road forks, she takes the route away from the sun because "by no other circumstances had I *will* to *decide* my *choice*" (pp. 282, 283, 372, 286, my emphases). Such an emphasis on her mental enervation attests to Jane's unconscious preoccupation with denying any active part in a decision-making process.

In spite of these attempts to escape self-hate, Jane is still its victim. Her rationalization that "God must have led me on" is rendered futile moments later when she says her prayers are "hopeless" and calls herself an "instrument of evil." Her self-contempt is not abated but augmented: "I abhorred myself. I had no solace from self-approbation: none even from self-respect. . . . I was hateful in my own eyes" (p. 283). It is highly significant that a year later Jane does not remember God leading her but a "revengeful fury tracking and scourging me, on the morning I fled from Thornfield" (p. 372). This fury is the self-hate threatened by any choice between conflicting needs. It is this fury—not a domineering Rochester or the moral law—which causes Jane to run "fast, fast," to "crawl forwards" on her hands and knees "eager and . . . determined" to escape (p. 283).

But Jane cannot escape her fury. Leaving Thornfield does not mark the end of battle, but gains her only a temporary truce by removing her from one particular field of combat where an immediate decision was necessary. Jane's fury is driven underground but is not disarmed. Her private hell is "the burden which must be carried" to Moor House (p. 286), and her personal fury is ready to surface at the slightest provocation.

5

Jane's relationship with St. John stirs up the smouldering ashes of her conflict to a white heat, and the fury is let loose again to reign supreme over the raging flames of Jane's personal hell. Although St. John is different from Rochester in obvious ways, he has the same basic characteristics; and Jane is both attracted to and repelled by him for the same reasons that she felt ambivalent toward Rochester. Primarily, she is drawn to his expansiveness. A "leader and superior" like Rochester, St. John is "of the material from which nature hews her heroes"; he is destined for "scenes of strife and danger—where courage is proved, . . . energy exercised, and fortitude tasked" (p. 346). Also like Rochester, St. John has high standards, he does not tolerate inferiority in any form, and he is highly selective of associates. He makes Jane feel special, as Rochester did, by singling her out and recognizing all her attributes—her intelligence, her usefulness, and her rectitude. Thus, it does not take long for Jane to become as dependent on St. John for approval as she had been on Rochester. Not only does she "daily [wish] more to please him" (p. 351); but indeed, she confesses that "when he said 'go', I went; 'come,' I came; 'do this,' I did it" (p. 350).

Jane's dependency on St. John brings her needs into conflict. Although St. John's tendency to master is the very characteristic which draws Jane to him like a moth to a flame, the power she has given him over her threatens her freedom. To avoid self-hate for putting herself in this vulnerable position, Jane exaggerates St. John's domineering nature as she had exaggerated Rochester's; but it is really the "iron shroud" of her own need to submit which "contract[s] round her" and results in her morbid dependency (p. 355).[15]

Jane's turmoil is increased as it was in her relationship with Rochester when St. John's proposal forces her to choose among moral perfection, independence, and love. If Jane refuses St. John, she will prove herself " 'worse than infidels' " in his eyes (p. 360). Because she has transferred her pride to him and desperately needs his approval, she is compelled to comply. But to choose to do so would not only be a deliberate violation of her independence but a complete renunciation of her hopes for love. St. John has made no bones about assuring Jane that it is not she but the missionary in her whom he wishes to wed. He urges her to sacrifice heart, home, and friends for a martyr's life in India. As previously, Jane is paralyzed; and instead of deciding, she hesitates, vacillates, and attempts to escape responsibility for making a choice. She builds cases for both sides of the issue; and again, it is important to understand that these cases are based on rationalizations.

In an attempt to avoid having to choose among her contradictory needs, Jane tells herself that it is the spiritual glory of the missionary's life which tempts her to adopt it: "Is not [this] occupation . . . truly the most glorious man can adopt or God assign?" Although Jane's answer is affirmative, she follows it with a second question which indicates that a glorious occupation is only a substitute for the love she really wants: "Is . . . [this occupation] not, by its noble cares and sublime results, the one best calculated to fill the void left by uptorn affections and demolished hopes?" (p. 356). Regardless of her efforts, Jane cannot suppress the fact that it is not God's glory but St. John's love and approval which she craves: "If I *do go* with him—if I *do* make the sacrifice he urges . . . I will throw all on the altar—heart, vitals, the entire victim. . . . By straining to satisfy St. John till my sinews ache, I *shall* satisfy him to the finest central point and farthest outward circle of his expectations. . . . He will never love me; but he shall approve me" (p. 356).

Significantly, Jane talks about her sacrifice conditionally. Because she desperately needs *both* love and approval, she simply cannot choose to make such a "monstrous" sacrifice (p. 356). But neither can she refuse St. John. Therefore, she must rationalize her hesitation. She convinces herself that she would go with St. John on the condition that he rescind the requirement that she marry him. Since St. John is certain to refuse this condition, Jane has managed not only to prolong a stalemate but also to transfer the responsibility for her indecision to St. John. The marriage question is really a smokescreen thrown up by Jane to avoid self-hate by blinding herself to her indecisiveness. Her sophistry is evident. She tells herself that to go to India as St. John's wife would force her to stifle her feelings whereas to go with him as his sister or curate would leave her "heart and mind . . . free"—"all would be right" (p. 359). But it is simply not true that her freedom is contingent on whether or not she marries St. John. The "fire of [her] nature" could hardly be more "checked" as St. John's wife than it is now when she forbears showing so much as a sign of "vivacity" because it is "distasteful to him" (p. 359). Moreover, St. John has pointed out that to work together in India unmarried would " 'fasten injurious suspicions on us both' " (p. 359). Given Jane's fear of the world's scorn, she could never risk such defamation.

Jane's dilemma is complicated by St. John's contradictory needs, just as her former conflict had been reinforced by Rochester's. Like Rochester, St. John needs Jane to be strong and weak at the same time. He reinforces Jane's independent spirit because it is precisely the quality which fits her for the rugged life of a missionary, but he also insists that Jane be dependent on him so that he " 'can influence [her] efficiently in life and retain [her] absolutely till death' " (p. 357). Furthermore, St. John needs Jane's love; but because his own heart is " 'no more than a sacrifice consumed' " (p. 323), he is incapable of accepting it. To persuade her to marry him, he appeals to her " 'woman's heart' " after he has already rejected it by admonishing her to " 'wrench . . . [her] heart from man, and fix it on . . . [her] Maker' " (p. 358). Finally, St. John needs Jane to be morally strict and lax at the same time. He exhorts her to martyr herself for God but makes it clear that her sacrifice will really be to his own "insatiable" ambition (p. 330); and because he is as fastidious about appearances as Jane is, he requires her to violate the sacrament of marriage as the first step in spreading the gospel. These contradictory demands pull Jane in opposite directions and also diminish St. John's power to force her compliance. When Jane discovers "his imperfection," she believes that she "might resist" him (p. 358).

But Jane can no more resist St. John than she can submit to him because, as we have seen, she desperately needs to do both. When Jane is finally "thrust . . . to the point" of choice "so long shunned," she is almost torn apart by indecision as she was in the crisis with Rochester. The difference between the present crisis and the previous one is that the balance in Jane's needs is reversed. Since her needs for independence, goodness, and resignation were all satisfied at the cost of love when she left Rochester, her need for love was intensified by its frustration. Since St. John has repeatedly frustrated it and now threatens the annihilation of any possibility that it will ever be fulfilled, Jane's need for love has become urgent. Because of this urgency, she grows "pliant as a reed under [St. John's unaccustomed] kindness." Jane's pliancy in response to St. John's tenderness is reinforced by her compulsive attraction to his powerful magnetism. She is completely caught up in "veneration" and "aw[e]" of St. John's "sublim[ity]." Because the self-effacing side of her personality wants to yield to St. John's "gentleness" and be subsumed by his strength, Jane is almost overwhelmed by the temptation to "rush down the torrent of his will into the gulf of his existence, and there lose my own." But at the very moment she is ready to capitulate, St. John breaks the spell of his "hierophant's touch" by assuming that Jane's decision is already made. When he ejaculates, " 'my prayers are heard!' " and "claim[s]" Jane for God, he makes the "difference" between tender feeling and his ambitious fervor so obvious that Jane can no longer blind herself to the proof that although St. John acts "*almost* as if he loved me," he in fact does not. Coupled with this undeniable proof of St. John's lack of love is a dramatic demonstration of his threat to Jane's freedom when he "surround[s]" her "with his arm," not in a caress, but in an act of possession (pp. 368, 369).

St. John's assumption that Jane has decided puts an end to her vacillation. She must find an immediate escape or be forever lost. The way out is conveniently provided by the "mysterious summons." The summons parallels the vision of the moon goddess in Jane's previous crisis; for it allows Jane to escape making a decision and to avoid responsibility for her flight while at the same time it allows her to appear to be doing the right thing. Jane gets to return to Rochester, but she need not hate herself. Brontë has opted for love, but Jane has not. She has made absolutely no conscious decision among the alternative issues at hand. She certainly does not reject St. John. What she does do is to refuse to be forced by him into making a decision. It is highly significant that on the morning of her departure from St. John, Jane is very careful to make clear that *her decision is yet to be made.*

> "My Spirit . . . is willing to do what is right; and my flesh, I hope, is strong enough to accomplish the will of Heaven, when once that will is distinctly known to me. At any rate, it shall be strong enough to search—inquire—to grope an outlet from this cloud of doubt, and find the open day of certainty." (p. 370)

6

Jane could not possibly choose to return to Rochester and revive the conflict which had almost torn her apart. That she now has money and a family does not change the fact that she would be scorned by the world as an adulteress if she lived with Rochester. If Jane could choose to be Rochester's mistress and bear such scorn, she would have returned before now. But it is Jane's urgent need for love which now drives her to Rochester in spite of the problems that await her. Horney points out that when a person is driven to satisfy an immediate need, he "does not think in long-range terms" but "find[s] an alibi of some sort" to justify whatever he must do to fulfill the immediate need (*NHG*, p. 108). Jane's alibi is that she only wishes to discover information about Rochester's well being. When this excuse loses its viability upon her passing the inn near Thornfield where she could make inquiries, she must find another justification for continuing all the way.[16] Ultimately, she escapes responsibility for her return just as she had escaped responsibility for her flight by crediting it to instinct. Comparing herself to a "messenger pigeon flying home," she observes that she was "in the midst of" Thornfield's grounds "ere I well knew what course I had resolved to take" (p. 372). In this way, Jane holds the coming conflict at bay, but she would face the same dilemma she had originally run away from were Rochester in the same circumstances. Because Jane has not changed, she is no more equipped to resolve her conflict now than she was then.

But Brontë too closely identifies with her heroine either to leave Jane torn by an unresolvable conflict or to reduce her character to a mere illustration of theme. St. John once said of himself, " 'Well, propensities and principles must be reconciled by some means' " (p. 313). But St. John could not reconcile them, and neither could Brontë solve Jane's problems, reconcile her mimetic character with the novel's theme, and clear up the confusion in the theme. It is to the credit of Brontë's intuitive psychological genius that she did not force an aesthetic unity at the expense of mimetic characterization by having Jane either capitulate to traditional values or defy them. Brontë preserves the integrity of Jane's character at the cost of leaving the theme confused. However, she manipulates the plot to vindicate Jane.[17] She eliminates the conditions that gave rise to Jane's conflict so that it appears to be resolved when it has really been evaded. Jane still has the same needs, but they are not in opposition because they are all fulfilled. The drastic measures required to meet all Jane's needs attest to their irreconcilability on a real level.

The best of all possible worlds is realized for Jane. Bertha Mason is conveniently disposed of to remove the moral obstacle to Jane's and Rochester's marriage. The timely award of an inheritance makes Jane " 'an independent woman now,' " secure enough to take the risk of a total surrender in love (p. 382). Moreover, the coincidental discovery that the Riverses are Jane's close relations, whose loyalty is purchased with her inheritance, ensures Jane of familial love should Rochester reject her. Such insurance is gratuitous, however, for Rochester himself has been molded ideally to suit Jane's needs.[18]

As a "sightless Samson," Rochester combines the strength and weakness to satisfy Jane's contradictory needs. His strength makes him a "safe . . . prop" for Jane to lean on and live through; it allows her to look up to a "Master" and to have her pride reinforced by a superior (p. 391). No longer the "fierce falcon" he once was, Rochester is still a "royal eagle"; the significant difference is that he is now "chained to a perch" and "forced to entreat a sparrow to become . . . [his] purveyor" (pp. 101, 387). Rochester's weakness both ensures Jane's independence and calls out the best in her. He needs her sympathy, understanding, and devotion—qualities on which Jane has always prided herself. By being Rochester's eyes, his hands, and his comforter, moreover, Jane feels more secure in Rochester's love because she is indispensable to him. In short, Rochester's mutilation and dejection render it safe and rewarding for Jane to sacrifice herself for love. When Rochester accuses her of " 'delight[ing] in sacrifice' " (p. 392), Jane denies that she makes any sacrifice at all. Long ago Jane told Rochester, " 'I'd give my life to serve you' " (p. 179); that she at last has the opportunity to give it is the " 'indulge[nce] . . . [of her] sweetest wishes' " (p. 397). "Love *is* sacrifice" for the self-effacing person, says Horney (*NHG*, p. 220); and this is certainly true for Jane, who told Helen Burns that " 'to gain some real affection' " she would " 'submit' " to torture (p. 60). Jane does not have to undergo torture, but she gets the kind of pay-off for sacrifice she has always wanted when her selfless devotion to Rochester is rewarded with an ideal marriage—a total merging of the self by which Jane becomes "absolutely bone of . . . [Rochester's] bone and flesh of his flesh" (p. 397).[19]

Not only are Jane's attributes set off to the greatest advantage by Rochester's misfortunes, but Rochester's and Jane's isolation at Ferndean eliminates any chance that Jane's social deficiencies might be exposed. Contrary to Helene Moglen's and Armour Craig's assertions, Jane's "absolute isolation" from society is not "the price" she pays for happiness; it is part of the remuneration.[20] Because Jane's idealized image incorporates both resignation and expansiveness, she has always preferred fantasy to reality; for the demands of these contradictory solutions can both be met in a dream world where romantic adventures have all the excitement with none of the risks the real world involves. Ferndean incorporates the best of both worlds. It has a real hero in Rochester who approximates all the romantic qualities of a dream hero. Yet, Ferndean does not have the judging eyes, the responsibilities, and the chances for failure of the real world. Moreover, because Jane's situation does not appear "too sweet," she need not dare fate or fear disappointment (p. 75). For the first time in her life, Jane can enjoy being happy.

The icing is put on the cake when in addition to getting everything she wants at the end, Jane *appears* to have made the right decisions all along. Rochester's apparent conversion justifies Jane's initial flight from him as well as her return.[21] Moreover, St. John's letters indicate that he does not believe Jane to be numbered among the infidels. His respect for her and his premature death suggest that she was right in not going with him to India.[22] Brontë's vindication of Jane is so thorough that it justifies Frederick Karl's irritation with a novel of moral evolution in which the heroine is "inflexibly right from the beginning." Indeed, it proves that the novel is not a *bildungsroman.*

Jane, of course, has done the right thing all along, but only because Brontë makes it turn out that way. Jane has made no deliberate decisions, and her ultimate happiness is contingent upon her being in a position in which there is no necessity to choose. The many critics who postulate Jane's victory over circumstances do not see that she is *awarded* the laurels of victory. She does not win them by "ruthless egoism," a "triumphan[t] impos[ition] of her will," a refusal to "sacrific[e] a grain of her Jane Eyre-ity," or an assertion of her "integrity to *be.*" Nor does she triumph by means of her "self-knowledge," her "transcendence with a vengeance," her ability "to divide and conquer," or by any other means.[23] Jane does absolutely nothing to solve her own problems.[24] Instead, she "wait[s] [for] some impossible change in circumstances" (p. 356). The "impossible change" occurs and Jane's bargain with fate works because Brontë is the divine agent.

NOTES

1. For notation of aesthetic weaknesses, see David Cecil, *Victorian Novelists* (Chicago and London: University of Chicago Press, 1935); Joseph Prescott, "Jane Eyre: A Romantic Exemplum with a Difference," in *Twelve Original Essays on Great English Novels,* ed. Charles Shapiro (Detroit: Wayne State University Press, 1960), pp. 87–102; and the essays by David Crompton, Elizabeth Rigby, W. C. Roscoe, and Mary Ward in *Charlotte Brontë, Jane Eyre and Villette: A Casebook,* ed. Miriam Allott (New York: Macmillan, 1973). For two of the best recent studies noting weaknesses, see Richard Benvenuto, "The Child of Nature, The Child of Grace, and the Unresolved Conflict of Jane Eyre," *ELH* 39 (December 1972): 620–38, and Barbara Hardy, *The Appropriate Form: An Essay on the Novel* (London: Athlone Press, 1964), pp. 61–70.

For support of aesthetic control, see Charles Burkhart, *Charlotte Brontë, A Psychosexual Study of Her Novels* (London: Victor Gollancz, 1973); John Halperin, *Egoism and Self-Discovery in the Victorian Novel* (New York: Burt Franklin, 1974); Robert H. Heilman, "Charlotte Brontë's 'New' Gothic," in the Norton Critical Edition of *Jane Eyre,* ed. Richard J. Dunn (New York: Norton, 1971), pp. 457–62; Earl A. Knies, *The Art of Charlotte Brontë* (Athens: Ohio University Press, 1969); Dale Kramer, "Thematic Structure in *Jane Eyre,*" *Papers on Language & Literature* 4 (1968): 288–98; M. H. Scargill, "Poetic Symbolism in *Jane Eyre,*" *University of Toronto Quarterly* 19 (1950); Mark Schorer, *The World We Imagine: Selected Essays* (New York: Farrar, Straus and Giroux, 1948); and Ruth Bernard Yeazell, "More True Than Real: Jane Eyre's 'Mysterious Summons,'" *NCF* 29 (1974): 127–43.

2. Burkhart, *A Psychosexual Study,* p. 69.
3. Knies, *Art of Charlotte Brontë,* p. 109.
4. See Kramer, "Thematic Structure in *Jane Eyre,*" for an illustration of this approach.
5. For a representative study postulating Jane's Christian conversion, see Lawrence Jay Dessner, *The Homely Web of Truth: A Study of Charlotte Brontë's Novels* (Paris: Mouton, 1975). For a representative study postulating Jane's triumph, see Armour Craig, "The Unpoetic Compromise: On the Relation Between Private Vision and Social Order in Nineteenth-Century English Fiction," in *Society and Self in the Novel,* ed. Mark Schorer (New York: Columbia University Press, 1956), pp. 26–50. A few critics view the ending as marred by Jane's capitulation to a patriarchal world.

Representative of this view is Richard Chase, "The Brontës, or Myth Domesticated," in the Norton Critical Edition of *Jane Eyre,* pp. 462–71.

6. Frederick A. Karl, *A Reader's Guide to the Nineteenth Century British Novel* (New York: Noonday Press, 1965), p. 98.

7. *Charlotte Brontë: The Self Conceived* (New York: Norton, 1976), p. 131. Moglen maintains that Jane resolves her inner conflict between passion and reason but that Jane's conflict with a patriarchal world is not resolved but "eradicated" by her isolation at Ferndean (p. 142).

8. Karen Horney, *Neurosis and Human Growth* (New York: Norton, 1950), p. 18. Hereafter cited in the text as *NHG.*

9. The Norton Critical Edition of *Jane Eyre,* ed. Richard J. Dunn (New York, 1971), p. 10. Hereafter cited in the text.

10. Jane's fear of failure also arises from her self-effacing feelings of inferiority. Moreover, her need to act *en règle* comes into play here. To seek adventure in a man's world would mar Jane's image as " 'quite a lady,' " which she must preserve at all costs.

The feminists' argument along these lines is that Jane cannot realize an expansive life in Victorian England because of the social limitations imposed on women. Even Jane laments the prejudices that prevent the recognition that "women feel just as men feel" (p. 96). Of course, these limitations existed; but regardless of them, Jane is incapable of pursuing adventure. In the course of her life, she is given the opportunity to travel over Europe and to live in India. Both prospects are terrifying to Jane because of her feelings of inferiority and compulsive resignation, and it is with immeasurable relief that she escapes the opportunities "to seek real knowledge of life amidst its perils" (p. 74). For a representative feminist study, see Harriet Björk, *The Language of Truth: Charlotte Brontë, The Woman Question, And The Novel,* Lund Studies in English, 47 (Lund: Gleerup, 1974), p. 95.

11. Rochester uses this justification during the proposal scene (cf. p. 225). He also makes a point of reminding Jane the morning after their engagement that " 'it was you who made me the offer' " (p. 230).

12. That Jane is wary of taking such a risk is indicated by her assertion: "I had a theoretical reverence and homage for beauty, elegance, gallantry, fascination; but had I met those qualities incarnate . . . , I should have known instinctively that they neither had nor could have sympathy with anything in me, and should have shunned them as one would fire, lightning, or anything else that is bright but antipathetic" (p. 99). Although Jane takes pride in being above caring for vain elegance, she has a repressed feeling of inferiority for lacking it. This feeling was generated by the Reeds' emphasis on her plainness and moroseness as proofs of her worthlessness and is illustrated by Jane's own contrast of her deficiencies in beauty and social graces to the superiority in these qualities of both Georgiana Reed and Blanche Ingram. Jane has nothing in common with an aristocratic society that values these qualities; and although she believes that Rochester also "is not of their kind," she feels "estranged" to him in social gatherings because she does not have "his force to influence" and "spell to attract" (pp. 154, 153).

13. Jane is often referred to as a child both by herself and by Rochester. Thus, there is good reason to assume that the child in her dreams is Jane (cf. pp. 272, 247–49, 252, 260).

14. When Jane does not need to see herself as helpless, she is well aware of the power she holds over Rochester and is even intrigued by exerting it (cf. pp. 241, 266). However, many critics have assumed Jane's blind spots and, taking the cue from her, have grossly maligned Rochester by crediting him with the evil intentions of a Bluebeard, Lovelace, and Satan. See Elaine Showalter, *A Literature of Their Own: British Women Novelists from Brontë to Lessing* (Princeton: Princeton University Press, 1977), p. 122: Patricia Beer, *Reader, I Married Him: A Study of the Women Characters of Jane Austen, Charlotte Brontë, Elizabeth Gaskell and George Eliot* (New York: Barnes & Noble, 1974), p. 104; and John Hagan, "Enemies of Freedom in 'Jane Eyre,' " *Criticism* 13 (1973): 351–76. For other attacks on Rochester, see Moglen, *The Self Conceived,* p. 129; Jane Millgate, "Jane Eyre's Progress," *English Studies, Anglo-American Supplement* 50 (1969): xxvi; and F. A. C. Wilson, "The Primrose Wreath: The Heroes of the Brontë Novels," *NCF* 29 (1974): 45.

15. That St. John does not generally dominate women is evident by his powerlessness before Rosamond Oliver and by the fact that he asks neither of his sisters to learn Hindostanee because he knows they would refuse. He urges Jane to become a missionary, not because he is domineering, but because he " 'recognised a soul that revelled in the flame and excitement of sacrifice' " (p. 355). Moreover, just as Jane exercised her power over Rochester, she is quite capable of asserting herself with St. John when her pride is crushed in the proposal scene and when she is pushed to desperation in the crisis (cf. pp. 359, 370).

16. Another alibi she uses is that no one would be hurt by her seeing Rochester again (cf. p. 373). That this is the same argument used by Rochester does not indicate that Jane has come round to his "way of thinking" as Maria Yuen maintains, nor does it support Arnold Shapiro's contention that Jane has rejected traditional morality for "human-heartedness" (Yuen, "Two Crises of Decision in Jane Eyre," *English Studies* 57 [1976]:225; Shapiro, "In Defense of Jane Eyre," *Studies in English Literature* 8 [1968]: 681). Jane agreed with Rochester's argument from the first, but it did not suit her needs to act on it; now it does. This is not the first time Jane has made expedient use of someone else's argument.

17. Yeazell, "More True Than Real," and Scargill, "Thematic Structure," argue that these plot manipulations reflect a transformation in Jane; to the contrary, they are a substitute for growth, not a reflection of it.

18. Dale Kramer maintains that "on all the levels of their [Jane's and Rochester's] relationship, Brontë emphasizes balance rather than forced adjustment" (p. 297). What Kramer does not see is that this "balance" is made possible by a great deal of "forced adjustment." The perfect balance of Jane's and Rochester's relationship would not be possible if Rochester were not maimed and blinded. " 'I was forced,' " says Rochester, " 'to pass through the valley of the shadow of death. *His* chastisements are mighty; and one smote me which has humbled me for ever' " (p. 393).

19. It is requisite to the fulfillment of Jane's opposing needs that she totally lose the self at the same time that she maintains her independence. The novel's fantasy ending makes this possible. However, only one set of Jane's contradictory needs is considered by critics such as Moglen; Yuen; Yeazel; Adrienne Rich, "The Temptations of a Motherless Woman," *Ms*, October 1973, pp. 68–72, 98; and Hazel Mews, *Frail Vessels: Woman's Role in Women's Novels from Fanny Burney to George Eliot* (London: Athlone Press, 1969). To support their contention that Jane grows by asserting her independence and integrity, they choose to ignore Jane's own statement that she merges with Rochester. They praise Jane erroneously for attaining a healthy detachment that precludes her making such a declaration as Catharine Earnshaw's " 'I *am* Heathcliff.' "

20. Moglen, *The Self Conceived*, pp. 142–43; Craig, "The Unpoetic Compromise," p. 41.

21. M. A. Blom is correct to question Rochester's conversion by pointing out that at the moment of repentance Rochester calls on Jane rather than on Christ and names Jane instead of Christ his Alpha and Omega. " 'Jane Eyre': Mind as Law Unto Itself," *Criticism* 15 (1973):350–64.

22. The few critics who note Jane's final tribute to St. John are correct in noting its importance, but they mistake its relevance. Harriet Björk concurs with Arnold Shapiro that it demonstrates a human-heartedness resulting from Jane's happy marriage which allows her to "describe St. John without rancor" (Shapiro, "In Defense of Jane Eyre," p. 697), and Jean Sudrann contends that it proves Jane is still a victim of a patriarchal world that has frustrated her expansive ambitions ("Hearth and Horizon: Changing Concepts of the Domestic Life of the Heroine," *The Massachusetts Review* 14 [Spring 1973]: 235–55). These critics do not see that Jane's tribute to St. John functions to reinforce her pride. In Jane's eyes her veneration of God's disciple and St. John's respect for her prove her perfection. We must remember that as far as Jane is concerned she never rejected St. John. She still had her decision to make when she left Moor House.

23. Rich, "The Temptations of a Motherless Woman," p. 107; Blom, "Mind as Law," pp. 364, 355; Schorer, *The World We Imagine*, p. 90; Halperin, *Egoism and Self-Discovery*, p. 48; Craig, "The Unpoetic Compromise," p. 39; Karl, *A Reader's Guide*, p. 94.

24. M. A. Blom represents the feminist argument that Jane "has bettered her chances of achieving a love involving no personal risk" because "during her absence [from Rochester] she has proved

herself, having earned a living, made friends, found loving relatives, and most significantly, inherited money" (p. 362). Contrary to Blom's assertion, these facts do not represent Jane's growth. She earned a living and won friends both at Lowood and Thornfield. That she does so at Moor House, therefore, does not indicate any change in her. Jane's finding relatives and inheriting a fortune, moreover, are the result of circumstances, not of Jane's "proving herself." Indeed, instead of developing healthier human relationships and learning to manage her own life, Jane is still so dependent and vulnerable that she gives away three-fourths of her inheritance in an attempt to buy love.

5

The Lost Self of Esther Summerson: A Horneyan Interpretation of *Bleak House*

Patricia R. Eldredge

> How is it possible to lose a self? The treachery, unknown and unthinkable, begins with our secret psychic death in childhood—if and when we are not loved and are cut off from our spontaneous wishes. . . .
>
> . . . . Everything looks normal; no crime was intended; there is no corpse, no guilt. All we can see is the sun rising and setting as usual. But what has happened? He has been rejected, not only by them, but by himself. . . . What has he lost? Just the one true and vital part of himself: his own yes-feeling, which is his very capacity for growth, his root system.[1]

To examine Charles Dickens' *Bleak House* from the perspective of Third Force psychology is to explore a deeper mystery than that of the plot, the mystery of self-alienation. The world of the novel, with its images of decay, disease, and death, is a smothering, ossified society that is perniciously destructive to human growth. Most of the sixty-odd characters who dwell in the Chancery environment are clearly understood by their author to be damaged human beings. Probing to find the source of this evil, Dickens, disturbed all his life by his own early humiliations, paid particular attention to adverse influences in childhood: *Bleak House* is full of neurotic parents and parent surrogates who are responsible for the "psychic deaths" of the children in their care. Esther Summerson, the heroine and second narrator, is one victim of a detrimental home; and in her case the implications are, I think, more serious than her creator, though he characterized her with unfailing accuracy, could consciously admit. Her lost self may be called the novel's unresolved mystery; for with her failure to outgrow her past and shine forth as an example of spontaneous goodness, Dickens' solution to social evil collapses and fog closes in again where sunlight is desired.

These conclusions—that Esther is a successful mimetic character, that she does not change significantly in the course of the novel, and that her characterization conflicts with the final thematic statement—must be supported within the context of a long and continuing controversy over the nature of Esther and of her narrative role. From the first appearance of *Bleak House* to the present, numerous critics have regarded her as a failure in characterization and have seriously questioned Dickens' judgment in choosing her to narrate half the novel. Phrases such as "cloying sentimentality," "tedious goodness," "false humility," and "tiresome efficiency" describe Esther for these readers. Sylvère Monod makes a concise enumeration of the main charges against her: her "naively surprised" way of proving her perfection through the praise of others; her tearfulness and sentimentality, made more perceptible by the powerful voice of the impersonal narrator; her coy modesty whenever love is mentioned; her seeming insincerity in speaking kindly of people whom she is actually judging severely; and her general artificiality as a narrator who has no special qualifications as a story teller. She is, Monod concludes, "probably one of the most unpopular figures of Victorian literature."[2]

A second group of critics defend Esther as narrator but deny that she is, or should be, a complex character; they seek to demonstrate that she is, instead, a function, not a flaw, in the organic unity of a great novel. Thus W. J. Harvey praises an Esther who is "as lucid and neutral as a clear window." Because she is devoid of any significant personality, he argues, she cannot color or distort the events she narrates; and this very lack of a Jamesian dramatization of consciousness is appropriate to the populated world of *Bleak House*.[3] Her tedious goodness, says Robert Donovan, may be considered part of her choric function "to provide a sane and wholesome standard of morality in a topsy-turvy world."[4] Joseph Gold emphasizes her symbolic function, calling her "the embodiment of love and compassion and humility that bring meaning and order out of chaos" and disregarding the psychological effects of her illegitimacy when he speaks of "her native ability (as a love-child?) [sic] for dispelling not only mud and fog, . . . but also the gloom that was part of her upbringing."[5]

The most recent critical position is to maintain that we have in Esther a complex psychological portrait. Of a fair number of provocative articles that support this thesis, Alex Zwerdling's "Esther Summerson Rehabilitated"[6] is, to my mind, by far the most convincing. Zwerdling responds directly to Harvey's "clear window" argument: "We are asked to look very much *at* Esther rather than through her, to observe her actions, her fantasies, even her verbal mannerisms with great attention."[7] Proceeding with just such careful attention to all these aspects of personality, he shows us an Esther who has deep inner conflicts and who has adopted "self-denigration" as her "essential life-style."[8] Unlike many other readers, he does not believe that Esther resolves these conflicts by the end of the novel. Yet because he thinks Dickens is being consciously clinical in portraying her, he finds one glaring inconsistency: "I have tried to show how psychologically plausible Dickens' portrait is, but there is one crucial fact this analysis has ignored: that a child brought up in a totally loveless home, as Esther was, is almost surely doomed to grow up unable to love anyone. Yet Esther is an open, affectionate, thoroughly responsive person."[9] Here Dickens' realism, he concludes, is sacrificed for his myth of the innocent child.

I believe that Zwerdling grasps Esther's essential personality and also that he correctly identifies a tension in *Bleak House* between theme and mimesis. However, he is wrong, I think, in his assertion that this tension produces elements of inconsistent characterization. His numerous insights into Esther's conflicts remain fragmented and incomplete for want of an adequate psychological model; and it is this much-needed model that Karen Horney's theory can provide. In the following study, I will use her psychology to explain an Esther who only *seems* (not *is*) genuinely open and loving. I will argue for a thoroughly consistent character, created with intuitive accuracy rather than with clinical consciousness. The tension between myth and realism appears, I feel, not in faulty characterization but in unrealistic plotting and thematic confusion, problems which may also be helpfully illuminated by Horneyan criticism.

Translating Zwerdling's "self-denigration as life-style" into Horney's terms, I propose that Esther has adopted a self-effacing solution as her major defensive strategy. I shall show, first of all, how the basic anxiety that she develops in her unhappy childhood causes her to reach out frantically for love and therefore to make those initial extreme and rigid moves toward other people that mark the beginning of compliant behavior. I shall then explain how this early development becomes part of a pride system, a "search for glory" that leaves her as deeply disturbed, in her own way, as Richard, Tulkinghorn, or Lady Dedlock are in theirs. This search for glory includes a fantasy of vindictive triumph which Esther shares with her author; I shall discuss how this fantasy colors her narrative, affects her relationships, and replaces growth toward self-realization. Finally, I shall use the Horneyan method as a way of understanding the implied author and his conflicts, trying, as I do so, both to look at him honestly and to appreciate his profoundly human struggle more fully.

1

Karen Horney's psychological theory begins with the presupposition that each human being possesses unique potentialities, a *real self*, and is capable of healthy self-realization provided he is fortunate enough to find a warm, secure environment in which to grow. If, however, he is surrounded by adults who are absorbed in their own conflicts to the point where they can neither love him nor even see him as an individual, he will experience his environment as hostile and himself as isolated and helpless. Horney uses the term *basic anxiety* for the "profound insecurity and vague apprehensiveness" that are felt when "the child does not develop a feeling of belonging, of 'we'."[10] In the face of this intolerable anxiety, a child first abandons his real feelings and unconsciously looks for defensive strategies with which to handle his hostile world.

Esther Summerson, according to the opening pages of her narrative, is given the most damaging message any child can receive: she should not have been allowed to exist. An illegitimate child, she is raised in strict secrecy by a stern, unloving aunt. Miss Barbary, acting out of a Calvinistic sense of duty, comes to regard herself as a suffering martyr and Esther as a living symbol of sin, the object of her offended morality and bitter resentment. On the traumatic occasion of the child's uncelebrated birthday, she declares: " 'It would have been far better, little Esther, that you had had no birthday; that you had never been born!' "[11] Instead of freedom to grow as a unique individual, the aunt offers Esther a life of " 'submission, self-denial, diligent work' " (p. 13) as a means by which she can perhaps earn her right to be.

The child Esther feels isolated, guilty, and worthless to the point of becoming dangerously withdrawn. Her only sense of "we" is found in confiding to her doll because "I was such a shy little thing that I seldom dared to open my lips, and never dared to open my heart, to anybody else" (p. 11). She repeatedly wonders why she is "so different" from others and concludes that she must be morally and mentally inferior to them. When the aunt forbids any socializing with schoolmates, Esther thinks her sense of separation from other children is caused by "their being far more clever than I was, and knowing much more than I did" (p. 12). This same insecurity is present in the older narrator, who declares, "I have a great deal of difficulty in beginning to write my portion of these pages, for I know I am not clever" and who keeps apologizing for being in the story at all, promising, "But my little body will soon fall into the background now" (pp. 11, 20).

Esther's tendency to relieve her anxiety by moving toward others in a compliant and clinging way is first seen in her relationship to her aunt. She regards the self-righteous Miss Barbary as a "good, good woman" and concludes that the lack of love between them must be the result of her own badness: "I felt so different from her, even making every allowance for the differences between a child and a woman; I felt so poor, so trifling, and so far off" (p. 12). Instead of showing, or even letting herself feel, any hostility, she appeases this threatening adult by being as submissive and diligent as is demanded. With the dying aunt and with the uncaring housekeeper, Mrs. Rachael, she displays profuse affection for those who have always treated her so coldly: "Mrs. Rachael was too good to feel any emotion at parting, but I was not so good, and wept bitterly. . . . I felt so miserable and self-reproachful, that I clung to her and told her it was my fault, I knew, that she could say goodbye so easily!" (p. 17). What at first reads as an ironic contrast between a child's natural affection and an adult's hard-heartedness is better understood as Esther's indiscriminate and guilt-ridden bid for love, and as a defense against the anger and blame that she would much more naturally feel in this situation.

Long before her aunt's death, Esther strikes a bargain with her fate that will henceforth govern every aspect of her behavior. She repeats over and over to her doll "that I would try, as hard as ever I could, to repair the fault I had been born with . . . and would strive as I grew up to be industrious, contented, and kind-hearted, and to do some good to some one, and win some love to myself if I could" (pp. 13–14). This is Esther's project throughout the novel. On the surface it appears to be a modest goal and one that is achieved miraculously well. First at boarding school, then in the home of her guardian, and finally as the wife of Allan Woodcourt, she is surrounded by a circle of admirers who feel she has earned their love and respect. " 'You do not know,' " says Allan as he proposes to her, " 'what all around you see in Esther Summerson, how many hearts she touches and awakens, what sacred admiration and what love she wins' " (p. 630). As far as the plot is concerned, fate, in the hands of the implied author, honors her bargain and rewards her efforts. She seems to outgrow the past and find her true identity through love.

It is the appeal of love that beguiles Esther, her friends, her readers, and even her author into mistaking self-effacement for self-realization. Love may, of course, be a genuine emotion and a positive value. But for the compliant person love tends to become an over-valued and confused concept, synonymous with a helpless dependency on others (*NHG*, p. 215) and with compulsive self-sacrifice and suffering (*NHG*, pp. 220, 225). It lacks the spontaneity, depth, and sincerity of feelings and values that originate in the real self (*NHG*, p. 165). Esther does not learn to love from the vital core of her being; she begins with the belief that, because she is unworthy of love, she must make herself into a good and loving being. Love is something for which she must constantly strive, under the direction of a set of powerful inner dictates which Horney calls "the tyranny of the should" (*NHG*, p. 65).

Esther achieves her two everyday virtues, dutifulness and cheerfulness, under the rigid command of her "shoulds." Both qualities are essential to her bargain: she *must* be dutiful to obtain love and keep it, and she *must* be cheerful to prove to herself that she has it. She must never, through a single neglected effort or even a momentary despondency, appear ungrateful to those who love her. She has a habit of addressing herself at moments when special effort is needed: " 'Once more, duty, duty, Esther,' said I; 'and if you are not overjoyed to do it, more than cheerfully and contentedly, through anything and everything, you ought to be' " (p. 407). That dictating voice is irrational; it disregards feasibility and realistic conditions for the fulfillment of its commands (*NHG*, p. 66). It also operates with a total disregard for the person's psychic condition (*NHG*, p. 67). Whenever Esther is sad or depressed, she can expect a sharp self-rebuke: "For I naturally said, 'Esther! You be low-spirited. *You!*' And it really was time to say so, for I—Yes, I really did see myself in the glass, almost crying. 'As if you had anything to make you unhappy, instead of everything to make you happy, you ungrateful heart!' said I" (p. 179).

As far as the inner dictates are concerned, nothing is impossible for oneself (*NHG*, p. 68). When Jarndyce cautions Esther, not long after her illness, that her daily trips to London to help Caddy will prove exhausting, she replies, " 'Not for me, dear Guardian . . . for I never feel tired' " (p. 516). But what human being can be always content, always busy, never depressed or fatigued? Esther is far from being her genuine self, which would be, among other things, a self fulfilled within realistic human limitations. Instead, she insists on believing that she can be, with ceaseless effort, a paragon of spotless conduct, steadfast good nature, and unfailing gratitude. Her virtues are humble, but they mask, as her more negative critics have always suspected, a subtle and insidious pride.

Esther's pride is more difficult to spot than that, say, of a Lady Dedlock because, as a self-effacing person who equates love with submissiveness and selflessness, she must have taboos on all aggressive and selfish impulses (*NHG*, p. 216). Pride is always present and yet must be constantly shunned and denied. Esther even apologizes for the possibility of unconscious pride: "I have mentioned, that, unless my vanity should deceive me (as I know it may, for I may be very vain, without suspecting it—though indeed I don't), my comprehension is quickened when my affection is" (p. 12). The language here suggests that this apology is not just excessive humility; her "yes—maybe—no" vacillation indicates that she is dimly aware of a submerged conflict. Her pride is largely unconscious, and yet it is often expressed in indirect ways that even she finds disturbing. When she apologizes for mentioning herself ("I mean all the time to write about other people, and I try to think about myself as little as possible" [p. 85]), she suspects, and the reader knows, that she is actually thinking of herself a great deal.

Since her taboo on pride allows her neither to acknowledge her expansive impulses nor even to believe in her real accomplishments, Esther's hunger for self-esteem is fed by the recognition she receives from other persons, which she can allow herself to accept if she calls it "love." Personal praise is recorded in a tone of guilty enjoyment: "Well! It was only their love for me, I know very well. . . . I must write it, even if I rub it out again, because it gives me so much pleasure. They said there could be no East wind where Somebody was; they said that wherever Dame Durden went, there was sunshine and summer air" (p. 324). Sometimes she experiences a commendation even more indirectly by converting it into a virtue of the giver, as when Ada first praises her: "My simple darling! She was quite unconscious that she only praised herself, and that it was in the goodness of her own heart that she made so much of me!" (p. 32).

As she receives more and more such praise for her devotion to others, Esther begins to speak of a "conspiracy" to keep her happy and good-humored. The word suggests multiple unconscious meanings: denial that the praise is deserved, suspicion of the real motives of others, a fantasy that others are taking an extraordinary interest in her, and also an oblique admission that she needs special efforts to keep her happy. We begin to see the inconsistency that points unmistakably to her conflict—she feels simultaneously exalted and oppressed, undeservedly happy and secretly miserable. Her original solution to her basic anxiety has grown into a fantastic system that leaves her torn apart and constantly vulnerable to the very terrors she has sought so desperately to avoid.

2

When Esther leaves her childhood home, she attempts to bury her real self as surely as she does her beloved doll. Facing the world with a frighteningly inadequate sense of identity, she creates the false self-image which Horney calls the *idealized self* (*NHG*, p. 23) and begins the hopeless task of molding herself to fit it. For her, this idealized self is an infinitely loving and lovable person, endowed with all the qualities that self-effacing people typically associate with love: "unselfishness, goodness, generosity, humility, saintliness, nobility, sympathy" (*NHG*, p. 222). Unconsciously, out of her deep insecurity and insatiable needs, she desires to perfect these qualities in herself.

Yet the inevitable result of this shift to a false identity is a divided self-image and increased conflict. Esther's quest for perfection makes it certain that she will come to hate the person she actually is and continue to reject the real self that she could be. Since she cannot help but fail to live up to her idealized image and since she incessantly shrinks her self-esteem through her taboos on pride, she still feels like the helpless and worthless being she is trying to lose, while the resulting panic drives her all the more frantically toward her proud self. Therefore two equally unreal and seemingly opposite images, her *idealized self* and her *despised self*, make up a *pride system* that operates in a "vicious circle" of self-glorification and self-contempt (*NHG*, pp. 111, 137).

This structure of Esther's unconscious conflict is remarkably revealed in the dreams she has during her illness. "In dreams," Horney writes, "we are closer to the reality of ourselves" (*NHG*, p. 349). When inactivity and delirium break down her usual defenses, two dreams tell Esther the truth about herself, were she able to understand it.

> I am almost afraid to hint at that time in my disorder—it seemed one long night, but I believe there were both nights and days in it—when I laboured up colossal staircases, ever striving to reach the top, and ever turned, as I have seen a worm in a garden path, by some obstruction, and labouring again. . . . I would find myself complaining "O more of these never-ending stairs, Charley,—more and more—piled up to the sky, I think!" and labouring on again.
>
> Dare I hint at that worse time when, strung together somewhere in great black space, there was a flaming necklace, or ring, or starry circle of some kind, of which *I* was one of the beads! And when my only prayer was to be taken off from the rest, and when it was such inexplicable agony and misery to be a part of the dreadful thing? (p. 370)

She cannot, of course, read her dream symbols, though she longs to, musing: "It may be that if we knew more of such strange afflictions, we might be the better able to alleviate their intensity" (p. 370).

Self-idealization is an attempt to escape isolation and helplessness by lifting oneself *above* others (*NHG*, p. 21). Horney calls this effort "the search for glory," and she finds it in every neurosis: "All the drives for glory have in common the reaching out for greater knowledge, wisdom, virtue, or powers than are given to human beings; they all aim at the *absolute,* the unlimited, the infinite" (*NHG,* p. 34). In his own mind, the individual achieves godlike power and a cosmic significance. The most striking feature of Esther's dreams is the cosmic imagery: she must climb stairs piled to the sky to reach her destination, she is part of a starry circle high above the earth. The goals that appear so modest and realistic in everyday life ("I thought it best to be as useful as I could . . . and to try to let that circle of duty gradually and naturally expand itself" [p. 80]) are accurately seen in the dreams as endeavors to place herself high above other people and assume a godlike responsibility for others.

In her dreams, however, as in her waking life, Esther *feels* more like her despised self than her idealized self. She is a plodding little being, trying to reach the top and never making it. She associates this with being *like a worm* that is forever encountering obstacles and having to crawl around them. And supposing she did reach the top, what would it be like? In the second dream, we sense a repressed response to the compulsive circle of duty, as though her imagination projects her present life into an eternity of angelic servitude and finds it a hell. The dream also speaks of her perpetual fear of her own pride, which would make the very attainment of her desire a torture. The "starry circle" reminds us of the "vicious circle" of pride and self-hatred, the painful dilemma of a person who is caught "between having to reach the peak and having to keep himself down" (*NHG,* p. 318).

Finally, the dreams offer Esther a potentially constructive insight. They let her feel just how oppressive her compulsive activity really is; they suggest that she should break out of this vicious circle that is both higher and lower than the fully human. The central inner conflict, Horney came to realize, is not the one between the false selves but the one between the entire pride system and the real self (*NHG,* p. 368). Dreams show just how accurately our every thought or action "registers"—they testify to a sense of the real self that can be deeply buried but never entirely destroyed. Esther's psyche is still capable of a healthy protest; but the protest goes unheeded when, after her illness, she adheres more rigidly than ever to her usual defenses.

Esther's proud and despised selves do not confine their fantastic role-playing to her dream life. As her idealized self, for example, she often tries to be the perfect mother, even though she is not one, has no model for such a role, and yearns herself for the mother she lacked in childhood. This endeavor is pathetic, but it is also extremely successful in terms of her solution because it appeals to other people's needs and therefore does win "love." The children at the boarding school, the orphans Ada and Richard, and Mrs. Jellyby's unfortunate offspring are the objects of her unfailing devotion and reward her with appropriately childlike affection. Her other group of admirers consists of lonely men: Mr. Boythorn, Mr. George, John Jarndyce, and Allan Woodcourt. The fatherly Jarndyce makes her his surrogate helpmate, a confusing role that encourages her to assume infinite parental responsibilities while at the same time she feels herself to be his dependent child.

Esther's friends have their own idealized view of her and thus unwittingly contribute to her fantasies. They even use cosmic symbols in praising her: she is to sweep the cobwebs from their sky (p. 74); she is the sunshine of their lives (p. 324). Their "sacred admiration" (p. 630) elevates her to a kind of sainthood, perhaps yet another self-image symbolized by the starry circle of her dream. (Is she part of the circle of the blessed? Will there be stars in her crown?) In many respects she is, apart from her realistic characterization, the Victorian ideal of the angel in the home; and we must continue to suspect the implied author of participating in this fantasy. He, after all, chose to call her Esther Summerson (summer sun).

There is, nevertheless, an ambiguity in Esther's situation at Bleak House. The same friends who encourage her to be her ideal self also contribute to her sense of being her despised self. Although she is always treated as a daughter or a partner by Jarndyce and as a sister by Ada and Richard, still the position of housekeeper indicates a servant role; and there is an unspoken assumption that as an illegitimate child she must be content to be the helpful spinster in someone else's home. As she starts her duties, she calls herself "a methodical, old-maidish sort of foolish little person" (p. 70) in a self-disparaging description that is soon reinforced by the nicknames her friends give her. After telling how Jarndyce likens her to the little old woman who will sweep the clouds out of the sky, she adds: "This was the beginning of my being called Old Woman, and Little Old Woman, and Cobweb, and Mrs. Shipton, and Mother Hubbard, and Dame Durden, and so many names of that sort, *that my own name soon became quite lost among them*" (p. 74, my emphasis). William Axton, in his excellent study of these nicknames, has pointed out how they deny Esther's individual identity and how, with their uniform references to witches, hags, and comic old dames, they reinforce her fears of being forever worthless, repulsive, and unloved.[12]

A further example of the conflict between pride and self-contempt is seen in Esther's attitude toward her physical appearance. Though she claims after her illness, "I had never been a beauty, and had never thought myself one" (p. 382), the indirect evidence contradicts her perception. The fact that in both face and figure she bears a striking resemblance to her handsome, aristocratic mother, Lady Dedlock, plays an important part in the plot and is immediately obvious to outsiders like her admirer, Mr. Guppy. She is not, then, merely pretty, but has much the same beauty and carriage that enable her mother to triumph in fashionable society. We may infer from her rather numerous references to mirrors and from her pleased denial when Allan assures her she is " 'prettier than . . . ever' " (p. 665) that she sometimes contemplates her appearance with guilty pride. When she first sees her mother's face, she experiences a shock of recognition as she vaguely associates it with her own (pp. 190–91). This is the closest she ever comes, however, to consciously acknowledging the likeness between them. Dame Durden, the despised illegitimate child, cannot believe herself beautiful and thus eligible for romantic love. Moreover, the pride of beauty must look like the most dangerous of temptations to Esther, the very one that led to the sinful act which gave her birth. The resignation with which she meets her eventual disfigurement is telling; for her scars, the visible marks of her shame, seem to ease her conflict by deciding it in favor of the despised self and affording her the safety and satisfaction of being a martyred beauty.

From the reader's point of view, Esther's rejection of her intelligence is particularly important because of all the implications for her role as narrator. Once we realize that the denial of her good mind, through the endless repetition of "I am not clever," is yet another act of self-disparagement, we are rescued, at least, from taking her own evaluation seriously. As a mimetic character and not merely the glass through which Dickens' own intelligence shines, she has the gifts of alert observation and potentially keen perception that make a good storyteller. And these very gifts expose her to the greatest of all her dangers: that she may destroy her own defense system by seeing and knowing too much.

Esther admits that she developed a habit of observation during her isolated childhood: "I had always rather a noticing way—not a quick way, O no!—a silent way of noticing what passed before me, and thinking I should like to understand it better. I have not by any means a quick understanding. When I love a person very tenderly indeed, it seems to brighten. But even that may be my vanity" (p. 11). She compartmentalizes her intelligence by carefully separating "noticing" from "understanding," keeping love as the magic power which will allow her some limited insight under safe circumstances. In her narrative she is, in many ways, very much a person "on whom nothing is lost." But when what she is seeing begins to become threatening, she unconsciously refuses to understand. There is no real contradiction between a perceptive Esther and a confused Esther; the confusion always occurs right at the point where her most accurate insights begin to emerge. For example, when Allan Woodcourt's mother is overly nice to her and yet keeps dropping hints about the importance of good birth, Esther is "uncomfortable."

> She was such a sharp little lady, and used to sit with her hands folded in each other, looking so very watchful while she talked to me that perhaps I found that rather irksome. Or perhaps it was her being so upright and trim; though I don't think it was that, because I thought that quaintly pleasant. Nor can it have been the general expression of her face, which was very sparkling and pretty for an old lady. I don't know what it was. Or at least if I do, now, I thought I did not then. Or at least—but it don't matter. (p. 313)

How much pride, guilt, and hostility would surface here if Esther consciously admitted what is going on!

In one of the most recent studies of Esther's character, Judith Wilt "proposes to explore the possibilities of strategic confusion, Esther's resourceful refusal to close in on judgment."[13] She views such confusion as a source of "fruitful power": "Esther holds fast to her Confusion, lest fear or anger or frustration or condemnation subvert her other, major power, her Affection."[14] Wilt thus correctly identifies confusion as one of Esther's main defenses but, in placing all the evil outside the character, essentially "buys into" her solution: a wronged but innocent woman who shuts her eyes to everything but love will both survive and transform a corrupt world. This is indeed how Esther idealizes herself, and this novel will always tempt its readers to participate in that fantasy.

The Horneyan critic, however, in all sympathy for Esther's problems, must call the god Confusion simply "muddled thinking" that is designed to "befog" this character's conflicts so that she will not have to face them squarely (*NHG*, p. 335). Such confusion helps preserve Esther's equilibrium and keep her solution from collapsing (*NHG*, p. 180); it certainly defends her against tensions she is unable to handle. But like all fears of knowing, it is, in the long run, a destructive process. Its healthy opposite is an openness to experience—to the inner self and to the world around one[15]—that an Esther will never have unless she can outgrow her pride system.

3

Esther narrates her story with a confused vision of reality in a novel that takes confusion, the fog in which humanity gropes and flounders, as one of its main themes. Nevertheless this does not mean that Dickens, in his desire to dispel confusion, handles his narrator either clinically or ironically. Seeing more than she does, he knows that she is a victim of injustice and that she suffers; apparently he does not see that she is as psychologically damaged as a Richard or a Harold Skimpole. Like many of his readers, the implied author mistakes the self-effacing solution, which adapts to defensive purposes such Christian values as sympathy, selflessness, and humility, for spontaneous goodness. His plot is a fantasy in which he manipulates fate to reward Esther's suffering and to allow her an innocent revenge.

A major element in the search for glory is the drive toward a vindictive triumph. Karen Horney uses the term "vindictiveness" for those impulses which have as their chief aim the desire to put others to shame and to make them suffer. She emphasizes that all such vindictiveness stems from the need to take revenge for humiliation experienced in childhood (*NHG*, pp. 26–27). We should not be surprised, provided we are willing to grant him his own human conflicts, to find that an author so preoccupied with early humiliations cherishes a fantasy of vindictive triumph over parental oppressors and the hostile human environment. He gives Esther similar impulses, consistently portraying her as the self-effacing person for whom "vindictive drives remain unconscious and can only be expressed indirectly and in a disguised form" (*NHG*, p. 219). Once again the characterization is flawless, but the handling of theme and plot implies that Dickens cannot interpret Esther's subtle vindictiveness objectively because he identifies too closely with her role as deprived child.

For signs of Esther's vindictiveness, we should note particularly the irony in her narrative, a tone ranging from the mildly humorous or mischievous to the wry and sardonic. The irony itself is not entirely unconscious: Esther may deliver satirical comments from behind a mask of innocence, express half-conscious amusement at disturbing incongruities, or even, in rare moments of aroused indignation, voice totally conscious ironic judgments. Vindictive intent, however, is an attitude she never knowingly assumes. As the common blind spot of character and author, the self-effacing solution frees her to ridicule "innocently" those do-gooders and parasites whose expansive and detached solutions appear so irresponsible compared to her own. The most frequent objects of her irony also classify as negligent parents—Mrs. Pardiggle, Mrs. Jellyby, Mr. Turveydrop. When ironic vision becomes too threatening for her defenses, she often retreats into sentimentality, focusing exclusive attention on neglected children and other downtrodden victims.

The account of Mrs. Pardiggle and the visit to the brickmaker's is an excellent example of the typical pattern of Esther's irony. Mrs. Pardiggle, a formidable and humorless do-gooder who takes great pride in her compulsive religious activities, is a woman who would surely arouse Esther's unconscious resentment by reminding her of her aunt. Through an ostensibly self-effacing apology for not being equally active in charitable projects, Esther condemns Mrs. Pardiggle and exalts herself.

> I then said . . . that I had not that delicate knowledge of the heart which must be essential to such a work. That I had much to learn, myself, before I could teach others, and that I could not confide to my good intentions alone. For these reasons I thought it best to be as useful as I could, and to render what kind services I could, to those immediately around me; and to try to let that circle of duty gradually and naturally expand itself. All this I said, with anything but confidence; because Mrs. Pardiggle was much older than I, and had great experience, and was so very military in her manners. (p. 80)

Secure in her moral superiority, the narrator now enjoys a series of ironic gibes. She offers a caustic description of the oppressed Pardiggle children: "I never underwent so much, both in body and mind, in the course of a walk with young people, as from those unnaturally constrained children when they paid me the compliment of being natural" (p. 80). Telling of the scene at the brickmaker's, she dares a satirical metaphor with the wordy and self-conscious delight of one unaccustomed to drawing such comparisons: "Mrs. Pardiggle . . . took the whole family into custody. I mean into religious custody, of course; but she really did it, as if she were an inexorable moral Policeman carrying them all off to a station-house" (p. 82). She even sympathizes with the husband's anger and sarcasm, and acutely observes Mrs. Pardiggle's "forcible composure, calculated, I could not help thinking, to increase his antagonism" (p. 82). But with her taboos on assertive action, this is as close as she dares come to the darker ironies of social injustice implicit in the scene. With the death of the baby, the attack on Mrs. Pardiggle gives way to a sentimental recollection of Ada's tears.

Similar combinations of irony and sentimentality are found in the descriptions of the Jellyby family, only here, because the relationships are more intimate, Esther's irony tends to be more indirect and anxious. For the most part, she silently condemns Mrs. Jellyby's lack of mothering by taking upon herself the care of Caddy and Peepy. When a bluntly ironic response does surface, it is pointedly a secret thought shared only with the reader: "It struck me that if Mrs. Jellyby had discharged her own natural duties and obligations, before she swept the horizon with a telescope in search of others, she would have taken the best precautions against becoming absurd; but I need scarcely observe that I kept this to myself" (pp. 407–8). When Caddy acquires a parasitic father-in-law, Esther experiences an uneasy enjoyment of someone else's vindictiveness: " 'The airs the fellow gives himself!' said my informant, shaking her head at old Mr. Turveydrop with speechless indignation as he drew on his tight gloves. . . . 'O!' said the old lady, apostrophising him with infinite vehemence, 'I could bite you!' I could not help being amused, though I heard the old lady out with feelings of real concern" (p. 146). Subsequently, Caddy's blind obedience and self-sacrifice in Mr. Turveydrop's home have Esther's blessing: "And if there seemed to be but a slender chance of her and her husband ever finding out what the model of Deportment really was, why that was all for the best too, and who would wish them to be wiser? I did not wish them to be any wiser, and indeed was half ashamed of not entirely believing him myself" (pp. 254–55). Esther could encourage Caddy's rebellion against her mother because it was motivated by the girl's love for Prince, but now she regards submission to an equally foolish parent as the sacrifice necessary to protect that love. She has guided her friend to the self-effacing solution; like Esther, Caddy is now free to be cheerfully overworked.

Esther's sentimentality is not surprising from one who overvalues love; it is the appropriate tone for her expressions of excessive sympathy and gratitude. It may also mask hostility and resentment. We find ambivalence, for example, in her accounts of her most sentimental relationship, her attachment to her friend Ada Clare. As a character, Ada is poorly developed; we know only that she is a beautiful golden girl in whom Esther claims to see nothing but goodness and truth. Through idealizing her, Esther externalizes and most fully experiences her own idealized image. She endows Ada with angelic beauty and virtue and vicariously participates in the girl's pure and selfless love for Richard. Ada is unreal in the narrative because, instead of being a true Other, a living and separate self, she is more like Esther's old doll, a possession that can become daughter, sister, or mother according to its owner's needs. After her disfigurement, especially, Esther needs to preserve her idealized fantasies through Ada and feel accepted by this projection of her "best" self, which is why their emotional reunion is so important to her: "O how happy I was, down upon the floor, with my sweet beautiful girl down upon the floor too, holding my scarred face to her lovely cheek . . . and pressing me to her faithful heart" (p. 392).

Yet Ada also plays a part in Esther's continuing humiliation. As Alex Zwerdling points out, although Esther is almost as young and quite as beautiful as her friend, no one for a moment thinks of her, the illegitimate, as a match for Richard.[16] She begins her involvement in the Ada-Richard romance—as helper, confidante, the "maiden aunt" of their future home—with depression and inexplicable tears (p. 179). Because she thinks of Ada as an inseparable part of herself, she can avoid having to confront her beloved friend as a rival. The crisis comes when Ada acts like a separate self by secretly marrying Richard. Her departure leaves Esther stunned and incomplete: "O how I cried! It almost seemed to me that I had lost my Ada for ever. I was so lonely and so blank without her" (p. 529). Here, as so often happens, the narrator stops just short of a significant insight when she wonders why she misinterpreted Ada's sadness as grief over her own secretly regretted engagement to Jarndyce: "How I persuaded myself that this was likely, I don't know. I had no idea that there was any selfish reference in my doing so. I was not grieved for myself; I was quite contented and quite happy" (p. 520). It is a fertile moment for realizing that she has seen this other person only in the light of her own needs.

Instead, the implied author allows Esther to evade even the limited growth of learning to live without her alter ego. In the end, the girls switch places in what proves to be one of several vindictive triumphs for the heroine: Ada, the widow, returns to live with Jarndyce, while Esther, the predestined spinster, is the one to marry and live happily ever after. The outcome is satisfying to Esther in every respect.

> I think my darling girl is more beautiful than ever. The sorrow that has been in her face—for it is not there now—seems to have purified even its innocent expression, and to have given it a diviner quality. Sometimes, when I raise my eyes and see her in the black dress that she still wears, teaching my Richard, I feel—it is difficult to express—as if it were so good to know that she remembers her dear Esther in her prayers. (p. 665)

Ada is thus permanently enshrined as the image of innocence purified through suffering. Esther continues to disregard the boundaries between them; and with her "*my* Richard," she appropriates for herself the one thing of Ada's that she still lacks, a son.

Her failure to change in this relationship is only one of many signs that Esther does not outgrow her conflicts by the end of the novel. Careful observation does not support claims that she becomes a "fully integrated person" through her ability to "confront evil, grapple with it, and emerge victorious"[17] or that her "final recognition of her mother liberates her from the self-effacing role she chose as a child."[18] Instead of openly acknowledging the discovery of her parents and facing the implications of that discovery for her personal identity, she exonerates herself through her suffering, which for the self-effacing person is the most acceptable way of expressing vindictiveness (*NHG*, p. 235).

The revelatory scene with Lady Dedlock occurs just as Esther is trying to adjust to her disfigurement. On the surface the meeting is sentimental; two strangers are united at once by the "natural" love of mother and child. But beneath the sentimental rhetoric, Esther experiences a flood of resentment as she listens to her mother's voice, "so unfamiliar and so melancholy to me; which in my childhood I had never learned to love and recognise, had never been sung to sleep with, had never heard a blessing from, had never had a hope inspired by" (p. 388). She finds some satisfaction in learning from her mother's letter that she was not knowingly abandoned. Then her new knowledge reawakens all her old anxiety, and she is overcome with self-hatred.

> I hope it may not appear very unnatural or bad in me, that I then became heavily sorrowful to think I had ever been reared. That I felt as if I knew it would have been better and happier for many people, if indeed I had never breathed. That I had a terror of myself, as the danger and the possible disgrace of my own mother, and of a proud family name. That I was so confused and shaken, as to be possessed by a belief that it was right, and had been intended, that I should die in my birth; and that it was wrong, and not intended, that I should be then alive. (p. 389)

These were her "real feelings," she tells us, but she now avoids any reference to anger at her parents. As her despised self she bears all the blame, to the point of suicidal despair.

What follows is a reaffirmation of her solution that testifies anew to its ingenuity as a defensive system. To alleviate her self-contempt, she considers that her fate—her happy life and the way things have "worked together" for her—proves her right to be; and she renews her resolutions, her old bargain with that fate. As always she opposes the despised self with a glorified image: "I knew I was as innocent of my birth as a queen of hers" (p. 391). Most significantly, she recalls once more her "comforting reconcilements" (p. 391) to her disfigurement. With her scars to evoke the Christian myth as a powerful support for the transformation of the despised self, she goes humbly forth to live for others in self-denial and willing suffering, carrying her mother's shameful secret like a cross: "It was a weight to bear alone; still my present duty appeared plain" (p. 392).

From this point on, Esther says little about her parents. When she accompanies Bucket on the search for her missing mother, the journey is dreamlike; and there is no recorded affect when she finds her mother dead. Her father she never specifically mentions, though by now the reader knows a good deal about him. We are left to contemplate the process by which the Dickens version of fate, as it draws the dying Lady Dedlock to Captain Hawdon's grave, avenges their innocent and forsaken child, while that child turns away to pay yet another tribute to the love of her friends (p. 615). The novel continues beyond that point to reward her innocence, not to integrate her experience.

The climax of Esther's personal story, according to William Axton, "centers on a choice between lovers."[19] But Esther does not choose, and her inability to do so is still further evidence of her lack of healthy growth. As a compliant person, she surrenders her freedom of choice to others, giving them the right to control her destiny. She becomes, in her own mind, too indebted to her guardian, John Jarndyce, and too dependent on his fatherly protection, ever to oppose him.

Jarndyce, a gentle and eccentric man, is another predominantly self-effacing character. It is his humble refusal ever to accept thanks for his acts of charity that makes things especially difficult for Esther. When she arrives at Bleak House, she already feels deeply indebted to him for providing her schooling, but his attitude makes it almost impossible for her to express it. The more he multiplies his kindnesses to her in the course of the novel, the more her gratitude becomes a burden. After he has comforted her about the discovery of her mother, she wonders, "how could I ever be busy enough, how could I ever be good enough, how in my little way could I ever be forgetful enough of myself, devoted enough to him, and useful enough to others, to show him how I blessed and honoured him" (p. 460). Therefore when, shortly after this, he proposes to her, it is as if he has suddenly sent the big bill, and what can Esther do but pay? "Still I cried very much . . . as if something for which there was no name or distinct idea were indefinitely lost to me. I was very happy, very thankful, very hopeful; but I cried very much" (p. 463). When Allan Woodcourt, unaware of the secret engagement, also proposes, she is conscious of her love for him but has no idea that she might act from it; it does not remotely occur to her to ask Jarndyce to release her.

The *deus ex machina* that rescues her is Jarndyce himself. He outdoes her in self-effacement and gives her up when he realizes the true state of things, exacting as the only price for his sacrifice a period of time in which he can play God. As the author's instrument for rewarding Esther's virtue, he makes all her decisions for her, surprises her with a home furnished to all her tastes, and hands her over to Allan and happiness. Jarndyce and the author also see to it that she gets a vindictive triumph over those who have openly insulted her. Mr. Guppy, who injured her pride with a proposal of marriage and then hastily retreated when she was disfigured, comes with his mother in tow to renew his offer, only to be sent away looking more ridiculous than ever. Allan's mother, who, in her pride of lineage, despised Esther's illegitimacy, is now forced to sit on the sidelines and watch how "completely . . . entirely . . . religiously" Esther will sacrifice her love for Allan "to a sense of duty and affection." Self-effacement, equated with innocence, is thus made a proof of "true legitimacy" (p. 650).

With Allan, the dark young physician, Esther fulfills her desire to merge as much as possible with the beloved one and experience her pride through him: "The people even praise Me as the doctor's wife. The people even like Me as I go about, and make so much of me that I am quite abashed. I owe it all to him, my love, my pride! They like me for his sake, as I do everything I do in life for his sake" (p. 665). She continues to live only through others, subjecting herself to them and yet clutching them possessively. If *my* dearest pets, *my* darling, *my* husband, *my* guardian are beautiful, she asks in her closing words, what does my own beauty matter?

4

We are often guilty of critical *hybris,* Michael Steig has recently reminded us, when, having psychoanalyzed a text, we insist the author was unconscious of its implications. We grant, from the very nature of our work, that "the text knows." "Yet when the text is so aware of what it is doing, do we not lack humility if we insist that *we* know things about Dickens' art of which he himself was unconscious?"[20] In the case of *Bleak House,* I reply that the text both knows and does not know; it tells us the truth about Esther, but it lies about her as well. It is this internal evidence of conflict, of an implied author not "in harmony with himself,"[21] that interests the Horneyan critic. Though his is a waking fantasy, Dickens is to his novel much as Esther is to her dream: we see conflict symbolized and can perhaps identify the germ of a healthy solution, but there is nothing to assure us that the implied psyche knows what it knows in a way that can resolve the conflict. What Dickens the man may have learned from his own novel we cannot, from *Bleak House* alone, presume to judge.

Northrop Frye writes that with Dickens' use of the New Comedy plot, "the comic action . . . moves toward the regrouping of society around the only social unit that Dickens really regards as genuine, the family."[22] But a new society crystallized around Esther, in her "rustic cottage of doll's rooms" (p. 648) that is the new Bleak House, is far from satisfying even before we begin to scrutinize her self-effacing values. Once we demonstrate that she is not a reliable source of goodness and virtue, we are left with two alternatives: either we accept Ellen Serlen's suggestion that Dickens offers us a "bleak and sordid reality" "under the protective cover of scathing irony"[23]; or else we follow Bernard Paris's lead and grant that even a great novel like *Bleak House* may contain a disparity between "the implied author's attitudes toward the experience that he represents" and "the novel's total body of represented life."[24] I believe that our best evidence supports the latter position.

Bleak House, we all know, has another narrative voice that we have thus far ignored. This other narrator sees and knows far more than Esther does. He is capable of a prophetic challenge like the one that follows his account of Jo's death: "Dead, your majesty. Dead, my lords and gentlemen. Dead, Right Reverends and Wrong Reverends of every order. Dead, men and women, born with Heavenly compassion in your hearts. And dying thus around us every day" (p. 492). Actually this passage is quite exceptional, but it is so memorable and epitomizes the narrator's vision so perfectly that few readers disagree about its effect on the whole novel—*Bleak House* cries out for justice and demands social action. How can we doubt that the juxtaposition of this vision and Esther's narrow, confused perspective was intended to make her look pathetic, if not absurd?

The problem is that the demand for assertive action is never met in the novel, nor can we see how it possibly could be. Though he displays expansive impulses, the implied author seems to fear expansiveness quite as much as Esther does. He understands neurotic pride as it manifests itself in the expansive solution exceedingly well; he also punishes it without mercy by making sure that each of its victims is either comically ridiculed or tragically destroyed. Tulkinghorn, the arrogant-vindictive villain, and Richard, the narcissistic hero, are both understood, and doomed, in terms of their search for glory. Expansiveness in women, in any form that takes one beyond the confines of the home, is strictly condemned: Lady Dedlock sought social triumph, and no power on earth can save her; Mrs. Jellyby and Mrs. Pardiggle, those "women with a mission," are foolish and dangerous, a root of the evil that creates unhappy childhoods.

Most disturbingly, those characters who attempt to exercise active control over their lives in more positive ways are also doomed to failure. Gridley dies because he insists on his rights in court instead of detaching himself from legal conflicts as John Jarndyce does. Mr. George dares to leave his mother and very nearly perishes before, in middle age, he is safely restored to her arms. Attempts have been made to defend Inspector Bucket, but I continue to find the argument that he is actually characterized as one more "passive-aggressive manipulator" more convincing.[25] Even if he is not, Hortense's scoffing questions—" 'But can you res-tore him back to life? . . . Can you make a honourable lady of Her?' " (p. 562)—ring true. Bucket's mastery of the situation may expose the evil, but he cannot undo it. If his handling of the Dedlock case leaves us uneasy, we may even suspect that he increases that evil.

Bucket's ambiguity and his dilemma have, in turn, implications for that fictional *persona* commonly called the "omniscient" narrator. As long as he remains safely *above* the world of the novel (the symbolic position, significantly, of the idealized self), he can denounce injustice in godlike tones; but if he descended into the confusion of the action, what would he do about it? The fear that pervades the novel is that no one can act decisively without proving himself, as Bucket does, more devil than angel, or, perhaps worse, simply making himself ridiculous. Caught in his own conflict between compliance and aggression, our implied author is divided and paralyzed. In his nightmare, the powerful prophet floats helplessly in space, while the helpless Esther has the only power on earth.

In *Bleak House,* the fantasy of self-effacing innocence is Dickens' major attempt to resolve this conflict. Again I am indebted to Alex Zwerdling for the implications of the novel's central myth:

> Esther . . . is an example of Dickens' myth of the innocent child, whose goodness must be absolute. Her harsh upbringing can leave her incomplete and vulnerable, but not selfish or corrupt. Dickens' vision of society depends on the idea of victimization, on the absolute separation of the oppressors from the oppressed. That the oppressed can go on to become oppressors in their turn is an example of the sort of pessimistic conclusion his fantasy exists to deny.[26]

We must add, however, that the author is perfectly aware of a negative innocence that may be carried over into adult life; this is clear from his portraits of Harold Skimpole and Mr. Jellyby. What he wants to believe is that we have in Esther, Ada, and Charley the miraculous survival, in some social victims, of the feeling self. A compassionate and responsible innocence, the pure motives of childhood producing quiet but meaningful actions in adult life, then rescues others from among the oppressed. Since Dickens' division of the world into good people and bad people is largely a division between the self-effacing and the expansive solutions, there is no other means of social redemption in his fictional universe.

Charles Dickens saw with great clarity the injustice of a society in which, to survive, nearly all of us reject our real selves; this is the inestimable value of the *Bleak House* vision. By demythologizing self-effacement, Karen Horney's psychology, as this study has demonstrated, calls attention to the blind spot in this vision and presents a strong argument against Dickens' only source of hope. On the other hand, Horney does not deny the goal that Dickens desires. She believes in the original "innocence" of the real self with all its constructive energies; and she also believes that the "lost" self can be found and restored to spontaneous growth (*NHG,* p. 15). She does not, however, offer us any magic preservation of our innocence, nor does she find any value in an injured innocence that fixes the blame on others. The painful and difficult way back to ourselves lies in the opposite direction from the route Esther takes—it is a reorientation through self-knowledge, and only this, which can enable us to give up our pride systems and rediscover our capacities for growth and love.

NOTES

1. Anonymous, "Finding the Real Self," a letter with a foreword by Karen Horney, *American Journal of Psychoanalysis* 9 (1949): 3.

2. "Esther Summerson, Charles Dickens and the Reader of *Bleak House*," *Dickens Studies* 5 (May 1969): 17–20.

3. "Chance and Design in *Bleak House*," in *Dickens, A Collection of Critical Essays*, ed. Martin Price (Englewood Cliffs, N. J.: Prentice Hall, 1967), pp. 139–40.

4. "Structure and Idea in *Bleak House*," *ELH* 29 (1962): 201.

5. *Charles Dickens: Radical Moralist* (Minneapolis: University of Minnesota Press, 1972), pp. 188–89.

6. Alex Zwerdling, "Esther Summerson Rehabilitated," *PMLA* 88 (1973): 429–39.

7. Ibid., p. 429.

8. Ibid., p. 430.

9. Ibid., p. 438.

10. *Neurosis and Human Growth: The Struggle Toward Self-Realization* (New York: Norton, 1950), pp. 17–18. Hereafter cited in the text as *NHG*.

11. Charles Dickens, *Bleak House*, ed. Morton Dauwen Zabel (Boston: Houghton Mifflin, 1956), p. 13. Hereafter cited in the text.

12. "Esther's Nicknames: A Study in Relevance," *The Dickensian* 62 (September 1966): 159–60.

13. "Confusion and Consciousness in Dickens's Esther," *Nineteenth-Century Fiction* 32 (December 1977): 286.

14. Ibid., pp. 293, 294.

15. Bernard J. Paris, *A Psychological Approach to Fiction: Studies in Thackeray, Stendhal, George Eliot, Dostoevsky, and Conrad* (Bloomington: Indiana University Press, 1974), pp. 48–50.

16. Zwerdling, "Esther Summerson Rehabilitated," p. 431.

17. Trevor Blount, "Chancery as Evil and Challenge in *Bleak House*," *Dickens Studies* 1 (September 1965): 119.

18. James H. Broderick and John E. Grant, "The Identity of Esther Summerson," *Modern Philology* 55 (May 1958): 256.

19. "The Trouble With Esther," *Modern Language Quarterly* 26 (December 1965): 547.

20. "Dickens' Characters and Psychoanalytic Criticism," *Hartford Studies in Literature* 8 (1976): 43.

21. Paris, *A Psychological Approach to Fiction*, p. 14.

22. "Dickens and the Comedy of Humors," in *Experience in the Novel*, ed. Roy Harvey Pierce (New York: Columbia University Press, 1968), p. 63.

23. "The Two Worlds of *Bleak House*," *ELH* 43 (1976): 565.

24. Paris, *A Psychological Approach to Fiction*, p. 14.

25. Michael Steig and F. A. C. Wilson, "Hortense Versus Bucket: The Ambiguity of Order in *Bleak House*," *Modern Language Quarterly* 33 (1972): 298.

26. Zwerdling, "Esther Summerson Rehabilitated," p. 438.

6

Browning's Guido: The Self-Fictionalizing Imagination in Crisis

Catherine R. Lewis

Most critics of *The Ring and the Book* agree that Browning wants us to judge Count Guido Franceschini as morally reprehensible; as Honan puts it, Guido "appear[s] to be prejudged by Browning," so that we are "never really left in doubt as to what to think of him."[1] There is far less agreement, however, about the psychological realism of Guido's two monologues, book 5, his testimony at his trial for the murder of his wife Pompilia and her parents, and book 11, his speech to his confessors before his execution. For many, Guido is less a mimetic character than a personification of evil, "the devil incarnate" or a "monster" motivated solely by "love of evil."[2] Their experience supports Fairchild's contention that Browning is "so much the warm-hearted moralizer" in presenting Guido that his usual attention to psychological realism is "supplant[ed]."[3] Other readers, however—notably Roma King—find in these monologues "a human figure" with "an explainable, believable inner life."[4] From this viewpoint, to interpret Browning's mimetic portrait of his villain, to understand the "real" Guido, is an essential task.

Yet the uncertain truth status of the monologues may preclude such a psychological interpretation. Book 5 is usually regarded as the false self-presentation of "the villain in disguise."[5] If in book 11 Guido "exposes his own character completely" and "finally speaks the truth," as many assume,[6] then the problem posed by the monologues' inconsistencies[7] is certainly lessened. However, even in book 11 it is frequently "difficult if not impossible to distinguish sincerity from show."[8] Guido himself, for example, admits that his "tale" would have been different if Pompilia had died immediately and claims that his "first true word" occurs in the last seven lines of his second monologue.[9] Other monologuists contradict Guido—and contradict each other. As Slinn rightly argues, "Browning's mimetic method . . . imitates not the world but men thinking about the world," so that *The Ring*'s speakers "retell the story according to need and predilection," "absorb[ing it] into [their] structure[s] of explanation."[10] The resulting epistemological problem is that we know Guido's self-characterization is a fiction: he is "invent[ing] himself,"[11] "telling a story" in both senses of the phrase, as he repeatedly implies by referring to himself as a rhetorician and orator (5.78; 11.174, 851, 1293). But we know, too, that external evidence, though it encourages a negative judgment of Guido's character, may not offer reliable insight into his character structure. How, then, is Guido's true identity to be known?

Third Force psychology, as represented by Karen Horney's personality theory, is well equipped to deal with the epistemological problems raised by a character like Guido, about whom we have little psychological evidence other than his "own" fiction. This theory accounts for the process of self-fictionalization as characteristic of neurotic development, in which the imagination plays a crucial role. As such development begins, a person's needs for "*integration,*" "self-confidence," superiority, and "*a feeling of identity*" are met "through imagination": it "creates in his mind an *idealized image* of himself."[12] Later "the individual may come to identify himself with his idealized, integrated image," turning it into "an *idealized self*" (*NHG,* p. 23) which he attempts to realize by embarking on a search for glory. Because the idealized self is unreal, "the whole search for glory is bound to be pervaded by fantastic elements." The imagination must continually generate "subtle and comprehensive distortions of reality which [the neurotic] is not aware of fabricating." It "turn[s] his needs into virtues or into more than justified expectations [claims]"; it "turn[s] his intentions" into realities, "his potentialities . . . into factual achievements," his "beliefs" about the world into a form consistent with his needs, and "his feelings" into those the idealized self should have (*NHG,* pp. 31–34). The search for glory is thus "a creative process" which "allows him to live in a world of fiction" (*NHG,* pp. 176, 64). Horney's theory makes psychological sense of observations such as Yetman's: Guido seems to be "his own controlled creation," yet "unconsciously" this created self becomes "a projection of the speaker's actual view of self."[13]

Each typical direction of neurotic development involves a typical kind of idealized self, or fiction of the self, which is identifiable and intelligible within the framework of the theory. Every neurotic is in a sense "telling a story," to himself and to the world, as Guido does; Horney gives us a way to interpret that story, and so to understand the teller, even when external confirmation or disconfirmation of the story is unavailable, inadequate, contradictory, or possibly unreliable.[14] Thus analysis of Guido in terms of Third Force psychology seems to offer important advantages. Both his monologues occur in situations that are particularly likely to evoke distortions: in book 5, he is trying "to save [his] neck" (5.8); in book 11, he is faced with death. Because within its theoretical framework possible untruth can nevertheless be informative, Horneyan analysis can yield inferences about Guido's character regardless of whether the abundant details he gives are objectively accurate. Deliberate or unconscious distortions reflect, for example, what the individual believes others will accept as exculpatory or what he perceives as persuasive; so even a group of statements *all* of which could be untrue may reveal patterns whose psychological significance can be inferred. Thus, by taking the contents of both books as phenomenologically revealing data, we can see Guido's monologues as different "voice[s]" of "the same man" (1.1285) rather than treating them as though there were really "two Guidos."[15] Horneyan analysis will allow us to appreciate the essential psychological continuity of books 5 and 11, to perceive, beneath their surface inconsistencies, the radical unity of Browning's mimetic portrait of Guido.

Such an analysis reveals one psychologically intelligible Guido. His dominant solution is arrogant-vindictive, but he has strong self-effacing trends as well. He scorns them, as they conflict with his self-idealization; but they influence him throughout his development. In fact, his self-effacing trends fuel the "need for vindication, revenge, and triumph" that is the "main motivating force" of an arrogant-vindictive person (*NHG*, pp. 203, 197). Crises threatening Guido's dominant solution account for his crime and for his reaction to impending execution. His inner conflict and his need for vindictive triumph are first intensified to the point of crisis in the course of his relationship to the Comparini family. His vindictiveness is discharged in the triple murder, and his neurotic pride and arrogant-vindictive idealized self are restored. A second crisis develops, however, as Guido anticipates execution. In response to escalating threats to his dominant solution, he reconstructs his idealized self in a form intended to banish his self-effacing trends and to accommodate death as a means to realization of a more powerful and perfect vindictiveness.

1

In Guido's arrogant-vindictive defense system, his family background both serves and fuels his neurotic needs. The arrogant-vindictive person finds "[t]he appeal of life . . . in its mastery" (*NHG*, p. 192); thus the idealized self that he attempts to realize demands that he always be superior and master life. He must suppress self-effacing attitudes such as compliance, dependence, and appeasement of others and maintain instead a "permanent vindictiveness . . . toward people," which he cultivates by "treasur[ing] and keep[ing] alive injuries received" so that he can justify his vengefulness (*NHG*, pp. 199, 201). Guido's family background, as he interprets it, serves all these needs. His family's social position and its former wealth and power have provided him the materials for constructing his proud, superior idealized self. His interpretation of the family's loss of its wealth and power serves his need to dissociate himself from self-effacing attitudes by scorning them. At the same time, he uses family training as an excuse for his self-effacing behavior and, when this behavior does not work, turns his potential "self-accusations, self-doubts, [and] self-contempt" (*NHG*, p. 192) into the justifications he needs for his vindictiveness and neurotic claims. At the same time, his background drives Guido to attain an external goal that will fulfill his need for vindictive triumph. This drive for triumph, ironically, plays a crucial role in his quadruply fatal decision to connect himself with the Comparini family.

The Franceschini's social position and their former wealth and power are central in the glorious idealized self that Guido strives to realize. He emphasizes that he is "representative of a great line"; "his 'scutcheon [is] full / Of old achievement and impunity" as exemplified by his grandfather, who "stabbed knave / For daring throw gibe—much less, stone—from pale" (5.140; 11.93–105). Guido identifies with his grandfather because such an exploit shows that the arrogant-vindictive solution works. The arrogant-vindictive person feels he should always take revenge, always be "self-sufficien[t]," always be "invulnerab[le]" to hurt; and he claims for himself "immunity and impunity" (*NHG*, pp. 204–5). Guido's grandfather has followed these shoulds, and his claims have been honored. Of course Guido's identification with this side of the family past contains, as Sullivan suggests, "an element of wishful thinking";[16] he knows that their position has changed and, as we shall see, he turns that fact to other uses. But his family's "old achievement" represents to Guido what he should be: strong, proud, immune to retaliation.

Reinforcing Guido's choice of what to emulate in his family history is his analysis of the family's loss of its monied, powerful position: the self-effacing values and behavior of some of his ancestors ruined "the Franceschini's once superb array" (5.40). They did nothing "but give, give, give / In blood and brain, in house and land and cash" (5.161–62) The example of his father proves to Guido that such self-effacing behavior does not work. His father, "the easy-natured Count before this Count," "let the world slide," giving lavish gifts to his subordinates even when the family was near ruin (5.45–47, 298–335). Guido consciously despises the self-effacing values that have left his family, once "great and rich" (5.352), with almost nothing. He has decided not to act in these ways, "Being not quite the fool [his] father was" (11.1878). Thus he uses the shabby side of his family history to justify his dominant solution and to keep down his self-effacement.

Guido also deals with his underlying tendencies to comply with others' expectations and to follow the rules in order to get rewarded (self-effacing behavior that puts him in danger of hating himself) by using his family training as an excuse for his compliance.[17] When this behavior does not work, he turns his suffering into justification for vindictiveness against society and into claims for restitution to himself as family representative. This dynamic is epitomized in Guido's admonition to the judges that they should "Weigh well that all this trouble has come on me / Through my persistent treading in the paths / Where I was trained to go" (5.123–25). This kind of statement seems at first glance simply an attempt to manipulate the court. But if it were a well-controlled rhetorical ploy, surely he would not describe his self-effacing behavior as that of a simpleton who was led astray by values such as service to others and duty to family.

Faced in his teens with poverty, Guido considered " 'soldiership' " and the priesthood as possible ways of getting ahead in the world. Men from his town who succeeded in these fields " 'got rewarded,' " his elders told him (5.193–211). But because Guido had been taught his responsibilities as " 'The eldest son and heir,'" he dutifully sought his fortune as a layman "Close to the Church" (5.212, 269). Arriving in Rome at fifteen, Guido says, he thought to himself,

> "Here wait, do service,—serving and to serve!
> "And, in due time, I nowise doubt at all,
> "The recognition of my service comes.
> "Next year I'm only sixteen. I can wait."
>
> I waited thirty years, may it please the court.
> (5.288–92)

The young Guido apparently made an essentially self-effacing bargain with himself and with life: he would serve, and he would be rewarded. He performed "functions to no end / I' the train of Monsignor and Eminence, / As gentleman-squire"; "Humbly I helped the Church," he says, "till here I stand" (5.337–39, 247).

At some "turning-point" when his "gorge gave symptom it might play [him] false" (5.342–49), Guido's original bargain failed and his repressed arrogant-vindictive side became dominant. Now, seeing himself as having tolerated subordination for thirty years and thus threatened by self-hate, he cannot afford to admit to himself that he complied because part of him is compliant. So he blames society for the fact that "'success'" was not "'attendant on [his] desert'" (5.1413); he paints himself as having been "deceived by principles and individuals commonly reckoned the touchstones of responsible attitudes and conduct."[18] Thus he turns potential self-hate into justified vindictiveness that supports his present dominant solution.

Guido's family background serves in another, more direct way to justify his vindictiveness. When he compares his circumstances to those of his ancestors, he resents his lack of the position and prosperity for which he was "born" (5.171–81). That they were "great and rich" indicates to Guido that he "should be rich" (5.352, 168). To see his reduced circumstances as unfair not only justifies his general vindictiveness but also fuels his hatred for others of lower social origins whose status is rising above his. Guido's life in Arezzo has been poisoned by resentment that his neighborhood is filling with such people, who "like building where they used to beg" (5.258). In Rome, too, Guido has seen "many a denizen o' the dung / Hop, skip, jump o'er [his] shoulder, make him wings / And fly aloft" while he has not advanced (5.293–95). He is eaten up by the arrogant-vindictive person's "bitter envy" of anyone who is happy (*NHG*, p. 211), and his resentment is multiplied by his feeling that by inheritance, he has a better right to the world's good things than do such lower-class people.

Guido also uses his family's history and status to justify his neurotic claims. Although he mocks his father's generosity, his own suppressed self-effacing attitudes, as we have seen, can trigger a transformation of self-effacing expectations (rewards for goodness) into arrogant-vindictive claims. Thus Guido turns his father's gifts into debts the recipients owe him. Several now-successful men have incurred Guido's wrath by failing to repay his father's past kindness to them (5.298–334). Guido bases other claims on family status, too. He claims "old . . . impunity," such as his grandfather had; and he expects that "Honour of birth" should bestow "privilege" and have a "value" exchangeable for whatever he wants (11.94; 5.439–65).

Guido's family background, finally, has determined his main life goal: to preserve his superior social status and to restore the external appearance befitting it. He pursues this goal compulsively because he has centered so much of his neurotic pride and based so many of his claims on the fact that he is "a nobleman" (5.351). As Horney explains, the neurotic "must build up in his mind an airtight case in order to make [his claims] entirely legitimate"; and having done this, he must protect the basis for his case, for example his "superiority" (*NHG*, pp. 52–53). In Guido's project, then, what is ultimately at stake is his idealized self.

2

When Guido decides to leave Rome and return to Arezzo, his defense system is in a precarious state. Rome has neither confirmed his idealized self nor rewarded his service; he is no closer to his goal than he was thirty years earlier. He has only a set of conflicting trends, an accumulation of vindictiveness, and a backlog of unhonored claims. At this juncture, he marries.

As Guido tells it, he does so because marriage, like his service in Rome, is a " 'duty' " he has been "taught from [his] youth up" (5.213, 434). In addition, his marriage and the dowry are supposed to offer a consolation for his otherwise fruitless service in Rome (5.403–11). Guido expects the dowry to restore his material status. He also expects his wife and her parents to appreciate their "Incorporation with nobility" (5.515). This expectation suggests that Guido wants them to treat him in accordance with his claims and at the same time to fulfill covertly his underlying self-effacing needs; for as Horney points out, the arrogant-vindictive person wants "recognition" because it confirms his superiority and "holds out the additional lure of being liked by others and of being able in turn to like them." That is, being looked up to allows the arrogant-vindictive person to fulfill his suppressed self-effacing needs without conflict.[19] Guido wants to get this pay-off while reserving the option of vindictive response to any disappointment of his expectations. Altogether, he feels his marriage should compensate him for all his previous frustrations and injured pride and allow him to triumph after all.

Of course no marriage (except perhaps the one he later fantasizes, to Lucrezia Borgia) could do so. His needs for vindictive triumph, like all neurotic needs, are insatiable and compulsive; he wants to get the rewards of self-effacing behavior (love, acceptance, appreciation) without having to behave in self-effacing ways that he scorns; and he cannot attain the compensation he desires no matter what anyone does: for example, he wishes to have back his youth (11.1077–79). But his marriage not only fails to reward and compensate Guido; it assaults him at his most vulnerable points and thwarts both his arrogant-vindictive and his self-effacing needs. His claim to the court that it was a mental torture—compared to which "This getting tortured merely in the flesh" is "almost an agreeable change" (5.23–24)—may well be true.

Pompilia's parents, the Comparini, rank lower than Guido socially but are wealthier. They are the kind of "ambiguous insects" (11.1263) whose financial and social progress has always offended Guido. Yet they complain about and publicly expose Guido's constricted circumstances and personal deficiencies. They "Mimic" him, accuse him of having misrepresented his finances, and spread Pompilia's complaints about him as a lover so that "Good folk begin at" him with advice about how to manage his sex life (5.51, 17–47; 11.1059–72). Guido's pride is assaulted by reminders of how very different his idealized self is from the Guido others see. The Comparini "remind him of failure,"[20] causing him to externalize his resultant self-hate.

The Comparini also fail to provide the means for Guido to preserve and restore his social status. They break the "bargain" Guido thinks he has made, "the exchange of quality for wealth." He has "Delivered" (5.500–16), but the Comparini renege and instead tell the world that Pompilia is really the daughter of a prostitute. This news threatens Guido's hopes of collecting the dowry and taints the family honor. He raves at the very thought of it:

> Pompilia, I supposed their daughter, drew
> Breath first 'mid Rome's worst rankness, through the deed
> Of a drab and a rogue, was by-blow bastard-babe
> Of a nameless strumpet, passed off, palmed on me
> As the daughter with the dowry. Daughter? Dirt
> O' the kennel! Dowry? Dust o' the street! Nought more,
> Nought less, nought else but—oh—ah—assuredly
> A Franceschini and my very wife!
>
> (5.768–75)

Guido has been "fooled," a terrible humiliation for an expansive person (*NHG*, p. 193); everyone, even his friends, laughs at him (11.1234–35); and his family, basis of his neurotic pride, is contaminated.

But these circumstances surrounding Guido's relationship to Pompilia are only part of his marital "torture," for Pompilia herself does not satisfy his emotional needs. He denies, of course, that he has such needs; he "should remain aloof and detached" so he can "give free range, at least in his mind, to his ample supply of bitter resentment" (*NHG*, p. 203). So he says, "How I see all my folly at a glance! / 'A man requires a woman and a wife': / There was my folly; I believed the saw" (11.161–63). Previously Guido has blamed his training for his service in Rome and has turned his potential self-hate into resentment against society; the same mechanism operates here. Unable to admit that he needed a wife, Guido convicts himself of the lesser sin of having "believed the saw" that a man needs a woman and thus adds his marriage to the list of injustices others have done to him. This dynamic signals that, despite his denials, he has needed things from Pompilia.

As Guido explains matters, of course, he had no needs, but rather standards of performance for Pompilia, standards that simply involved her recognizing his due as her master and superior. His "obligation . . . was just / To practise mastery, prove [his] mastership:— / Pompilia's duty was—submit herself" (5. 716–18). She should have shown "loyalty and obedience,—wish and will / To settle and suit her fresh and plastic mind / To the novel, not disadvantageous mould!" (5.578–80). She should have rejected her parents when they turned against him (5.785–832). She should have " 'exaggerate[d] chastity' " so as " 'to disprove the frightful charge' " about her parentage (5.887–88). She was supposed to " 'desire [his] love, /'Yield [him] contentment and be ruled aright!' " (11.1309–10). If she "Can . . . feel no love," then "Let her show the more, / Sham the worse, damn herself praiseworthily!"; his "slave" should do no less (11.1408–9, 1420). Clearly, Guido has wanted Pompilia to confirm by her behavior that he has the mastery, superiority, and irresistible will of his idealized self.

But Guido seems to have other, underlying needs generated by his suppressed self-effacing trends. He has wanted Pompilia to see, beneath his physical unattractiveness, "the wrought man worth ten times the crude" (11.1027). Her acknowledging his worth, he has felt, would rejuvenate him, "prick[ing] on the soul to shoot / New fire into the half-used cinder, flesh!" (11.1030–31). Guido has wanted to satisfy secret, self-effacing needs to feel worthy of love and "to make the partner love him" (*NHG*, pp. 240, 242). In particular, his obsession with her sexual faithfulness appears as partly a self-effacing need for reassurance about his attractiveness.

Guido's fantasy of the wife he would really like further demonstrates how both arrogant-vindictive and self-effacing trends have shaped his image of the perfect relationship. The fantasy wife would bring "a husband power worth Ormuz' wealth!" She would see him as " 'law, right, wrong, heaven and hell!' " If anyone dared to " 'frustrate' " Guido, she would get him whatever he wanted, even if she had to betray a " 'fair' " young man. She would be uninhibitedly sensual, but only toward Guido; she would say to him, " 'Let us blend souls, blent, thou in me, to bid / 'Two bodies work one pleasure!' " With her, Guido would have no trouble being "the burning bridegroom" (11.2184–2220). This Lucrezia Borgia figure would fulfill Guido's arrogant-vindictive needs by serving his desires, being ruled by his standards, and providing the means to demonstrate his superior status. At the same time, she would satisfy his self-effacing needs. She can play Delilah to any Samson, but considers only Guido worthy of her love. Guido could merge with her and have her supply anything he wants (typically self-effacing desires) without having to ask: Lucrezia is the one who yearns to merge with and serve Guido. She would allow him to be both masterful and passive, rather like an enormous infant whose nurturing mother removes every frustration and urges him to " 'take the breast shall turn a breast indeed!' " (11.2205). The fantasy wife, in short, would fulfill Guido's self-effacing needs while he remained his arrogant-vindictive idealized self.

Thus Guido has expected Pompilia to fulfill a set of powerful, conflicting needs, needs which have gone thirty years without gratification. Under these conditions, they have developed into sadistic trends that color his expectations. The sadistic person, according to Horney, is driven by "vindictive needs" for which he seeks an outlet (*NHG*, p. 199n.); thus Guido's cruelty to Pompilia gives him "a feeling of strength and pride" (*OIC*, p. 207) by venting his vindictiveness and allowing him to triumph. But the underlying dynamic involves more. The sadist is "a desperate individual who seeks restitution for a life that has defeated him" (*OIC*, p. 216); feeling "futil[e]," "forever excluded, forever defeated," and "hopeless" (*OIC*, pp. 201, 192), he "make[s] an attempt at restitution by living vicariously" (*OIC*, p. 192). As we have seen, Guido expects restitution when he marries, and he attempts to get it by typical sadistic means: by "enslav[ing] the partner," by "molding or educating the victim," by subjecting her to "possessive jealousy" so strong that to hold on to her is more important than living his own life, and by *"playing on the emotions"* of the partner (*OIC*, pp. 193–95). Thus Guido has expected Pompilia to be his "slave," to fit herself into his "mould," to "exaggerate chastity" so as to appease him, and to be terrified by his threats. Such behavior allows him to "fill out a life that is emotionally empty" by "feed[ing], vampire-like, on [Pompilia's] emotional vitality" (*OIC*, p. 197). Because Guido needs to fill his "empty heart" after having " 'bid hope good-bye' " in Rome, he wants Pompilia to be his "refreshment" (5.694, 366; 11.1092); but if not that, he wants her to supply intensity by sinning or revolting, as Caponsacchi and the Pope understand (6.1795–99; 10.603–10).

Given Guido's needs, one can see why, as Pompilia says, "Nothing about me but drew somehow down / His hate upon me" (7.1725–26). She "refused . . . / Either in body or soul to cleave to" Guido, "confirm[ing his] doubt" about his attractiveness (5.608–9; 11.1000) and making him feel like a "failure" both "as man and lover."[21] Feeling hurt by Pompilia's revulsion cracks Guido's invulnerable shell, exposing his despised self-effacing side; to defend himself from the resulting self-hate, he must turn it on her. But the sadistic need for vicarious participation in others' "emotional vitality" (*OIC*, p. 197) must be taken into account to explain why Guido could not bear Pompilia's eventual resignation. She would do nothing of her " 'own accord,' " but was "cold and pale and mute as stone," offering Guido no "fair sport" (11.1311–34).[22] He has "judged, sentenced and punished her" (11.1432) as much for what she lacked as for what she was. To say that Guido hates Pompilia because she is good and he evil, as several other speakers in the poem and many critics do,[23] is to miss the psychological complexity of Guido's sadism and the constellation of needs that have been frustrated in his marriage.

Pompilia's escape and the birth of her son, Gaetano, bring Guido's already great need for vindictive triumph to a crisis. Caponsacchi takes Guido's victim away from him, while Guido has failed in his plots to entangle Pompilia with Caponsacchi. To be thus outmaneuvered threatens Guido's view of himself as the smartest person around. His humiliation is especially painful because Caponsacchi embodies much that Guido envies and wants to feel that he is. Not only is the priest "the man-lover he would like to be";[24] in addition, his family's higher rank encroaches upon Guido's idealization of himself as socially superior to everyone. Guido's self-idealization is further threatened when his fantasized revenge on Pompilia and Caponsacchi falls flat. Instead of "surpris[ing]" them in bed together "And pinn[ing] them each to other partridge-wise," Guido has to be saved when Pompilia snatches his sword (11.1540–42; 6.1544–49). She humiliates him and plays out the arrogant-vindictive person's deep fear that his victims "may retaliate for the offenses he perpetrates on them" (*NHG*, p. 206). Finally he is exposed to more gossip and laughter, both when he discovers the elopement and when, returning to Arezzo after the unsatisfying trial of the runaways, he feels actuely "the archway's grin" and "the length of sarcasm in the street" (5.995–1029, 1267–68). He is especially vulnerable to this ridicule because his position in Arezzo is crucial in his self-idealization and because the people there, being most aware of his family's decay, are the very ones to whom Guido most needs to prove himself effective. Instead, they now see final proof of his inability even to control his wife.

The elopement episode also brings Guido closer to psychological crisis because he experiences the outcome of Pompilia and Caponsacchi's trial as another betrayal by the system and as a result, his inner conflict is exacerbated. Once more attributing his compliance to his training, Guido claims that he took the matter to court because he was "brought up at the very feet of law" (5.1106). He really hoped, of course, to have the law mandate the revenge that he failed, and was afraid, to take. He is then enraged that the culprits receive a token sentence by which "No particle of wrong [done to him] receive[s] . . . / One atom of right" (5.1946–47). He has "played the game [social authorities] warrant wins," but the court has not saved him from the "plague" of inner conflict which is "Breaking [his] tree of life from root to branch" (11.1526; 5.1950–51). He is still torn between his inner dictate that he should take revenge, on the one hand, and on the other, his fear of doing so and his wish to be protected by someone else.

Soon, Guido receives news that heightens this conflict: he has lost his divorce suit, and Pompilia has been allowed to go home to her parents (5.1307–42). Again, the law has thwarted Guido and excused his enemies. At the same time, his brother Paul, who has been handling Guido's " 'tangle of affairs,' " leaves Italy for parts unknown. Just when Guido's drive for revenge is intensified, the person who has been his " 'single prop and stay' " deserts him (5.1343–73). His vindictiveness increases, but so do his fear and insecurity.

As a result, Guido sinks deeper than ever before into hopelessness, "an ultimate product of unresolved conflicts" and of "despair" at the unconscious feeling that he will never "measure up to the idealized image" of himself (*OIC*, pp. 183–84) that he has struggled for so long to realize. His description of the period between the failed divorce suit and his son's birth closely resembles Horney's description of the hopeless person's conscious feelings.

> A person may have a pervasive sense of doom. Or he may take a resigned attitude toward life in general, expecting nothing good, feeling simply that life must be endured. Or he may express it in philosophical terms, saying . . . that life is essentially tragic and only fools deceive themselves about man's unalterable fate. (*OIC*, p. 182)

Similarly, Guido describes himself as having felt " 'irremediably beaten,' " " 'caught . . . in the cavern where I fell, / 'Covered . . . / 'With an enormous paving-stone of shame,' " beyond " 'human aid.' " " 'Half below-ground already,' " he has been in "the stoic's mood," ready to " 'let all end here.' " He has not " 'claim[ed] escape from man's predestined lot / 'Of being beaten and baffled.' " He has thought that no new " 'injury' " could arouse him (5.1390–1466). Yet when he hears that Pompilia has had the baby, he is aroused to the point that his need for revenge finally overcomes his fear of retaliation. Why?

One reason, of course, is that the news fuels the vindictiveness and sadistic trends that are concomitants of his hopelessness. The vindictiveness he already feels at the Comparini's having cheated him out of Pompilia's dowry increases, for through Gaetano, they now have a claim on his estate as well (5.1468–70). His outrage at the corruption of his honor by Pompilia's bastardy increases, for now Gaetano "shall keep displayed / The flag with the ordure on it" (5.1490–91). Because Guido associates the child with Caponsacchi, whom he half believes to be the father (5.1498–1503), his sadistic "possessive jealousy" (*OIC*, p. 194) increases. The possibility that the baby might be legitimate also feeds Guido's sadism by confirming that he really is "forever excluded" (*OIC*, p. 201) from what is rightfully his. Though he cares little about the baby, I think, he feels a great deal of the sadist's "burning envy" (*OIC*, p. 201) toward the Comparini. In Rome before the murders, he first waits in Paul's "hateful house," now "empty" and haunted by "the ghost of social joy" (5.1588–90). At last, outside the Comparini's villa, he thinks of Pompilia and her parents cozy inside, perhaps sitting around the fire and having wine with some friends to celebrate " 'the babe's birth' " (11.1586–91). The two houses objectify his envy: " 'they' sit at the table while he goes hungry; 'they' love, create, enjoy, feel healthy and at ease, belong somewhere" (*OIC*, p. 201). Guido's response to this vision carries out literally the sadist's "impulse to thwart others—to kill their joy" (*OIC*, p. 197).

A second reason for Guido's taking revenge now is that his increased sadistic vindictiveness causes his inner conflict to become so urgent that he must resolve it. According to Horney, "sadistic strivings" "generat[e] . . . anxiety" because the sadist "fears that others will treat him as he treats them—or wants to treat them" (*OIC*, p. 208); and fear in turn stirs up Guido's self-effacing trends. The heightened inner conflict that follows is reflected in Guido's view of the child both as a tiny "filthy pest," eating at him, and as himself, "ma[d]e . . . anew" to be "crush[ed]" by an enormous "reptile" that "coil[s]" all around him (5.1539, 1958–62). He feels both like a great, strong creature who can rid himself of a little nuisance and like a weak baby held helpless by a monster. Similarly, he is torn between the image of "Satan and all his malice" and the image of "the Holy Infant," which must age, suffer, and die before he can act (5.1577, 1598–1608). Guido tries to interpret Satan as the evil that he will destroy; but the psychic meaning of his vision appears to be that his arrogant-vindictive side (the devil, with whom he later identifies) must overcome his self-effacing side (the infant, associated of course with Christian values) before he can take revenge.

Given this level of inner conflict, it is little wonder that finally (as Guido puts it) " 'Some end must be!' " (5.1612). Yet must the " 'end' " be triple homicide? His vindictiveness is great, and his neurotic pride would make it difficult for him to back away from revenge in front of his lower-class accomplices. On the other hand, the nine-day wait in Rome indicates that his self-effacing side has had a good chance of winning the inner conflict. Certainly for Guido to have heeded his fear of committing murder would have been a more realistic, self-preserving move.

Here a pattern of inner dynamics discovered by Dr. Andrew K. Ruotolo in pretrial examinations of nine murderers—eight who killed their victims and one who did not succeed, but "not for lack of genuine trying"[25]—strikingly parallels Guido's experiences during the crucial period before the crime. Ruotolo reports that "hopelessness and contempt for one's own life" are "common precursor[s] of homicide."[26] This notion is consistent with Horney's observation that increasing hopelessness leads to "the recklessness of a person who has nothing to lose" (*OIC*, p. 204). Guido's growing despair prior to the murders thus has not only increased his sadistic vindictiveness, but has loosened the grip of his fear upon him, making him feel that his "life was valueless"; he says to the court, "Judge for yourselves, what life seemed worth to me / Who, not by proxy but in person, pitched / Headforemost into danger as a fool" would do (5.1738, 1715–17).

What precipitates such a pitching into danger, according to Ruotolo, is "A shattering blow . . . to the [murderer's] pride system," a blow resulting in "enormously intense self-hate" which he "externalize[s] to the victim." A second result is "A radical move . . . away from a formerly held major neurotic solution into a repressed solution such as from expansiveness to self-effacement" (*DSM*, p. 173). Sometimes this move seems to be "in the direction of health relative to [his] habitual psychic [position]" (*NPH*, p. 15). But the move "set[s] off intense, overpowering conflict with inevitable anxiety" (*DSM*, p. 173). The person desperately needs to escape this anxiety by "lurch[ing] precipitously back to" "the pseudo-safety of his major neurotic solution"; but first the "symbolic or actual impediment to [his] return" to this safe position "*ha*[*s*] to be eliminated": the murder victim (*NPH*, p. 15; *DSM*, pp. 173–74).

Guido's case illustrates this process quite well. The Comparini, especially Pompilia, have assaulted his pride for years, but the news of Gaetano's birth is the "shattering blow." Guido cannot avoid realizing how long he has waited for revenge: throughout Pompilia's pregnancy. The way he paints the response of his "serving-people" to the news indicates that he feels his delay to be a shameful failure to do what these peasants would have done immediately (5.1550–60). His shoulds torment him into self-hatred that, according to his habit, he externalizes to the Comparini. His move in Rome toward self-effacement (with its implication of relatively healthy impulses to self-preservation) precipitates increasingly severe inner conflict and anxiety. Ruotolo helps us to understand that for Guido, given these conditions, safety seems to lie not in refraining from murder, but in removing the Comparini so that he can return to his major solution.

That the murders allow Guido to resume and reinforce his arrogant-vindictive stance is evident from his reactions to his crime. He feels that he has done justice as "law's mere executant" (5.2003); this is the arrogant-vindictive notion of justice: "triumphing by hitting back harder" than one was hit (*NHG*, p. 203). The murders assert Guido's claim of privilege and immunity and reinforce his identification with his grandfather's arrogant-vindictive example: they are "some prank my grandsire played" (11.111). They restore his pride, being deeds which "manly men / Approved," deeds in which "strength, being provoked by weakness, fought / And conquered" (11.43–44, 1283–84). They eliminate the three major sources of his humiliation and give him a great vindictive triumph over everyone he hates: over the Comparini; over Caponsacchi (5.1692–93); and over all his friends who have laughed at him (11.1238–42). The murders even triumph over the institutions and authority figures who thought to "Baulk [the] fulness of [Guido's] revenge" (11.1495–99). By the time Guido flees the villa, he feels that

> unbrokenly lay bare
> Each taenia that had sucked me dry of juice,
> At last outside me, not an inch of ring
> Left now to writhe about and root itself
> I' the heart all powerless for revenge! Henceforth
> I might thrive: these were drawn and dead and damned.
> (11.1605–10)

His revenge completed, Guido is "Redundantly triumphant" (11.1624).

His immediate response to triumph, as he describes it in book 5, is an inflated sense of well-being and confidence. "I was my own self, had my sense again" (5.1677). He feels "whole": with "Health . . . returned, and sanity of soul," he can "live again" (5.1700–7, 1740). These feelings result from his having resolved his inner conflict and found a way back to his dominant solution and the false integration provided by his idealized self. He feels alive because in the sadist, "almost all feelings except those of anger and triumph have been choked off. He is so dead that he needs these sharp stimuli to feel alive" (*OIC*, p. 207).

Guido seems confident, looking down at the court from the heights of his self-idealization, that his superior intellect can produce the "right interpretation" to excuse his "irregular deed" (5.113–14). This "right interpretation" reflects the "air-tight case" (*NHG*, p. 52) that Guido has long been building to justify his claims and his vindictiveness to himself. To the degree that the case is effective, it is so, I suspect, because Guido is sharing the phenomenological reality of his experience, the way his life feels to him. However, the rhetorical weaknesses of his "interpretation" seem equally the product of his neurotic solution. For example, he cannot resist mentioning that he intends to manipulate his auditors (asides that assert his superiority over them) and cannot see the hazards of an analogy between a listening judge's regret at his purchase of a painting and Guido's rage at having bought an unsatisfactory wife (5.483–92). At such points, Guido's blindness to the possibility that his auditors could be something other than fools or knaves is best explained by the arrogant-vindictive person's tendency to assume that others do indeed fall into one of these extreme categories (*NHG*, pp. 199, 207–8). The same inability to escape the attitudes associated with his dominant solution dooms Guido's calculated attempts to paint a self-effacing portrait of himself and of his purported attachment to his family, particularly his poor old mother. The false sentiment of his concluding plea to be released and given his son (whom he has described earlier as a "bastard" and "filthy pest"—5.1537–39) is comically evident. Guido's idea of how to play at familial and social piety is apparently to burlesque Tennyson.[27] Altogether, the strengths and weaknesses of Guido's rhetoric in book 5 are precisely those one would expect of an arrogant-vindictive rhetorician who is experiencing himself as his idealized self. If his persuasion fails, its failure will be intimately related to the structure of his defense system.

3

When Guido reappears in book 11, his conviction, the failure of his appeal to the Pope, and the prospect of execution are precipitating a second psychological crisis. The court has discounted Guido's self-justifications; the Pope has rejected his claims for "A little indulgence to rank, privilege" (11.1778). He is enraged that his "blood" should "end / This way" and that the Christian value system he despises has triumphed: the Pope has "revert[ed] . . . / To the good and right, in detriment of [him]" (11.15–17, 81–82). Underlying Guido's resentment of the Pope is anger with himself for having wasted his energy serving the church. His claim of clerical privilege—supposedly "Firm should all else . . . fail" (11.47)—has failed. Guido must externalize the self-hate generated by this final evidence of the folly of his service and must prove to himself that it did not reflect what he is really like. So he tells the Cardinal and Abate that if he had another chance "to choose," he would "be free / Your foe," not "subsidized your friend forsooth!" (11.831–33). Guido feels that he has not done what he should have done to realize his idealized self; he has been too timid. His pride is hurt, for he has not "assert[ed his] claims effectively" (*NHG*, p. 92). And his bargain has not worked. The arrogant-vindictive person's bargain, as Paris has described it, is a "convi[ction] that he can reach his ambitious goals if he remains true to his vision of life as a battle and does not allow himself to be seduced by the traditional morality."[28] Guido feels that by committing the murders, he lived up to his shoulds; but now his triumph has been denied him. Instead, he is to be punished. For all these reasons, his solution is seriously threatened. If it is to remain intact, Guido must somehow make it work, find a way to feel like his idealized self once more. Since he cannot escape death, his remaining alternative is to find a way to turn it into a triumph of his idealized self.

But early in book 11, two things are interfering with Guido's pursuit of this triumph. The first is that he is terrified of death. This normal fear constitutes a threat to the dominant solution which for Guido is his identity: if he is overcome by fear, his idealized self will be lost. The arrogant-vindictive person, though always secretly "afraid of people," would violate his shoulds if he were to "admit to himself" that he is afraid (*NHG*, p. 206); he defends himself by developing an "unconscious conviction of his own inviolability." But if something shatters this conviction—in Guido's case, rejection of his final appeal—"his pseudo security is shattered and he is likely to be seized by acute panic" (*OIC*, p. 209). Guido's vivid account of Mannaia (the guillotine) reflects this panic, as do his compulsive references to broken necks throughout the book. If he is to turn his death into a triumph of his idealized self, he must find a way to reconstruct his sense of inviolability and thus conquer his fear.

The second thing interfering with Guido's holding on to his idealized self is the emergence of his self-effacing trends when he panics at the thought of Mannaia. Guido excoriates himself for having ever believed he needed a woman, for he has just discovered that "woman's in the man!" (11.166).

> Overmuch life turns round my woman-side:
> The male and female in me, mixed before,
> Settle of a sudden: I'm my wife outright
> In this unmanly appetite for truth,
> This careless courage as to consequence,
> This instantaneous sight through things and through,
> This voluble rhetoric, if you please,—'t is she!

> Here you have that Pompilia whom I slew,
> Also the folly for which I slew her!
>
> (11.168–76)

Because Guido hates Pompilia, partly for her compliance, he identifies the surfacing of his hated self-effacing side with turning into her.

It makes sense that Guido sees a threat to his dominant solution as a threat to his maleness, for he equates arrogant-vindictive behavior and values with masculinity, a position that no doubt has received considerable validation from the violent, male-dominated culture he lives in. Manliness for Guido implies, among other things, deceit, well-calculated, successful plotting, and self-control. He must defend himself from self-hate if he ever fails in these "manly" activities. Thus, for example, he must make excuses for having confessed under torture and must blame bad "luck" for the debacle at the inn and "the spite of fortune" for his bungled escape after the murders (5.18–19; 11.1567, 1674). When panic makes Guido feel he is losing his "manly" self, he attributes to his "woman-side" those "unmanly" traits that are the opposites of deceit, calculation, and self-control: an "appetite for truth," indifference to "consequence," and "voluble rhetoric."

Guido attributes "sight through things and through" to his woman-side because he associates Pompilia's sight and her eyes with a type of experience that seriously threatens an arrogant-vindictive person: having "guilt feelings or . . . self-doubts" about his treatment of others. For a person like Guido, "Any [such] doubt . . . would . . . sweep away his whole artificial self-assurance" (*NHG,* pp. 208–9). In the past, Guido has been threatened by this disaster when Pompilia has looked at him (11.1373–74); thus to have Pompilia's sight, which sees the soul (11.987–88), would mean seeing himself as guilty, losing his arrogant-vindictive "armor of self-righteousness" (*NHG,* p. 208), and being assaulted by self-hate.[29] Again, Guido's feeling that he has turned into Pompilia signals inner conflict.

With his dominant solution thus threatened by fear and by his self-effacing side, Guido might respond either by breaking down or by adopting another solution; what he does, however, is to construct a more inflated idealized self that will be the "truth" to "save" what Guido calls "my soul" (his dominant solution).[30] It will make him the ultimate in arrogant-vindictive potency, strong enough for "one good grapple, I with all the world!" (11.460–65). He prepares to enter the ring by metaphorically exposing this greater idealized self, dropping his "sheepskin-garb" to "show [his] shag!" (11.443–44). To fight him, it will be necessary not only to face a wolf, but even to "exorcize the devil, for here he stands . . . !" (11.555).

Book 11 records how Guido constructs this terrifying new idealized self. One of his major strategies is to elevate his rage and vindictiveness to the status of an indestructible life force.[31] He extols his "overplus" of vitality, his "manifold and plenitudinous life, / Prompt at death's menace to give blow for threat" (11.144–55). Here Guido intensifies the identification of vitality and vindictiveness that operated in his response to the murders. He sees his life as feeding upon the vindictiveness directed against him: "I do get strength from being thrust to wall, . . . / By this tenacious hate of fortune, hate / Of all things in, under, and above earth" (11.1796–99). The more he is hated and the more he seems defeated, the stronger and the more vital he really is. Thus Guido reassures himself that his vitality, identified with his vindictiveness, can overleap the world's last act of hatred, his execution. It is the "something changeless" that will survive death (11.2394). As Hymes observes, "Guido's imagination will never let him die."[32]

A second major strategy in Guido's creation of his ultimate idealized self is to expand his observations of hypocrisy and evil into an indictment of society and religion in general. He can escape his weakening self-hate and even feel superior to everyone else if he shows that others (particularly religious authorities) are really just the same as he is, but that he is "the one person who is above common hypocrisy" (*NHG*, p. 207). Much of Guido's social analysis in book 11 serves this defensive purpose. He has a vested interest in being, as the Pope complains, a man who "believes in just the vile of life" (10.512). This stance allows him to see his execution as final proof that his superior honesty has frightened the "' "wise men" '" of Rome: they *have* to get rid of him because he has "'reveal[ed their] mystery'" (11.2034, 2012). Through this logic, Guido can regard his death as evidence that he has actualized his terrifying idealized self.

Despite these strategies, the greatest barrier to Guido's construction of the supremely vindictive idealized self remains: his self-effacing side. He deals with it by building on his identification of that side with Pompilia. He hates his self-effacing trends by hating her; he gets rid of his attraction to pity, love, and forgiveness by emphasizing these qualities in her, then rejecting her. He recalls how Pompilia disgusted and infuriated him, proving to himself that she was "a true stumbling-block" to him (11.1523). Then he contrasts himself with her. Pompilia has "excused" his crime; he warns his mental image of her, "Beware me in what other world may be!— / Pompilia, who have brought me to this pass!" (11.941, 2102–3). He is not like her; he is "Implacable, persistent in revenge" (11.2107). He knows that "There was no touch in her of hate: / And it would prove her hell, if I reached mine!" (11.2089–90). He is not like her. If he had "an outlet for escape to heaven," he would stay in hell "if such flight allowed my foe / To raise his head" (11.2096–99). He will thus be where Pompilia is not, even after death. He must escape her image: "Away with the empty stare! Be holy still, / And stupid ever! Occupy your patch / Of private snow," but "freeze not me, / Dare follow not another step I take" (11.2077–82). By banishing Pompilia, Guido hopes to conquer the side of himself that stands in the way of his being the "veritable wolf"—his preferred "image . . . at every turn" (11.1178–79).

Guido's strategies for dealing with his fear and his self-effacing trends have not dealt with a final problem which he faces toward the end: his actual self. Guido stumbles onto this barrier when he tries to free himself from the indignity of "mak[ing] . . . suit to live" (11.1812) by proving to himself that he does not want or need life. If he were pardoned, he says, his future would be "sad and sapless," full of "things grown grey." People would never appreciate the heroism of the murders. His "brothers quietly would edge [him] out / Of use and management of things called [his]," always mocking and squelching his attempts to "command," to "Show anger," to "advise." His son, young and strong, would rise above his father; Guido would "lack courage" to satisfy his appetites (11.1821–1910). At this point Guido seems to be seeing his actual self (and other people) rather clearly. He has apparently been ineffective for most of his life. He has been unable to get promotion in Rome. His younger brothers have shown little respect for his competence and intelligence: Paul has stage-managed Guido's marriage and his lawsuits in Rome; back in Arezzo, Girolamo has not hesitated to make advances to Pompilia under Guido's very nose. Guido's attempts to entrap Pompilia and Caponsacchi in Arezzo and at the inn have failed. His one effective act, the murders, nonetheless left Pompilia alive long enough to ruin him; and even had he not forgotten to obtain the pass he needed for escape, he would not have escaped his peasant accomplices, who were obviously less than overawed by his authority and prowess. If his past is any indication of Guido's capacity for actual greatness, he is correct to doubt that more of life would validate his idealized self. Once Guido sees this, his remaining alternative is to conceive of an afterlife in which he will achieve such validation.

Guido makes his case for this alternative by first concluding that his entrapment in his mortal state is responsible for the discrepancy between his projected earthly future and the idealized self he "really" is. Combining this idea with his notion that his vindictive life force is indestructible, Guido envisions a next life in which he will not only survive, but be free to be his ultra-idealized self. There he will "turn wolf, be whole, and sate, for once"; he will "Wallow in what is now a wolfishness / Coerced too much by the humanity / That's half of me as well!" (11.2056–59). His "honest instinct, pent and crossed through life," will burst into "Fire for the mount" (11.2064–72), the volcano to Pompilia's "patch / Of private snow." This vision does not represent the truth about Guido, as a number of critics have contended;[33] rather it is Guido's fantasy of total realization of his highly idealized self. The "honest instinct" that has been frustrated is his neurotic search for glory. To be "whole" is to be—completely, without conflict, and eternally—his idealized self. To be freed of "humanity" and be a wolf or volcano is to be forever rid of his actual self, with the hated self-effacing trends that have so hampered his neurotic aspirations.

Briefly glorying in the illusion that he is about to become the visionary wolf, Guido denounces Pompilia and fantasizes the Lucrezia Borgia-wife, shocking his confessors and reassuring himself that he "should not change, / And shall not" (11.2223–24). The visionary self is precious to Guido, for it will achieve what he has aspired to: a powerful, perfect vindictiveness. No longer troubled by his "blunderer's-ineptitude," he will triumph over "that particular devil whose task it is / To trip the all-but-at perfection" and to "Inscribe all human effort with one word, / Artistry's haunting curse, the Incomplete!" (11.547, 1555–61). About to rise above being merely human, Guido must indeed be determined not to change, for in his mind at this moment, as Sullivan says, he is close to the "magnificence in evil" which he so desires.[34]

But as the hour of execution approaches, Guido's elaborate structure of defenses and self-idealization, his fiction, is subverted by its internal contradictions. It is all very well to envision glory in the afterlife, but one must first die to get there; at the peak of his vision of greatness, Guido cannot quite forget that his "head shall drop in pannier presently" (11.2267), and he is afraid. To complicate matters further, his now-essential belief in an afterlife is not firmly grounded in his past beliefs. It has been his habit to believe in "solid earth, not empty air"; so he has always chosen " 'Faith in the present life, made last as long / 'And prove as full of pleasure as may hap' " (11.2008, 725–26). Even if he can now believe in an afterlife, his God is full of "wrath," vindictiveness, and destructiveness (11.921–27), not One to fall all over Himself to grant posthumous fulfillment of Guido's wishes. Like Browning's Caliban, Guido habitually thinks of God as an omnipotent version of himself, or rather in Guido's case, of his idealized self. Ironically, then, the idealized self that he wishes to become has led him to project a God Who is very likely to thwart him.

Given these weaknesses in Guido's fiction, it is not surprising that the wolf wavers; conflict sets in again. Guido feels that he "should not change," but attempts a last appeal—offering to "serve" the Cardinal (11.2255–86). Scrambling to recover his wolf-confidence, he attempts to think of God as "conserv[ing] his work," making each creature with "its proper instinct of defence" (11.2302–3). And my instinct is the wolf's, he says grandly: "The last bad blow that" brings death will "be cheated of a pang / If, fighting quietly, the jaws enjoy / One re-embrace in mid backbone they break"; for "That's the wolf-nature" (11.2312–18). But a second later he admits, "My fight is figurative" (11.2320); the vindictive triumph is after all only imaginary. Again Guido scrambles: "I begin to taste my strength, / Careless, gay even. What's the worth of life?" Having temporarily thrust back his fear, he vindictively taunts the Cardinal and Abate with their imminent defeats (11.2330–47). Yet within moments, he speaks sentimentally of death as the "foil" to "nobleness" and "faith and love" on earth, and he announces himself ready to "acknowledge" the "new rule" of God "In heaven" (11.2376–92). Again snatching himself away from such compliant thoughts, he reasserts his vindictiveness.

> Nor is it in me to unhate my hates,—
> I use up my last strength to strike once more
> Old Pietro in the wine-house-gossip-face,

> To trample underfoot the whine and wile
> Of beast Violante,—and I grow one gorge
> To loathingly reject Pompilia's pale
> Poison my hasty hunger took for food.
> (11.2400–6)

Now he consolidates his arrogant-vindictive position: "I lived and died a man, and take man's chance, / Honest and bold: right will be done to such" (11.2412–13). He seems prepared to hold on to his idealized self to the very end.

But it is not to be. The conflict manifested in Guido's rapidly changing attitudes has exhausted his "last strength." Now, as the Brotherhood of Death approaches his cell, his solution collapses. He disowns his neurotic fiction: "All was folly—I laughed and mocked!" (11.2419). His fear of death betrays him into the very submission he most loathes and can least afford to feel.

> Don't open! Hold me from them! I am yours,
> I am the Granduke's—no, I am the Pope's!
> Abate,—Cardinal,—Christ,—Maria,—God, . . .
> Pompilia, will you let them murder me?
> (11.2424–27)

Guido's fear, one of the most human things about him, has defeated his aspiration to be his inhumanly strong, invulnerable, and implacably vindictive idealized self. His fiction has not withstood the test of his experience.[35]

The final stage of Guido's inner development remains mysterious. Its outward manifestation, his public behavior before his execution (book 12), has been interpreted in various ways. Altick and Loucks believe Guido convincingly "play[s] a sanctified role" at his execution. Jack thinks that Guido dies "boastful and unrepentant." Langbaum, on the other hand, points out that Browning "uses" the source material on Guido's Christian death "without casting doubt upon it." King argues that the execution scene is deliberately "ambiguous," either the "signal" of a real inner "transformation" or "hypocritical bravado."[36] I find that the poet simply has not provided the rich mimetic details—the "facts from within," to borrow Langbaum's phrase[37]—that would allow psychological insight into Guido's behavior in book 12. In the absence of such information, any of the readings I have cited is at least possible. The epistemological problems posed by Guido seem most resistant to satisfying solutions not when we are confined to his point of view, but when we are denied access to the kind of "unreliable" phenomenological data available in his monologues.

A Horneyan approach to Guido's monologues allows us to appreciate Browning's genius and integrity as a mimetic artist. In writing *The Ring and the Book,* his moral intention clearly was to vindicate Pompilia and Caponsacchi. Further, he almost certainly had a considerable psychological stake in glorifying this couple whom he identified with Elizabeth Barrett and himself.[38] Yet he has made his villain a believable human being: morally outrageous, cruelly violent, and revoltingly blind to both these qualities; but motivated by understandable human needs, the conflict and frustration of which have made him what he is. He is a liar, but his lies are of a piece with the inner logic of his neurotic solution. With the help of a theory equipped to allow us insight into the psychological meaning of his necessary fictions, we find that even those "tell a truth / Obliquely," as the poet says his art does (12.859–60).

Guido is intelligible as a suffering human being whose need for triumph twists and thwarts his need for love; whose despicable behavior issues from his sense of failure, of unattractiveness, and of ineffectiveness at controlling his life; and whose deepest deceits are the self-deceits through which he attempts to avoid being devastated by his self-hate and his fear of death. Browning made his Guido not a conveniently inhuman monster, but a man: a terrible man, to be sure, but one whose basic needs and fears are uncomfortably familiar to us all. Given a situation in which his own moral convictions and psychological needs would have been well served by a Guido both inexcusable and inexplicable, Browning made his Guido still inexcusable, but psychologically explicable through the details and patterns of his voluminous self-fictionalizations.

NOTES

1. Park Honan, *Browning's Characters: A Study in Poetic Techniques* (New Haven: Yale University Press, 1961), p. 205. See also Robert Langbaum, "*The Ring and the Book:* A Relativist Poem," *PMLA* 71 (1956); reprint, in Robert Langbaum, ed., *The Victorian Age: Essays in History and in Social and Literary Criticism,* 2d ed. (New York: Fawcett, 1967), p. 226; Wendell Stacy Johnson, "Marriage and Divorce in Browning," in *Sex and Marriage in Victorian Poetry* (Ithaca: Cornell University Press, 1975), p. 227.

2. Richard D. Altick and James F. Loucks, II, *Browning's Roman Murder Story: A Reading of* The Ring and the Book (Chicago: University of Chicago Press, 1968), p. 52; Hoxie N. Fairchild, "Browning the Simplehearted Casuist," *University of Toronto Quarterly* 18 (1949): 239, Johnson, "Marriage and Divorce," p. 227, and Honan, *Browning's Characters,* p. 205; A. K. Cook, *A Commentary Upon Browning's* The Ring and the Book (1920; reprint, Hamden, Conn.: Archon Books, 1966), p. 235. Similar views are stated by Henri A. Talon, "*The Ring and the Book:* Truth and Fiction in Character-painting," *Victorian Poetry* 6 (1968): 358; Langbaum, "A Relativist Poem," p. 226; William C. DeVane, *A Browning Handbook,* 2d ed. (New York: Appleton-Century-Crofts, 1955), p. 336.

3. Fairchild, "Browning the Simplehearted Casuist," p. 239.

4. Roma A. King, Jr., "Immortal Nakedness: *The Ring and the Book,*" in *The Focusing Artifice: The Poetry of Robert Browning* (Athens: Ohio University Press, 1968), p. 140.

5. Altick and Loucks, *Browning's Roman Murder Story,* p. 79. Cf. Johnson, "Marriage and Divorce," p. 232, and Richard D. McGhee, "'The Luck That Lies Beyond a Man': Guido's Salvation in *The Ring and the Book,*" *Browning Institute Studies* 5 (1977): 88.

6. Ian Jack, *Browning's Major Poetry* (Oxford: Clarendon Press, 1973), p. 91; Boyd Litzinger, "The New Vision of Judgment: The Case of St. Guido," *Tennessee Studies in Literature* 20 (1975): 70. Cf. DeVane, *A Browning Handbook,* p. 336, and Honan, *Browning's Characters,* p. 305.

7. Cook, *A Commentary,* p. 92, outlines some of these inconsistencies.

8. Altick and Loucks, *Browning's Roman Murder Story,* pp. 71–72.

9. Robert Browning, *The Ring and the Book,* vols. 5 and 6 of *The Works of Robert Browning,* Centenary Edition (London, 1912; reprint, New York: Barnes & Noble, 1966), Bk. 11, lines 1704–5, 2420. Hereafter *The Ring* is cited in the text.

10. E. Warwick Slinn, *Browning and the Fictions of Identity* (Totowa, N.J.: Barnes & Noble, 1982), p. 110. Slinn sees in *The Ring*'s "predetermined and clearly enunciated authorial attitude . . . a standard for measuring moral behaviour" and argues that this standard, by showing "the limits to [each character's] perspective," offers a way out of the poem's "epistemological ambiguity" (pp. 126–27). However, if the epistemological problems concern the mimetic, psychological level of the monologues, as I think they do, the availability of a moral standard would seem to contribute little to our ability to understand the characters in psychological terms.

11. Morse Peckham, "Personality and the Mask of Knowledge," in *Victorian Revolutionaries: Speculations on Some Heroes of a Culture Crisis* (New York: George Braziller, 1970), p. 117.

12. Karen Horney, *Neurosis and Human Growth: The Struggle Toward Self-Realization* (New York: Norton, 1970), pp. 20–22. Hereafter cited in the text as *NHG.*

13. Michael G. Yetman, " 'Count Guido Franceshini': The Villain as Artist in *The Ring and the Book,*" *PMLA* 87 (1972): 1094.

14. Bernard J. Paris, "The Withdrawn Man: *Notes From Underground,*" in *A Psychological Approach to Fiction: Studies in Thackeray, Stendhal, George Eliot, Dostoevsky, and Conrad* (Bloomington: Indiana University Press, 1974), pp. 191–92, 201–2, discusses the appropriateness of Horneyan analysis for "first person narrations . . . in which we are totally dependent upon an untrustworthy narrator."

15. Cook, *A Commentary,* p. 235. The phrase is adopted by Roy Gridley, "Browning's Two Guidos," *University of Toronto Quarterly* 37 (1967): 51–68, and Mary Rose Sullivan, "The Two Guidos," in *Browning's Voices in* The Ring and the Book: *A Study of Method and Meaning* (Toronto: University of Toronto Press, 1969), pp. 137–63.

16. Sullivan, "The Two Guidos," p. 160.

17. For an interpretation of Guido's references to his training as a way to "claim implicit freedom from responsibility," see Slinn, *Browning and the Fictions of Identity,* pp. 115–17.

18. Joseph A. Dupas, "Guido Franceschini's Verbal Flourishes for 'Something Changeless at the Heart,' " *Renascence* 29 (1977): 68.

19. Karen Horney, *Our Inner Conflicts: A Constructive Theory of Neurosis* (New York: Norton, 1966), p. 70. Hereafter cited in the text as *OIC.*

20. King, "Immortal Nakedness," p. 142.

21. Ibid., p. 142.

22. Cf. Sullivan, "The Two Guidos," p. 160.

23. Langbaum, "A Relativist Poem," p. 227; Cook, *A Commentary,* p. 235; King, "Immortal Nakedness," p. 142.

24. King, "Immortal Nakedness," p. 143.

25. Andrew K. Ruotolo, "Dynamics of Sudden Murder," *American Journal of Psychoanalysis* 28 (1968): 162. Hereafter cited in the text as *DSM.*

26. Andrew K. Ruotolo, "Neurotic Pride and Homicide," *American Journal of Psychoanalysis* 35 (1975): 14. Hereafter cited in the text as *NPH.*

27. Cf. esp. "Locksley Hall," lines 181–83 with 5.2036 and *In Memoriam,* sec. 106, lines 13–24 with 5.2037–47, where Guido reverses Tennyson's message but not its tone.

28. Bernard J. Paris, "Bargains with Fate: A Psychological Approach to Shakespeare's Major Tragedies," *Aligarh Journal of English Studies* 5 (1980): 149.

29. Cf. Robert Langbaum, "Is Guido Saved? The Meaning of Browning's Conclusion to *The Ring and the Book,*" *Victorian Poetry* 10 (1972): 301: "Guido's disturbance over Pompilia's look is a sign of the conscience that makes him redeemable."

30. Cf. Slinn, *Browning and the Fictions of Identity,* p. 123: In book 11 Guido is "constructing for himself whatever images will defend his self-respect."

31. Cf. Gridley, "Browning's Two Guidos," pp. 51, 57: Guido's "improvising upon the theme that he is a life-force" is "a defiant verbal assertion of his existence, his identity." In the same context Dupas, p. 59, speaks of Guido's "almost maniacal efforts to prevent the dissolution of his selfhood."

32. Allan Hymes, "'A New Rule in Another World': Guido's Experience of Death in *The Ring and the Book*," *Thoth* 14 (1974): 9.

33. Langbaum, "A Relativist Poem," p. 227; Cook, *A Commentary*, p. 92; Honan, *Browning's Characters*, p. 308; King, "Immortal Nakedness," p. 141; Yetman, "Villain as Artist," p. 1093.

34. Sullivan, "The Two Guidos," p. 159.

35. Cf. Honan, *Browning's Characters*, p. 290, who describes Guido's state as "complete mental disintegration."

36. Altick and Loucks, *Browning's Roman Murder Story*, p. 225; Jack, *Browning's Major Poetry*, p. 292; Langbaum, "Is Guido Saved?" p. 293; King, "Immortal Nakedness," p. 164.

37. Robert Langbaum, *The Poetry of Experience: The Dramatic Monologue in Modern Literary Tradition* (New York: Norton, 1963), p. 78.

38. J. E. Shaw, "The 'Donna Angelicata' in *The Ring and the Book*," *PMLA* 41 (1926): 69; Norton B. Crowell, *The Convex Glass: The Mind of Robert Browning* (n.p.: University of New Mexico Press, 1968), pp. 185–86.

7
Lawrence's "The Princess" and Horney's "Idealized Self"

Barbara M. Smalley

1

D.H. Lawrence's harsh treatment of the women in his stories and novels has caused many readers, including a number of eminent critics, to view him as the archetypal male chauvinist. Kingsley Widmer, for example, writes of Lawrence's "mystical mysogyny" and of Lawrence's view of woman as man's "nemesis," a "subtly diabolic" creature.[1] Repeatedly, Widmer says, Lawrence employs female characters "to dramatize the sicker forms of destruction."[2] Lawrence's portrayal of women, in the opinion of Charles Rossman, at times suggests a degree of hostility toward them "verging on sadism."[3] Harry T. Moore maintains that Lawrence in his own person shared his male characters' dread of domination by strong-willed women in their "implementation of pure will."[4] Mark Spilka discovers in Lawrence's postwar fiction a sensational variety of means by which male characters endeavor to subdue resistant females. These include resort to "drugs, murder, rape, sexual cannibalism, soul-absorption, wish-fulfillment, [and] pond-stoning argument."[5] Lawrence's emasculating females play, indeed, an impressive part in his fiction. They come from a wide range of socioeconomic backgrounds. Some are maternal; others are decidedly nonmaternal. A list would include such notable portrayals as Gertrude Morel in *Sons and Lovers,* Hermione Roddice in *Women in Love,* Paul's mother in "Rocking-Horse Winner," Pauline in "The Lovely Lady," Mrs. Bodoin in "Mother and Daughter," Mrs. Gee in "Two Blue Birds," and Annie Stone and her female friends in "Tickets, Please."

In the view of some critics, Dollie Urquhart in "The Princess" is simply another of Lawrence's strong-willed women subjected to intense cruelty through their own perverse struggles to exert dominance over their male counterparts. Charles Rossman sees in Dollie Urquhart "an emotionally sterile, willful, 'unfeminine' woman" who, through her own obstinancies "suffers repeated rape."[6] Kingsley Widmer holds that Dollie Urquhart's destruction of her satanic "demon lover" in the final scenes of the work symbolizes the triumph of will over passion.[7] Graham Hough views Dollie Urquhart as yet another in Lawrence's long catalog of women seeking dominance over males only to suffer the author's "doctrinaire cruelty" meted out as a form of vengeance upon "cold, white women."[8]

Critics who see Dollie Urquhart in such terms base their opinions on the final scenes of the story. In these final pages, Dollie and her "blood-conscious" primitive Latin guide Domingo Romero travel to a cabin high in the mountains of New Mexico where, miles from cultivated life, they have a sexual encounter. Dollie tells Romero that she finds him sexually unsatisfactory, whereupon he repeatedly "rapes" her in an attempt either to win her or to break her spirit. When Romero is later shot down by rangers, Dollie seems to have emerged triumphant from her contest of wills. She seems Kingsley Widmer's "willful witch"[9] epitomized.

Such a reading, however, does not take into account the underlying *causes* for Dollie's appearing to exert willfulness in the final pages of the tale. When the work is considered as a whole, "willfulness," I shall attempt to show, is not an exercise of will but an expression of a response conditioned by a pervasive pattern of her childhood training, a pattern that Lawrence treats with much greater subtlety than has been credited to him. I believe that Karen Horney's theories are valuable for an understanding of Lawrence's portrayal of Dollie Urquhart's behavior in "The Princess." In order to find the causes for the compulsive behavior Dollie manifests in the final pages of the work, it is necessary to begin at the beginning of the story and to focus on her father's neurotic personality structure.

2

In the first part of "The Princess," Lawrence creates in Colin Urquhart the kind of neurotic Karen Horney terms "detached." These individuals studiously avoid entangling relationships with other people and value their freedom from such intimacies above everything else. Actually their need to keep emotional distance between themselves and others is caused by the intense anxiety they feel in situations that require relatedness to other people. These individuals have learned to deny in themselves their basic human need for emotional involvement with people and have learned to withdraw (to "move away")[10] from others. In an attempt to avoid the feelings of insecurity they experience in situations requiring give-and-take relationships, they have created an idealized self that does not need to engage with other people—a self that is independent and self-sufficient. By presenting this grandiose image to the world, they attempt to avoid the anxiety they feel in interaction with others.

Characters in "The Princess" who attempt to establish a relationship with Colin, even in the years before Dollie is born, find themselves blocked by this elegant product of Colin's imagination. The role Colin plays habitually and compulsively is that of a charming, ineffectual gentleman of high birth. He is consistent in his "never arriving anywhere, never doing anything, and never definitely being anything." Colin imagines himself to be a descendant of "Scottish kings" and imagines that "the blood of Scottish kings" flows in his veins. He assumes that his royal heritage entitles him to the prerogatives of rank ("claims").[11] Consequently, he maintains social distinctions and keeps distance between himself and other people. The narrator informs us, however, that "Colin was just a bit mad," and that Colin's American relatives said that he "was just a bit 'off' " in his claims of royal blood.[12]

Colin assiduously avoids making any "decisive connection" with others (p. 473). His aloofness and inaccessibility do not prevent women from being fascinated by him, however, and when he is nearly forty, Colin marries a girl of twenty-two. It is not long before his wife finds that she has sought an intimate connection where none can exist. Colin's feelings of superiority due to his imagined royal heritage prevent him from taking seriously the concerns of his young wife. He must maintain his dignified exterior at all costs. "Mrs. Urquhart lived three years in the mist and glamour of her husband's presence. And then it broke her. It was like living with a spectre. . . . He was always charming, courteous, perfectly gracious in that hushed, musical voice of his. But absent. When all came to all, he just wasn't there" (pp. 473–74). He seemed "like a living echo." When his young wife became angry with him, Colin "just opened his wide blue eyes wider, and took a child-like, silent dignity there was no getting past" (p. 474). After his wife's death, Colin spends some time with her relatives, but he wards off all attempts at intimacy. He persists in maintaining his regal role. Her relatives remain for him "just casual phenomena, or gramophones, talking-machines that had to be answered. But of their actual existence he was never once aware" (p. 474).

Colin refuses to recognize in himself any need to establish close human ties with other people (to "move toward" them).[13] His personality demonstrates what Horney means when she says that the person who is alienated from himself (his real feelings and wishes) may work, talk about himself, even engage in sexual relations with another person without showing anything of his spontaneous real self. His relation to himself and to his whole world "has become impersonal" (*NHG,* p. 161).

The narrator of "The Princess" does not present material from Colin's childhood that would help explain why he feels he must keep emotional distance between himself and others. We do not learn why he believes he must act according to the dictates of the arrogant role he has assumed. However, when Colin takes over the upbringing of his two-year-old daughter Dollie after the death of his wife, the narrator presents with almost textbook precision the process whereby a parent perpetuates his own neurosis through his child by giving her conditional "positive regard," i. e., awarding her his approval only if certain conditions are met.[14]

Unable to accept his daughter's individuality, Colin makes his regard for her contingent upon her *appearing* to be the ideal child he creates in his imagination. In order to win the approval of her father, Dollie learns to act not in accordance with her own wishes and feelings, but in accordance with the glorified Princess role her father prefers. Thus Dollie becomes alienated from her own perceptions and values, her "real self," and becomes committed to acting according to the requirements (the "shoulds")[15] of a royal Princess image. She learns to reject her spontaneous, authentic reactions, and like her father, she becomes committed to "appearing" rather than "being." The relationship between father and daughter graphically portrays what Horney means when she says that the neurotic process "is a process of abandoning the real self for an idealized one; of trying to actualize this pseudoself instead of our given human potentials" (*NHG*, p. 376).

Carl Rogers, who shares the views of Horney and other Third Force theorists concerning the constructive forces inherent in the newborn child, writes of the process through which a child rejects his own innate potential for psychological growth and maturation (his "real self") and becomes committed to appearing as someone else wishes him to be. According to Rogers, the need for positive regard from someone whose love the child needs (a "significant social other") is more compelling for the child than his "own organismic valuing process." Consequently, the child may learn to reject his own values—values that are an expression of his own real needs and beliefs—in an attempt to secure the regard of a "social other" (often the child's mother). Thus the child becomes guided in his behavior "not by the degree to which an experience maintains or enhances his own organism," but by the probability of receiving approval and love from such "significant others." He learns to view himself and his behavior in the same way these individuals do: he now regards some of his behaviors positively that are "not actually experienced as satisfying," and he now regards some behaviors negatively that are not "actually experienced as unsatisfying." When the child behaves in "accordance with these introjected values," he has acquired "conditions of worth." He can no longer "regard himself as having worth unless he lives in terms of these conditions." Now the child avoids or carries out certain behaviors "solely because of these introjected conditions of self-regard, quite without reference to the organismic consequences of these behaviors." He has learned to falsify some of the values he experiences and to perceive them "only in terms of their value to others." Consequently, he is not "true to himself," to his own natural "organismic valuing of experience."[16]

In his presentation of the relationship between Dollie and her father during her childhood, Lawrence dramatizes the process whereby a child gives up her "own organismic valuing process" and becomes, in Horneyan terms, "alienated" from herself. Colin teaches his daughter that his regard for her depends on her appearing to be the superior, idealized self—the Princess self—he creates for her. He instills in her the belief that she must be worthy of her eminent position and that she must adhere to certain rules ("*noblesse oblige*"): she must maintain social distinctions and never become emotionally involved with "commoners"—a category including all people except the Princess and himself. Another requirement ("should") is that she treat the "vulgar" masses with politeness, gentleness, and kindness. He warns her, however, that she must never try to think of inferiors (all other people) as if they were "like" her, "the last of Princesses."[17] She must always remain in the isolation of her regal role, he admonishes her, for if she trusts other people and reveals her *"great secret,"* her royalty, dire consequences will result: others will "envy" her and will try to "kill" her (pp. 475–76).

As a result of her father's indoctrination, Dollie learns to perceive other people as common, vulgar, and even as potential murderers. Moreover, her father teaches her to dehumanize herself and other people in her imagination and to think of people as "demons" rather than as human beings. This kind of perception of other people as objects or things is discussed in especially enlightening terms by R. D. Laing in regard to the schizoid individual. Laing points out that the schizoid "fears a real live dialectical relationship with live people. He can relate himself only to depersonalized persons, to phantoms of his own phantasies (imagos), perhaps to things, perhaps to animals."[18]

In order to secure her father's regard, Dollie becomes alienated from her real self. She learns to deny in herself her basic human need for ties of affection with others. Her spontaneous impulses are now held in check by an automatic control system. Impulses and feelings of affection, trust, and relatedness—feelings incompatible with her solitary regal role—are held in check or denied. She now reacts to people and situations as she "should" in order to live up to her glorified self and to please her father. Her behavior becomes compulsive. She now displays the rigidity that Horney says is "inherent in all neuroses" (*OIC*, p. 81).

Afraid to trust other people and to relate to them in a meaningful way, the Princess presents a seemingly impervious facade to the world. She possesses a "cold elfin detachment." Something seems to have "crystallised in her character," the narrator tells us. She has become "clear and finished" and "impervious as crystal" (p. 476). She has abandoned her spontaneous self to become an unnatural creature—"something like a changeling, not quite human" (p. 477).

As a result of her father's training, Dollie becomes imbued with neurotic pride, pride based on attributes she arrogates to herself in her imagination (*NHG*, p. 90). She assumes that her superiority entitles her to be exempt from the give-and-take relationships of human experience.[19] She assumes that her "slightly benevolent politeness" will be adequate acknowledgement of other people (p. 476). She assumes that others will be aware of her rank and will not attempt to overstep social barriers and become familiar with her.

Other people, however, do not share her glorified image of herself. They sense her unrelatedness, and they resent her armor of indifference. When she visits her American relatives, they are "infuriated" by her "condescension" and her "inward coldness" (p. 476). When she travels, her "peculiar condescension" earns her "strange antipathies" (p. 477). *Macho* Latin porters and cabmen especially dislike her, for they sense her "sterility," and her insensitivity to their "*beauté male.*" When they are alone with her, they show their resentment by treating her with "brutal rudeness." The Princess, however, is unaware of them as individuals. She negates them in her mind, classifying them as "types" she has read about in Maupassant and Zola. She looks at a "lusty, sensual Roman cabman as if he were a sort of grotesque, to make her smile" (p. 477).

The Princess keeps emotional distance between herself and *all* people except her father, not merely members of the opposite sex. Even after she has had the same female companion for many years, she rigidly insists upon class distinctions. They "were always Miss Urquhart and Miss Cummins to one another, and a certain distance was instinctively maintained" (p. 480). The Princess becomes so isolated and emotionally impoverished that eventually she becomes psychologically detached even from her father, whose unhealthy perceptions of himself and others have led him into increasingly neurotic behavior and even into "fits of violence" (p. 479).

3

The Princess is "relieved when her father die[s]," but his death compels her to ask herself what she must do with the remainder of her life. At thirty-eight she is without purpose. She cannot admit to herself that she is afraid to give up her solitary lifestyle and engage with people. She avoids acknowledging her fears by imagining that she is "becoming vulgarised" through her exposure to the "vulgar crowd." She then begins to think of marriage as an escape from the sullying effects of contact with the masses. However, she psychologically distances herself from the thought of marrying by thinking of marriage in the "blank abstract." She decides that marriage is the thing she "ought to *do.*" By thinking of marriage as a duty she imposes on herself, the Princess avoids acknowledging her need for a meaningful relationship with another person. In spite of her need to feel that she is independent and self-sufficient, however, the images she associates with her own nature are dependent and sexual: she thinks of herself as "an unstoppered bottle" and as an "empty vessel in the warehouse of the world" (p. 480).

The Princess is convinced that she does not feel "any sudden interest in men" and that she is not "vitally" attracted to them. However, she now begins to look at men with a "shrewder eye," an "eye toward marriage" (p. 480). She even goes to a ranch in New Mexico so that she can meet suitable candidates. When any of these wealthy and eligible men hint "marriage at her," however, she resents their presumptuousness. Her neurotic pride is offended, and she finds their proposals "rather preposterous, quite ridiculous, and a tiny bit impertinent on their part" (p. 482).

The only man the Princess finds herself attracted to at the ranch is not of royal birth. He is a Mexican peasant, Domingo Romero, a guide at the ranch.

Since he has his clearly-defined subordinate role as an employee, the Princess does not feel threatened by him. He is hired to serve her, and she feels in control of him and of herself. However, in spite of her need to deny in herself any dependency needs, she begins to trust Romero's judgment and to rely on him. She accepts him as an authority in matters pertaining to ranch life, and she allows him to teach her some of the skills necessary for living on a ranch. Soon the Princess experiences feelings for Romero that are a threat to the neurotic defenses she has maintained since childhood. She becomes vitally attracted to him. She likes his appearance, his voice, "his presence." She imagines that there is even a wordless communication between the two of them as between kindred natures, as if he sends her "*from his heart* a dark beam of succour and sustaining. She had never known this before, and it was very thrilling" (p. 485). Since her neurotic pride in her own imaginary superiority compels her to believe that anyone who interests her must be decidedly superior, she includes Romero in her imaginary realm of gentility. She persuades herself that she perceives in Romero something like the aura of nobility that surrounds her own personality as a Princess—a special spark in Romero's eye that sets him apart from all commonplace persons. Others are too crass to recognize his authentic gentility as the descendant of the Spanish family that had once owned not only the area of the ranch but "miles of land" thereabout (p. 482). The Princess imagines that she sees in Romero a special elegance, dignity, and gentlemanliness. Regardless of her desire to maintain her self-sufficiency and her independence, she eventually relaxes her guard and becomes emotionally involved with Romero; it is Romero's attendance upon her that makes her feel like "her true Princess self" (p. 485).

In spite of her feelings for Romero, the Princess cannot consider marrying him. She cannot overcome the fear and distrust of other people instilled in her by her father. The idea of a sustained relationship based on trust and intimacy (and vulnerability) is frightening to her. In her fear of committing herself to a relationship based on closeness to another person, the Princess demonstrates what Horney means when she writes that the "detached" type of neurotic fears "ties" with people. Even at the beginning of a relationship he is often concerned with devising ways for extricating himself. His fear of a "lasting tie" may cause him to panic at the thought of marrying (*NHG*, p. 266). The narrator makes it clear that the Princess' reluctance to marry Romero is not due to "conventional" ideas concerning their class differences. Nor is it due to economic reasons, for the Princess has "plenty of money for two." However, Romero's presence puts to flight "the *idée fixe* of 'marriage'. For some reason, in her strange little brain, the idea of *marrying* him could not enter. Not for any definite reason. He was in himself a gentleman. . . . There was no actual obstacle" (p. 485).

In an attempt to allay the anxiety she feels in a person-to-person relationship with Romero—a relationship that reawakens her childhood fears—the Princess utilizes a technique her father taught her for maintaining psychological distance from people: she dehumanizes herself and Romero in her imagination. She imagines that both she and Romero are kindred "demons." Romero becomes much less threatening as a thing, a "demon" divorced from ordinary human context rather than a person capable of destroying her independence and her Princess facade. It was "as if their two 'daemons' could marry, were perhaps married. Only their two *selves,* Miss Urquhart and Senor Domingo Romero, were for some reason incompatible" (p. 486). The defense mechanism here utilized by the Princess is the same as that often employed by schizoid individuals. Laing writes that the self of the schizoid person avoids "being related directly to real persons." Instead, the self of these individuals posits an object of its imagination and then relates to it. *"The self can relate itself with immediacy to an object which is an object of its own imagination or memory but not to a real person."*[20]

The Princess insists that Romero, in his hired position as a guide, accompany her and Miss Cummins on an overnight journey to a remote place known only to Romero. Even after Miss Cummins is forced to turn back due to her horse's lameness, the Princess insists that she and Romero complete the hazardous journey, alone. The Princess has a momentary awareness that she and Romero will be isolated from other people, but she is very "sure of herself," and she is convinced that Romero is "not the kind of man to do anything to her against her will" (p. 493). On the conscious level, the Princess is convinced that she and Romero are on an educational mission: she tells herself that she wants to learn about animals as they exist in their native habitat. As the Princess and Romero take their Conradian journey away from the restraints of civilization, the scenery strongly reflects the Princess' unconscious feelings. The journey up the mountain is fraught with sexual imagery, and the trip is a metaphor for the Princess' sexual attraction to Romero: the Princess wants to see "animal" life. She insists on taking the trip so that she can observe the animals moving about in their "wild unconsciousness" (p. 488). Her "fixed desire" is to go "over the brim of the mountains, to look into the inner chaos of the Rockies." The Princess comes close to acknowledging her real feelings for Romero when she decides that he should accompany her through this wild primitive scenery because there is a "peculiar kinship" or "peculiar link" between the two of them (p. 493).

Imagery of death and decay figure prominently in this section of the work. As noted earlier, Romero is one of the last descendants (who are now "just Mexican peasants") of a Spanish family that had once owned many miles of land. The white man and "fatal inertia" have finished Romero's family line. Romero dresses in black; there is a resigned, hopeless quality about him. He seems to be waiting "either to die or to be aroused into passion and hope" (p. 482). As Romero and the Princess travel through parts of the mountains, around them "lay patches of white snow." It was all so "anti-life." Everything was "grey and dead around them"; they saw "silver-grey corpses of the spruce" and heard the "huge, monstrous, mechanical wind" in the mountains, which were "empty of life or soul" (p. 496). The virgin Princess' emotional sterility and barrenness are symbolized by the "debris" of the virginal forests they pass through: a chill enters her heart as she realizes "what a tangle of decay and despair lay in the virgin forests" (p. 490).

During their trip Romero maintains a respectful distance from the Princess. It is the Princess, not Romero, who initiates their first sexual encounter. She dreams of snow and coldness. Awakening in the ice-cold room, she complains of the cold to Romero. When he asks her pointedly if she wishes him to "make her warm," she responds with a single "yes." She "wanted warmth, protection, she wanted to be taken away from herself." It is at this point in the story that the Princess loses her rigid control over her feelings: *"And she was given over to this thing"* (pp. 503–4, my emphasis). The Princess tries to reconcile her spontaneous reactions to Romero with her compulsive need to keep emotional distance between herself and others and to maintain control of herself. On the one hand she "had *willed* that it should happen to her. And according to her will, she lay and let it happen." Diametrically opposed to these thoughts are those that cause her to deny to herself that she is responsible in any way for their sexual encounter: "But she never wanted it. She never wanted to be thus assailed and handled, and mauled. *She wanted to keep herself to herself*" (p. 504, my emphasis).

What ensues between the Princess and Romero seems on the surface to be only another power struggle between a sensuous untutored male and a sterile willful Anglo-type female—the kind of combat that appears so notably in *Sons and Lovers* and in different guises throughout the canon of Lawrence's works. In "The Princess," however, a great deal of the conflict between Romero and the Princess is due to the conflict within the Princess herself. By initiating their sexual encounter and then losing control over herself, the Princess has reactivated her childhood conflict between what she really feels and what she believes she *should* feel—a conflict she put out of operation when she learned to deny in herself her basic human needs for ties of affection with other people and committed herself to appearing as the solitary self-sufficient Princess preferred by her father. A relationship based on honesty and authenticity would leave her vulnerable to rejection, for she has been taught that she is basically unlovable, that she cannot be esteemed if she removes her Princess mask. She must maintain the defenses provided by her Princess role. She must "keep herself intact" (p. 503). She must *"regain possession of all herself"* (p. 505, my emphasis).

In an attempt to deny in herself any feelings and wishes that are incompatible with her idealized self, the Princess begins to think of herself as a victim and to blame Romero for the violation of her Princess self that has taken place. Their moments of sexual intimacy she can view only as Romero's triumph over her: she "could feel a curious joy and pride surging up again in him *at her expense. Because he had got her* . . . and he was exulting in his power over her, his possession, his pleasure" (p. 504, my emphasis).

When in the morning Romero asks whether she had "liked" the previous night, the Princess' fear of intimacy underlies her hostile behavior toward him. She tells him with intentionally insulting coldness that she had not enjoyed their sexual experience. She feels that she is establishing emotional distance once more, that she is "getting her own back." Nevertheless, she is not convinced that she has severed all bonds with him, for she senses that *"in some mysterious way"* he possesses *"some part of her still"* (p. 505, my emphasis).

The Princess' hostile vindictive feelings are alien to the serene unruffled Princess she aspires to be.[21] If she were not emotionally involved with Romero, she could have resorted to any one of a number of stratagems to induce him to take her back to civilization: she could have feigned sexual satisfaction; she could have agreed (disingenuously) to marry him. Once again under the protection of the law, she could easily have extricated herself from Romero's attentions. However, she cannot evaluate the situation dispassionately and react in her usual emotionally detached manner. She must wound Romero in retaliation for the wrong she would like to believe he inflicted on her. By telling him that he is sexually inadequate, she has dealt Romero "a cruel blow" (p. 505).

The effect of the Princess' declaration upon Romero goes beyond anything she could have expected. Romero, despite his humble position at the ranch, possesses a pride in his Mexican *macho* self-image so extreme as to verge on severe neurosis. Saying that he will "make" her love him, Romero gathers all her clothing and, breaking a hole for the purpose, throws the garments under the ice of the pond. He then—in an even more reckless defiance of consequences—tosses both her saddle and his beneath the ice.

The Princess is more in control of the situation than she can admit to herself. By provoking Romero to prove his masculinity, she can see herself as an unwilling victim, thus allowing her to deny to herself that she is in any way exercising choice. She tells Romero that he can never "conquer" her. Romero continues to be vulnerable to her attacks on his maleness, for in response to her remarks, his face registers many emotions—"wonder, surprise, a touch of horror, and an unconscious pain" (p. 508). After the Princess defiantly informs Romero that he can never get her under his "will," she is forced to submit to his sexual performances. "In a sombre, violent excess" Romero "tried to expend his desire for her. And she was wracked with agony, and felt each time she would die." Then the narrator points out that her agony is due to her losing control of "some unrealised part of her" of which she does not wish to be aware: *"Because in some peculiar way, he had got hold of her, some unrealised part of her which she never wished to realise"* (p. 509; my emphasis). The part of her that she does not wish to realize is her real self. By reacting spontaneously and naturally to Romero, the Princess has acted according to the needs of her real self—the self that she became alienated from as a child in order to secure the conditional "positive regard" of her father. Her father taught her to have contempt for her real self and to believe that she is not acceptable when she acts in accordance with her real wishes and feelings. Consequently when she reacts naturally and authentically, she has feelings of worthlessness and fears of being rejected by others.

When the Princess begins to weep, Romero no longer approaches her. She is now free from the anxiety she feels in a relationship that threatens the neurotic defenses she has built up against acknowledging her needs for closeness to other people. The Princess and Romero "were like two people who had died. He did not touch her anymore. . . . His desire was dead" (pp. 509–10).

The Princess' ambivalence toward Romero persists, however. Even when he is preparing to shoot at the rangers who have come to find her, she still has feelings for him that are unacceptable to her solitary idealized self. She "wondered why she did not feel sorry for him. But her spirit was hard and cold, her heart could not melt. *Though now she would have called him to her, with love*" (p. 510, my emphasis).

When the rangers who have killed Romero are in the process of approaching the camp, however, it is her idealized Princess self that dominates her consciousness rather than horror at what has just taken place. Romero has undergone sexual death, spiritual death, and ultimately physical death during their relationship, but she is once more chiefly concerned with the proprieties surrounding her regal status. It is unseemly for a woman of her position to have a man lying dead at her feet. As a Princess, she feels a loss of caste and hurt pride at being beheld deprived of her clothes, her status symbols, under humiliating circumstances: "Oh, the sense of ridicule she felt!" (p. 511).

The Princess' experiences with Romero have been harrowing in the extreme, but they have not dislodged her from the role she has assumed and believed in and found a specious and self-betraying kind of protection in since childhood. Unable to accept responsibility for her contributions to Romero's death, Dollie distorts in her mind the details of his firing at the rangers and his death in the ensuing gunfire. She explains to herself and to others the scene as it *should* have happened, with herself assigned an appropriately regal part: "a man went mad and shot my horse from under me," she is accustomed to explaining once she has returned to the East, "and my guide had to shoot him dead" (p. 512). She is still "appearing" rather than "being." She is once more "the Princess, and a virgin intact," the narrator assures us (p. 512). She is still the Princess who looks sardonically "out on a princeless world" (p. 479). One recalls that early in the work the narrator notes that "no one, to her dying day, ever knew exactly the strange picture her father had framed her in *and from which she never stepped*" (p. 476, my emphasis).

NOTES

1. Kingsley Widmer, "Lawrence and the Fall of Modern Woman," *Modern Fiction Studies* 5, no. 1 (1959): 48.

2. Kingsley Widmer, *The Art of Perversity* (Seattle: University of Washington Press, 1962), p. 76.

3. Charles Rossman, " 'You are the Call and I am the Answer': D. H. Lawrence and Women," *The D. H. Lawrence Review* 8, no. 3 (1975): 257.

4. Harry T. Moore, "Bert and Lady Jane," in *Lawrence and Women,* ed. Anne Smith (London: Vision Press, 1978), p. 182.

5. Mark Spilka, "On Lawrence's Hostility to Wilful Women," in *Lawrence and Women,* ed. Anne Smith (London: Vision Press, 1978), p. 198.

6. Rossman, "D. H. Lawrence and Women," p. 257.

7. Widmer, *The Art of Perversity,* p. 85.

8. Graham Hough, *The Dark Sun* (London: Gerald Duckworth, 1968), pp. 179–80.

9. Widmer, "Lawrence and the Fall of Modern Woman," p. 48.

10. Karen Horney, *Our Inner Conflicts* (New York: Norton, 1972), p. 73. Hereafter cited in the text as *OIC.*

11. Karen Horney, *Neurosis and Human Growth* (New York: Norton, 1950), p. 41. Hereafter cited in the text as *NHG.* Horney uses the term "claims" to designate the neurotic's unrealistic expectations: when the neurotic imagines he really is his glorified self, he expects "special attention" and "deference" from others. He believes that "he is entitled to be treated by others, or by fate, in accord with his grandiose notions about himself."

12. D. H. Lawrence, "The Princess," in *The Complete Stories of D. H. Lawrence* (London: William Heinemann, 1963), 2:473. Further references to "The Princess" will be to this edition and will be cited in the text.

13. Horney writes that "in a healthy human relationship, the moves toward, against, or away from others are not mutually exclusive. The ability to want and to give affection, or to give in; the ability to fight, and the ability to keep to oneself—these are complementary capacities necessary for good human relations" (*Neurosis and Human Growth,* p. 19).

14. Carl Rogers utilizes this term in his analysis of the process whereby a child gives up his own "organismic valuing process" in an attempt to secure the regard of a "significant social other." (See n. 16, below.)

15. Horney writes that the imperative "shoulds" or coercive "inner dictates" are "an expression of the individual's . . . drive to make himself over into something he is not" (*Neurosis and Human Growth,* p. 374). Adherence to his "shoulds" renders the neurotic's behavior rigid and inflexible. In any given situation he cannot express his real feelings and wishes by behaving spontaneously and naturally. Instead, he will react as he "should," i. e., in compliance with the demands of his imaginary grandiose self (*Neurosis and Human Growth,* pp. 73–74).

16. Carl Rogers, "A Theory of Personality," in *Theories in Psychopathology,* ed. Theodore Millon (Philadelphia: W. B. Sanders, 1967), pp. 263–66, passim. For another discussion of the process through which a child gives up his "self" in an attempt to win the approval of those individuals whose regard he needs, see Abraham Maslow's *Toward a Psychology of Being* (New York: Van Nostrand, 1968), pp. 51–52.

17. Horney utilizes the term "search for glory" to designate the neurotic's desire to feel superior. The neurotic's compulsive drive for "indiscriminate supremacy" causes him to be "indifferent to truth, whether concerning himself, others, or facts" (*Neurosis and Human Growth,* p. 30).

18. R. D. Laing, *The Divided Self* (Baltimore: Penguin Books, 1974), p. 77.

19. The Princess' assumptions are her "claims." See n. 11, above.

20. Laing, *The Divided Self,* p. 86.

21. The neurotic has a "degraded image" of himself and that is one reason why he "clings so tenaciously" to his glorified self. When he fails to measure up to the rigid demands (his "shoulds") of his grandiose self, he is overwhelmed by self-contempt (*Neurosis and Human Growth,* p. 137). He may then externalize his self-hate and become quite abusive toward others (*Neurosis and Human Growth,* p. 121).

8

A Psychological View of Priesthood, Sin, and Redemption in Graham Greene's *The Power and the Glory*

Joe Straub

Like any other set of relatively new ideas, Third Force psychology works in antithesis to what has come before it. Western culture, secularized as it now is, remains a culture based on values we call Judeo-Christian; Third Force psychology, as an outgrowth of that culture, works within the same value system as the Judeo-Christian, and yet stands in antithesis to certain fundamental tenets of it. In questions of human ethics, there is little difference between modern psychology and traditional religion: for both, the various shades and permutations of murder, theft and false witness are the kinds of behaviors to avoid; where the two differ is in how such behaviors are to be avoided. The Christian doctrine of the Fall of Man suggests that people, being basically wicked, *want* to murder, steal and lie, and that they require an outside authority—the Church, or Divine Grace—to deter them from such acts. For the Third Force psychologist, a person's most basic drives are toward healthy life and good interpersonal relationships, and so a wholesome fostering of those drives would preclude anyone's desire to act destructively in the first place. The Third Force model suggests that an individual person may *be* good; the "Fallen Man" model suggests that people can only be coerced into acting as *if* they were good, by restraints imposed from outside. So, from the Christian point of view (or more specifically, in this essay, from the Roman Catholic point of view), a person cannot be saved in this life; he can only be made to act in certain ways that would effect his salvation after this life. The important psychological implication of that idea of salvation is that it makes a person's immediate sense of his own self less important to him than his adherence to behavior dictated by outside authorities.

The protagonist in Graham Greene's *The Power and the Glory* is a Roman Catholic priest who suffers from such a split between his sense of self and the authority in which he believes. The novel is the tragedy of a man who gives his life over to the finest ideals he can imagine, but loses his sense of self in doing so. He loses the ability to make decisions based on his own strength and intelligence, or based on his own "self," and his ideals—fine as they are, in his mind—are not enough to replace his authentic self; they cannot help him to live, they can only help him to choose a death that seems glorious to him. The central argument of this essay is that the priest's loss of self is encouraged by Roman Catholic doctrines about salvation and the priesthood, and I use the ideas of Third Force psychologists, Horney, Fromm, and Maslow, to illustrate how these Catholic doctrines can aggravate self-alienation. By juxtaposing the two metaphors of personality development—"self-actualization" and "salvation"—I hope to show that some basic Roman Catholic doctrines, when adhered to in an extreme and literal fashion, lead to an unhealthy glorification of what Karen Horney calls the "idealized self" at the expense of the "real self." In doing that, the essay spends as much time on Church teaching as it does on the character of the priest. The diversion into Church doctrine is necessary, though, since the priest's character is shaped around his priesthood, and the conflict in the novel results from his difficulty in adjusting his personal actions to his social and religious role as a priest.

Graham Greene wrote that this conflict is central to the "thesis" of *The Power and the Glory:* "I think *The Power and the Glory* is the only novel I have written to a thesis. . . . I had always, even when I was a schoolboy, listened with impatience to the scandalous stories of tourists concerning the priests they had encountered in remote Latin villages (this priest had a mistress, another was constantly drunk), for I had been adequately taught in my protestant history books what Catholics believed; I could distinguish even then between a man and his office."[1] So it serves Greene's rhetorical purpose to make his priest a sinner, or even a neurotic, because in that way he glorifies the social function of his protagonist, rather than the protagonist himself. Greene underscores the point with his creation of an antagonist for the priest, the police Lieutenant. In his travels in Mexico, Greene says, "I had not found the idealism or integrity of the Lieutenant of *The Power and the Glory* among the police and *pisteleros* I had actually encountered—I had to invent him as a counter to the failed priest: the idealistic police officer who stifled life from the best possible motives: the drunken priest who continued to pass life on."[2] Greene has deliberately made the role each character fulfills more significant than the men themselves.

Greene's statement that the priest passes life on is a curious one, since he has gone out of his way to make the priest as objectively useless as possible; by his drunkenness and fathering of a child, the priest sets a miserable example of priesthood for the people to whom he ministers; he is unable to feed or protect his people; and he is the indirect cause of the deaths of hostages. The only thing he passes on to people is Roman Catholic ritual, and the only kind of life he actually enhances is the abstract "life" of the priesthood and the Church. Greene implies, as does Church doctrine, that this abstract life is the only kind that matters. When Greene glorifies the Church and the priesthood at the expense of both the priest and his parishioners, and when the Church offers rewards in the next life, they are both advocating a way of life in which people disregard their own intelligence, emotion, and initiative, in favor of an external authority. Such a world view is tantamount to a denial of the value of individual people. Greene's priest is an example of a person who has been persuaded to give up his own individuality in favor of his office; in terms of Third Force psychology, he has also been persuaded to turn his back on his "real self" in favor of a highly glorified "idealized self." By the end of the novel, the priest welcomes death as a release from the unhappiness of life under the power of such an idealized image.

It could be argued that the priest is simply a hero, that he dies for the Church as he has suffered for the Church, and that he simply makes a decision that the Church is worth dying for. But his character is depicted in enough detail that we can form some ideas about his motivation, and it is clear that the priest's mental state is such that he would be incapable of making a clear, conscious decision about anything. He does not take his own volition into account at all; whatever free will he has is at the service of the best idea he can make of God's will, based on "signs." He thinks that his escape "couldn't be anything else but a sign—an indication that he was doing more harm by his example than good by his occasional confessions."[3] Throughout the novel, he looks for a sign from God, that he should escape, or return, or go to a particular village. He does not consciously choose to act, but waits for the choice to be made for him. His actions therefore become random, rather than being designed for the sake of service, and the suffering he undergoes becomes an end in itself, rather than a means to the end of serving the Church.

Suffering appeals to him for its own sake. When the Lieutenant says that he wants to remove suffering from the lives of the common people, the priest replies enigmatically and illogically, "But if they want to suffer . . ." (p. 184). When he gives a sermon on the value of suffering, he feels "an immense satisfaction that he could talk of suffering to them now without hypocrisy" (p. 66). The priest is clearly proud to be suffering as he is, but whenever he becomes aware of his pride he denies it. He says, "Saints talk about the beauty of suffering. Well, you and I are not saints. Suffering to us is just ugly" (p. 122). He cannot admit pride, because even though pride exists, it is contrary to his self-effacing ideal of himself.

Horney says of the self-effacing person, "his very image of saintliness and lovableness prohibits any *conscious* feeling of pride. . . . the exclusion of pride from awareness belongs to his way of solving the conflict."[4] The denial of pride, Horney says, is often rationalized into a kind of self-hate: "When, despite all these difficulties, a piece of work is finished, well done, and well received, the self-disparagement does not end. 'Anybody could have achieved the same thing with so much work put in.' "[5] The priest rationalizes in exactly the way Horney describes. Even considering that he has been operating under threat of death, he thinks, "How little his pride had to feed on—he had celebrated only four masses this year, and he had heard perhaps a hundred confessions. It seemed to him that the dunce of any seminary could have done as well—or better" (p. 89).

In the self-effacing neurotic's effort to eradicate even healthy pride in real virtues, Horney says, he is quick to admit any fault of which he is accused, regardless of the truth of the accusation. The priest responds to accusations in this way. When he senses that the mestizo is a threat to him, he cannot bring himself to think ill of the man; rather, he allows the mestizo to manipulate him by accusing him of ingratitude: "His conscience began automatically to work: it was like a slot machine into which any coin could be fitted, even a cheater's blank disk. The words proud, lustful, envious, cowardly, ungrateful—they all worked the right springs—He was all these things" (p. 83). He thinks of his sensitive conscience as a mechanism, although he does not spell out the kind it is, a defense mechanism, which transforms pride into self-hate by automatic guilt reactions.

Not only must the priest repress all conscious pride, he must also eliminate feelings of anger and suspicion. The only person he is allowed to hate is himself, so he assumes a saintly, forgiving attitude toward everyone else. The people around him hunt him, reject him, insult him, and betray him, and he must feel some anger. But even with the mestizo who turns him in for a reward, the priest discovers a way to avoid hate or even resentment. The mestizo "had so much excuse—poverty and fever and innumerable humiliations. . . . When you visualized a man or woman carefully, you could always begin to feel pity . . . it was impossible to hate. Hate was just a failure of the imagination" (p. 123). With the use of imagination, he thinks, you can transform hate into pity.

The inability to distinguish real from imagined emotions is one sign of domination by the idealized self. Horney says that "the creation of make-believe feelings is most striking in those whose idealized image lies in the direction of goodness, love, and saintliness. They should be considerate, grateful, sympathetic, generous, loving."[6] The priest does manufacture feelings of pity and charity, but he has trouble expressing genuine love, for his ideal of saintliness requires him to love absolutely or not at all; he is allowed to love the human race, but not a single human. Praying for his daughter, he is filled with conflict: " 'O God help her. Damn me, I deserve it, but let her live for ever.' This was the kind of love he should have felt for every soul in the world: all the fear and wish to save concentrated unjustly on the one child. . . . He thought: This is what I should feel all the time for everyone" (p. 197).

The priest's creation of artificial feelings, his repression of genuine feelings, and his unnatural addiction to suffering for its own sake are all indications that he is incapable of genuine altruism or service because he is not motivated by genuine feelings. He is not capable of carrying out any genuine wish to help people, because he is primarily at the service of an idealized self whose dictates are not in the interests of any real person, but are in the interests of furthering the ideal itself. The needs of individual people are irrelevant, most especially his own needs. When he escapes the Red Shirts, he finds that his ideal makes a peaceful life empty for him: "It ought to be possible to be happy here, if he were not so tied to fear and suffering—unhappiness too can become a habit like piety. Perhaps it was his duty to break it, his duty to discover peace" (p. 164). The priest does not "want" to be happy; instead, he feels that "perhaps it was his duty" to be happy. He would not actually desire happiness for himself, but if a higher authority were to require it of him, he would be obedient to duty. He is so alienated from his "real self" that even a simple desire for happiness has to be projected outside him, to his duty, to a higher authority than himself.

This is not the result of his enslavement to the idea of "authority" in general—if that were the case, then nothing would be simpler than for him to give in to the government. But instead, he gives himself over to the service of a different, very particular authority, which he thinks of as his duty, or the will of God, or the will of the Church. It is around these ideals that his idealized image takes its shape, and it is the requirements of duty, God, or the Church that make up the dictates which constitute the "tyranny of the should" under which the priest lives.

The tyranny of the should is Karen Horney's term for the manner in which the idealized self enforces its dictates. The foundation of the tyranny is self-hate complemented with a search for the glory that is necessary to alleviate that self-hate, as the priest's life illustrates: on the one hand, his fornication and alcoholism show him to be the essentially weak and degraded creature that the Church says all men are since the Fall; on the other hand, his adherence to duty even to the point of death would glorify him as a martyr and a saint. For the sake of its own self-preservation, the idealized self must perpetuate a cycle of emotional confusion in the priest. It must ensure that his self-hate is so strong that he will never be satisfied until he reaches his ideal, and it must also ensure that his ideal is so unrealistic that he will never reach it. It is Horney's contention that although such a cycle of self-hate and self-glorification is common, it is unnatural and unnecessary; it must be learned by a person. Usually such learning is unconscious, but in the case of the priest, his personality and his self-image have been formed under the influence of the Church, which has a stake in cultivating an idealized image in its members, to ensure their loyalty. Jesuit schoolteachers used to claim that, given a child to the age of eight, they could ensure his loyal Catholicism for life. It seems clear that one does not win an eight-year-old over to a religion by the use of reasoned theological arguments; it has to be done by manipulation of the child's emotions.

The way the Church is able to control a person who is weakened by an idealized image can be illuminated by Erich Fromm's discussion of conscience in *Man For Himself.* Something like the tyranny of the should operates in the kind of conscience Fromm calls "authoritarian" as opposed to "humanistic." According to Fromm, the authoritarian conscience originates outside a person, in the dictates of religious or political lawmakers or of parents, and becomes internalized in the course of a person's life so that it exercises control even in the absence of the originating authority. The humanistic conscience differs in that it originates not from external authorities, but from a person's awareness of what is "conducive to the proper functioning and unfolding of our total personality."[7] Such a humanistic conscience would clearly aid the actualization of the real self in the same way that an authoritarian conscience would reinforce the power of the idealized self.

The authoritarian conscience demands obedience, and more important, submission and humility; pride is automatically *overweaning* pride, because it might suggest independence from the authority. This demand creates emotional confusion, according to Fromm: "The authoritarian guilty conscience is a result of the feeling of strength . . . while the authoritarian good conscience springs from the feeling of obedience, dependence, powerlessness, and sinfulness. . . . The paradoxical result is that the (authoritarian) guilty conscience becomes the basis of a 'good' conscience, while the good conscience, if one should have it, ought to create a feeling of guilt."[8] Such a paradox is not only confusing but it also reinforces the power of the authority, by ensuring guilt. Just as the idealized self is reinforced by its own guilt-producing dictates, the authoritarian conscience draws strength from a person's guilt over failing to live up to the dictates of the conscience. Both the idealized self and the authoritarian conscience depend on self-hate and guilt, for as Fromm says, "Not only do guilt feelings result from one's dependence on an irrational authority and from the feeling that it is one's duty to please that authority, but the guilt feeling in its turn reinforces dependence."[9]

Fromm points out that sexual repression is an excellent way to reinforce an authoritarian conscience; since the sex drive is universal, sexual guilt can be made universal, and so can dependence on the authority that has the power to absolve guilt. Whether the Church teaches sexual repression—or only sexual restraint—is a matter of opinion; but it is a fact that the Church links not only sex drives to guilt but virtually all basic drives. One teaching is that "the chief sources of actual sin are: pride, covetousness, lust, anger, gluttony, envy and sloth."[10] Except for "sloth," perhaps, these capital sins, as they are called, are just the basic human instincts, given names that connote excess. They represent the negative side of the healthy motivations that Abraham Maslow arranges in a "hierarchy of needs" in *Motivation and Personality.*[11] Maslow says that people have basic drives to achieve physiological satisfaction, safety, social belongingness, and self-esteem; the frustrations of these drives, he says, are obstacles to actualization of the self. Maslow and the Church are working with similar ideas here. Where the Church says that lust and gluttony cause sin, Maslow says that unsatisfied physical needs fixate a person at the physical level, and prevent him from rising above that level. The Church says covetousness and envy cause sin; Maslow says that security needs, if thwarted, prevent a person's healthy actualization of self.

Naturally enough, the Church and Maslow both base their psychologies on human instincts, but they are saying almost the opposite things about instinct. Maslow's idea is that the healthy satisfaction of needs is what saves us from excesses, that the best way to avoid gluttony, for instance, is to avoid excessive hunger of an emotional or physical kind. But the Church prescribes overcoming the instincts by sheer will power: "We must all be on our guard against capital sins. . . . It is not sufficient to resolve not to give in to capital sins—we must strive to practice the opposite virtues. . . . Everyone should honestly examine his own character and find out his predominant passion—that is, the type of sin to which he is most inclined—and try earnestly to overcome it."[12]

By linking a person's "predominant passion" with his sinful nature, the Church is suggesting that real feelings, and therefore the real self, must be buried in favor of the ideal. And the Church recommends that we overcome instinct, passion, sin, by placing the will over the emotions: "God will not forgive us any sin, whether mortal or venial, unless we have true contrition for it. . . . A feeling of sorrow is not necessary for true contrition, for contrition is an act of will, not of the feelings."[13] This repression not only of actions but of instinct as well denies the real self by denying real feelings, and it creates an inescapable sense of moral failure; one can refrain from violent acts by the use of will power, but one cannot refrain from feeling anger, except by the unhealthy repression of genuine emotion.

One of the ways that the Roman Catholic Church capitalizes on guilt is through ritual, such as confession, or "Penance." Once a person has accepted the idea that his basic instincts lead inevitably to sin, he is trapped by the Church, because he needs the ritual of Penance to relieve the guilt that arises from virtually any self-motivated action at all. Another ritual that reinforces the guilt-dependence cycle is the central Catholic ritual, the Holy Mass. The Mass is a commemoration of the death of Christ, for which all of us, as sinners, are responsible, and for a Catholic to miss this commemoration on even a single Sunday is a mortal sin—a sin punishable by eternal damnation—as is a Catholic's failure to receive Holy Communion at least once a year. Communion is the symbolic consumption of the body of Christ, but the cannibalism suggested by this act goes beyond symbolism, for Catholics; the Church makes a great deal of the idea that the bread consumed does not *represent* the flesh of Christ—it *is* the flesh of Christ, only disguised as bread.

Requiring people periodically to reenact a bit of deicide and cannibalism, even symbolically, is bound to generate a great deal of guilt, especially for people whose ethic is ostensibly based on nonviolence, on the love of God and man. The ritual forces people to recognize on a subliminal level that they are murderous and cannibalistic as a group, and that they can never live up to the Church's ideal of Christlike love. It reinforces dependence on the Church by reinforcing guilt and the need for salvation through the Church.

The priest in Greene's novel, having celebrated the Mass hundreds of times in his life, would have received the full emotional force of the daily killing and eating of God; a priest is actually said to stand in for Christ during the Mass, when he says, "All of you take and eat of this. For this is my body." Greene's priest finally makes the ultimate identification with Christ by allowing himself to be made, literally, into a human sacrifice. In doing so, he satisfies his need to believe that he suffers for others, and at the same time he resolves the tension created by his failure to live up to his impossible ideals. That tension is greater for him than for most Catholics, because priesthood is glorified so much that his simple moral lapses create a tremendous rift between his actions and his ideal of himself; and that great rift demands great suffering to secure divine forgiveness, to quiet the voice of his authoritarian conscience. Greene hints at the coming sacrifice at the end of the first chapter, when he says that the priest "was like the King of a West African tribe, the slave of his people, who may not even lie down in case the winds should fail" (p. 15). Greene's African background shows here, for his description of the African king is an accurate one.

According to Sir James Frazer, one example of the African slave/king is "the priestly king Kukulu, [who lives] alone in a wood. He may not touch a woman nor leave his house; indeed he may not even quit his chair, in which he is obliged to sleep sitting, for if he lay down no wind would arise and navigation would be stopped."[14] The African king is "responsible for the weather and the crops, and . . . he may justly pay with his life for the inclemency of the one or the failure of the other."[15] Greene says that the priest is like an African king, and what African kings do is to live in slavery to their office and die for their people in times of tribulation.

This view of kingship is in line with the view of priesthood implied in Greene's "thesis" that a man and his office are separate entities. Primitive Africans routinely killed the physical person of their kings so that the spiritual function of the king could continue unabated by physical infirmity of age or disease on the part of the living king. This paradox, and the presence of king and slave in one person, can only be resolved by a mystical leap of faith in the invisible, even for the Africans. Geza Roheim says of the typical African monarchy, "The king is not himself, not what he seems to be, but the representative of an ancestral god, a being who lived in the infancy of humanity."[16] Believers need to make a distinction between the natural man who happens to be king, and the power he is believed to hold over nature. It is almost like two personalities living in the same body, one of them mortal and fallible, and the other omnipotent, not residing in one king, but existing eternally in the kingship as passed from one man to another.

The Roman Catholic Church has a similar difficulty in its doctrine concerning the priesthood, and the Church resolves it in exactly the same way as primitive people do. To explain the contradiction of a priest like Greene's, "a damned man putting God into the mouths of men" (p. 56), and to make possible the demand that a priest exercise supernatural powers with supernatural humility, the Church posits a double identity in each of her ordained priests. Ordination to the priesthood gives the priest "a character, lasting forever, which is a special sharing in the priesthood of Christ and which gives the priest supernatural powers . . . which can never be taken away."[17] When a priest remits sins, or transforms bread into flesh, he is able to do so not through his own power, but through the power of Christ that resides in him. The priest in the novel says that this distinction between the priest and priesthood is the greatest virtue of the Church: "It doesn't matter so much my being a coward—and all the rest. I can put God into a man's mouth just the same—and I can give him God's pardon. It wouldn't make any difference to that if every priest in the Church was like me" (p. 185).

This doctrine is necessary to unravel the paradox that one sinner could grant absolution to another sinner. But like the doctrine of Original Sin, it creates a chasm between a man's sense of himself and his ideals. By making the ideal of his office semi-divine, it makes the ideal absolutely unreachable. But if the doctrine saddles the priest with greater guilt than most Catholics, it also allows him the opportunity for redemption through greater suffering than most Catholics are capable of. The doctrine allows him not only to suffer and die for the sake of others, but also to accept eternal damnation for them. A curious double-bind inherent in Church doctrine is that, even though a priest's power to save souls cannot be taken away regardless of his state of salvation, any priest who performs a sacrament while in the state of mortal sin is committing the serious sin of sacrilege. For the priest in the novel, "There was a time when he had approached the Canon of the Mass with actual physical dread—the first time he had consumed the body and blood of God in a state of mortal sin: but then life bred its excuses—it hadn't after a while seemed to matter very much whether he was damned or not, so long as these others . . ." (pp. 65–66).

The priest willingly reaffirms his damnation every time he ministers to the soul of anyone else. He trades his own eternal suffering for the release of others from the same suffering. In a grotesque version of what Horney calls the "bargain with fate," the priest asks, "O God, give me any kind of death—without contrition, in a state of sin—only save this child" (p. 76). He is the quintessential suffering, self-effacing person, and his unique position allows him to feed his pride and his sense of guilt at the same time, feeling that he must suffer supernaturally in order to fulfill the duties of priesthood. There is something circular in the priest's suffering for the sake of a priesthood one of whose functions is to reinforce the emotional need for redemption through suffering.

I do not think I misread the novel when I say that Greene is glorifying suffering for its own sake, for the sake of the relief that suffering brings to a guilt-ridden person. And that kind of suffering as an end in itself is inherent in the Church's doctrine about sin and redemption. A story about Saint Francis of Assisi shows how meaningless suffering can be glorified. St. Francis tells a young monk that he should hope to suffer unjust punishment; for example if the porter at the monastery should fail to recognize them, repeatedly turn them away cold and hungry, and then, if at their final dying request to be admitted, "the porter should be enraged with us, and coming out with a great knotted stick . . . throw us in the snow and beat us until we were all over wounds and bruises . . . then believe, O Leo! that we have found ecstatic joy; for all the gifts [Christ] will give to His servants, the greatest of all is to overcome themselves and to suffer."[18] The Church's commentary that accompanies that story says, "It is by hitching ourselves to such a sublime ideal that we are aided in the struggle to become fit instruments to meet our Maker and be assigned by Him to places of Honor in His Celestial Kingdom."[19] These quotations recommend suffering as a "sublime ideal" that leads to a place of honor in a "Celestial Kingdom": those terms sound reminiscent of Karen Horney's description of the "search for glory" in the self-effacing neurotic. The saint recommends that we reach our glory by overcoming ourselves. Horney might ask, which self?

She distinguishes among various kinds of "self." In her scheme, the "real self" is the vital inner force that wants to be actualized; the "ideal self" is made up of a person's ideas about what he should be; the "actual self" has attributes of both the real and ideal, and expresses both healthy and neurotic drives. When St. Francis says that we should overcome ourselves, he means that we should bury our real selves in favor of the glory to be had in following the dictates of a self-effacing ideal. In Horney's scheme of the personality, to do that would be to live a self-alienated, neurotic life that centers around the impossible "shoulds" of a tyrannical idealized image.

The Roman Catholic Church did not invent free-floating guilt or the idealized image, but the doctrines of sin and redemption, and the Fall of Man and the coming Judgment, raise those psychological forces to the level of myth, and the Church has traditionally exploited those forces to elicit loyalty from its members. By creating tension between a Christlike level of aspiration and a degraded image of actual mankind, the Church reinforces guilt and fear of divine punishment. As an escape from guilt and punishment the Church provides ritual and an intricate system of law, the essence of which is obedience to an internalized authoritarian conscience, the performance of roles rather than the actualization of self, the exercise of the will and the suppression of the emotions, the aspiration to the Christlike ideal of mankind and rejection of the "fallen" reality. But the Christian ideal of perfection is designed to be so stringent that no human will ever live up to it; salvation comes through *believing* in the perfectly self-effacing ideal self, not through *achieving* it. If the ideal were realistic enough so that people actually reached it, then the glory would be theirs, not God's, and the tension between the actual and the ideal—and the guilt arising from that tension, which the Church uses to motivate people—would be destroyed.

The Church has had absolute success in securing the loyalty of the priest in *The Power and the Glory.* He overcomes himself; he suffers and dies for the glory of the Church. The sad thing about his death is that it lacks purpose of any humanistic kind. His reasons for accepting death do not seem to be genuinely idealistic; his motivation is too self-involved for idealism, too closely bound to his need for the gratification he receives from suffering. A way of illustrating the difference between idealistic self-sacrifice and enslavement to a self-effacing idealized image is to compare the priest's death to the death of another fictionalized martyr, Sir Thomas More in Robert Bolt's play, *A Man for All Seasons.* The comparison is especially illuminating because the deaths of the two men are superficially similar. Both are profoundly religious Roman Catholics who are executed for resisting the encroachments of a secular authority on the prerogatives of the Church. Both therefore become Christian martyrs, but aside from that, there is hardly any similarity between the two men and their motivations for accepting death.

In an earlier essay in this volume, Bernard Paris argues that, unlike most literary characters who accept death, Thomas More does so—in the play, at least—out of a need to preserve his real self: More is forced to choose between death and the denial of his essential integrity, and he chooses death as the lesser evil. Many fictional deaths, Paris says, allow the protagonist a simple solution to personal conflicts, and permit him to actualize his idealized image in the final moment, in a way that a less glorious but more pragmatic solution would not. I believe that the martyrdom of the priest in *The Power and the Glory* is this kind of death, a glorification of the priest's pernicious self-image, a glorification of the simplicity of death as a solution to conflict, and a refutation of the possibility of taking reasonable action in this life to resolve conflict.

The conflict the priest suffers is between himself and his ideal, specifically between his degraded view of himself as a person and his glorified view of his role as priest. That conflict makes it hard for him to make practical decisions based on sound reasoning. In deciding whether to escape or not, he tries to find a rationale that acknowledges his personal worthlessness at the same time that it defends the supreme importance of his office: "When he was gone it would be as if God in all this space between the sea and mountains ceased to exist. Wasn't it his duty to stay, even if they despised him, even if they were murdered for his sake, even if they were corrupted by his example?" (p. 60). His beliefs about himself and his priesthood will not even allow him to consider a practical resolution to the conflict, that first, he might conduct himself in such a way that he does not corrupt by his example, or second, that even if he left, God would not really cease to exist there; other Christians and other priests could fulfill God's plan for Mexico—if it really is God's plan, and not the priest's.

The priest shows enormous self-glorification in raising his own simple decision—go or stay—to one of cosmic significance; he disguises that glorification by attributing the glory to his office rather than himself. And he is willing that people be murdered or corrupted for the sake of his office because to him, murder and corruption are unavoidable in the fallen real world. He does not perceive the world as a place where particular good things are won by particular efforts; he sees instead a strict dichotomy between degraded humans living in a fallen world and the absolute perfection of sainthood and heaven. In a world view like that there really is no choice; a person with any moral sense at all would naturally choose ultimate perfection over ultimate degradation. For the priest, that means to discard the possibility of human choices, and to adhere to the will of God. So he waits for a sign from God, the capture or escape that would demonstrate God's will empirically.

In contrast, Thomas More takes conscious actions for conscious reasons, based on his own intelligence. He cannot make himself swear to an oath that he believes is false because such an oath would deny his ability to distinguish right from wrong. He believes the oath is false because his own powers of reason tell him so; the important thing, he says, is "not that I *believe* it, but that *I* believe it."[20] In taking that position, More is as loyal to the Church and to God as Greene's priest is, but More acknowledges that the responsibility for his actions is his own, not God's. He submits to the will of God, in refusing to perjure himself, but he does not even toy with the idea that he should submit to death as a sign of obedience: "If He suffers us to fall to such a case that there is no escaping, then we may stand our tackle as best we can. . . . But it is God's part, not our own, to bring ourselves to that extremity. Our natural business lies in escaping."[21] When his death comes, it is King Henry who orders it, not God, and More does everything his sense of morality will allow to prevent his death.

And unlike the priest, More does not allow the needs of his office to overrule his personal conscience. When More realizes that his position requires him to go against his deeply held beliefs, he hesitates only a moment before he removes the chain that signifies his office. Greene's priest is unable to make such a choice between himself and his office, because for him, the office is all that matters. Priesthood has endowed him with a second, supernatural self that is infinitely more important than his natural, individual self. This makes his personal conscience meaningless, compared to the duties of the priesthood. His conscience tells him, for instance, that it is wrong to abandon his daughter, but he is unable to entertain the idea of taking her away, of raising her or finding a better home for her; his idea of priesthood does not include such a pragmatic, humanistic expression of love for people. The priest knows also that the rituals he performs are causing suffering and death at the hands of the Red Shirts, and he feels terribly guilty over that, but the rituals are too important for him to give up. In every case, his personal conscience surrenders to the needs of his office.

Like the people around the priest, More's friends and family also suffer because of his ideals, but they suffer only because More has miscalculated the extent of King Henry's rancor. His error is a practical one, an error of intelligence rather than emotion, and he does not become emotionally attached to his error—he does not rationalize, as the priest does, by trying to believe that suffering is part of God's plan, and that suffering is therefore good. To More, his own death and the suffering of the people he loves are tragic and unjust—but unavoidable—results of his insistence on preserving his essential integrity, his real self. To the priest, his own death is a glorious thing, an escape from his real self, and a chance to give reality to his idealized self.

But the greatest difference between Thomas More and Greene's priest is in the nature of the lives they lead, rather than the deaths they suffer. More lives in the world he sees; the priest—to a greater extent than More, or than most other people—lives in the world he needs to believe is there, whether he sees it or not. More's life is not perfect, but he does not expect perfection. For him, life is a mixture of good and evil; he does not see life the way the priest does, as a choice between degradation and sainthood. The priest's polarized way of seeing the world and himself prevents him from making choices between relative good and evil; he can see the world only in absolutes. Since choices in this life are seldom between polar opposites, the priest is ill-equipped for real life, for a life not confined to the role of persecuted priest.

When he escapes his persecution, he also loses the security of a world divided clearly between persecutors and victims. In the relative peace of the Lehr's ranch, he is undone by his division of the world into good and evil, and by the similar internal schism between his saintly idealized self and his degraded view of his actual self. First, the relative freedom of the place allows him to backslide—he starts drinking and chiseling baptismal fees again, so he has evidence of his worthlessness. And second, no one wants to make a martyr of him there, so he has no hope of achieving enough glory through suffering to counteract his low self-esteem. Since after years of being denied his real self has no force in his life, he finds that he *has* no life, outside the pursuit of his ideal of sainthood. He feels that "perhaps it was his duty" to be happy, but he does not believe he ever will be. The only way left to him for salvaging any self-esteem at all is to actualize his ideal self, which requires, by then, that he give everything, that he become a sacrificial victim. As he returns with the mestizo, knowing he will be arrested and probably shot, his depression lifts; he starts to whistle; "the oddest thing of all was that he felt quite cheerful" (p. 171). He is made happy by his approaching death, because his loss of self has made real life meaningless to him.

His decision to return is inevitable; the cowardice of refusing the last rites to the dying American gangster would have destroyed forever his belief in himself as a priest. He has no choice at the end of the novel but to die so that even if his own life is worthless, his ideal of the priesthood will survive.

That is, Greene leaves him no choice but to die. Greene has set the priest up for death and Greene himself has chosen to make the death a futile one. Even from a Catholic point of view the priest's return is ineffective; he is unable to make the gangster repent, so the gangster is not saved, unless by God's grace, and he had access to that without the priest. What the priest's death does uphold is the unswerving performance of duty, the absolute adherence to the requirements of office.

At the end of the novel, when young Luis gives obeisance to the new priest, the implication is that the boy, and by extension Mexico, is given a renewed faith in the priesthood, but nothing more than that. Greene chooses to give his priest a death that is specifically for the sake of priesthood as an abstraction. Greene's thesis for the novel is that a man and his office are not the same; he implies that the office is greater. The priest in the novel believes that the priesthood must go on even if people despise it, are corrupted by it, are murdered for it.

The sad thing about the ideal the priest dies for is that it denigrates people and glorifies abstractions. The priest's ideal of service to people has become warped so that people become secondary to the ideal itself. And that is a fair statement of the difference between idealism and emotional bondage to an idealized image. The priest's ideal has very little to do with people; real needs and real altruism mean nothing to the ideal; what matters is that service must take place; people must be served even if they do not want that service, and even if it kills them.

An ideal like that is a form of madness, and madness can only grow in a suitable environment. The barbarity of the Mexico of the novel is a perfect setting for the priest's embracing of death. Not coincidentally, that fictional Mexico is a little bit like the collapsed empire that provided fertile ground for the spread of Christianity throughout Europe. Legitimate authority has broken down; physical danger and starvation are constant threats; local strong men replace the disappearing moral order with military power. As society decays, every level of Maslow's hierarchy of needs is undermined. And without empirical reinforcement, self-esteem and confidence in real human nature disappear and are replaced with imagined ideals of absolute perfection.

Attempting to reconcile people to that kind of world, the Church posits the dichotomy between degraded reality and the glorious ideal; but Church teachings are only part of the equation. For the split to work and to be maintained, the world has to appear to be a degraded place. It is the fact that people so often act as if they were fallen from grace, and people's awareness of their own disgraceful actions, that make the fallen man theory and its degraded image of mankind seem plausible.

In the poverty and oppression of a place like the Mexico in the novel, the fallen man theory can only flourish. In a world peopled with oppressors and victims, it is easy to split reality into pure good and pure evil, and it is easy to glorify the victim in that scheme. It is easy to believe that suffering, being universal, must be an expression of God's will, a great gift that allows one to overcome himself—his degraded view of himself—as St. Francis affirms, and as the Church at least does not deny.

In fairness to the Roman Catholic Church, I should say that the religious works I quoted were published in the thirties and forties, about the same time as *The Power and the Glory.* Great changes have taken place in the Church since then, since the humanizing influence of Pope John XXIII, and it is likely that Church writings have also changed.

And in fairness to Graham Greene, I should say that although he is a devout Catholic, he is not an orthodox one—in *Ways of Escape,* one volume of his autobiography, he writes that he doubts the reality of eternal punishment for sinners. So it would be unfair to both Greene and the Church to attribute all of the beliefs of either one of them to the other. *The Power and the Glory,* in fact, was listed in the 1948 edition of the Vatican's *Index of Forbidden Books.* The reason the novel was banned is not clear—it does not advocate heresy; it is not a pornographic book; and it does not glorify violence. It may simply be that, to the Vatican censors, the novel depicted the psychology of priesthood too honestly for comfort.

NOTES

1. Graham Greene, *Ways of Escape* (New York: Simon and Schuster, 1980), pp. 88–89.
2. Ibid., pp. 88–89.
3. Graham Greene, *The Power and the Glory* (New York: Bantam Pathfinder, 1972), p. 125. Hereafter cited in the text.
4. Karen Horney, *Neurosis and Human Growth* (New York: Norton, 1950), p. 223.
5. Ibid., p. 140.
6. Ibid., p. 83.
7. Erich Fromm, *Man for Himself* (New York: Holt, Rinehart and Winston, 1947), p. 159.
8. Ibid., p. 150.
9. Ibid., p. 155.
10. Francis J. Connell, *The New Baltimore Catechism* (New York: Benziger Brothers, 1943), p. 43.
11. Abraham Maslow, *Motivation and Personality* (New York: Harper and Row, 1954).
12. Connell, *The New Baltimore Catechism,* p. 45.
13. Ibid., pp. 265–66.
14. Theodore H. Gaster, *The New Golden Bough: A New Abridgement of the Work by Sir James Frazer* (New York: Mentor, 1964), p. 188.
15. James George Frazer, *The Dying God,* vol. 3 of *The Golden Bough* (London: Macmillan, 1963), p. 165.
16. Geza Roheim, *Animism, Magic and the Divine King* (London: Broadway House, 1930), p. 225.
17. Connell, *The New Baltimore Catechism,* p. 310.
18. David Goldstein, *Campaigners for Christ Handbook* (Boston: Astor Post Press, 1937), p. 3.
19. Ibid., p. 3.
20. Robert Bolt, *A Man for All Seasons* (New York: Random House, 1960), p. 91.
21. Ibid., p. 126.

9

"Keep Your Muck": A Horneyan Analysis of Joe Christmas and *Light in August*

Marjorie B. Haselswerdt

1

When Alfred Kazin describes the "pinched rotted look"[1] of Faulkner's *Light in August,* he is referring to the influence of the depression on the atmosphere of the novel. But his words have a resonance for the story of Joe Christmas that goes far beyond the superficial. *Light in August* looks "pinched and rotted," it seems to me, not only because its characters live stark, luxuryless lives on a barren landscape but because it contains buried within it an aversion to life, a profound inability to confront human existence with openness and joy. Though Faulkner's public utterances on the novel give heavy emphasis to Lena Grove, her "courage and endurance" and her pagan joy in giving birth,[2] the novel itself embodies a denial of those things that Lena represents which is only partly compensated for by her rather bewitching presence. In fact, it is Joe Christmas—cold, violent, driven—and not the gentle Lena who dominates *Light in August,* and he dominates it not only because his is the central story but because his personality finds striking parallels in the implied world view of the novel as a whole.

Joe Christmas is a highly complex and difficult fictional character. Though Faulkner has presented him in great detail, his motives and reactions often seem bizarre and puzzling. Before we can understand his relationship to the atmosphere and significance of *Light in August,* we must understand Joe himself in some systematic way. I propose to analyze his character from the point of view of the Third Force psychology of Karen Horney,[3] and to move from this analysis to a consideration of the relationship between Joe and his creator, and the effect of this relationship on the novel itself. Wayne Booth tells us that every novel implies an author, a guiding consciousness who is responsible for the "core of norms and choices" that shapes the novel, and who uses rhetorical devices to influence his readers to share his perspective on the world he has created.[4] In the case of *Light in August,* as we shall see, this "implied author" gives evidence that his relationship to life is at times as troubled and contradictory as that of Joe Christmas, indeed that there is a kind of collusion between him and Joe that has a great deal to do with the vision of the world he ultimately portrays in the novel.

The detailed Horneyan analysis that follows indicates that Joe Christmas is a type of aggressive personality that Horney labels "arrogant-vindictive."[5] A person afflicted with this kind of neurosis is consumed with the desire to seek vindictive triumph. His ideal self is immune to human attachments and needs and he seeks to quell his inner conflicts by focusing on his need to achieve revenge for the wrongs done him in childhood and since by a world he sees as hostile. He externalizes his own feelings of hostility and convinces himself that the world is hateful and mean—if he were not convinced of this, his solution would not "work" and he would be beset by the anxiety that accompanies inner conflict. Thus he sees all attempts by others to "move toward" their fellow man as hypocritical and revolting. In himself, self-effacing tendencies are deeply buried, and if he is threatened with their emergence he will feel intense shame and self-hate, perhaps in the form of rage. Self-effacing "shoulds" generally influence his behavior in a negative way. Whatever a loving or loyal or trusting person "should" do in a given situation is what he must avoid doing in order to avoid anxiety. Nevertheless, as we shall see, in a crisis his repressed desires to "move toward" others, to seek their acceptance and love, may emerge to haunt him, causing him to feel guilt for his aggressive behavior and motivating him to act in ways inconsistent with his dominant solution.

By analyzing Joe Christmas's nature and behavior in terms of Horney's theories about this particular type, we shall be able to understand much about him, and to appreciate Faulkner's artistry in creating a character of such vividness and coherence. And once we understand Joe's inner conflicts and the "solutions" that he brings to bear on them, we shall be able to study the conflicts present in *Light in August* itself, and thus to identify and analyze the bleakness that pervades it in spite of all that Lena's quiet cheerfulness can do and the energy that hums through its pages, holding the reader in thrall. While most of Faulkner's work ostensibly espouses "self-effacing" values, asking us to empathize with sensitive and/or helpless victims like Quentin Compson or Darl Bundren, and his public pronouncements on his work virtually always emphasize humanist themes such as the importance of love and of endurance in the face of trial, *Light in August* is permeated with an aggressive attitude which resembles that of Joe himself.

2

Like Jason Compson's, Joe Christmas's adulthood is made up of attempts to achieve revenge against and mastery over those people and forces responsible for his mistreatment and frustration as a child. As Horney describes it, the arrogant-vindictive person's development

> started in childhood—with particularly bad human experiences and few, if any, redeeming factors. Sheer brutality, humiliations, derision, neglect, and flagrant hyprocrisy, all these assailed a child of especially great sensitivity. . . . He may make some pathetic and unsuccessful attempts to win sympathy, interest, or affection but finally chokes off all tender needs. He gradually "decides" that genuine affection is not only unattainable for him but that it does not exist at all. (*NHG,* p. 202)

"Memory believes before knowing remembers,"[6] begins the chapter on Joe's childhood, indicating that Faulkner means to trace the unconscious legacy of the child to the man. And what a legacy it is. No child-victim of Victorian literature ever had a worse time of it than Joe. Imprisoned behind the bleak, soot-blackened walls of the orphanage, "small, still, round-headed, round-eyed" (*LA,* p. 117), Joe grows to the age of reason without love, his only treat an occasional "pink work" of the dietitian's toothpaste. One older girl he likes "well enough to let her mother him a little" (*LA,* p. 127), but she suddenly disappears (not t.b. or small pox, adoption). Like many another little victim he has someone assigned especially to hate him, Doc Hines, the racist lunatic who devotes his life to the destruction of the "abomination" that is Joe. In addition, he suffers the derision of his fellow inmates who, out of some natural but obscure evil impulse, since he does not then and never will look black at all, call him "nigger."

As the toothpaste episode unfolds, we see that Joe has very early (he is now five) come to see punishment and persecution as the central facts of his life. When the dietitian tries to bribe him instead of beating him, he becomes profoundly confused, and his mistrust of his fellow men increases. By the time he is adopted by the McEacherns he has taught himself not to expect anything good from life, in fact to defend himself from disappointment by hating, as Hyatt Waggoner says, "not *even* those who love him but *especially* those who love him."[7] He has learned to deny the very existence of the love that has been denied him, and seems not to hope for any positive results from the adoption. He does not reach out at all to McEachern during their long ride to his new home, sitting, a silent little bundle in the wagon, even more taciturn and unresponsive than McEachern himself. But it is Mrs. McEachern's welcome—the attempt to carry him to the house, the washing of his feet, the watching by his bedside—that is most wasted on him; he can only wait for "the part that would not be pleasant" (*LA,* p. 156) to begin. Already he has taught himself not to believe in the genuineness of human affection, so her actions, the "trivial, clumsy, vain efforts" (*LA,* p. 157), can only mystify and eventually disgust him.

His initial response to his foster mother is the first indication we have that Joe will make the transition from victim to victimizer typical of the arrogant-vindictive type. The real turning point occurs on a Sunday when the eight-year-old Joe is beaten and starved by his Calvinist foster father in an attempt to get him to learn his catechism. Unable to prevent the beatings, he accepts them without emotion, "with a rapt expression like a monk in a picture" (*LA*, p. 140). He is calm because McEachern's treatment of him corresponds to his view that life consists of a series of punishments, and because by remaining "rapt" he can refuse McEachern mastery over him. After his inevitable collapse he awakens feeling "quite well," at peace, as if he has just made an important decision. Looking back on this day he thinks, "On this day I became a man" (*LA*, p. 137), and it becomes apparent that at this moment, starved and aching from repeated beatings, he embarks on the search for vindictive triumph that will lead him to murder at least twice. Unable to revenge himself as yet on McEachern, he lashes out at his foster mother, violently rejecting her offer of love and comfort in the form of food by dumping the tray of secretly prepared dishes in the corner, only later, when it is just food and no longer a tangible symbol of the love in which he cannot believe, kneeling over it and eating, "like a savage, like a dog" (*LA*, p. 146). The events of this day establish the pattern of Joe's life. He will for the rest of his days accept, and even seek out, punishment, taking his revenge where he can, and behaving with particular violence in response to offers of love or aid.

Once, however, taken off guard by the exigencies of adolescence, Joe displays the vulnerability to human feelings that his "solution" denies him. In his relationship with Bobbie Allen we find the lessons of his childhood confirmed, and the hardening process completed. Falling in love with a peculiarly stunted blonde waitress with oversized hands, Joe risks a partial abandonment of his drive for mastery and his need to deny and repress positive feelings, only to be taught again that there is not really any such thing as love. At first he is caught up in the mystery of Bobbie and of sexual love in general, but his belated discovery that Bobbie is a prostitute imported from Memphis (though, as the older blonde woman complains, in Joe's case she has brought "it" all the way down to Jefferson just to give it away) leads him to compensate for this vulnerability by aggressive behavior. Now he smokes and drinks and "in his loud drunken despairing young voice" (*LA*, p. 187), calls Bobbie his whore.

It is in the midst of his sexual initiation into adulthood that Joe finds an opportunity for vindictive triumph. His murder, or attempted murder, of McEachern, and his brutal robbery of Mrs. McEachern free him from the role of victim and release him forever from the standards of behavior that govern mere mortals. On his way back to Bobbie, "The youth . . . rode lightly, balanced lightly, leaning well forward, exulting perhaps at that moment as Faustus had, of having put behind now at once and for all the Shalt Not, of being free at last of honor and law" (LA, p. 194). For the moment he is his idealized self, but, as his haste to return to Bobbie indicates, he is not yet completely hardened.

Bobbie takes care of that. In the scene that follows Joe's heroic journey to her house with Mrs. McEachern's egg money, Bobbie provides Joe with the experience that finally "choke[s] off all tender needs," and leads him to behave for the rest of his life as if "genuine affection is not only unattainable for him but . . . does not exist at all." Her feelings presumably wounded by McEachern's rather polite reference to her as a "harlot," Bobbie has exchanged her usual cowlike demeanor for that of a cornered rat. Her rejection of Joe's offer of matrimony is ugly and vicious: " 'He told me himself he was a nigger! The son of a bitch! Me f—ing for nothin a nigger son of a bitch that would get me in a jam with clodhopper police. At a clodhopper dance!' " (*LA*, p. 204). No, Bobbie does not want to get married, and Joe's last attempt to win affection is rewarded by several cruel blows to the face. Now, with the taste of bitter rejection mingling on his tongue with the flavor of vindictive triumph, Joe embarks on his adult journey, "the street which was to run for fifteen years" (*LA*, p. 210), and then for three more before Percy Grimm's knife and gun bring it to a close. During these years he systematically denies his connection to men of any race, and searches out opportunities for reenacting the punishment and revenge pattern established in his childhood.[8]

We get our closest look at the adult Christmas during the three years that he spends in Jefferson before the murder of Joanna Burden. During this time he exhibits virtually every personal quality ascribed by Horney to the arrogant-vindictive type: arrogance, envy, the need to frustrate others, the inability to feel sympathy, the inability to ask for or receive aid graciously, the tendency toward uncontrollable rage. His need to keep others at bay, or, when he has the chance, to make them the recipients of his contempt, to triumph over them with tongue or fist, governs his every action. He manages to repress thoroughly all self-effacing or loving tendencies, thus avoiding the intense self-hate that would accompany any violation of his solution.

Appearing on the Jefferson scene, Joe is "sullen and quiet and fatal as a snake" (*LA*, p. 41). The men at the mill know him by his "darkly contemptuous expression," and the "silent and unflagging savageness" with which he shovels sawdust. These are apparently enough to keep them at bay, but with the arrival of Brown, made of denser stuff, Joe resorts to blows, curses, and murder threats.

But it is in the portrait of Joe's most "intimate" relationship that Faulkner shows most vividly the emotional paralysis and the compulsive need to deny others warmth that are the inevitable adjunct to the search for vindictive triumph. Joe first encounters Joanna Burden when she finds him standing in her kitchen, surreptitiously eating the food that he could have had for the asking. At first, their relationship is based on her supplying him with the food and shelter that he needs but will not ask for. It is not much of a connection, but it is enough to make Joe uncomfortable, especially when he realizes one day, "liplifted," that she has put herself above him by not inviting him into the "house proper." He revenges himself by raping her, unfeminine and unattractive as she is, but his triumph is rendered incomplete by her failure to disintegrate at his touch. Her surrender is "hard, untearful and unpitying and almost manlike" (*LA*, p. 221), and thus he is compelled to try again. This time he approaches her "in a quiet rage," determined to "show the bitch," but he meets neither enthusiasm nor resistance, and so is, again, denied the triumph that would allow him to leave her alone. "It was as though some enemy upon whom he had wreaked his utmost violence and contumely stood, unscathed and unscarred, and contemplated him with a musing and insufferable contempt" (*LA*, p. 224). Eventually he rids himself of this sense of her contempt in a scene reminiscent of Catechism Sunday. As he sniffs and audibly identifies each dish of food that has been left for him before he sends it crashing into the kitchen wall, he feels an exhilarating sense of vindictive triumph. It is no accident that this is one of the few times in the novel that Joe really seems to come alive, to do more than cast a baleful shadow on the page. These are the moments for which the arrogant-vindictive type lives: the moments that deny his dependency on others and establish his ascendancy over them, the glittering prizes that inspire his search for glory.

Now that he has caught on to the way to establish his ascendancy over Joanna, Joe can stay on at her place and wait for her complete surrender, a surrender that comes in the form of a grotesque middle-aged sexual awakening: "In this way the second phase began. It was as though he had fallen into a sewer" (*LA*. p. 242). The words "fallen" and "sewer" are important here. What happens to Joe in his relationship with Joanna is that her "surrender" threatens to confine him. In the "sewer" of her sexuality he might be trapped, and as Horney observes, "all human ties . . . are felt as restraints on the path to a sinister glory" (*NHG*, p. 203) by the arrogant-vindictive type. Joe is wary, and tries to preserve his distance by having no daytime contact with Joanna at all, scarcely, indeed, exchanging any words with her at any time except for the obscenities that she perversely demands. And he is able to resume his progress down the path toward aggressive triumph when, following Faulkner's rather bizarre notion of female sexuality,[9] Joanna abruptly becomes asexual at the onset of menopause, and insists on praying over Joe and trying to reform him. Now she is vulnerable because she is asking for something that he is adept at denying, expressing a need that he is indeed compelled to frustrate, just as he was compelled to frustrate Mrs. McEachern's need for affection. Again the "need for triumph and the need to deny positive feelings" (*NHG*, p. 203) come into play at the same time. Now Joe can taste his triumph over Joanna, thinking, "There is something I am going to do." Now he can deny her any feelings of love or respect, "his lip lifted into the shape of a soundless and rigid snarl," saying, " 'You just got old and it happened to you and now you are not any good any more' " (*LA*, p. 262).

He hates her now "with a fierce revulsion of dread and impotent rage" (*LA*, p. 257) for threatening his solution by caring for him. His rage, maybe not really so impotent, leads him to tote his razor up her stairs and slit her throat so thoroughly that the country man who finds her body will be afraid to pick it up for fear that her head will stay behind. The intensity of his rage is partly a response to her determination to deny him mastery, but it is primarily his reply to her attempts to be a loving mother to him. *"All I wanted was peace,"* he thinks, " 'She ought not to started praying over me' " (*LA*, p. 104). By praying over Joe, Joanna, like Mrs. McEachern before her, violates Joe's "peace," threatening his vindictive solution by implying that the world is not entirely hostile, and reviving suppressed conflicts between his hated and repressed self-effacing shoulds and his need for vindictive triumph. Like any other human being, Joe has a deep-seated need to give and receive love, but if he recognized this aspect of himself at this point in his life, it would lead to the disintegration of his neurotic personality—the "solution" that allows him to function (albeit on a pitifully restricted level) without the agony of inner conflict. His fear of such conflict is reflected in the intensity of his rage, an intensity that eventually makes murder inevitable.

In examining Joe's relationship with Joanna we have seen all of the elements of his disturbed personality revealed. But his neurosis is not confined to one relationship—all of his contacts with the people of Jefferson reflect his compulsive need to move against others. To begin with, there is his consistently arrogant and rude demeanor. This is the result of his need to externalize the self-hate that is the inevitable concomitant of the gap between his actual self (a two-bit drifter) and his idealized self (the young Faustus above honor and law). It also serves his need to deny positive feelings, to reject the self-effacing strategies that his childhood taught him were ineffective, and his need to intimidate others into allowing him the vindictive triumph that is his only source of satisfaction. All who come in contact with him—the McEacherns, the mill workers, "Joe Brown"—are treated with the same distancing coldness and contempt. He establishes around himself an impenetrable aura of sullenness.

Then there is his tendency to respond violently to the friendly gesture, his inability to ask for or receive help graciously, because to do so would be to admit a failure of mastery and to recognize the existence of the humane values that he must deny in order to protect his neurosis. This is especially evident in his response to proferred food. We have seen what he does with Joanna's and Mrs. McEachern's carefully prepared meals, and when Byron Bunch offers his lunch pail, Joe's response is again violently negative. " 'I ain't hungry,' " he says, " 'Keep your muck' " (*LA*, p. 31). This tendency also extends to money. He is careful to remind Mrs. McEachern as he steals her little hoard that he has not accepted it as a gift: " 'I didn't ask, because I was afraid you would give it to me. I just took it. Dont forget that' " (*LA*, p. 196). It is important to note that this inability to take from others is compulsive, and not a healthy desire to "live on the terms of his own self-definition," as John Lewis Longley, Jr., describes it.[10] Joe does not merely refuse aid, he responds with fury, with physical or verbal violence when it is offered. He does so because of a need to reassert the false feeling of superiority that is threatened when people behave as if they think he needs help, and because such offers of aid remind him of the despised and repressed part of himself that would depend on others for love, approval, or aid.

Joe's relationship with Joanna also brings into clear perspective another pattern of dealing with others typical of the arrogant-vindictive personality. As we have seen, his most common stance is that of a highly controlled sullenness. But in opposition to this guardedness we find a tendency toward violent and uncontrollable rage. The vindictive type, though he may be very unpleasant indeed, ordinarily does not express much of the hostility that he feels (this would be too dangerous). But on occasion his compulsions overwhelm him, and he feels rage as something impinging on him from outside, something over which he has no control, something which frightens even him. These occasions arise when there is a clear threat to his idealized image, when his mastery or his freedom from positive feelings is threatened. When Brown laughs at him and calls him "nigger," Joe comes close to killing him, seeing his actions as out of control, as coming from another source: "*Something is going to happen to me. I am going to do something*" (*LA,* p. 97). When he goes for a walk in Freedman Town and encounters some blacks talking and laughing, he almost cuts a man with his razor: " 'What in hell is the matter with me?' " he wonders. Then, "*Something is going to happen to me*" (*LA,* p. 110). As they are throughout the book, blacks here are a reminder to Joe of his despised actual self, the self that he is afraid might be black, and thus, in his mind, inferior. As we have seen, Joe's murder of Joanna is also the result of vindictive rage, a rage so far out of control that he begins to think of the murder as past before it has even happened: " 'Maybe I have already done it,' " he thinks. " 'Maybe it is no longer now waiting to be done' " (*LA,* p. 104). Again we must note a flaw in Longley's argument that Joe is an existential hero. His acts of violence are not evidence of rebellion against a controlling society. They are evidence of a profound loss of choice emanating from an irrational rage at those who threatened his identification with his ideal self.

Faulkner's portrayal of Joe Christmas builds to a climax in the description of his relationship with Joanna, but the events following the murder are also of importance to our understanding of his character and its significance. Once "something" has indeed happened, and Joanna's throat is slit, Joe's revenge for the damage done him in childhood is almost, but not quite, complete. He has destroyed the punishing man (McEachern) and the confining women (Joanna and Mrs. McEachern), but one more threat remains. He still has to triumph over the spectre of his weakness and inferiority, the "actual self" that he has come to associate with blacks. To this end, he bursts in upon a black church, cursing God, slapping the minister, knocking a seventy-year-old man "clean down into the mourner's pew," fracturing the skull of that man's six-foot grandson with a bench leg. " 'I'll cut a notch in it tomorrow' " (*LA,* p. 308), he thinks and, close to laughter for the second time in the novel, says, " 'Have a butt, boys,' " as he flicks his cigarette into the bushes where the mystified and frightened black men wait. The next time we see Joe it is at dawn, and he is feeling a sense of peace and exhilaration, the rewards of complete vindictive triumph. His dragons slain, Joe need fight no longer.

Joe's passive surrender to the law, and then to the gun and knife of Percy Grimm, may seem to be grossly inconsistent with his character as I have described it, but in fact his martyrdom is readily explicable in Horneyan terms. Every arrogant-vindictive type, as I have mentioned, harbors powerful self-effacing trends. They are part of the actual self that he is compelled to despise. They threaten him with helplessness, and they cast doubt on the "truth" of his solution, but they remain to tempt him with a means of obtaining the affection and acceptance that he was first denied and has since denied himself. Drawing on her psychoanalytic experience, Horney describes the frequent reaction of a patient whose vindictive trends are brought to light by analysis: "a period ensues when he feels altogether contemptible and helpless and tends to prostrate himself for the sake of being loved" (*NHG*, p. 207). This extreme response is, in a sense, paralleled by Joe's response to the fulfillment of his vindictive desires. Once he has succeeded in slaying all of his demons—the confining women, the threat of negritude, the spectre of his helplessness in a hostile world—Joe has carried his aggressive solution to its logical conclusion. He has achieved a palpable vindictive triumph, and like Horney's patients who suddenly turn against their own solutions, he now feels compelled to allow his submerged needs for love and approval to surface. The self-effacing shoulds that he has so brutally repressed and violated are now the source of a guilt that must be expiated. That Joe that we see shaving and combing his hair, preparing himself, the town says, like a bridegroom, for death, is a Joe who has satisfied his compulsion to make others suffer, and has been overcome by that hitherto submerged part of his personality that wishes suffering on itself and cannot allow itself to fight back. As we shall see, this sudden emergence of Joe's self-effacing trends is part of his creator's plan to elicit our sympathy for and identification with Joe, but first let us understand the psychological implications of his surrender.

The suffering that Joe undergoes during his "passion" and death is, it is clear, very real suffering indeed. Nevertheless, in the context of Faulkner's characterization, it is "neurotic" or "functional" suffering in that Joe seeks it out deliberately, and uses it with the apparent object of "dying on the doorstep" of the world that has abused him for so long. Functional suffering, a prominent aspect of self-effacing neurosis, has as its purpose the accusing of others and the excusing of oneself (*NHG*, p. 235), and Joe's sudden switch from murderer to passive victim can be understood as a product of his need to do just that. He is reacting to the fulfillment of his drive for vindication in the same way that Horney's patients react to the vision of their own vindictiveness: by switching the emphasis onto himself as needy victim and sufferer in order to mollify those self-effacing shoulds that he has repressed for his entire adult life but never eradicated. Captured in Mottstown, Joe allows Halliday to hit him in the face, "acting like a nigger" (i.e., prostrating himself) for the first time, according to the town (*LA*, p. 331). He escapes, apparently only in order to increase his suffering, to hurry his martyrdom, and does not defend himself against Grimm even though he is carrying a loaded pistol. Faulkner describes his castration and death in a remarkable passage:

> For a long moment he looked up at them with peaceful and unfathomable and unbearable eyes. Then his face, body, all, seemed to collapse, to fall in upon itself, and from out the slashed garments about his hips and loins the pent black blood seemed to rush like a released breath. It seemed to rush out of his pale body like the rush of sparks from a rising rocket; upon that black blast the man seemed to rise soaring into their memories forever and ever. They are not to lose it, in whatever peaceful valleys, beside whatever placid and reassuring streams of old age, in the mirroring faces of whatever children they will contemplate old disasters and newer hopes. It will be there, musing, quiet, steadfast, not fading and not particularly threatful, but of itself alone serene, of itself alone triumphant. (*LA*, p. 440)

Once again we are witness to the successful completion of the search for glory, but this time the reward is the crowning glory of martyrdom rather than vindictive triumph. This glory is bought with suffering rather than mastery, and it is shown to be a thing greatly to be desired. Those who have neglected and persecuted Joe, who have denied him love and understanding, are now never to lose the memory of his suffering, the image of his martyred face.

3

Thus far my analysis has been restricted to making psychological sense of Faulkner's portrait of Joe Christmas. It would appear that his character is psychologically explicable as that of a man whose horrendous childhood has caused him to behave in rigidly prescribed patterns—first as avenging angel, then as suffering martyr—patterns responsive not to objective reality, but to his unrealistic vision of his idealized self. But we are left with some questions. We have evaluated Joe's motives and behavior from an objective standpoint, but we have not evaluated them in the context of *Light in August* as a whole. How is the reader to view Joe's troubled life and ultimate martyrdom? With admiration, or sympathy, or with the amiable condescension of the sociologist? And what of the other characters in the novel, particularly what of Lena Grove and Byron Bunch? How does their story of birth and love and ongoing life relate to Joe's story of death and death-in-life? In other words, what does the guiding consciousness of *Light in August* want us to think about the characters and events of the novel?

As we shall see, this question is not easily answered. An analysis of the subtle rhetoric of *Light in August* reveals that the author that it implies is, like Joe Christmas, a being in conflict. Like the Joe we have observed, he is ultimately torn between a need to deny positive feelings and pursue triumph over the weak, and a need to compensate for this aggressive activity. In fact, we can find much rhetorical evidence for the theory that Joe's creator identifies with him and with his world view. *Light in August* is primarily an aggressive novel that seeks to compensate for its tendency to "move against" humanity by martyring its aggressive protagonist, and by making various mostly halfhearted and unsuccessful attempts to affirm the value of life and love.

We can begin our analysis of the implied author and his intentions by examining his relationship to his protagonist. As we have seen, he has painted in Joe a portrait of a very disturbed man. But instead of always seeing Joe for what he is, he seems at times to see him for what he would be, to mistake his idealized for his actual self, and particularly to overemphasize his role as victim and martyr as a way of excusing his aggression. As we shall see, this treatment of Joe is reflected in the thematic structure of *Light in August* as a whole.

Though it is quite rare in Faulkner's major works to encounter lines or descriptions that do not ring true to the characterizations of which they are a part, this does happen, it seems to me, in the case of Joe Christmas. Occasionally he is given a line to speak that strikes a false note in relation to the rest of his characterization. These lines seem designed to ask our participation in his irrational sense of injury, to encourage us to identify with him, and to prepare us to accept his "apotheosis" at the end.

For example, there is Joe's plaintive reaction to Bobbie's rejection of his proposal of marriage: "*Why, I committed murder for her. I even stole for her*" (*LA*, p. 204). As Waggoner points out, the effect of this passage is sentimental because Faulkner seems to ask us to accept this assessment of the situation, to pity Joe for being betrayed, when, in fact, what he says is a lie.[11] Joe killed McEachern, gleefully, for revenge, and he stole from Mrs. McEachern, not to get the money for Bobbie, because he could have had it for the asking, but to demonstrate his complete rejection of his foster mother and her way of being. But putting this unlikely line in Joe's mouth (his motives seem clear enough to him moments before), Joe's creator is asking us to play down Joe's victimization of others.

A similar situation occurs when Faulkner has Joe ask Joanna, after hearing the story of her ancestors, " 'Just when do men that have different blood in them stop hating one another?' " (*LA*, p. 236). Hitherto Joe's only contribution to brotherly love between the races has been to hate whites for being white and blacks for being black. And the Joe Christmas that Faulkner shows us would never have said those words—self-pity and humanism are most definitely not his style. Here, as in the jarring passage that describes Joe as being "sick for two years" after sleeping with an unsegregated prostitute, his creator is asking us to give more weight to Joe's distress over his racial ambiguity than it will bear. He does so, I think, in order to increase our sympathy for and involvement in Joe's plight.

This sentimentalization of Joe's role as victim culminates in his final martyrdom. As we have seen, Joe's "conversion" itself is psychologically explicable.

He is driven from one neurotic solution to another by an overwhelming sense of guilt that is brought on by repeated and flagrant violations of his deeply buried but still active self-effacing trends. But in attempting to discover what the author of *Light in August* wants us to think of all this, we find that he seems to share in Joe's desires to accuse others and excuse himself through suffering, that he too sees Joe's life as justified by his end, that, in fact, he sometimes sees Joe as his idealized self, as a god.

There is much discussion among critics as to whether the parallels between Joe and Jesus Christ are meant to be ironic or not. It seems clear to me that they are not. The language used to describe Joe's death, the idiotic cruelty of Percy Grimm, the ugliness of the lynch mob, the sympathy due Mrs. Hines, the dignity of Joe: these are just a few of the things that encourage our positive identification of Joe with Jesus. The religious imagery surrounding Joe's death has been heavily documented. There are angels and halos; there are "slashed garments," and a wound to the body. The language used to describe Joe's death makes it obvious that he is to be identified with the Jesus who ascended into heaven to sit at the right hand of His Father. When, on the geyser of "pent black blood" from his loins, Joe seems to "rise soaring into [the] memories forever and ever" of the men who are watching him; when his face is immortalized, "of itself alone serene, of itself alone triumphant," it becomes clear that his death is meant by his creator to justify all that has gone before, in fact, to accuse others and excuse Joe. Like that of Jesus, Joe's martyrdom is seen as willed and redemptive. The compulsions shown to have been set in motion by his childhood are now forgotten as he soars into our memories, purified and glorified by his suffering. Critics have found this apotheosis difficult to account for, and no wonder. As our psychological analysis of Joe's character allows us to see, it is possible for a man like Joe to feel driven to martyrdom, but highly unlikely that he should achieve such glorious results (based on fantasy, like all other manifestations of the neurotic search for glory, such attempts at martyrdom are unlikely to buy one the kind of eternal life granted to Joe). Joe's soaring departure is made possible not by the realities of his characterization, but by the tendency of Joe's creator to mistake Joe's idealized self for reality, and to manipulate his fictional world to honor Joe's neurotic bargains with fate.

The emphasis on Joe's role as victim and martyr is evidence of the partial identification of Joe's creator with his creation, an identification the reader is invited to share. Though the implied author of *Light in August* never addresses the reader directly, an analysis of some of the patterns of imagery in the novel and of the treatment of some of the characters other than Joe will reveal that the novel often asks the reader to participate in the same denial of "weakness" and search for "triumph" that govern Joe's life until the bench leg comes in contact with Roz Thompson's head.

It has often been pointed out[12] that for Faulkner women represent that aspect of humanity which is most basically human: physical as opposed to intellectual, realistic as opposed to idealistic, enduring as opposed to vengeful, accepting as opposed to aggressive. In Horneyan terms, women in his novels are ordinarily seen as superior to men because they tend to embody the self-effacing values espoused by his humanist themes. But if we look closely at the treatment of women in *Light in August,* we find that instead of representing the "weaker" (that is to say more human, more accepting, less aggressive) aspects of humanity in a positive sense, they are presented as by and large the objects of squeamishness and contempt.[13] Their physical selves, accepting and giving rather than moving against, are either malfunctioning or nauseating; their attempts to love or to be kind are generally awkward, ridiculous, and unsuccessful. In other words, the novel as a whole tends to share Joe Christmas's perspective on women rather than the perspective of the public Faulkner. In the novel, as in Joe's mind, they are associated with "muck," this four letter word referring not only to their association with food but to their sexuality and to their tendency to try to make positive human connections.

Here is what happens to you if you are a female character in *Light in August.* If you are past menopause you are asexual; you are ugly; you dress funny; you wear your hair in an unattractive "tight screw" at the back of your head, and your gestures of kindness or affection are "savage," "clumsy," even ridiculous. If you are young and do not have sex then you look "frozen and skinny," are driven to run off to Memphis where you can get what you need, have a nervous breakdown in church, and finally feel so guilty that you jump out a hotel window. If you are young and do have sex then maybe you are the "prone and abject" recipient of organized fourteen-year-old lust, or maybe you are unnaturally short and have great big hands "dead and pale as a piece of cooking meat" (*LA*, p. 202), the outer signs of your "inner corruption of the spirit" (*LA*, p. 161). Or maybe you are a "pinksmelling" wild-eyed young woman willing to destroy a child's life to keep your activities secret. Or just maybe you can give off the air of an unravished bride of quietness even while eight months pregnant and demonstrate your "courage and endurance" by pursuing across three states a man who does not want you and would not be worth catching even if your "slow time" did not make it seem highly improbable that you would do any such thing. But if you are a middle-aged woman who has sex, then you are in real trouble, because while a man's "sin" can be "healthy and normal," making love with you is like falling into a sewer. You will try to draw a man into the "black thick pool" of your sexuality. You will be afflicted with that ghastliest of infirmities, nymphomania, and will cast yourself about in wild poses and shout obscenities. You too look funny in your clothes, but underneath is a "rotten richness ready to flow into putrefaction at a touch" (*LA*, p. 247). Eventually you will reach menopause and make a fool of yourself by suddenly thinking you are pregnant. Then you will lose all interest in sex and absurdly transfer your energies to a scheme to send your ignorant mill-hand lover to law school, that is before you go completely nuts and try to shoot him with an old pistol that does not work. Then you will get your throat slit and look funny lying on the ground for all the world to see with your head turned around completely backwards (if you'd been able to do that before, they say, maybe you wouldn't be doing it now). As Albert J. Guerard points out, "The misogynous imagination selects for its female victims appalling situations and punishments."[14] These things do not happen to Joanna Burden by chance. They happen to her because her creator manipulates her world to make her appear ridiculous and contemptible. It would seem that the guiding consciousness of *Light in August,* far from setting himself to admire the "courage and endurance" of women, wishes to reject or deny or ridicule the messy humanity that they represent. Their sexuality in particular is shown to be the source of corruption, ugliness, stupidity, mean-spirited behavior, and bad smells.

To a lesser extent the blacks of the novel are also the objects of this compulsive rejection of all that is "weak" or "inferior" in humanity. It has not gone unnoticed that there are some blatantly racist descriptions in the novel, such as that which refers to the "vacuous idiocy" of "idle and illiterate" (*LA,* p. 53) Negro nursemaids, or the "fumbling and timeless Negro fashion" (*LA,* p. 68) of a black expectant father. But there is also a consistent pattern of imagery that places blacks in the messily human, and thus despicable, category of women; their alleged inferiority and tendency to connect with others (they seem to crowd together and are over and over again described as "fecund") qualifying them to be the recipients of the implied author's contempt. Like women, blacks are associated with smells and unpleasant enclosure. Freedman Town is like "the bottom of a thick black pit" (*LA,* p. 107). This echo of the description of Joanna's sexuality is no accident; a walk here is like a return to "the lightless hot wet primogenitive Female" (*LA,* p. 107) and, as we have seen, that is like a stroll through the sewer. Joe can hardly breathe lying next to his ebony carving of a common-law wife, and blacks are smelled before they are seen. The air around whites is "cold and hard," and, if they are male, presumably odor-free.

Just as Faulkner's public statements ask us to see *Light in August* as a celebration of womanhood, however, some elements of the novel ask us to see it as a sympathetic tract on the race question. The novel seems at times to ask the question so improbably attributed to Joe, " 'Just when do men that have different blood in them stop hating one another?' " As we have seen, Faulkner's portrayal of Joe asks for our sympathy for the outsider, the "nigger," the victim of the lynch mob, the man unjustly hated because of the "curse" of his alleged black blood. But at the same time we are subtly asked to despise all those who do not pursue mastery and deny positive feelings, and thus the black race, condemned to an inferior position and prone to close associations, is seen as fumbling, stupid, and smelly.

A look at the positive imagery associated with aggression in the novel confirms our theory that it tends to encourage aggressive fantasy. When Samuel A. Yorks points out that in the world of *Light in August* it seems "better to be castrated than seduced,"[15] he is obliquely referring to the way the novel continually contrasts the admirably "clean" tendency to move against people or things, or to separate oneself from them, as opposed to the "messy" tendency to move toward them, to make physical or emotional connections.

When Joe violently removes his undergarment in a bizarre "streaking" episode, his right hand slides "fast and smooth," striking the remaining button a "light, swift blow" (*LA*, p. 100). Then the dark air breathes "smoothly" around his male nakedness: it is "soft" and "cool." This is his answer to the "thick still black pool of more than water" (*LA*, p. 99) that is the image for Joanna's frantic attempts to move toward him. This same contrast of phallic with womb-sewer imagery is encountered in the description of Joe's trip through the black section of town. Here Joe is the "lone telephone pole," connoting something "clean, hard, and dry,"[16] as Yorks points out, while, as we have seen, the black area where people are gathered closely together, presumably in the process of being "fecund," is like the womb, "lightless, hot, wet," like "the bottom of a thick black pit." The contrast also appears in the description of Joe's response to Bobbie's explanation of menstruation. Nauseated, he runs to the woods where he takes brief solace in the "hard trunks" of the trees, "branch shadowed, quiet, hardfeeling, hardsmelling, invisible" (*LA*, p. 197), and then seems to see a row of misshapen urns (the shape of the womb, the functions of which are to give and receive rather than move against): "Each one was cracked and from each crack there issued something liquid, deathcolored, and foul" (*LA*, p. 178). Naturally, Joe vomits. But then he buys a nice new rope with which to escape from the house at night, and the next time he sees Bobbie manfully hauls her off to the woods with no preliminaries.

In the description of Joe's childhood the imagery used in connection with McEachern and his cruelty towards Joe tends to be more positive than that connected with Mrs. McEachern's ineffective attempts to move toward him. Mr. McEachern is frequently described by terms like "hard" and "vigorous." He is "rocklike," indomitable. He smells of the "clean hard virile living leather" with which he beats Joe coolly, without heat or anger (*LA*, p. 139). Mrs. McEachern, on the other hand, is a "stiff caricature" when she reaches out her hand to Joe. She is "shapeless, a little hunched" (*LA*, p. 145). She hovers, she fumbles, and she huddles, like some unattractive little bird. This imagery is not wasted on Longley, who refers to her "sickening attempts to make [Joe] as cringing as herself."[17] It is Joe, of course, who accepts and models himself after his foster father and despises his foster mother because he cannot understand or believe in love, but the novel seems to lend some support to his choice.

Even in Percy Grimm's final pursuit of Joe we see that the imagery gives a positive connotation to aggression and a negative connotation to its opposite. Grimm's face is "rocklike," "bright." It has "that serene, unearthly luminousness of angels in church windows" (*LA*, p. 437). The rest of the community, on the other hand, huddled together, look at "his tense hard young face," their own faces "blanched and gaped with round, toothed orifices" (*LA*, p. 434). And Hightower, who frantically and ineffectively tries to give Joe aid, has "[a] bald head and [a] big pale face" (*LA*, p. 438).

Light in August presents a world where the warm gesture, the act of giving or physical union, and the source of life itself are seen as unbeautiful, awkward, even "foul," while the tendency to move against others, or at least to maintain a "clean" and "hard" separateness, is invested over and over again with a certain beauty. Like Joe Christmas, the consciousness that has created this world seems to have a compulsive need to deny the reality and efficacy of human bonds, and to indulge in pleasurable fantasies of triumph and separation. The novel also presents a world where human physical and emotional ties are warmly, if a bit condescendingly, accepted, but though this seems designed to compensate for the strain of aggression that we have been observing, it is undercut in various ways and does not do so effectively.

I am not the first to notice that the thematic impact of Byron and Lena is reduced by their creator's tendency to make light of their crises and motivations, to place himself and the reader at a distance from them for the sake of comic effect. Though Lena, for example, seems to be presented as an important thematic force when she draws Hightower into life through the birth of her baby, this impression is undercut[18] when we see her reduced to a comic figure (in the Bergsonian as well as the conventional sense) as she mechanically resumes her pursuit of Lucas after he jumps out the window. " 'Now I got to get up again' " (*LA*, p. 410), she says out loud to herself. And in the scenes that portray a Lena who could not resist the callow Burch rejecting the advances of Byron, her devoted protector, it is obvious that the implied author is more concerned with humor than with theme. The humor is very good, and Lord knows it is welcome, but it has a rather negative effect on Lena's status as a redeemer. The qualities that she represents—loyalty, endurance, an accepting spirit—are a little hard to take seriously. Her loyalty is misplaced, her endurance seems to be the result of a one-track mind, and her accepting spirit begins to seem primarily comic and mechanical, as she continues to ignore the negative aspects of her situation and extol the virtues of traveling. There is much to be said for Lena's enjoyment of her situation, and much to be appreciated in her characterization, but there is also in the novel at least a partial denial of the positive feelings that she represents, a denial which coincides with the strain of aggression that we have been tracing. Her creator is obviously smitten with her, but he demonstrates a certain contempt for her as well. Her femininity and fertility are the source of jokes, and her treatment of Byron puts her in a category with other women of loose morals and bad taste in men.

The strain of aggression is even more clearly at work in the novel's treatment of Byron Bunch. The original description of Byron is flavored with sentimentality. He works six days a week, not for money or pleasure, but because working is somehow the thing to do, and because it keeps him out of "trouble." On the seventh day, not content to go to the local church of his choice, or even to ride two hours to a different one like McEachern, he rides *all night* Saturday and *all night* Sunday in order to lead the choir at an *all day* country church service, only to be on hand with "clean overalls and shirt" when the mill whistle blows Monday morning. He eschews "meanness" to the extent that he does not even know who the local moonshiner is, and his only friend is an ex-minister who is neglected and persecuted by the rest of the town. He stumbles on this man's doorstep every time he goes to visit him until, transformed by love and a newly found decision-making ability, he is able on one occasion to stride right in. This portrait is sentimental because it is based on exaggeration and cliche. Unlike the Faulkner of *Snopes* who was able to create in V. K. Ratliff a "good" man of many dimensions, a character who gets right up and walks off the page, the implied author of *Light in August* seems only able to define a healthy lack of aggression in a character by relying on stereotype.

As Slatoff[19] points out, Faulkner allows Byron a brief gain in stature (as he arranges for Lena's lying-in and defies the Mrs. Grundies of Jefferson, he stands up straight and has a "new air born somewhere between assurance and defiance" [*LA*, p. 295]). But in the final chapter he is greatly reduced. The furniture dealer, rather a wonderful narrator, describes Byron as "the kind of fellow you wouldn't see at first glance if he was alone by himself in the bottom of a empty concrete swimming pool" (*LA*, p. 469), and says it is impossible to imagine "any woman knowing that they had ever slept with him, let alone having anything to show folks to prove it" (*LA*, p. 470). He "trots" into the store and, over-eager, comes out with so many bags that, little as he is, he can hardly see over them. He is a "durn little cuss" about to "burst out crying" because of sexual frustration. He is not only rejected by Lena, but is hoisted out of the truck by her as if he were a six year old. I submit that in these scenes Byron's creator has castrated him just about as effectively as Percy Grimm castrates Joe Christmas. His thematic role as a man who accepts and involves himself in humanity is seriously undercut. He becomes first and foremost a "little" man, cute and amusing, but eunuchlike and ineffective.

We have seen that the desire for aggressive triumph and the need to deny positive feelings play important roles in the guiding consciousness of *Light in August.* But we have also seen that the canonization of the aggressive protagonist (with whom the implied author seems to identify) is bought with his suffering, with his ultimate assumption of the role of passive victim. And we have seen that various attempts (mostly half-hearted or unsuccessful) are made throughout the novel to portray the importance of positive feelings. What can we hypothesize about the implied author in relation to these conflicting aspects of the novel?

It seems to me that the occasional attempts to espouse nonaggressive values in *Light in August* are meant to serve the same purpose for the novel as a whole as Joe's "passion" and death serve in relation to his character. By showing Joe's assumption of a self-effacing value system at the end, and by closing the book with Hightower's conversion and the coziness of the furniture dealer's narration, the implied author is attempting to compensate for the intense aggressiveness of the novel. Guerard attributes much of the appeal of Faulkner's work to "highly liberated fantasy."[20] It is my view that the central fact about *Light in August,* its source of appeal, the quality that makes it fairly hum with forbidden energy, is its "highly liberated" use of aggressive fantasy. Joe may be made to wonder why the blacks in the cabin are "of their brother afraid" (*LA*, p. 317); Hightower may come to see that he was wrong to neglect his wife; Mrs. Armstid may demonstrate the fundamental generosity of her kind by giving away her egg money; but these moments do not define the essence of *Light in August.* It would be more accurate to say that they seek to compensate for it. The essence of the novel is found in the disturbing and vicious chapters on Joe's affair with Joanna Burden, in the portrayal of his stand-off with McEachern and his cruel treatment of Mrs. McEachern, in Doc Hines's excruciating narration of his attempts to destroy "God's abomination," in the image of the bloody butcher knife in Percy Grimm's hand. These passages, permeated with a consciousness that is drawn again and again to the aggressive vision, appeal not to our reason, our social conscience, or our admiration for Nobel-Prize-speech sentiment, but to our less wholesome impulses.

NOTES

1. Alfred Kazin, "The Stillness of *Light in August,*" in *Faulkner,* ed. Robert Penn Warren (Englewood Cliffs, N.J.: Prentice-Hall, 1966), p. 161.

2. Quoted in *Faulkner in the University,* ed. Frederick L. Gwynn and Joseph Blotner (Charlottesville: University of Virginia Press, 1959), pp. 74, 199.

3. My critical method (the use of Third Force psychology to analyze fictional characters, implied authors, and other elements of fiction) is adapted from that of Bernard J. Paris and is most fully outlined and justified in his *A Psychological Approach to Fiction* (Bloomington: Indiana University Press, 1974). See also my "On Their Hind Legs Casting Shadows: A Psychological Approach to Character in Faulkner," Ph.D. diss., Michigan State University, 1981.

4. Wayne C. Booth, *The Rhetoric of Fiction* (Chicago: University of Chicago Press, 1961), p. 86.

5. Karen Horney, *Neurosis and Human Growth* (New York: Norton, 1950), p. 18. Hereafter cited in the text as *NHG.*

6. William Faulkner, *Light in August* (New York: Random House, 1932), p. 111. Hereafter cited in the text as *LA.*

7. Hyatt Waggoner, *William Faulkner* (Lexington: University of Kentucky Press, 1959), p. 103.

8. The question of Joe's race must be introduced into any discussion of the formation of his adult personality. It seems to me that Joe's possibly "mixed blood" has only a peripheral effect on the *formation* of his personality. Though the hatred of Hines, an important part of the atmosphere of his childhood, might be attributed to his racial ambiguity, the crucial turning points in the development of his neurotic "solution" cannot be. The central fact of Joe's life is that he has been injured and thus seeks to injure others and to deny his connection with them. The possibility of his "mixed blood" provides him with a means of denying others closeness and thus of denying the

existence of values like love and kindness, and it provides him with opportunities for perpetuating the compulsive pattern of punishment and revenge, but it is not the *cause* of his alienation.

9. A possible source for Faulkner's notions about middle-aged women is suggested in Ilse Dusoir Lind, "Faulkner's Women," in *The Maker and the Myth: Faulkner and Yoknapatawpha,* ed. Evans Harrington and Ann J. Abadie (Jackson: University Press of Mississippi, 1978). Lind says that the theories of Havelock Ellis and Louis Berman are responsible for the portrayal of this aspect of Joanna.

10. John Lewis Longley, Jr., *The Tragic Mask: A Study of Faulkner's Heroes* (Chapel Hill: University of North Carolina Press, 1963), p. 195.

11. Waggoner, *William Faulkner,* p. 116.

12. See for example the writings of Cleanth Brooks, in this case most notably "The Community and the Pariah," in *Twentieth Century Interpretations of* Light in August, ed. David L. Minter (Englewood Cliffs, N.J.: Prentice-Hall, 1969), pp. 55–70; Sally R. Page, *Faulkner's Women* (DeLand, Fla.: Stetson University Press, 1972); or Linda Welshimer Wagner, "Faulkner and (Southern) Women," in *The South and Faulkner's Yoknapatawpha,* ed. Evans Harrington and Ann Abadie (Jackson: University Press of Mississippi, 1977), pp. 128–46.

13. The misogyny of *Light in August* has been much discussed. See for example Samuel A. Yorks, "Faulkner's Women: The Peril of Mankind," *Arizona Quarterly* 17 (1961): 119–29; Jackson W. Heimer, "Faulkner's Misogynous Novel: *Light in August,*" *Ball State University Forum* 14 (1973): 11–15; or Leslie A. Fiedler, *Love and Death in the American Novel* (New York: Criterion Books, 1962), pp. 309–10. Some critics defend Faulkner against charges of misogyny. See for example Lind, "Faulkner's Women"; Wagner, "Faulkner and (Southern) Women"; and Page, *Faulkner's Women.*

14. Albert J. Guerard, *The Triumph of the Novel: Dickens, Dostoevsky, Faulkner* (New York: Oxford University Press, 1972), p. 110.

15. Yorks, "Faulkner's Women," p. 210.

16. Ibid., p. 125.

17. Longley, *The Tragic Mask,* p. 197.

18. Walter J. Slatoff makes this point in *Quest for Failure: A Study of Faulkner* (Ithaca: Cornell University Press, 1960), p. 177.

19. Ibid., p. 178.

20. Guerard, *The Triumph of the Novel,* p. 4.

10

I'd Rather Be Ratliff: A Maslovian Study of Faulkner's *Snopes*

Marjorie B. Haselswerdt

The nature of the "good" character has changed considerably as the novel has developed. In *Clarissa,* as well as in many Victorian novels, the good characters represent a religious ideal. Paul Dombey, Dorothea Brooke, Fanny Price, Maggie Tulliver, Amelia Sedley—all of these characters are models of Christian self-sacrifice who disregard their own needs and desires in favor of those of someone else. Henry James moves away from the religious overtones of the traditional nineteenth-century novel, but retains the assumption that the most self-sacrificing character is the most honorable. Isabel returns to Osmond, Strether returns to the United States, Adam Verver gives up his daughter—all of these characters renounce their desires in order to conform to a stringent code of behavior. As twentieth-century readers we are often hard pressed to admire the saintly self-denial of a Strether or a Dorothea. Our own notions of appropriate behavior are colored by our attachment to the anti-hero who, far from sacrificing himself to save his society, or to live up to a moral code, chooses escape or rebellion. The more sympathetic our twentieth-century hero, the less likely it is that he will be a smoothly functioning, contributing member of his society. The emphasis of our century is not on codes of behavior, but on means of survival and self-expression.

The early and "major phase" writings of William Faulkner are very much a part of this tradition. Quentin Compson chooses not to live in a world dominated by time and marred by sisters gone wrong. Joe Christmas passes his short life alternately rebelling against and escaping from the necessities of his existence. But in his later work, *Snopes* and *The Reivers* particularly, Faulkner departs from the mainstream. In these works, as other critics have pointed out,[1] he is struggling to present his readers with codes of behavior, with notions of how it is "good" for men to behave. It is my view that some of the critical resistance to these later novels is related to the lack, in the novelistic tradition of the twentieth century, of a commonly accepted notion of human virtue. I believe that by viewing *Snopes* in the light of a twentieth-century standard for human behavior that replaces the nineteenth-century preoccupation with self-sacrifice, and transcends the twentieth-century preoccupation with the anti-hero, we can better assess Faulkner's unique purpose and achievement.

I will focus on V. K. Ratliff, the itinerant sewing machine salesman of the Snopes trilogy. Faulkner himself thought highly of Ratliff and considered him a model for human conduct, saying that his work was done for those who would say, "Yes, it's all right. I'd rather be Ratliff than Flem Snopes. And I'd still rather be Ratliff without any Snopes to measure by even."[2] Not all critics have shared Faulkner's enthusiasm. They have found Ratliff too strong and assertive,[3] too capitalistic,[4] too much of the victim of his own neurotic drives,[5] or too fondly indulged by his creator.[6]

On the other hand, some critics have seen Ratliff's potential as a new kind of twentieth-century hero. Joseph Trimmer sees him as a character in pursuit of "knowing" in the Conradian sense, a uniquely creative man who "welcomes the relativity of knowledge since it allows for the continuously exciting game of reassessment and recreation."[7] Edwin Moses points to Ratliff's "passionate humanity" and to his "staggering list of gifts and virtues," the greatest of which is his ability to identify himself wholeheartedly with his fellow man without losing his necessary detachment.[8] Benjamin McClelland sees Ratliff as one of the results of Faulkner's attempt to create "a redeemer for modern man," who would embody the combined virtues of Christianity and stoicism,[9] and Warren Beck refers to him simply as the "epitome of humanity."[10]

The great claims made for Ratliff by these critics in contrast to his otherwise lukewarm reception encourage us to define further his virtuousness and worth as a human being. I propose as a means of doing so a consideration of his character in light of psychologist Abraham Maslow's theories regarding self-actualization in mentally healthy human beings.[11] Maslow, like Faulkner, approaches the problem of virtue in the modern world and offers a solution. While Faulkner's solution, it seems to me, is embodied in the character of Ratliff, Maslow's solution comes as the result of his research into the behavior and attitudes of exceptional human beings, and is approached with the tools of social science rather than art.

> Every age but ours has had its model, its ideal. All of these have been given up by our culture; the saint, the hero, the gentleman, the knight, the mystic. About all we have left is the well-adjusted man without problems, a very pale and doubtful substitute. Perhaps we shall soon be able to use as our guide and model the fully growing and self-fulfilling human being, the one in whom all his potentialities are coming to full development, the one whose inner nature expresses itself freely, rather than being warped, suppressed, or denied.[12]

The resemblance of Faulkner's solution to Maslow's, of Ratliff to the "fully growing and self-fulfilling human beings" of Maslow's study is the subject of this essay.

Maslovian theory is based on the concept that human beings are governed by a hierarchy of biologically based needs. The hierarchy begins with the most basic requirements of the human animal for survival—food, shelter, and safety—and proceeds through the middle needs for love and belonging to the highest needs, those for self-esteem and self-actualization. These needs are hierarchical in the sense that the lower ones must be satisfied before the higher ones are felt. A man who does not have food, for example, does not feel a strong need for love, while a man whose physiological and safety needs are satisfied will feel a strong desire for the regard of his fellow men. Likewise, a man who feels secure in his relationship with his fellows will feel a desire to raise himself in his own regard, and a man who is able to think well of himself will desire to fulfill his potential as a human being, to "actualize" his self. Although the higher needs are not as strongly felt as the lower ones, all of them are "instinctoid" in that they are included in man's biological makeup. They are part of the biologically based "inner nature" of mankind, which is "in part unique to each person, and in part species wide" (*PB*, p. 3).

Maslow's work is primarily concerned with that part of human motivation and behavior which is based on the higher needs. In other words, he is interested in the process of self-actualization, in the movement that a healthy person makes toward "the actualization of [his] potentials, capacities and talents" (*PB*, p. 23). His findings indicate that a human being whose lower needs are satisfied will strive for what the existentialists refer to as authentic humanness, will actively seek a kind of mental health far more profound than our common notion of "normality," which, according to Maslow, is nothing more than a "psychopathology of the average" (*PB*, p. 16). The healthy person will be occupied not with controlling the urges of his id, or with becoming "well-adjusted" to his society, but with cultivating the development of his real self, his human nature. He will be open to himself, and this openness will be "manifested in his greater congruence, his greater transparence, and his greater spontaneity."[13] In other words, he will know what he thinks and feels, express his feelings and thoughts honestly in actions and words, and behave spontaneously according to his inner dictates. By observing such people, according to Maslow, we should be able to draw conclusions about what human nature is, and thus about what it means to be a good or a healthy human being. He says that "We can discover (rather than create or invent) which values men tend toward, yearn for, struggle for, as they improve themselves, and which values they lose as they get sick" (*PB*, p. 167); and he further maintains that from our discoveries we should be able to develop a "scientific ethics, a natural value system, a court of ultimate appeal for the determination of right and wrong" (*PB*, p. 4). Though the development of this "natural value system" was still in the formative stages at the time of Maslow's death, I hope to make it clear that his work in this area is of great value in the study of literature, particularly with regard to that kind of literature Faulkner considered to be the most worthwhile, that which deals with "the old verities and truths of the heart."[14]

In *Motivation and Personality* and in *Toward a Psychology of Being*, Maslow published the results of his research on self-actualizing people, listing and explaining the qualities that typically accompany this high state of human development. Since mental health, unlike "normality," is a comparatively rare phenomenon, and since mentally healthy people are usually reluctant to talk about themselves, Maslow's task was difficult. He had hoped, he says, to use for illustrative purposes some characters from modern literature, but could find none that he considered "usable."[15] I assume that he overlooked Faulkner's triology since my work indicates that the rich characterization of Ratliff sheds light on and adds depth to the theory of self-actualization. Though this is primarily an essay in literary criticism, it has value for the psychologist as well as for the student of literature.

Maslow's primary insight about the mentally healthy person is that his perceptions are clearer and more efficient than those of the average person, perhaps because "the effects of wish, desire, prejudice upon perception . . . should be very much less in healthy people than in sick" (*MP,* p. 154). For the most part, the people of Frenchman's Bend and Jefferson see things as they expect, want, or need to see them. Ratliff, whose perception is seldom affected by his expectations or needs, recognizes this when he says,

> what somebody else jest tells you, you jest half believe, unless it was something you already wanted to hear. And in that case you dont even listen to it because you had done already agreed, and so all it does is make you think what a sensible feller it was that told you. But something you dont want to hear is something you had done already made up your mind against, whether you knowed-knew it or not; and now you can even insulate against having to believe it by resisting or maybe even getting even with that-ere scoundrel that meddled in and told you.[16]

A notable instance of the influence of this phenomenon of "insulation" in Frenchman's Bend concerns Eula. Gavin cannot understand until it is too late that what Eula needs is someone "brave enough" to accept her love. He is too involved in his own concept of himself as a latter day Don Quixote to admit to the real human needs of a woman; his self image requires that she be simply pure and in need of defense. It is up to Ratliff to say "Maybe she was bored" (*T,* p. 258), implying that by ignoring her humanity the men in Eula's life left it empty and ultimately not worth the living. Since he bases his self esteem neither on his chivalry as does Gavin, nor on his virility as does de Spain, Ratliff can see Eula herself more clearly, and he is the first one to come up with a good explanation for her suicide.

Another example of Ratliff's superior ability to perceive reality clearly is found in the famous "Spotted Horses" episode of *The Hamlet.* While all the other men allow themselves to be duped by Flem and the gingersnap eating Texan into bidding on horses that not only are not broken, but are actively mean, Ratliff has enough sense to leave the area for the day. "A fellow can dodge a Snopes," he points out, "if he starts lively enough."[17] He knows that Flem's plan is to use the weak perceptions of the other men (their ability to see clearly is distorted by their need to prove their masculine ability to trade shrewdly and handle horses competently) in order to line his pockets.

Of course the men all buy horses, and the horses all escape, and Will Varner thinks that it is all right because "They'll get the money back in exercise and relaxation" (*H*, p. 308) trying to catch them; but Ratliff does not agree.

> "That's one way to look at it, I reckon," [he says.] "In fact it might be a considerable comfort to Bookwright and Quick and Freeman and Eck Snopes and them other new horse-owners if that side of it could be brought to their attention because the chances are aint none of them thought to look at it in that light yet." (*H*, p. 308)

Again Ratliff's perceptions are the clearest. Will Varner, since he has connections with Flem, prefers to look on the whole thing as a rather good joke; but Ratliff, who has no stake in the matter, perceives it clearly, and, in his gently ironic way, refuses to deny the suffering involved.

Maslow writes of the "unusual ability" of the self-actualizing person "to detect the spurious, the fake and the dishonest" (*MP*, p. 153). Obviously this is part of what Ratliff demonstrates in the "Spotted Horses" episode, and it is this ability that Faulkner relies on as his counter to the fundamental spuriousness and dishonesty of Flem Snopes, who, if he doesn't ever shortchange his customers, does with his every action deny the concept of honorable and open interaction between human beings. It has been pointed out that "Flem Snopes never appears in any work which does not include Ratliff."[18] Faulkner realized that he needed as an antidote to Flem a character whose own needs would not distort his perceptions.

Another aspect of what Maslow calls the self-actualizing person's "superior relationship with reality" is his ability to accept it without categorizing it. The healthy man has the "innocent eye," the ability to look at the unknown without feeling the desire to apply to it some preconceived cultural notion, and without feeling threatened by it (*MP*, p. 154). Ratliff is often described as "innocent," and Faulkner makes it very clear that the sewing machine salesman is intrigued with, rather than put off by, that which is outside the expectations of his culture.

In *The Mansion*, when Ratliff accompanies Gavin to New York, it is quite obviously the first time he has been any farther than Memphis. But, thrown in with people and ideas very different from anything he could have met with before, Ratliff is perfectly at his ease—still "affable," still speaking in his undefensive, unpretentious way, telling the owner of an exclusive tie store that he makes his own faded blue shirts: " 'I sells sewing machines. First thing I knowed I could run one too.' "[19] When Barton Kohl shows him some very avant garde (and apparently bawdy) sculpture and asks, " 'Shocked? Mad?' "

Ratliff counters, " 'Do I have to be shocked and mad at something jest because I never seen it before?' " (*M*, p. 73). He looks at it for a while and thinks maybe he "recognizes" what some of it is, but then he realizes that recognition isn't the important thing.

> Because anybody can see and hear and smell and feel and taste what he expected to hear and see and feel and smell and taste, and wont nothing much notice your presence nor miss your lack. So maybe when you can see and feel and smell and hear and taste what you never expected to and hadn't never even imagined until that moment, maybe that's why Ol Moster picked you out to be one of the ones to be alive. (*M*, p. 173)

And Barton, realizing that Ratliff is capable of finding beauty in the unrubricized, bequeaths him one of the sculptures.

Ratliff's sense of humor is an integral part of his character; and although it occurs side by side with a lot of robust, slapstick folk humor, it is very definitely in the "unhostile," "philosophical" mode that Maslow associates with the humor of the self-actualizing man. His "voice" is part of this humor; never strident, or cruel, or frantically witty, it consistently delights us with its homespun judgments of men and situations. Gavin, for instance, is described as incapable of a secret life, "a feller that even his in-growed toe nails was on the outside of his shoes" (*T*, p. 342). And Flem, on the rise in Jefferson, is

> a banker now, a vice-president, not to mention being the third man, after the Negro that fired the furnace and the preacher his-self inside the Baptist Church ever Sunday morning, and the rest of his career in Jefferson doomed to respectability like a feller in his Sunday suit trying to run through a field of cuckleburs and beggarlice. (*M*, p. 57)

This is what Maslow calls the "humor of the real," which "consists in large part in poking fun at human beings in general when they are foolish, or forget their place in the universe, or try to be big when they are actually small" (*MP*, p. 169). Ratliff undercuts Flem's attempt to be "big," not with a cruel or bitter attack, but with his easygoing, drawling talent for humorous comparisons. And he uses the same technique to poke fun at Gavin's vision of himself as capable of carrying on dignified romantic intrigues. It is impossible to do justice to this kind of humor, since it is so well integrated into the context of the novels, but I should point out that it comes out of Ratliff in a steady stream throughout the trilogy.

He is not, however, a compulsive humorist. He is occasionally "sober," and he realizes that sometimes you run across something that "soon as you set down to laugh at it, you find out it aint funny a-tall" (*T*, p. 257). Warren Beck points out that he is fundamentally "serious minded" in spite of his ability to be funny.[20] He is often described as having an "almost smile" on his face, but he really laughs only a few times in the trilogy. As Maslow says, the humor of the self-actualizing person is more likely to elicit a smile than a belly laugh (*MP,* p. 170).

Ratliff's humor is closely related to his role as a purveyor of unpretentious wisdom. Maslow maintains that all self-actualizing people are "in one sense or another philosophers, however homely" because they live in the "widest possible frame of reference," and are concerned with basic issues and eternal questions" (*MP,* p. 160); and Ratliff is no exception. Consistently he relates the progress of Snopesism and other events in Frenchman's Bend and Jefferson to the human condition in general. When he and Will Varner are talking at the very beginning of *The Hamlet* about the alleged Snopes proclivity for barn burning, Ratliff says,

> "It wasn't proved. . . . Of course, that's the trouble. If a fellow's got to choose between a man that is a murderer and one he just thinks maybe is, he'll choose the murderer. At least then he will know exactly where he's at. His attention aint going to wander then." (*H,* p. 26)

A little amateur psychology emerges from what is just gossip before Ratliff comes upon it. And in *The Town,* after Eck Snopes is blown to bits, Ratliff explains his fate by standing back and looking at the exigencies of Snopesism and human existence in general.

> "Eck wasn't a Snopes. That's why he had to die. Like there wasn't no true authentic room for Snopeses in the world and they made theirselves one by that pure and simple mutual federation, and the first time one slips or falters or fails in being Snopes, it dont even need the rest of the pack like wolves to finish him: simple environment jest watched its chance and taken it." (*T,* p. 107)

The whole universe seems to be included in Ratliff's "frame of reference."

Their philosophic bent is part of the tendency of self-actualizing people to be "problem-centered rather than ego-centered" (*MP,* p. 159). While a person at a lower motivational level may be preoccupied with his own needs, the self-actualizing person, with his most powerful needs gratified, is able to turn his energies outward. The "problem" in *Snopes* is Snopesism, and from the beginning Ratliff devotes considerable attention to it, even launching a kind of crusade in opposition to Flem's carefully orchestrated assault on Frenchman's Bend and Jefferson. This is in contrast to the other characters of the trilogy who avoid the problem—" 'It aint right,' " says Tull, " 'But it aint none of our business' " (*H,* p. 71)—or see it through the haze of their own personal involvement, as Gavin does. It is this ability of Ratliff's to focus on the problem that Faulkner asks us to admire, not the efficacy of the crusade itself, since this, as various critics have pointed out, is hardly remarkable for its success.[21]

Ratliff's various plots to inhibit the spread of Snopesism reflect another quality that Maslow found to be common among his self-actualizing subjects:

focusing on ends rather than means. The plot to end Clarence Snopes' political career is a case in point. Rubbing a man's pant legs with twigs from a bush much frequented by dogs, so that all the dogs at the political picnic rush to pay their respects, may be an unconventional way to keep a man from running for Congress, but it works with Clarence, and the district will have an honest, nonracist congressman instead of the totally corrupt and bigoted C. Egglestone Snopes. Needless to say, Ratliff takes a bit of enjoyment in the "means" that he uses here, but he makes it clear that he is more concerned with the "ends."

> "It's a pure and simple proposition; there must be a pure and simple answer to it. Clarence jest purely and simply wants to get elected to Congress, he dont keer how; there must be some pure and simple way for the folks that purely and simply dont want him in Congress to say No to him, they don't keer how neither." (*M*, p. 131)

Maslow describes his self-actualizing subjects as strongly ethical. In the C. Egglestone episode Ratliff demonstrates his ethical sense along with his willingness to act; he believes in good and evil, and he believes that man can bring about the triumph of good, " 'providing [he] jest keeps his eyes open and uses what he has, the best he knows' " (*M*, p. 320). And provided he can learn to "trust in God without depending on him"—to believe in goodness without expecting its achievement to be easy (*M*, p. 321).

But since Ratliff's code of ethics, like those of so many self-actualizing people, is unconventional, some people find it difficult to accept all of its manifestations as good. One episode in particular, that concerning the idiot, Ike Snopes, and Houston's cow, has been the subject of critical controversy for this reason. Ike's hideous cousin, Lump, has set things up so that people can watch the idiot having intercourse with the cow, and this raises in Ratliff a sense of "baffled and aghast outrage" (*H*, p. 198). Though he recognizes Ike's genuine love for the cow, and is not a stranger to the rural sense of humor that has prompted the display (and indeed prompts Faulkner's conception of the whole episode), Ratliff's personal code of ethics requires that he put an end to this violation of human dignity.

> "You don't need to tell me he aint got nothing else. I know that. Or that I can sholy leave him have at least this much. I know that too. Or that besides, it aint any of my business. I know that too, just as I know that the reason I aint going to leave him have what he does have is simply because I am strong enough to keep him from it. I am stronger than him. Not righter. Not any better maybe. But just stronger." (*H*, p. 198)

Ratliff is ruthless in this case, but he is not compulsively aggressive. In spite of all his talk about strength, it is not mastery over Ike that he wants, but the "end" that his action will achieve. Ike's love affair, as Norman Farmer points out, has been "rendered obscene by those who have made it a spectacle,"[22] and thus it degrades human love and dignity and violates Ratliff's sense of the way things ought to be.

Joseph Gold does not share Ratliff's code of ethics, and so believes that he behaves wrongly in this case. Gold believes that love is the only alternative to Snopesism, and that therefore Ratliff was wrong to be "righteous" instead of loving.[23] Other critics have placed the same emphasis on the importance of love in Faulkner's works,[24] and certainly it is central to his vision. But in the context of the trilogy Ratliff's action appears worthy of our respect. I think that Maslow's theories of self-actualization help us to see that Faulkner portrays, through the character of Ratliff, the value of the potentially ruthless ethical man who does not deny love, but holds some values above it.

Part of Ratliff's moral effectiveness has to do with what Maslow calls the "quality of detachment" common to self-actualizing people. "My subjects," he writes, "make up their own minds, come to their own decisions, are self-starters, are responsible for themselves and their own destinies" (*MP,* p. 161). Having had their basic needs satisfied, these people no longer are dependent on others for approval or love (*MP,* p. 162) so they may appear detached to those around them. Ratliff is able to do what he does in the episode of Ike and the cow because he is dependent on no one's approval but his own. Even Mrs. Littlejohn's opposition does not deflect him from his goal.

In the matter of dress Ratliff follows the pattern described by Maslow in that he is "certainly not fashionable, or smart, or chic" (*MP,* p. 172). This unwillingness to dress as others dress is part of his refusal to be totally acculturated, a refusal common in self-actualizing people and made possible by their healthy detachment from society. As Ratliff tells the lady in the tie store, he makes his own "neat faded blue tieless shirts" which are apparently not much like anything that other people wear. And when Gavin sees the tie that he is planning to wear for their trip to New York he says, " 'I wont travel with you. I wont be seen with you' " (*M,* p. 165), indicating that his friend's accessory is neither conventional nor attractive. But Ratliff is perfectly satisfied with his tie, which he wears for his own reasons (as a sort of personal sign of respect for his ancestors, whose place of entry into the United States he is planning to visit) and refuses to mollify Gavin by removing it. He buys two beautiful and chic ties in New York, but they become artifacts rather than articles of dress for him. Unlike Flem, he has no need to dress the part in order to insinuate himself into society.

Although Ratliff avoids becoming acculturated, he is far from wishing to avoid contact with his fellow man. Like Maslow's subjects he has for humanity in general "a deep feeling of identification, sympathy and affection" (*MP,* p. 165), which exists alongside of the knowledge that he can see things that are for most people "veiled or hidden" (*MP,* p. 166). We see these two qualities at work in his relationship with Gavin. While he is sympathetic toward the learned lawyer, and devotes a lot of time to their friendship, he realizes that Gavin is not capable of understanding as quickly or as well what Flem is all about. Gavin himself wryly recognizes this when he says,

> I mean it had to be Ratliff who told me: Ratliff with his damned smooth face and his damned shrewd bland innocent intelligent eyes, too damned innocent, too damned intelligent. (*T*, p. 33)

Although Ratliff is at once more innocent (less weighted down with the patterns of his culture and his own needs) and more intelligent (perceptive) than Gavin, he never feels or demonstrates contempt for him. His attitude toward humanity is the thematic refrain of *The Mansion*, " 'the pore sons of bitches,' " and he agrees with Stevens that " 'People just do the best they can' " (*M*, p. 429). It is Ratliff who takes in Mink's wife and feels for her "a sort of shocked and sober . . . not pity: rather concern" (*H*, p. 259). He respects her ability to endure with her family "the old agonies: terror, impotence, hope" (*H*, p. 260), obviously seeing her as part of the same imperfect but marvellous species to which he belongs himself.

Ratliff is quick to understand the vindictiveness of a "soured" man like Ab Snopes, and slow to take offense from anyone. And he is very fond of the young. (Maslow says that self-actualizing people are often "easily touched" by children.) The rest of the town is caught somewhere between terror and amusement in reaction to the "Apache Snopeses," regarding them as some kind of weird and hilarious phenomenon. Ratliff, though he is as tickled as anyone by the situation, sees them as little people, and, in the only humane gesture made in this direction during their stay in Jefferson, brings them candy and gum and fruit for their journey home.

One of the most important things about Maslow's self-actualizing person is his "continued freshness of appreciation," his lack of "staleness" or cynicism (*MP*, p. 163). And there is a great sense throughout the trilogy that Ratliff enjoys his life. He continually finds things to appreciate that other adults might find routine, dull, or childish. Strawberry ice cream, for instance.

> "This here is jest about as pleasant a invention as any I know about. It's so pleasant a feller jest dont dare risk getting burnt-out on it. I cant imagine no tragedy worse than being burnt-out on strawberry ice cream." (*T*, p. 106)

He enjoys simple bodily pleasures also. He loves to cook and eat, and when he is recovering from his gall bladder operation he finds things to appreciate in the experience of convalescence,

> . . . the sheer happiness of being out of bed and moving once more at free will, in the sun and air which men drank and moved in and talked and dealt with one another. . . . He did not still feel weak, he was merely luxuriating in that supremely gutful lassitude of convalescence. (*H*, p. 68)

He enjoys the newness and freshness of the experience, not taking it for granted or being annoyed by it, reactions that one might expect from a less spontaneous man.

A spontaneous person is likely to be a creative person, and in Maslow's view all self-actualizing people are creative in one way or another (*MP,* p. 170). Certainly Ratliff is an artist. There are those shirts, after all, and there is his ability in the kitchen. And, as Cleanth Brooks recognized when he called him a "creator of myth,"[25] he elevates people-watching and gossip to the level of art. It is through his unique "innocence," what Maslow could call his "second naivete," that we come to see the significance of what happens in Frenchman's Bend and Jefferson during the time span of the trilogy. He does not just report the facts, he forms them so that they will have meaning. "I won't have nothing else for the simple dramatic verities" (*M,* p. 122), he says as he gives us his version of Eula's deflowering, "I jest simply decline to have it any other way except that one" (*M,* p. 123–24).

This recounting of the resemblance of Faulkner's favorite character to Maslow's description of his self-actualizing subjects is not meant to imply that Ratliff has achieved some ideal state wherein he sees everything clearly, deals with everyone fairly and humanely, never stoops to concern with the petty, and always rises above the personal to the universal. On the contrary, he falls for Flem's hoary salted mine plot, has to "fight like a demon, like Jacob with his angel" (*M,* p. 164) to resist the niggling temptation to say "I told you so," frustrates the reader by refusing to help the impoverished and overworked Mrs. Armstid, and is excessively proud of his reputation for being first with the news. Ratliff's mistakes and shortcomings are inevitable accoutrements of the twentieth-century hero as Faulkner sees him: the emphatically human redeemer, the equal participator in the human comedy. It is not a paragon of rarified virtue that Faulkner wishes to offer as an answer to Snopesism, but a man who, in the process of fulfilling his own potential, can demonstrate the potential of mankind as a whole.

Maslow believes that a "very important theoretical conclusion" arising from his study of self-actualizing people is that the dichotomies usually seen as part of human nature (e.g. masculine-feminine, head-heart, maturity-childlikeness) are resolved, are "merged and coalesced with each other to form unities" in the self-actualizing person (*MP,* p. 179). It seems to me that Ratliff provides resolutions for the dichotomies that structure the thematic material of *Snopes,* and that he can do this because he is self-actualizing and can find unity where others find only conflict.

For instance, the trilogy very clearly portrays a split between masculine and feminine "principles."[26] In "Spotted Horses," Henry Armstid and the other men play out the "masculine" concept of aggressive competition and self-assertion, while Mrs. Armstid and Mrs. Littlejohn display the "feminine" qualities of endurance in the face of hardship, common sense, and compassion. " 'You men,' " says Mrs. Littlejohn as she prepares to take care of Henry, whose leg has been badly broken, " 'Go outside. See if you cant find something else to play with that will kill some more of you' " (*H,* p. 305). Obviously she has more common sense than all of the men that Flem duped put together. And while her husband lies crippled by a horse he never should have gotten close to, let alone bought with the five dollars set aside for his children's shoes, Mrs. Armstid calmly doubles her already awesome work load. Certainly there is a gap between what Faulkner thought to be primarily the natural expression of the male and its female counterpart. But Ratliff's presence seems to provide a bridge. He explains Mrs. Armstid's plight to the other men. He seems to be the only one to realize the great extra burden that Henry has brought on her, just as he had earlier been the only one to resist the opportunity to enter into the aggressive competition of the horse trading. Although he is definitely "masculine" in that he does not hesitate to assert himself, he has the "feminine" qualities of common sense and compassion. By his very existence he shows the possibility of resolving the conflict Faulkner portrays.

Faulkner also seems to see spontaneity and a willingness to deal with the unknown as "feminine" qualities. It is women, he has Ratliff say, who "don't need reasons" (*M*, p. 117) because they function from necessities. But Ratliff also is guided by necessities rather than reasons. Throughout the trilogy he accepts what is necessary in the human condition, that which " 'couldn't nobody help nohow,' " the treachery, vindictiveness, ignorance, and blindness of his fellow man, as well as the "old agonies" inflicted on him by the universe, without expecting a "reason." And, as we have seen, he does not have trouble accepting things that he doesn't recognize, or can't place in a category. He describes a gap between men and women, but he himself bridges it.

Self-actualizing people, as Maslow points out, can "admire and enjoy one another in a nondoing or nongetting way" (*MP*, p. 197), and this is how Ratliff seems to enjoy women. He has neither the aggressive sexuality of de Spain, nor the romantic devotion to the idea of womanhood of Gavin Stevens. Instead there is in him "that hearty celibacy as of a lay brother in a twelfth-century monastery—a gardener, a pruner of vines, say" (*H*, p. 42), so that he can deal with women as human beings, instead of as the "enemy" in the battle of the sexes. Eula's suicide is the ultimate casualty of this battle as it is portrayed in the trilogy, but Ratliff's posthumous appreciation of her, represented in his "Eula Varner Room," holds out the hope of a truce.

But perhaps Ratliff's most important function as a dissolver of dichotomies is his demonstration that love and economics need not be at odds. Olga Vickery points out that these two elements are in conflict throughout the trilogy, and that Flem's fault is to isolate the economic values of society and refuse to "temper reason with emotion or self-interest with sympathy."[27] Ratliff, it seems to me, is the one who does the "tempering." At the same time that he is sympathetic and compassionate, he is a very shrewd businessman. Faulkner describes him at one point as "affable, bland, anecdotal . . . but . . . not to be denied" (*H*, p. 55). This makes him unpopular with some critics who view the trilogy as a denunciation of finance-capitalism.[28] But it is clear that Faulkner himself is sympathetic with Ratliff's approach to business matters, and does not consider the market place evil in itself. Ratliff never disregards anyone's humanity, never looks upon a person as an object whose existence has meaning only insofar as it enriches him. Flem does this consistently, and that is why he is considered evil by Faulkner, and would be considered "autocentric" and stunted in his psychological development by Maslow. Ratliff makes money at what he does without victimizing others, and this indicates that Faulkner sees no inevitable dichotomy between economic success and love. Self-actualizing people, as Ratliff shows us, can care for others without withdrawing from the world of competition. It is only the self-effacing neurotic who cannot do that, who needs to deny his competitive nature before he can feel "good." Because of his robust mental health, Ratliff can be both assertive and loving, and thus he is a suitable vehicle for Faulkner's resolution of the "love versus economics" dichotomy that looms so large in *Snopes.*

Maslow's description of self-actualization in *Motivation and Personality* suffers both from the limitations of his language (which lacks imagination and warmth) and the paucity of his examples. He seems really unable to describe his subjects in concrete and lively detail. Faulkner, on the other hand, is able to make Ratliff come alive, and it seems to me that in observing him we have gained a better insight into the way a self-actualizing man would meet with his surroundings and his fellow man than Maslow has given us. When we hear Ratliff say, "the pore sons of bitches," for instance, we understand much more completely what Maslow was trying to do when he quoted one of his subjects as saying,

> "Most people, after all, do not amount to much but they *could* have. They make all sorts of foolish mistakes and wind up being miserable and not knowing how they got that way when their intentions were good. Those who are not nice are usually paying for it in deep unhappiness. They should be pitied rather than attacked." (*MP,* p. 167)

This subject may be a very healthy and good person indeed but he does a poor job of explaining himself. He speaks in abstractions and ends up sounding patronizing, and we get no sense of the man behind the voice, whereas, having followed Ratliff through many different situations, and having been apprised of his various foibles and quirks, we understand exactly the nature of the compassion, understanding, and identification expressed in his inelegant phrase. Faulkner's mimetic genius tells us more about what the properly nourished inner nature of man consists of than Maslow's research does. But it is Maslow's research that allows us to recognize in Ratliff a unique kind of modern hero—a man who is living up to his own potential rather than filling a preconceived role.

As we have seen, Ratliff is not merely an isolated example of self-actualization, he is a successful literary character as well. In the artistic universe of *Snopes* he serves both structural and thematic functions—acting as a counter to the blankness and dishonesty of Flem, demonstrating man's ability to accept newness and motion, and embodying the resolution of the dichotomies that lend form and theme to the trilogy. Obviously he is a "hero" in that he illustrates Faulkner's affirmation of human goodness and strength. But his heroism is uniquely his own, resembling neither the self-sacrifice of a Dorothea, nor the defiance of an anti-hero. He is able to live in the world without denying his essence, to coexist with society without capitulating to it, to love other people without belittling himself, and to live up to an ethical code without stifling his natural impulses. It is no wonder that Faulkner was so pleased with him, and that we are willing to accept his judgment and think, "I'd still rather be Ratliff without any Snopes to measure by even."

NOTES

1. Cf. Panthea R. Broughton, *William Faulkner: The Abstract and the Actual* (Baton Rouge: Louisiana State University Press, 1974) or Benjamin McClelland, "Not Only to Survive, But to Prevail: A Study of William Faulkner's Search for a Redeemer of Modern Man," *DA* 32 (1972): 6438A (Indiana).

2. Quoted in Roger Lewis Davis, "Faulkner, V. K. Ratliff, and the Snopes Saga," *DA* 32 (1971): 3300A (UCLA).

3. Joseph Gold, "The 'Normality' of Snopesism: Universal Themes in Faulkner's *The Hamlet*," in *Faulkner: Four Decades of Criticism*, ed. Linda Welshimer Wagner (East Lansing: Michigan State University Press, 1963), p. 32.

4. James L. Roberts, "Snopeslore," *University of Kansas City Review* 28 (1961): 69.

5. Nancy Norris, "*The Hamlet, The Town,* and *The Mansion:* A Psychological Reading of the Snopes Trilogy," *Mosaic* 8 (1973): 213–35.

6. Joseph Reed, Jr., *Faulkner's Narrative* (New Haven: Yale University Press, 1973), p. 250.

7. Joseph F. Trimmer, "V. K. Ratliff: A Portrait of the Artist in Motion," *Modern Fiction Studies* 20 (1974): 452.

8. Edwin Moses, "Faulkner's *The Hamlet:* The Passionate Humanity of V. K. Ratliff," *Notre Dame English Journal* 8 (1973): 98–109.

9. See McClelland, "Not Only to Survive."

10. Warren Beck, *Faulkner: Essays* (Madison: University of Wisconsin Press, 1976), p. 645.

11. For the idea of using Maslow's theories as a critical tool, I am indebted to Bernard J. Paris, *A Psychological Approach to Fiction* (Bloomington: Indiana University Press, 1974).

12. Abraham Maslow, *Toward a Psychology of Being*, 2d ed. (New York: Van Nostrand, 1968), p. 5. Hereafter cited in the text as *PB.*

13. Paris, *A Psychological Approach to Fiction*, p. 46.

14. See Faulkner's Nobel Prize acceptance speech.

15. Abraham Maslow, *Motivation and Personality*, 2d ed. (New York: Harper and Row, 1970), p. 150. Hereafter cited in the text as *MP.*

16. William Faulkner, *The Town* (New York: Random House, 1957), p. 258. Hereafter cited in the text as *T.*

17. William Faulkner, *The Hamlet* (New York: Random House, 1956), p. 276. Hereafter cited in the text as *H.*

18. See Davis, "Faulkner, V. K. Ratliff, and the Snopes Saga."

19. William Faulkner, *The Mansion* (New York: Random House, 1965), p. 188. Hereafter cited in the text as *M.*

20. Warren Beck, *Man in Motion, Faulkner's Trilogy* (Madison: University of Wisconsin Press, 1963), p. 64.

21. Cf. John Owen White, "The Existential Absurd in Faulkner's Snopes Trilogy," *DA* 32

(1971): 3336A (Arizona State) or Walter Brylowski, *Faulkner's Olympian Laugh: Myth in the Novels* (Detroit: Wayne State University Press, 1968), p. 206. See also Reed, *Faulkner's Narrative,* p. 256.

22. Norman Farmer, Jr., "The Love Theme: A Principal Source of Thematic Unity in Faulkner's Snopes Trilogy," *Twentieth Century Literature* 8 (1962): 121.

23. Gold, "The 'Normality' of Snopesism," p. 325.

24. Cf. Lawrence Edward Bowling, "William Faulkner: The Importance of Love," *Four Decades,* pp. 110–16.

25. Cleanth Brooks, *William Faulkner: The Yoknapatawpha Country* (New Haven: Yale University Press, 1963), p. 171.

26. Sally R. Page in *Faulkner's Women: Characterization and Meaning* (Deland, Fla.: Stetson University Press, 1972) discusses this dichotomy in convincing detail, but does not mention the importance of Ratliff's role.

27. Olga Vickery, *The Novels of William Faulkner: A Critical Interpretation* (Baton Rouge: Louisiana State University Press, 1964), p. 168.

28. Cf. Gold, "The 'Normality' of Snopesism."

11
A Psychological Redefinition of William Styron's *Confessions of Nat Turner*

James R. Huffman

William Styron's best-seller, *The Confessions of Nat Turner,* was probably the most controversial American novel of the sixties. Praised by many white critics and damned by most black ones, the novel polarized the academic community and became a social issue related to civil rights in some circles. Reviewers felt more constrained to defend their ideological positions than to analyze the work. As a result, there has been little agreement on the presumed intentions of the novelist, let alone the social implications of the novel.[1] Styron's "meditation on history" has not been analyzed thoroughly enough as a novel to allow full consideration of it as a social phenomenon.

Yet most writers presume that the work has been more than adequately defined. After all, well-known casebooks and counter-casebooks have appeared on the subject. The book "has been reviewed widely, and the critics have inspected it in detail." However, as *Psychology Today* also recognized, "neither the psychologist nor the sociologist has looked into the implications of Styron's novel."[2] Unfortunately, the psychologist and sociologist commissioned by *Psychology Today* to remedy that lack have room only to begin the job, and black psychologist Alvin Poussaint adds only a little to their work.[3] On the basis of fewer than ten pages of analysis, some critics contend that it has been proven "clearly and in great detail that the novel is psychologically false through and through in terms of human motivation and psychological theory and is morally wrong as well."[4]

I dispute these conclusions. Critics of the psychology of the novel have taken far too simple a position. Just because they have no explanations for the behavior of Styron's main characters in controversial scenes, these critics assume that the scenes and characters are inexplicable or false. They feel that the characters are only superficial stereotypes. Finally, they conclude that because of this alleged superficiality and psychological falsity, the novel is racist and therefore immoral.

In contrast, I intend to show that Styron's main characters, particularly the controversial Nat Turner himself, are clearly understandable according to recognized psychological principles. Furthermore, I believe that these principles reveal how the novelist has depicted something deeper than stereotypes, namely, the psychological causes and structure of stereotypical personalities, the more complex realities behind the simple images. Finally, such analysis shows that, while the novel does not totally escape tinges of racism, its message is not nearly so negative and immoral as many believe. Until a thorough psychological analysis is undertaken, the novel cannot be accurately judged as a sociological artifact.

Styron's Nat Turner may well *not* be much like the historical Nat Turner, as most black critics argue. I wish Styron had chosen another name for his character, for the historical facts and emotion surrounding Turner's Rebellion simply cloud the issues and social truths Styron has perceived. Styron's violation of the literal and historically likely truth about the individual Nat Turner is not the main issue, however. *Of course* Styron's Nat Turner is false; he is a literary creation, the portrait of a "meditation on history," not a full-blown and painstaking portrait of an actual slave leader. The question is not whether the portrait has congruency with Nat Turner or any other slave leader, but whether the novel depicts accurately some of the likely psychological and social results of slavery and oppression. Styron's Nat Turner is a credible character *as literary character* (judged by tests of explicability and internal consistency), and he is also faithful to social and historical possibilities, if not to the real Nat Turner. Styron's figure would not likely have achieved the position of leader under slavery, though he could have; but slaves like him would quite likely have existed in significant numbers under any such oppressive social structure. Slaves like Hark, the "Sambo" figure so criticized in the novel, would likely have been even more numerous. I think Styron may have transplanted a twentieth-century phenomenon into the nineteenth century by making his black leader obsessed with white women, the most controversial aspect of the novel. But even this obsession is *possible*, has an important thematic role in the novel, and has been documented by many black writers as well.[5] In general, the novel has more social and psychological truth about oppressors and victims, whites and blacks, males and females, then and now, than most of us are willing to face.

The psychological analysis that follows logically leads to most of the general positions I have just outlined. It also takes the punch out of two major criticisms of the novel, which ought to be mentioned here due to their prominence in articles on the work: (1) the idea that the novel is totally governed by the Elkins thesis and (2) the charge that it follows a hackneyed Freudian formula. Perhaps the most common criticism of Styron's characterization, in addition to criticism of Nat's obsession with white women, is that his slave leader seems to be an embodiment of the "Sambo" figure, and thus supports the controversial Elkins thesis. Stanley Elkins, in his well known work *Slavery*, argues that slavery dehumanized many slaves, and not only produced the stereotype of the fawning, self-effacing Sambo, but made that stereotype a widespread social reality. In its most extreme statement, as formulated by one of its opponents, this "fraudulent and untenable thesis" argues that "American slavery was so oppressive, despotic and emasculating psychologically that revolt was impossible and Negroes could only be Sambos."[6]

I do not have room to refute or confirm the Elkins thesis here, of course. Like most historical theses of great generality, it has a good deal of truth, but it is not universally applicable. In response to this attack on Styron as a disciple of Elkins, I am arguing that the novel's position is more complex than the Elkins thesis or its opposition. Styron shows how the white-washed antebellum myth of slavery was in fact enforced by powerful external controls, and demonstrates further how forcing this myth on the slaves created powerful psychological shackles for many. The *Confessions of Nat Turner* does analyze the effects of slavery in perspectives similar to Elkins'. But Styron *represents* oppression in action as a dynamic process, rather than just talk about it as Elkins does. As a result, the novel takes the superficial stereotypes in that historical treatise and transforms them into broad and deep psychological portrayals of the nest of personalities described in Karen Horney's theory of anxiety neurosis.

The second major criticism of Styron's characterization of Nat Turner is that it follows hackneyed Freudian concepts. This view does not do justice to Styron's use of Freud, which is not slavish; and in any case Freud is not the only key to the novel. Although Styron consciously uses a Freudian perspective in several places, Karen Horney's theory of anxiety neurosis reveals Styron's intuitive grasp of human psychology in the novel more fully than Freud's. Her theory explains a number of otherwise inexplicable scenes in the work, and shows that Styron's so-called stereotypes, such as Nat and Hark, are complex manifestations of the presence of anxiety neurosis in American culture.

In order to establish the extent to which Styron's novel is psychologically credible, then, it is necessary to show how the book follows understandable psychological patterns. Many of these do not seem to be the result of explicit reading of psychology by Styron, in contrast to his use of Freudian elements, but appear to be intuitive representations of behavioral patterns that have also been described by psychological researchers. Correlations between the intuitive perceptions of an artist and the empirical or theoretical discoveries of psychologists tend to confirm the accuracy of both the novel and the research.

There are many examples of this kind of correlation in the novel. The simple idea of "pecking order" is illustrated in the hierarchy of power and violence in the novel. In any chicken yard there tends to be a single rooster who rules everyone, followed by a first lieutenant who pecks on everyone but the top rooster, and so on down to the most oppressed chick in the yard, whom everyone harasses. A more sophisticated version of this behavior pattern is obvious at Turner's Mill: the white male patriarchal masters control everyone, followed by a few of the more aggressive white women with social and economic status. Below them are the white overseers like McBride, poor whites like Moore and Reverend Eppes, black male overseers, and "house niggers" with more status than field hands. On the bottom are the overworked "field niggers," including black women who may be sexually exploited by anyone at any time. Violence increases the further down in the pecking order one goes, but harassment is common at all levels. Miss Maria Pope can literally run Hark up a tree, despite his desperate fear of heights. Lower-class whites and overseers whip the slaves with lashes, and the slaves in turn beat the mules that work under them.

Styron also parallels the discoveries of Penfield, whose electronic probings of the brain form the experimental basis for transactional analysis. According to Penfield's work, the right stimulus—electronic or sensory—can trigger nearly complete recall, not just abstract remembering. That is, a person whose memory is properly stimulated will not only remember past events, but relive them and feel now as he did then.[7] Nat Turner exemplifies this phenomenon whenever he smells pine scent, which is inextricably connected with his lone orgies in the carpenter's shop.

> It was always a nameless white girl between whose legs I envisioned myself—a young girl with golden curls. The shed smelled strongly of freshly hewn timber and there was a resinous odor of loblolly pine, pungent and sharp enough to sear the nostrils; and often in later times, walking through noontime heat past a stand of pine trees, that same spicy and redolent odor of cut timber would arouse my senses and I would feel a sudden surge and stiffening at my groin as I thought of the carpenter's shop and as the memory began achingly to return, mingling tenderness and desire, of my vision of the golden-haired girl with her lips half open and whispering, and my young self so many years before crouched panting in the pine-smelling sweetness.[8]

However controversial (and perhaps unrepresentative) it may be for a black slave leader to be portrayed as having sexual fantasies of white women, it must be admitted that the psychological mechanisms portrayed are accurate. In the finer details of representation, the novel holds up.

Determining how credible the characters in the novel are, however, requires a much deeper consideration of psychology than Penfield and pecking order. Psychological insights that are only incidental to the portrayal of Nat's character will not establish its credibility or accuracy. So to establish the mimetic accuracy of the novel, I shall now analyze the behavior of the characters from two more integral perspectives, the Freudian viewpoint that Styron seems to place at the center of the work, and the Horneyan one that he intuits so well.

Let me outline the Freudian framework Styron sets up, and show what it is supposed to explain. It is vitally important to recognize that Nat is *not* a consistent spokesman for the author in any section of the novel. That is, Nat does not lie to the reader, but he simply does not understand himself well enough for his "confession" to take on the status of straight, unironic explanation. Presuming that Nat speaks for Styron leads to great misunderstanding of the novel, particularly its ending. Styron stresses his ironic distance from his character starting with the very first scene of the novel, the Freudian dream or vision—Nat is never certain which—that so obviously serves as a symbolic key to the work.

Since this dream vision recurs so often and begins the important concluding section of the novel, its significance must be understood by the reader, even though it is never understood by Nat himself. Indeed, the prominence of the dream and Nat's constant bafflement over it show that Styron understands his character better than the character explains and understands himself, which is prime evidence that Nat cannot be Styron's spokesman. Clearly Styron wants the *reader* to understand Nat better than Nat understands himself, for Nat is to serve as an example of psychological problems that result from slavery. "There is no doubt, however, that it was all connected with my childhood" (p. 19), Nat says of the dream. This emphasis on the influence of childhood as the root of Nat's problems establishes the intentional pre-eminence of psychology in the structure of the work. Together, the prominence of the dream and emphasis on childhood also suggest that Styron is consciously relying on Freudian concepts in devising his main character. Consequently, understanding the key dream first requires analysis of a number of other Freudian elements in the work.

Styron invites a psychological interpretation most obviously in the portrayal of Nat's family—deviating markedly, by the way, from the circumstances of the historical Nat Turner in order to explore possible psychological relationships between blacks and whites. Like Huck Finn and a number of other figures in a long tradition of literary and psychological analysis, Styron's Nat Turner loses his father early. But Styron does not make the usual use of this loss, to show the weak black male deserting his family because he does not feel any masculine identity with them.[9] Instead, Nat's father is used to stress strong masculine pride in black men, the refusal to be slapped or disciplined in public by a white man, master or no master. Thus Nat's only knowledge of his father reinforces a sense of pride and dignity in black manhood, not a weak stereotype. Styron is not using his Freudian configurations tritely.

Nevertheless, this loss of the father creates several classic Freudian possibilities. First, the young Nat's passing through the Oedipal phase is heightened. After all, he now gets to sleep with his mother: "as she moves with a tired *slat-slat* of bare calloused feet from the kitchen, enters our tiny room, and lies down beside me in the dark, . . . I reach out and lightly touch the rough cotton shift above her ribs, to make certain that she is there" (p. 131). Nat is not simply replacing his father in bed, however. Having been abandoned by his father, Nat touches his mother to make certain that he has not also lost her. Instead of Nat's dreams of "inchoate promise and voiceless hovering joy" being part of Oedipal sexual rivalry, his dreams represent the fact that he is now the man in the family, or at least the man-to-be, in a nonsexual sense. He dreams of improving his social position, finding a glorious height that will prove him a man.

Sometimes when a boy loses his father, he feels guilty, Freud says, as though his desire that his father were out of the way somehow magically caused his disappearance. Since Nat's father apparently ran away before Nat was old enough to entertain any such wish, none of this guilt appears. However, the ambivalence toward father figures that is part of the Oedipal complex, the mixed admiration and resentment, is quite evident. Nat admires his main father substitute, master Samuel Turner, and wants to be like him. On the other hand, he resents the presence of McBride, the white overseer who exploits the slave women sexually. It is as though Nat would like the powerful social role a man may have, yet wants to deny the sexual one. The situation is more complex than this superficial splitting of his feelings suggests, however, especially since Nat also comes to resent Samuel Turner and involuntarily respects the power of even the drunken McBride. Since the old servant Little Morning is the only black man in the house, and since Nat feels superior to "field niggers," there are only white men left to serve him as masculine models. This condition is posited by Styron as a major cause of Nat's problems with identity and role.

Observe Nat's reactions in Styron's equivalent of a "primal scene." He comes upon McBride raping his mother in the kitchen. At first he is paralyzed, like Hamlet catching Claudius at prayer.[10] As in *Hamlet*, the theory of the Oedipal complex suggests that Nat is paralyzed partly because, although he would like to kill the intruder if he could, he would also like to take his place—a much more explicit scene here than in Shakespeare. But Styron does not imply this classic explanation simply; he goes beyond it. Nat is fascinated, only half understanding what is happening. Although he has seen some sexual activity by spying on slaves through the cracks in their cabins, Nat had previously thought that sex "was the pastime, or habit, or obsession, or something, of niggers alone" (p. 149). He reverses the famous duchess's attitude toward sex, that it is "too good for the peasants," because his religious training has taught him sex is a degrading activity, and because white people seem above sweat and bodily turmoil. Like parents, whom they substitute for, white people are not supposed to be sexual. He is disillusioned at the discovery that white men are sexual animals just as he will be disillusioned later when he finds the supposedly pure Southern belle, Miss Emmeline, enjoying a blasphemous orgasm with her cousin. Nat's first impulse on seeing his mother being raped is to flee, but he can't; there is nowhere a slave can go.

Yet the white man himself remains an ambivalent rather than a totally hated figure, due to his power and ability to take the place of Nat's father by force. When Nat returns to the house after the rape, "it is McBride alone who seems to fill the entire space within my sight, prodigious even as he stands weaving . . . prodigious and all powerful, yet mysterious in his terrible authority, filling me with dread" (p. 151). Nat's rhetoric here reminds one of Freud's connection of the image of God the Father with the image of fathers that develops during the Oedipal phase. If McBride is the feared Old Testament image, Samuel Turner becomes the New Testament counterpart, the admired and untainted, merciful yet powerful father. As Nat puts it, "at this time, my regard for him is very close to the feeling one should bear only toward the Divinity" (p. 130). Clearly Styron is using Freud, but is presenting a much more complex view than any simple formula.

This substitution of white father figures for his own father creates a great identity problem for Nat as Styron conceives him. Nat wants to believe he is white. Not only do he and Wash put mud on themselves and pretend to be white boys when it dries, but Nat strives to become in effect Samuel Turner's son. He is devastated to hear that he is a slave, and when Samuel must sell the mill, Nat pretends to be the owner and urinates in lordly style on the front steps, just as Benjamin Turner had done. "How white I was!" he says. "What wicked joy!" (p. 226). Styron uses implicitly the notion of father figures or father substitutes, and some characteristics of the Oedipal phase, to help make sense of Nat's identity problems. But the problems are not created by the Freudian concepts; Styron just implies the concepts to help clarify the problems. Nat is a credible figure, with or without Freudian concepts or implications.

The most crucial result of the Oedipal complex as portrayed in Nat is one that may well affect both white and black people in the South: the warped concept of women. Again the parallel in *Hamlet* is useful. Hamlet has two basic images of women; either they are totally chaste, or they are whores. Mothers are usually conceived as pure or even nonsexual. Due to the suppression of the threatening idea that a person's parents have sexual relations, most people desexualize their parents, not thinking of them at all as studs or nymphs. But Hamlet is forced to recognize Gertrude's sexuality, and so she appears to be a slut rather than a mother to him. Ophelia also becomes an ambiguous figure. He wants her to get to a "nunnery," which can be either a convent or a brothel in Elizabethan slang. The Oedipal complex tends to split women into just these two categories, madonnas and whores.

In *Portnoy's Complaint* Philip Roth presents a similar split in attitudes toward women, entitling one chapter after Freud's essay on "The Most Prevalent Form of Degradation in Erotic Life." To Alexander Portnoy, one of the "fragmented multitude" suffering from this complex, women like his mother are lovable but sexually unexciting, while sexually exciting women are unworthy of love. Roth adds an interesting racial element: women are either chaste Jewish mothers to Alex, or they are loose Gentile sluts.[11]

Styron's novel tends to present a similar racial paradigm: women are either chaste white Southern belles, or they are black nymphomaniacs. As Calvin Hernton points out, the old practice of white children having black mammies to nurse them may have helped reinforce this split in Oedipal-related images of women along racial lines; the white mother seems pure and aloof, while the black mammy is sensuous and available.[12] But notice that this perspective would be primarily that of a white male child. There is an uncomfortable possibility here that Styron has transferred illegitimately to a black man, Nat Turner, an attitude based on the Oedipus complex of the white man. But if this were the case, then the chaste Southern belles ought to be less sexually exciting than black women in the novel, which is not so. Indeed, Nat reverses Portnoy's psychology in this respect, in that it is the *chaste* image of white women that excites him, not the loose sexual image that arouses Portnoy. Nat's religious views could explain that reversal, since "bad" women would be morally distasteful to him. It seems most likely, however, that both Portnoy and Nat find the white woman or "shikse" attractive mainly because she is "forbidden fruit." Besides, as Joel Kovel has pointed out, the tendency to view black women as less attractive sexually is part of a Northern form of prejudice, "aversive racism," not Southern "dominative racism."[13] So his possible Southern biases just do not explain Styron's portrayal of black-white relations, as some critics have charged.

This portrayal of a black man as obsessed with white women and repelled by black women is the most controversial element in the novel. Black critics argue that it is prime evidence for deducing that Styron has put a "white" mind in a black body. But no clear authorial bias is necessarily evident in the portrayal of Nat's interest in white women. After all, black authors have often written about the same obsession, judging that dominant cultural values "brainwashed" many black men to prefer white women in this century. Whether this phenomenon would occur in the nineteenth century, without the mass media to help create it, is debatable, but not impossible to conceive. Since the United States is basically a patriarchal culture, the values of white men still generally pervade it, and affect all in the culture to some extent. Styron's emphasis on Nat's obsession with white women may result partly from his being a Southern white man, but the phenomenon does exist in American psychology. Besides, Styron portrays only Nat and Will as having strong interest in white women, so he does not seem to be stereotyping the trait for all black men. Rather, he is trying to isolate the factors that might cause the obsession, especially Nat's contempt for his own blackness, which seems to be projected onto black women and other black men.

That key symbolic dream I started with is now open for full interpretation. Nat is in a small boat, flowing with the current of a river toward the ocean. He does not have control over his direction or speed, suggesting the comforting idea that he is a pawn in the hands of God, just flowing with the tide of history, and thus not responsible for the destruction of whites and blacks that the rebellion involved. Above the silent river is a "promontory facing out upon the sea," and on the cliff stands a building "stark white and serene against a blue and cloudless sky."

> It is square and formed of marble, like a temple, and is simply designed, possessing no columns or windows but rather, in place of them, recesses

> whose purpose I cannot imagine, flowing in a series of arches around its two visible sides. The building has no door . . . it seems to have no purpose, resembling, as I say, a temple—yet a temple in which no one worships, or a sarcophagus in which no one lies buried, or a monument to something mysterious, ineffable, and without name. (p. 18)

The symbolism is not very obscure to an analyst, whether Freudian or not. Nat has placed white culture, especially white womanhood, in an ideal position, but to no purpose. He has no access to the status and wealth of that culture, nor to its women; there are no doors open to him, not even the body of a woman. So he worships outside the temple, unable to get in. It is the sarcophagus of his own dreams, a monument to his own futility. He does not want to recognize fully his obsession with whiteness, for if he does, the full responsibility of his acts will fall on him. That is, Nat would realize that his own needs made him an avenger, not God's call. Like the governess in *The Turn of the Screw,* Nat knows subconsciously that if his religious interpretation of his life is not accurate, then he must be mad. He avoids considering that possibility at all costs.

> But as is my custom whenever I have this dream or vision, I don't dwell upon the meaning of the strange building standing so lonely and remote upon its ocean promontory, for it seems by its very purposelessness to be endowed with a profound mystery which to explore would yield only a profusion of darker and perhaps more troubling mysteries, as in a maze. (p. 18)

Only by not interpreting this guiding vision of his life, the haunting and recurring symbol of his condition, can he retain the "emotion of a tranquil and abiding mystery" (p. 19) that keeps him from going insane.

Styron opens the culminating section of his book, in total only about 3000 words long, with his last version of this dream. By now the vision has become a death wish, the controversial Freudian Thanatos or return to the womb: "nothing disturbs me, I drowse in the arms of a steadfast and illimitable peace." Nat is facing his death by execution, symbolically the point at which the river meets the sea, yet the tide's "unhurried booming fills me not with fear but only with repose and slumbrous anticipation—serenity as ageless as those rocks, in garlands of weeping seaweed, thrown up by the groaning waves." Nat is returning to his historic womb, as he imagines "a cobalt sky arching eastward toward Africa" (p. 397).

Styron starts this short, crucial section of the novel with the vision to place his key symbolism before the reader once more, and to ensure that the reader will not mistake Nat's view for Styron's. "Again I cannot tell what it is or what it means," Nat says of the vision, and the building is still the "white inscrutable paradigm of a mystery beyond utterance or even wonder" (p. 398). Suffering not only from oppression and suppression but also internal repression, Nat never faces himself.

> Yet I cannot dwell on that place too long, for again as always I know that to try to explore the mystery would be only to throw open portals on even deeper mysteries, on and on everlastingly, into the remotest corridors of thought and time. So I turn away. (p. 398)

Unless this failure of Nat to understand himself is kept in mind, the reader is likely to misread the ending drastically.

Margaret Whitehead forms the controversial center of this ending. She is the only one Nat has killed, and the only one that he feels should have been spared. Although Nat does not presume that he will change color in the next world, his final vision of Margaret resembles Blake's poem on the black child who thinks that white children will love him in heaven because he will then be white: "*We'll love one another,* she seems to be entreating me, very close now, *we'll love one another by the light of heaven above*" (p. 401). Her voice recalls for Nat the other vision's "flowing waters, tumultuous waves, rushing winds," the signs of approaching death as well as sexual climax. In a very Freudian use of guilt as a motive, Styron implies that Margaret's fantasized forgiveness and love can assuage Nat's guilt if his death pays for her blood.

But is this Freudian interpretation of the ending sufficient to explain it fully? I don't believe it is. Obviously Nat's attitude is markedly changed in this section—so changed that many critics reject the change as impossible. Nat does not regret leading the rebellion, but his Old Testament prophetic stance has become transformed into a Christlike one. For the first time in the whole book the New Testament and its message of love and mercy find expression, and the name of Jesus is mentioned only in the final lines of the novel. What kind of change has Nat undergone, and what is Styron implying by it? An interpretation of the ending that does not take into account the ironic distance Styron sets up might presume that the novel is suggesting intermarriage as a simple solution to the racial problems portrayed. But even adding awareness of Styron's irony to the Freudian elements does not fully define the novel's impact and implications. Because this ending is so variously interpreted, I must go back and rebuild an interpretation from yet one more psychological perspective in order to do justice to its complexity. Although Styron implies some Freudian explanations, his intuitive perception goes beyond Freud. The following application of Karen Horney's theory of anxiety neurosis to the novel clarifies, deepens, and revises the simple Freudian view of the work.

Although several Horneyan studies of literature have appeared, Karen Horney's ideas are still not widely enough known for me to presume general understanding of them. In order to clarify my analysis of Styron's novel, at least a brief summary of the basic concepts in her description of neurosis must be given here. In *Neurosis and Human Growth,* Horney claims that anxiety neurosis is generally caused by a childhood environment that is hostile or threatening. Conflict with others creates a "basic anxiety" and sense of inferiority in the child, or at least the fear that he or she is inferior. To compensate for this sense of inferiority, the neurotic individual creates an idealized image of himself and tries to live up to it, embarking on a "search for glory" that will prove to himself and to the world that he is not inferior. The desires of his more genuine self may be suppressed as he remakes himself into the ideal image, and he ultimately begins to believe that he is ideal and to make neurotic claims on others to treat him as though he had a higher status than actual conditions show. He sets up impossible standards for his behavior ("the tyranny of the should"), which only reinforces his underlying feelings of inferiority. For whenever he fails to live up to the standards, his actual self proves to be less than ideal, and he feels worthless.

Depending upon what strategy he has found to be more effective in dealing with a hostile environment, the neurotic individual begins to build a total philosophy and life style around that technique for coping. If he is best able to avoid the conflict that makes him feel inferior by complying obsequiously with every request, he may develop a "self-effacing" personality that moves toward people and places a high regard on love and service. If he has found withdrawal more effective in his circumstances, he may move away from people and show a resigned attitude toward life, valuing personal independence rather than social ties. The third strategy, the aggressive or expansive solution, involves moving against people, handling the threatening conflict by conquering others. Those who gradually mold their personalities around this strategy for coping with the world become primarily (1) arrogant-vindictive conquerors, (2) absolute perfectionists, or (3) narcissistic charmers. In his lifetime an individual may try all of these strategies, moving from one to another particularly in times of stress, when the previous strategy is not working as well as usual. Each individual will mix his strategies and values according to his own needs and circumstances, but eventually a clear pattern of preference for one strategy or another will appear. Though he may go through "phases" before settling on a dominant mode, the individual will build his values and life style around a single strategy in most cases. Such strategies are not neurotic until they become *compulsive,* virtually automatic ways of dealing with others and protecting the self from situations which could unearth those devastating feelings of inferiority again. The neurotic individual may vacillate between despair and ecstasy, as his dissatisfaction with his actual self battles with his belief in his idealized image. If his dominant strategy fails, the person may undergo a crisis in which he switches strategies and values and life styles abruptly. Chances are, however, that no true internal change has taken place, and that the person is merely caught in another form of the vicious circle—the search for glory that ends in a feeling of worthlessness.[14]

It is not difficult to see these patterns at work in Styron's novel. Indeed, Nat himself describes at least two of the neurotic solutions explicitly.

> Certain Negroes, in exploiting their own particular niggerness, tell dumb jokes on themselves, learn to shuffle and scrape for their owners, wallowing in the dust at the slightest provocation, midriffs clutched in idiot laughter, or they master the rudiments of the banjo and the jew's harp or endear themselves to all, white and black, through droll interminable tales about ha'nts and witches and conjurs and the cunning little creatures of the swamp and woods. Others, by virtue of some indwelling grittiness and strength, reverse this procedure entirely and in *their* niggerness are able to outdo many white people at presenting to the world a grotesque swagger, becoming a black driver who would rather flog a fellow Negro than eat Smithfield ham, or at the most tolerable limit becoming a tyrannical, fussy, disdainful old kitchen mammy or butler whose very security depends upon maintaining without stint—safely this side of insolence—an aspect of nasty and arrogant dominion. (p. 260)

The directly opposing expansive and self-effacing solutions are obvious in this description. Certainly the third solution, resignation, is also apparent in the novel, as so many slaves resign themselves to their lot. Styron may be debatable when he attributes expansiveness to "some indwelling grittiness and strength," but he clearly sees the condition of "niggerness" for what it is, an oppressed state in which neurosis is all but unavoidable. Though he is comparatively pampered, the young boy Nat feels that "sense of my weakness, my smallness, my defenselessness, my *niggerness* invading me like a wind to the marrow of my bones" (p. 151). To be black is to face psychological devastation constantly.

The classic conditions for and symptoms of anxiety neurosis are present point by point. No environment could be much more hostile to a child than the condition of slavery. The fear of inferiority in the slave child is reinforced daily by the facts of social inferiority. Nat and his playmates are constantly threatened by authority, and are established as inferior "niggers" even by their mothers, who curse their "black souls" when they steal food. When he catches Nat with the stolen book, the old slave Little Morning tells the boy that his master is going to send his "thievin' black soul" to Georgia (p. 153). Like many twentieth-century black children, Nat hears "nigger" and "black" as negative epithets as often as endearing ones. He internalizes negative concepts of blackness fast, saying "daggone yo' no-good black soul" to Wash when that "field nigger" burns him while he sits in the outhouse (p. 140). Rather clearly, the hostile environment has produced in this black child the fear of inferiority and "basic anxiety" described by Horney.

Nat's fear of personal inferiority leads him to search for glory, first by learning "white English" and then by stealing a book and trying to read. His dreams of what he might become if he learned to read are naturally vague, for he has no clear model of a glorified position (other than the white master's) to aspire toward. Nevertheless, he knows that he must prove his superiority to the white world. He performs for the master before visitors by spelling "columbine," and that night the word is "still on my lips as I sink away into some strange dream filled with inchoate promise and a voiceless, hovering joy" (p. 131). Here Nat is an unformed self looking for an identity, an unknown slave looking for a way to glory.

As he creates an idealized image of himself to overcome his fear of inferiority and the sense of his actual status, a major complication enters. He begins to dissociate himself from the "field niggers," as his mother does ("Us house folks is *quality*"—p. 139), and feels superior to nearly all black field hands the rest of his life. More crucially, he nearly worships the white master (p. 130), and tries to make himself believe he is white. In other words, his idealized image, subconsciously, gradually becomes white. Just how successful Nat is in hiding his condition from himself is clear when he is shocked at overhearing himself called a "slave" (p. 164). But his actual self cannot possibly live up to his idealized white image, so he feels "black assed," as Hark puts it. In fact, nearly every time a white person comes around, Nat is uneasy, for even if he or she is sympathetic like Jeremiah Cobb or Margaret Whitehead, Nat is still forced to acknowledge his blackness in their presence (pp. 76, 63). Some of the other slaves perceive Nat's psychological problem. When he vindictively tells Raymond, who is in a slave coffle being sold down the river, that his master is going to set him free, Raymond sees right through him: "Yo' shit stink too, sugah," Raymond puts him down; "Yo' ass black jes' like mine, honey chile" (p. 198). Unlike the Freudian view, which makes this phenomenon a result of replacing a black father with a white father figure, Horneyan psychology explains Nat's identity problems as a natural result of being black in a particularly oppressive white culture. That is, a racist culture teaches a black person to some extent to hate his actual self just because it is black, regardless of the presence or absence of black parents. By intuiting this condition, Styron has struck a more generally applicable vein of human psychology than Freud.

One of the most difficult challenges Styron faces is in convincing the reader that a hater of black people could become a leader of them, that a psychological position that smacks of self-effacing subservience to whites could become expansive leadership against them. Once again Horneyan psychology explains how these anomalies can happen, and unravels one of the most controversial and supposedly incredible scenes in the novel.

While trying to work up a suitable idealized image to combat his sense of inferiority, Nat is strongly influenced by his religious training. His early intelligence makes his mother remark that he might become a prophet, and that glorified image appeals to his mind. Indeed, the Old Testament provides him with a glorified model of the arrogant vindictive personality in its image of the prophets and concept of Jehovah. But Nat regards blacks "as meaningless and stupid as a barn full of mules," and has learned to "hate them one and all," presumably including his actual self. How can this man become a prophetic leader of black people? While he is in church thinking these thoughts, his hatred of black people changes abruptly, and for many critics, incredibly. He sees Margaret Whitehead as she "carols heavenward, a radiance like daybreak on her serene young face." As a result of watching this greeting-card angel, Nat feels that "slowly and softly, like a gentle outrush of breath, my hatred of the Negroes diminishes, dies, replaced by a kind of wild, desperate love for them, and my eyes are wet with tears" (p. 109). Disbelieving critics are correct in seeing that this behavior of Nat's is not credible if taken as an unironic portrayal of truthful thought. But the portrayal is still psychologically accurate: Nat is just fooling himself about his love of black people. As one perceptive critic observes, "to believe that Nat completely could shift his allegiance from whites to Negroes and his hostility from Negroes to whites would be a mistake both from the point of view of the author's intentions and from that of understanding Turner's motivations."[15] Then how can Nat's apparent change from hating black people to loving them in this scene be understood? Horneyan psychology suggests a reasonable explanation: looking at Margaret Whitehead, so ideal in Nat's eyes, causes him to realize that his glory can only come from leading black people. The hymn Styron selects for this scene reveals his insight: "Can we whose souls are lighted / With wisdom from on high"—obviously implying the white congregation in its own estimation—"Can we to men benighted / The lamp of life deny?" (implying black slaves). This verse not only reveals the arrogance underlying the doctrine of the "white man's burden," but also suggests how such brainwashing of the slaves to believe in their inferiority might lead to Nat's desperate search for glory as a prophet. The concluding verse of the hymn, "From Greenland's Icy Mountains," reveals superbly Styron's intuitive grasp of Nat's search for glory: "Salvation, O Salvation! / The joyful sound proclaim, / Till each remotest nation / Has learnt Messiah's name." The Messiah's name, of course, will be Nat Turner. Margaret Whitehead has triggered his search for glory, and has started him on the gradual but essential course of changing his idealized image from white to black.

This scene is partly an example of a general truth Styron wants to show: there is often a great deal of difference between what is going on inside the slaves and what is allowed to come out overtly in everyday behavior. And it is here that Styron most deepens the Elkins thesis. The "Sambo" slave, best exemplified by Hark early in the novel, has become self-effacing as a protective device. Hark lived on a large, particularly oppressive plantation, and so he is one of the most extreme examples of self-effacement. His wife and child were even sold away from him. What Styron reveals is that this "obsequious coon," as Nat calls him, this "bootlicking Sambo," is in fact deeply enraged at his treatment. Scratch a "Sambo" below the surface, Nat finds, and you may well have a dedicated revolutionary.

Nat himself is an example of this phenomenon. He begins by being self-effacing and eager to please as a boy at Turner's Mill. By the time he is a man, however, his psychology has changed. He may still use the self-effacing manner to get something he wants, as in using black slang on "Marse Kitchen" to get some extra food or a blanket for Hark (pp. 22–23). But when he does, it is deliberate behavior, not automatic and compulsive scraping, as with Hark. After Nat has renounced the self-effacing solution as an affront to his pride, he will use it only consciously as a manipulative device when it is essential in order for him to get by. For example, Nat behaves self-effacingly when his illiterate master, Moore, is threatened by Nat's ability to read. Moore protects his own sense of self with cruel expansiveness, beating Nat until the superior slave cringes and acknowledges him "Master" (p. 244). The clearest case of Nat protecting his hidden expansive identity with a self-effacing cover is with Jeremiah Cobb. Nat is uncertain whether Cobb is sympathetic or is taunting him with his questions.

> But at this point it was not the possibility of humiliation I wanted to avoid so much as the possibility that having recently vowed that humiliation would never again be a constraint upon me, or a repression, I would be forced to surmount it by beating the man's brains out, thus completely wrecking all my great designs for the future. (p. 70)

In becoming more expansive, Nat is repelled by self-effacement. He is compulsively on the verge of violence, ready to strangle Cobb or clobber Moore with a stick of wood, but must master his compulsions with a semblance of compliance.

> I do not want to, but now, now if he forces me to spell the word I will have to try to kill him. I lowered my eyes again, saying more distinctly: "Don't mock me, mastah, please." (p. 76)

Styron clearly sees that, far from being a superficial stereotype, the "Sambo" pose is part of a deep psychological condition, whether deliberate as in Nat or automatic as in Hark. Horney makes Styron's perception of the self-effacing slave and the rebellious avenger analytically intelligible.

Indeed, Styron's Nat Turner is a classic Horneyan case. His idealized prophetic self and increasingly religious search for glory develop quickly: "I had begun to sense the knowledge that I was to be involved in some grand mission divinely ordained" (p. 265), he says, and sometimes during his frequent fasts "a mood of glory stole over me and I was filled with a strange radiance and a languid, blissful peace" (p. 266). Nat begins to make neurotic claims even on God based on his idealized image as a prophet, virtually demanding signs and visions. He sets impossible standards for himself (Horney's "tyranny of the should"), not only touching no liquor but touching no women; for in Nat's view a prophet with a mission must be virgin. Nat cannot meet his high standards, of course, which threatens his self-image. When he compromises his virginity in his Saturday masturbations, he rationalizes that the Lord will allow him that much—if he sticks only to Saturdays. Hopefully he can repent early on Sunday before God's wrath might strike. Similarly, when his standards break down in a homosexual act with Willis, he baptizes away their guilt.

The closer Nat gets to the day of reckoning, the more unstable he becomes. His mood becomes mercurial, now ecstatic as a sign justifies him, soon despairing as his plans are delayed. Horney gives a clear explanation of such manic depression; it occurs as a person is able to live up to his "shoulds" and maintain his idealized image (causing euphoria) or fails to be the person he wants to believe he is (causing total depression). When Nat can keep his rules and be a prophet, he is on top of the world; but whenever that idealized self is threatened, he is on the bottom again (pp. 334, 338). Above all looms the necessity to *act.* But in order to act against whites, Nat must change his idealized vision of them and get rid of the whiteness in his own idealized self. He is partly successful. His view of Margaret in church starts the process, but more must change. A series of visions of black angels triumphing in battle over white ones reveals Nat gradually darkening his idealized image, and transferring his conceptions of God from the white father figure Hark believes in to a vaguer figure (pp. 278–81).

White people accelerate this shift in idealized image and devaluation of whites by falling one by one from the pedestals Nat has placed them on: Samuel Turner falls from near godhood by failing to set Nat free as he had promised, a betrayal that makes Samuel the only white man Nat totally hates. Miss Emmeline falls from her chaste image when Nat accidentally catches her in the grass with her cousin (pp. 179–81).

However, Nat cannot overcome the idealized image of whites completely; Margaret Whitehead stands in the way, undefiled. She remains a pure, virginal image, the only white person who does not fall from Nat's idealized conceptions. If Nat were fully rational, he could justify killing Margaret as an unavoidable necessity if the rebellion is to succeed; no one who might warn others could be spared. But he has trouble convincing himself that innocent deaths are justified in any case. The only way he can be at peace is to assume that no white person is truly innocent or admirable. Throughout the novel Margaret is a constant threat to that view, for he identifies with her innocent sympathy involuntarily (p. 98). It is no accident that Nat kills Margaret of all white people in the novel. To rescue his vacillating leadership from the threat of the aptly named Will, Nat must show that he can kill a white person. Since he still partly wishes he were white, that is difficult. In effect he must kill this sympathetic image of white goodness not only literally, but in his own mind. The irony is that, by killing Margaret, Nat makes it impossible for her ever to fall from his psychological pedestal; she can never betray that ideal image once she dies. The manner of her dying makes things even worse. Her almost Christlike understanding of his killing her strikes him deeply. Since his first half-hearted blow does not kill her, Nat finally kills her out of love and mercy, putting her out of her misery just as he had killed the injured turtle at her request. Nat kills no other person, yet regrets killing Margaret so much that he lets another young girl escape to make up for her death. This act probably sinks the rebellion, for the girl apparently warns the countryside that Nat's army is on the move. He cannot become a glorious black prophet so long as part of his idealized self remains white. Instead his unworthy black self, a concept reinforced by Christian imagery, must fail and be punished.

The foundation is now prepared for a more complete interpretation of the controversial ending. Perhaps critics have been most misled by Nat's role as a Christ figure in the novel. He is 33 and a carpenter. Part 1, "Judgment Day," opens with an attitude of "My God, my God, why hast Thou forsaken me"; and part 4 is an explicit "It is finished . . ." parallel to Christ (p. 395). Even the scripture Styron uses as an epigraph to part 1 is postapocalyptic, implying a world after Christ's second coming. But Nat is partly an ironic Christ: he has a Messianic complex, but he is not a Messiah. Styron intends this viewpoint and takes pains to make his portrayal clear.

Again a Horneyan approach to the ending makes its point less confusing. Nat has been torn throughout the novel by inner conflict. Rejecting the self-effacing role his acculturation as a slave demands, he still cannot express openly the expansive reaction that he prefers. In trying to carry out his expansive role by becoming a "black Napoleon" (p. 316), he finds the role too much at odds with the rest of his character. His sympathy for the young girl that he lets go breaks his desire to conquer and humiliate white people for the moment, and his conflicts result in loss of will (what Will has), psychological paralysis, and resignation.

> I might have reached her in a twinkling—the work of half a minute—but I suddenly felt dispirited and overcome by fatigue, and was pursued by an obscure, unshakable grief. I shivered in the knowledge of the futility of all ambition. My mouth was sour with the yellow recollection of death and blood-smeared fields and walls. . . . Who knows but whether we were not doomed to lose. I know nothing any longer. Nothing. (p. 394)

Having suffered as a self-effacing Sambo, and having tried an expansive rebellion against his nature, Nat now gives classic expression to the resigned solution. Nat has simply come full circle in his inner conflicts, trying out all the neurotic solutions and finding them wanting.

Part 4 dramatizes the pathetic failure of his final psychological solution. No longer the expansive revolutionary, he sits in jail resigned to his fate. In Horneyan terms, he has adopted the resigned solution rather than the Freudian Thanatos. Still mixed with the resignation is part of the self-effacing value system of the New Testament, which Nat had suppressed in favor of Old Testament expansiveness throughout most of the work. Strangely, for a Messiah leading his people to freedom, Nat rarely emphasizes independence, a value most associated with the resigned solution. At most, freedom to Nat is what power makes possible, showing how much his values are governed by the expansive solution most of the time. By the end of the novel, however, he has had enough of the power to conquer and humiliate his enemies, and turns for fulfillment to love, the cardinal value of the self-effacing solution. His final position, then, is a mixture of self-effacement and resignation, the classic Christian approach to martyrdom.

Perhaps because Nat's attitude is so classically Christian, critics have not accurately measured the distance from classic Christianity that Styron sets up. Again I must stress Nat's unreliability even at this stage of the novel, his never understanding fully that final resigned vision. Furthermore, he has another key vision in this final section, tied to the first vision by its repetition of the motif, "Surely I Come Quickly," a reference both to Christ's second coming and to the approach of the executioner. This vision emphasizes Nat's switch from expansive to compliant feelings, as Nat envisions a religious/sexual encounter with Margaret, the first fantasy of a white woman in the novel that is not an expansive, desecrating forcible rape.

> *Then behold I come quickly. . . .*
>
> And as I think of her, the desire swells within me and I am stirred by a longing so great that like those memories of time past and long-ago voices, flowing waters, rushing winds, it seems more than my heart can abide. *Beloved, let us love one another: for love is of God; and everyone that loveth is born of God, and knoweth God.* Her voice is close, familiar, real, and for an instant I mistake the wind against my ear, a gentle gust, for her breath, and I turn to seek her in the darkness. And now beyond my fear, beyond my dread and emptiness, I feel the warmth flow into my loins and my legs tingle with desire. I tremble and I search for her face in my mind, seek her young body, yearning for her suddenly with a rage that racks me with a craving beyond pain; with tender stroking motions I pour out my love within her; pulsing flood; she arches against me, cries out, and the twain—black and white—are one. I faint slowly. My head falls toward the window, my breath comes hard. I recall a meadow, June, the voice a whisper: *Is it not true, Nat? Did He not say, I am the root and the offspring of David, and the bright and morning star?* (pp. 401–2)

What message is the reader to glean from this strategically placed fantasy? Critics who do not perceive the ironic distance Styron sets up presume that this ending leaves an "all we need is love" flavor, a simplistic solution to the problems presented by the novel. But if Nat's unreliability is kept in mind, the ironies of this fantasy become clear: the celibate apostle Paul hardly had a wet dream in mind when he enjoined Christians to "love one another: for love is of God." Instead of these scriptures being the voice of Paul or Jesus to Nat, they are the voice of Margaret, recalled from a past summer's day while he masturbates. Her voice has become the voice of Jesus, and her body is the way to heaven. Without "her that showed me Him whose presence I had not fathomed or maybe never even known," Nat would have "almost forgotten His name" (p. 403). Given the speed of Nat's ejaculation at the end of this short fantasy, one cannot help wondering if there isn't a bit of grotesque humor in the opening and closing line: "Surely I come quickly. . . ."

Throughout this ending Styron is *not* presenting a simple solution to racism, Christian or otherwise. Nat's idealization of Margaret would not lead to a stable relationship. Nor would her conscious inability to recognize that he is a male, as shown in the scene in which she tends him like an injured puppy while in her underwear, totally oblivious to his manhood as she could never have been with a white man (pp. 322–24). Perhaps Styron is saying that if we think interracial sex alone will solve the problem of interracial relations, then maybe we are dreaming just as much as Nat is. The unreality of Nat's idyllic martyrdom is brought sharply into focus by the quotation from Drewry's historical record of *The Southampton Insurrection* that Styron appends immediately after Nat's epiphany.

> The bodies of those executed, with one exception, were buried in decent and becoming manner. That of Nat Turner was delivered to the doctors, who skinned it and made grease of the flesh. Mr. R. S. Batham's father owned a money purse made of his hide. His skeleton was for many years in the possession of Dr. Massenberg, but has since been misplaced. (p. 404)

Styron wants us to see that we have not witnessed a glorious martyrdom, but a holocaust.

Despite the power of Horneyan psychology to make sense out of *The Confessions of Nat Turner*, the elements I have discussed in Nat's portrayal will no doubt remain among the most controversial points of the novel. As black psychologist Alvin Poussaint argues, "Styron may be guilty of projecting onto Nat Turner many of the classical white stereotypical notions about black people. . . . Styron's reconstruction of events is an example of the stereotyped belief that black people rebel primarily because of an unfulfilled psychological need to be white and not because of a sense of their own inner dignity."[16] Just how many slaves ever idealized themselves as whites is difficult to establish, but is it so strange to think that some members of an oppressed group might sometimes wish they had been born into the dominant group? Alexander Portnoy certainly wishes in some ways he were Gentile, some women have wished they were men, and some slaves surely would have preferred to be white. The terms "Uncle Tom" and "oreo" (black on the outside, white on the inside), used by black critics to castigate members of the black community in the twentieth century, suggest that the phenomenon exists even under more favorable conditions than slavery. Furthermore, some middle-class black people maintain attitudes toward blacks in the ghetto that are not very different from the "house nigger" / "field nigger" mentality. Styron's position seems to be that the "sense of inner dignity" is precisely what is so difficult to maintain under oppressive conditions. Poussaint is looking for the prodigious differences between Nat Turner and other slaves, "what really distinguished him." Styron seems to be trying to find out what psychological conditions slavery produced in blacks and whites, what Nat Turner may have had in common with other slaves. Poussaint is correct in saying that "it is just as reasonable, from a psychological viewpoint, to speculate that he did not hate his blackness and that it was self-love that made him a revolutionist revolting against the abominable institution of slavery." But Styron is equally entitled to his speculation in this "meditation on history," to see whether he is able to reveal something about the general social and psychological history of blacks and whites.

A psychological approach to Styron's *Confessions of Nat Turner* redefines the novel in terms rather different from earlier criticism. It underscores the fact that Nat is not psychologically stable, and was not intended to be a spokesman for Styron. He is, among other things, a social and psychological portrait of one of the most common effects of oppression, anxiety neurosis. Slaves like Hark and Will extend that portrayal of oppression, showing the self-effacing and arrogant-vindictive (or possibly even psychotic) variations of anxiety neurosis. Analysis of characters like Moore, Nat Francis, Miss Emmeline, and even Samuel Turner, would reveal that in Styron's view, psychological problems were not confined to black people under slavery, either. What Styron seems to be trying to show is the horrible social and psychological consequences of slavery for both black and white people in America. Examining Freudian elements in the novel, which Styron was surely aware of, reveals that Styron uses but is not confined to traditional Freudian concepts such as the death wish and the Oedipal complex. These elements emphasize the white patriarchal domination of American culture, and may have caused much of the reaction of black critics to the novel. But Styron's intuitive grasp of anxiety neurosis shows that he went well beyond the tenets of Freudian analysis and the biases of a white Southern man in portraying the characters of the novel. He may have placed too much emphasis on the sexual image of black women, the sexual preferences of black men, the pure image of Southern women, and the goodness of white masters because of being a white Southern gentleman. But he counters almost all these portrayals with contrasting representations of black and white people throughout the novel. He may not have captured the historical Nat Turner with accuracy, but he may well have caught a good deal of social psychology accurately for that point in history. He possibly distorts the nineteenth century somewhat by importing twentieth-century phenomena, such as the "black is beautiful" and "black power" rhetoric or the plight of the emasculated black man, into his portrayal of 1830s Virginia. But all these possibilities are just that: possibilities. A psychological approach can be used to support a number of these objections to the novel. But it mainly reveals the depth and breadth of Styron's understanding of American society. Perhaps we should not expect the novelist to be a perfect historian, a totally unbiased observer of society, an escapee from his own acculturation. Perhaps we should ask that he portray his own viewpoint, his own culture, and his own century in as complex a vision as he can. I think Styron has done that, and that any further historical or sociological interpretations of his novel will have to take into account the psychological complexity of his achievement.

NOTES

1. See John Henrik Clarke, ed., *William Styron's Nat Turner: Ten Black Writers Respond* (Boston: Beacon Press, 1968). In this volume Ernest Kaiser presents a good annotated bibliography of favorable and unfavorable reviews, esp. pp. 58–65. See also Melvin J. Friedman and Irving Malin, eds., *William Styron's Confessions of Nat Turner: A Critical Handbook* (Belmont, Calif.: Wadsworth Publishing Company, 1970).

2. See reviews by Lloyd Tom Delany and Gerald M. Platt, *Psychology Today,* January 1968, pp. 11–15.

3. Alvin F. Poussaint, "*The Confessions of Nat Turner* and the Dilemma of William Styron," in Clarke, *Ten Black Writers Respond,* pp. 17–22, does not begin to treat the psychology of the novel adequately.

4. Ernest Kaiser, "The Failure of William Styron," in Clarke, *Ten Black Writers Respond,* p. 64.

5. Famous examples include Rufus Scott in James Baldwin, *Another Country* (New York: Dial Press, 1962), and Eldridge Cleaver, *Soul on Ice* (New York: McGraw Hill, 1967).

6. See Stanley M. Elkins, *Slavery: A Problem in American Institutional Life,* 3d ed., rev. (Chicago: University of Chicago Press, 1976); and Kaiser, "The Failure of William Styron," in Clarke, *Ten Black Writers Respond,* pp. 50–65.

7. For further description of the Penfield experiments see Thomas A. Harris, *I'M OK—YOU'RE OK: A Practical Guide to Transactional Analysis* (New York: Harper and Row, 1969), chap. 1, or W. Penfield, "Memory Mechanisms," *A. M A. Archives of Neurology and Psychiatry* 67 (1952): 178–98.

8. William Styron, *The Confessions of Nat Turner* (New York: The New American Library, 1968), p. 172. Hereafter this reprint of the Random House edition is cited in the text.

9. Louise Meriwether, *Daddy Was a Number Runner* (New York: Prentice Hall, 1970), portrays James Adam Coffin as a black father who deserts his family because he cannot maintain the masculine image of breadwinner. The only masculine image left for him is the stud role, so he moves in with another woman.

10. Although Nat's mother's reaction to her rape can be understood in Freudian terms (she enjoys it because her husband ran away long before, because she has no consistent access to black men, and because she might as well submit since there is no way to avoid the rape), it is still disturbing. Even if some women under the right conditions might not only submit but respond sexually to rape, the fact remains that Styron portrays black women only as sluts in the novel. There are no Miss Jane Pitmans or other strong, nonprostituted black women in the work, which seems at least an indirect distortion.

11. Philip Roth, *Portnoy's Complaint* (New York: Random House, 1969).

12. Calvin C. Hernton, *Sex and Racism in America* (Garden City, N.Y.: Doubleday, 1965), pp. 107–10. I am endorsing neither Hernton's methodology nor some of his conclusions, but his analysis of the Oedipal phase as it relates to views of black and white women by Southern white men is appealing theoretically for its ability to explain these images.

13. Joel Kovel, *White Racism: A Psychohistory* (New York: Pantheon, 1970), pp. 177–211.

14. Karen Horney, *Neurosis and Human Growth: The Struggle Toward Self-Realization* (New York: Norton, 1950).

15. Platt, review in *Psychology Today,* January 1968, p. 14.

16. Poussaint, "The Dilemma of William Styron," in Clarke, *Ten Black Writers Respond,* pp. 18–20.

12

Two Consciences: A Reading of Tim O'Brien's Vietnam Trilogy: *If I Die in a Combat Zone, Going After Cacciato*, and *Northern Lights*

Marie Nelson

Tim O'Brien's *If I Die in a Combat Zone* was published in 1969, *Going After Cacciato* and *Northern Lights* in 1975. The three books are written in three different narrative modes, but all three grow out of O'Brien's war experience, and all three focus on a central question: What law must a man who wants to be good obey?

O'Brien says in *Combat Zone*, the overtly autobiographical member of the trilogy, that he read Fromm, and it is apparent that he deals with the Vietnam question in terms of whether it is better to obey, in Fromm's terms, an "authoritarian" or a "humanistic conscience." *Combat Zone* presents the conflict of the two consciences very directly, and it is reasonably clear that in choosing to fight in Vietnam rather than to run away to Sweden or Canada O'Brien was following the demands of an internalized voice of authority rather than the inner voice of his humanistic conscience. But the question is not really resolved. It comes up again in *Going After Cacciato*, which consists mainly of a fantasy of escape from the consequences of the choice to obey the demands of the authoritarian conscience.

Going After Cacciato, O'Brien said, grew from a question that he asked himself: What if he *had* deserted? What if he had carried out the plans he showed himself making in *Combat Zone*?[1] And *Northern Lights*, which I will discuss as the third member of the trilogy,[2] presents the question of conscience in another way: What if he had made a general decision to refuse to obey the demands of his authoritarian conscience? Would this have meant that he would leave the fighting for his brother to do? that he would reject his father's values entirely? And if it meant these things, could he then think of himself as a good and loving human being? In *If I Die in a Combat Zone* and *Going After Cacciato* the result of obeying the authoritarian conscience is a strong sense of guilt, and the result of *dis*obeying the authoritarian conscience is also a strong sense of guilt. *Northern Lights* shows, in addition, that simply refusing to obey the authoritarian conscience by no means constitutes the commitment to life and growth that obeying the humanistic conscience requires, and that failure to heed the inner voice of the humanistic conscience can also leave the human being who wishes to be good with a sense of having much to answer for.

In this paper I will discuss O'Brien's three books in terms of their presentation of responses to the demands of authoritarian and humanistic consciences. In discussing *Combat Zone* I will refer to Erich Fromm's definitions of the two consciences in *You Shall Be as Gods* and *Man for Himself*, to his definition of "benign aggression" in *The Anatomy of Human Destructiveness,* and to his discussion of the fear of aloneness in *Escape from Freedom.* In discussing *Going After Cacciato* I will use some of the suggestions for understanding symbolic language that Fromm makes in *The Forgotten Language. Going After Cacciato* includes a plea for peace and understanding to which its central character, Paul Berlin, is unable to respond. Finally, however, in *Northern Lights,* with the splitting of the central character of *Combat Zone* and *Cacciato* into a brother who went to war and a brother who stayed home, some of the difficulties that accompany efforts to respond to the inner voice of the humanistic conscience are overcome. In discussing *Northern Lights,* I will refer to Fromm's *Psychoanalysis and Religion*, in which the ethical question of whether it is better to follow an authoritarian or a humanistic conscience becomes a religious issue.

I begin with the question of whether it would be better to fight in Vietnam or to run away as O'Brien presents it in *If I Die in a Combat Zone.* O'Brien says that he and Erik Hansen, a friend he made at Fort Lewis, Washington, where both men were in training, joined to fight their own war, which was "mainly a coalition against the army."[3] The purpose was—"loosely," O'Brien says, and his style belies his seriousness—"to preserve ourselves." The purpose was to maintain their integrity in the face of a training that put a very heavy emphasis on obedience and humiliation. Then in the same paragraph O'Brien restates the purpose of the coalition: "It was a war of resistance. The objective was to save our souls" (*CZ*, p. 34), and the seriousness of their purpose shows through.

O'Brien shows himself carrying his doubts about whether he can fight in Vietnam and continue to respect himself as a person to the Fort Lewis chaplain. He presents his doubts with some diffidence.

> "All I want is some advice. I don't think we can convince each other of anything, not about politics. But assuming, sir—just assuming—that I truly believe the war is wrong—and maybe I'm wrong, I'll grant that—is it then also wrong to go off and kill people? If I do that, what happens to my soul? And if I don't fight, if I refuse, then I've betrayed my country, right?" (*CZ*, pp. 57–58)

The chaplain and O'Brien's commanding officer dismiss his problem as a matter of being afraid. Soldiers, of course, are human, and it is human to be afraid when one's life is threatened. Nevertheless, they are being trained to face threats to life, and when the fight-or-flight choice is posed on the field of battle a soldier fights. That response is part of the code that it is one of the purposes of basic training to teach. This, at least, was the official answer to O'Brien's question.

If it were this simple, following orders would present no moral problem. In following the demands of the authoritarian conscience, O'Brien and Hansen might have to kill to stay alive, but killing in self-defense would not violate the values of the humanistic conscience. According to Fromm's definition of defensive, or "benign aggression," killing in self-defense, like running away to save one's life, is a nonculpable act.[4] Benign aggression, whether in self-defense or in the defense of family or country, would not violate the values of the conscience that is always committed to life and growth.[5] O'Brien and Hansen could fight to defend home and family without denying their own inner sense of what it is right for human beings to do.

O'Brien's problem, however, goes beyond the question of whether it is right to perform acts of defensive aggression. He has a solid understanding of the values of his culture. His father served in World War II, and his mother was a Wave. He introduces himself to the reader with these self-identifying details, and his discussion of his doubts about serving in Vietnam shows that he has internalized the code that says young men must fight to defend their country. But he questions whether the acts he may be required to perform will *be* acts of defensive aggression. The Vietnamese have bombed no American ships, and they do not threaten to invade American territory. The domino theory notwithstanding, it is hard to see killing Vietnamese peasants as defensive and therefore justifiable aggression. The code he has internalized, if the war he is asked to fight is not a defensive war, would not seem to apply. Moreover, by virtue of being human, O'Brien hears an inner voice that says it is wrong to kill other human beings.

According to Fromm's definition, the authoritarian conscience, which he associates with Freud's superego, is an internalized voice of external authority.[6] This means that the individual makes his own the value system of parents, state, religion, or whatever the culture accepts as authority, and that he must live by that value system. He is obligated to follow the demands of an internalized voice, his authoritarian conscience, even if it commands that he do things he might otherwise regard as evil. The essential concept of this conscience, Fromm says, is a very narrow one: the authoritarian conscience is primarily a punishing conscience.

The humanistic conscience, on the other hand, is a very broad concept. This conscience, which Karen Horney calls the "intrinsic conscience,"[7] is responsive to the personality itself; and it responds to the whole range of capabilities that constitute human and individual existence. It does not have to speak in a loud voice, nor does it have to speak to us directly or even in a way that makes us aware that it is speaking, Fromm says, for us to be influenced by it. The voice of the humanistic conscience may be sensed as only a vague feeling of uneasiness. Then again, for the individual who has learned to listen to the voice of his inner self, it may provide a very strong sense of his own integrity. The humanistic conscience is realized in an individual's ability to say yes to himself; to respect his self; and to love himself, that is, to affirm his own potentialities.

Both the authoritarian and the humanistic conscience have prohibitions and obligations. Indeed, as Fromm points out, prohibitions like "thou shalt not kill" may be rules for both consciences. As a directive of the humanistic conscience, however, "thou shalt not kill" is responded to as a result of the individual's sense of responsibility to himself, whereas as a rule of the authoritarian conscience it requires submission to authority. The authoritarian (or "punishing") conscience places a heavy emphasis on thou-shalt-nots, but it also has its primary thou-shalt: thou shalt obey.

The humanistic conscience places a heavier emphasis on its thou-shalts than on its thou-shalt-nots, and it places a particularly heavy emphasis on its primary obligation: thou shalt have faith in a human potentiality for goodness. The man who follows the voice of his humanistic conscience is not simply forbidden to deprive another human being of life. He is obligated to *live,* and this means that he must live with the highest degree of emotional, intellectual, and moral awareness of which he is capable. This, as Fromm and other Third Force psychologists did not hesitate to acknowledge, requires a very large measure of strength and courage.

It is not surprising, then, that the very young Tim O'Brien of *If I Die in a Combat Zone* was not able to heed the inner voice of his humanistic conscience. He could, nevertheless, hear the inner voice just as clearly as he could hear the demands of his authoritarian conscience. He knew that to flee from his responsibility to defend his country would be to defy the internalized voice of authority, but he also knew that to kill innocent people in defense of his country's unprincipled politics would be to deny the moral authority of the inner voice. The consequence of acting against the apparent dictates of the authoritarian conscience would be to incur charges of cowardice, but the consequence of denial of the humanistic conscience would be to take on the unbearable guilt of unjustified killing. Since O'Brien and his friend Hansen were not convinced that the Vietnam war was being fought in defense of their country, their participation in that war would not be justifiable as benign, or defensive, aggression, and *would* violate the moral sense of the humanistic conscience. To kill in self-defense or to protect one's country might be justifiable, but for human beings to kill other human beings because they will be punished if they do not, O'Brien and Hansen agreed, was wrong. And yet O'Brien went to fight in Vietnam.

His decision was not an easy one. *If I Die in a Combat Zone* presents a detailed account of O'Brien's well-laid plans to escape. The self O'Brien presents here used a short leave to read about other soldiers who escaped to Paris or Sweden. He made plans to escape and kept them folded in his wallet. He sent home for his passport. He wrote letters of explanation to his family—and did not send them. He packed an AWOL bag. He rented a room in Seattle. He changed to civilian clothes there, but then returned to Fort Lewis and the duty the state imposed upon him. His explanation for his return was, "I was a coward. I was sick" (*CZ*, p. 65).

The complexities of human motivation being what they are, it is difficult to say whether O'Brien's return was motivated by a fear of consequences or by a response to conscience. If he returned simply because of fear of consequences—and he says later that he considered exile "a very heavy price to pay as a kid"[8]—his act would not, of course, in Fromm's terms, be a response to conscience. But his decision does not seem to have been based on a sense of weakness. The authority of the United States army was vested in men O'Brien could not respect—a chaplain who was not a man of God, an immediate superior who callously challenged his masculinity, and a commanding officer who assumed a false fatherliness. He did not fear *their* punishment or hope for *their* reward, and besides, he is sure he could have got away. Many others did, and he openly gives them credit. But, like Socrates (O'Brien includes Plato as well as Fromm in his account of formative reading), O'Brien felt that he owed his country something; and, like his friend Hansen, he was from a small town where everyone knew his family. They could be hurt by an act they did not understand and might take as a violation of shared values. It seems, then, that his return to Fort Lewis must have been motivated at least in part by a response to the internalized values of his authoritarian conscience.[9]

On the other hand, O'Brien's failure to run away, which he explains as an act of cowardice, could have resulted from a discovery that he was simply not strong enough to do what his humanistic conscience told him he ought to do. The last line of *Combat Zone*'s "Escape" chapter, "There was just no place to be alone" (*CZ*, p. 65), may sound like an ordinary complaint about the noisy barracks to which he returned, but he chose to return *from* a dirty room where being alone was very frightening.[10] He may not have been able to endure the prospect of the aloneness that following the inner voice of the humanistic conscience would require. And, of course, all three reasons—respect for the values of his authoritarian conscience, inability to do what his humanistic conscience would seem to have counseled, and fear of the aloneness of exile (which is obviously related to his difficulty in following the inner voice of the humanistic conscience)—may have been involved in O'Brien's decision to return to Fort Lewis.

O'Brien did go to Vietnam, he did serve his term there, and he wrote two books about it. The two not only cover roughly the same time period, they include the same kinds of events. *Combat Zone* has two set pieces, "Mori," in which an American soldier tries to ease the dying of a Vietnamese woman whom he has wounded, and "The Man at the Well," in which another American soldier humiliates an old man. Paul Berlin, in *Going After Cacciato*, remembers frisking an old man on a train as his only truly shameful act (*GC*,

p. 137).[11] Both books tell of purposeless shooting of animals, fragging of officers whose adherence to rules unnecessarily risked the lives of their men, and deaths in tunnels. The essential difference is that in *Cacciato* real life events like these become background for the main story, an account of a fantastic escape from Vietnam.

Combat Zone and *Going After Cacciato* have the same central character. As the consonants of the two names suggest, the Paul *Berlin* of *Going After Cacciato* is a transformation of the "I," Tim O'*Brien*, of *Combat Zone.*[12] O'Brien's description of his return to Fort Lewis suggests a very compelling reason for his failure to carry out his plans to escape—the aloneness that such an escape would require. The imaginary escape of Paul Berlin, however, does not require such aloneness. Paul Berlin stands guard alone, but during the six hours he stands guard his imagination enables him to escape the war in the company of his friends. The story of the night watch becomes a narrative frame for the fantasy of the pursuit of Cacciato, a soldier who has decided to hike the 8,600 miles to Paris. The fantasy not only enables Paul Berlin to escape in the company of his friends; it makes it possible for him to flee eight thousand miles in six hours.

Cacciato is introduced with strikingly realistic details. He gives Paul Berlin a piece of Doublemint chewing gum, comforting him in a time of terror; he fishes with a paper clip for a hook in a water-filled bomb crater in a place the soldiers call Lake Country; and he leaves candy wrappers and maps by his campfires. But as the fantastic flight that provides the basic core of the novel progresses by ox cart, by train, by boat, and by Chevrolet Impala, he also appears and reappears as the round-faced, moon-faced, jack o' lantern Cacciato. Thus Cacciato functions both as a character in the narrative of day to day war in Vietnam that intrudes into the fantasy of escape, and as a character born of the nighttime imagination of Paul Berlin. And this is true also of the group of soldiers who accompany Paul Berlin in the pursuit of Cacciato.

Any sane person wishes to escape death, but a sane person with an authoritarian conscience must wish to escape death without loss of honor. For a sane person with an authoritarian conscience even the temporary escape from fear of death that permits a dreamer to remain sane must be supported by defenses against charges of cowardice and disobedience. And here lies the great triumph of the basic plot of *Going After Cacciato.* It enables the pursuers of Cacciato to flee without a sacrifice of honor. *They* do not deny the supremacy of the authoritarian conscience. It is Cacciato who denies his responsibility to stay and fight a foolish war, and even Cacciato—since he is so stupid—is not to blame. But *Going After Cacciato* is more than a story of an imaginative flight from reality. It is also a story about "facing facts," to use Paul Berlin's own words.

The fictional means that makes it possible for O'Brien to accomplish his double storytelling purpose is a coordinate ordering of space and time.[13] The narrative of escape is ordered in terms of space, the narrative of facing facts in terms of time. The foreground narrative is an account of a journey from Vietnam to Laos; to Mandalay, where Paul Berlin and his cohorts stay at the Hotel Minneapolis; to Chittagong and Delhi in India; to a little town called Ovissil, where the mayor takes them in; to Kabul, Tehran, Izmir; then to Athens; and from there through the heartland of Germany (Giessen, Herborn, and Limburg fly by); and finally to Paris. And this story of escape from a barely endurable present is enclosed in a framing narrative that is told in ten "Observation Post" chapters that measure time in minutes. Speaking from his observation tower, that sundial of the night, Paul Berlin records their passing: "twelve-twenty, middle-hour guard"; "nearly one o'clock, one-twenty"; "one-thirty"; "three o'clock, the darkest time"; "four o'clock, no ten minutes to four"; "four-thirty"; "five o'clock sharp, he had to hurry"; and "six o'clock," when all the facts, not just the ones that can be endured, must have been faced and the work of introspection completed.[14]

Paul Berlin insists that the story he tells is neither a dream nor a madman's fantasy. He is not dreaming, not pretending, not crazy. What he is doing as he constructs his fantasy of escape out of the events of reality,[15] contradictory as it seems, is facing facts. As he keeps his double watch (he is so absorbed with his imaginative construction that he does not awaken his replacement), he uses a starscope, an instrument that literally uses the light of the stars to illuminate the surrounding darkness, and the suggestion is that the starscope lights up his inner experience in much the same way that Fromm, who uses the metaphor of the microscope, says a dream functions.[16] The young soldier is having desperate difficulties living up to the demands of his authoritarian conscience during his daytime hours, but during the hours from midnight to morning he is shut off from the outside world and in a state in which he can experience his unconscious. In this state he can bring charges of cowardice against himself, *and* he can defend himself against those charges. And this is precisely what Paul Berlin does as he constructs his fantasy of escape.

In the reality of day to day war Paul Berlin is continuously afraid. His comrades die one by one. Their deaths are facts that must be faced, and the temporary retreat from the real world that his fantasy provides gives Paul Berlin the bare modicum of emotional distance he needs to face them. He is afraid of death, he is afraid of being afraid, he is afraid of being known to be afraid. He fears that he will not be able to do what his authoritarian conscience says he has to do, that he will be recognized as a coward, and that he will suffer a coward's punishment—humiliation. His fantasy not only provides a brief escape from the fears that oppress him, but, by means of its power to incorporate both facts and fears in forms that can be faced, it also enables him to confront them.

Events from the recent past intrude into the narrative of the fantastic pursuit of Cacciato, but they come with their own defenses. The recurrence of a real event in language characteristic of fiction can make the event seem, if all too familiar, not totally real. The memory of "Billy Boy Watkins, who died of fear on the field of battle," cannot be put down, but the formulaic expression with which it recurs provides its own defenses; and the memories of the deaths of Frenchie Tucker and Bernie Lynn in the tunnel and of Buff in an above-ground explosion, presented in shocking detail as they are, similarly recede, with repetition, into the distance of unreality.[17] Even the terrible detail of Cacciato dumping Buff's face out of his helmet is pushed into the past with the laconic roll call of the dead with which the last Observation Post chapter begins. One memory, a vision of "Cacciato's right temple caving inward, silence, then an enormous explosion of outgoing brains" (*GC*, p. 15), comes just once, and then is firmly repressed.

Along with the defenses that accompany the memories that demand to be let in to the narrative of escape come defenses against the accusations of the authoritarian conscience. Reinforcements of the primary defense—escape as pursuit—take a variety of forms. Transferring guilt to Cacciato is just one answer to the charge that Paul Berlin and his fellow soldiers are guilty of cowardice and desertion. Harold Murphy, one of the small group that starts out in pursuit of Cacciato, turns back, and *he* is the deserter. Lieutenant Corson, an aging authority figure who has to be protected like a child, has another defense. When the group is formally charged with desertion he claims to have been kidnapped. Outrageous as this defense is, it is easy to see how it works: kidnappers act of their own volition, but the kidnapped are passive victims. Doc Peret, a figure of authority by virtue of his special knowledge, has a modern theory of humors that provides an explanation for Paul Berlin's fear. Fear is a result of the purple biles,[18] and therefore nothing to be ashamed of. Being afraid is as involuntary as the release of bladder and bowels in extreme situations. And euphemism provides another defense. Challenged to produce proof of identity in Tehran, Doc Peret's defense is a triumph of euphemistic evasion. The group does not need passports, he says. They are "travelling under certain military regulations," "mutual military travel pacts." They are "touring soldiers," "soldiers who tour, touring soldiers" (*GC*, p. 193). In contrast, Oscar Johnson, the sergeant of the group, relies on a crude passive, "We been screwed" (*GC*, p. 225), but again the passive functions as a denial of responsibility.

Defenses proliferate, and for good reason. The soldier who does not run away faces death, and the soldier who does run away faces death too—as a possible punishment for desertion. Paul Berlin's fear of being a coward, moreover, is as relentless as his fear of death. His fear of being afraid becomes most overt in the Tehran sequence, in which the group is imprisoned and interrogated. Here the metaphor for self revelation is a nakedness that goes beyond the nakedness of being stripped of clothing.[19] Paul Berlin has witnessed a punishment for desertion: a boy is first shaved and then beheaded in a public square. The following night he is awakened by "a sharpness against his neck, a swift scraping followed by the chill of melting snow" (*GC*, p. 222). The naked flesh is exposed, and then the naked self, or selves. All the soldiers—Paul

Berlin, the lieutenant, Doc Peret, Oscar, Stink, and Eddie Lazzuti—confess that pursuing Cacciato is an alibi and are forced to shout that they are clowns. At this point the primary defense visually asserts itself. The moon rises, Cacciato's round face is seen, an embodiment of simple-minded innocence, and they are rescued. They flee from their accusers in an old Impala that fortuitously appears. The fantasy of escape, momentarily threatened by a demand of the authoritarian conscience that cowardice be confessed, can continue.

Between the group confession and the rescue comes a flashback that requires its own defenses. The scene is Lake Country. Lieutenant Sidney Martin is insisting on following SOPs, Standard Operating Procedures. Tunnels must be searched first, then blown. After Bernie Lynn and Frenchie Tucker are killed because of Lieutenant Sidney Martin's insistence on SOPs, his men determine to kill him in what they consider to be self-defense.[20] Oscar, adding a desensitizing obscenity to the basic argument, uses the clichés of Darwinism to justify what he persuades the others to do: " 'Preservation . . . the survival of the species, which is us. . . . It's preservation. That's all it is—it's self-fuckin preservation' " (*GC*, p. 235). And the last defense against the possible accusations for what they are about to do is unanimity. If everyone agrees that something must be done, no one can be held responsible for the deed. Even Cacciato, whether he understands the gesture or not, must touch the grenade that kills Lieutenant Sidney Martin.

This is the ultimate disobedience of the authoritarian conscience, and, if one takes into account Cacciato's insistence that what happened to Sidney Martin was sad, it is also a violation of the humanistic conscience. Sidney Martin, wrong or not, was a human being. From such responsibility as this, even if it is shared, there is no defense but flight, and there is no denial that what the group is doing is running way. "Flee, fly, fled"; "speed, sped, spent"; "run, running, running"—this is the basic grammar of flight as Paul Berlin drives across moonscaped plains in the old Impala, running from the shame of running and from the guilt of killing an officer. For a time there is no elaboration of defenses. The primary defense itself breaks down as the pursuers of Cacciato are pursued, but they find temporary sanctuary in a town called Ovissil and at last they reach Paris, where peace talks are being held.

The word "Ovissil" recalls "officer," but not so strongly that men fleeing from their consciousness of having committed an act of ultimate disobedience cannot find temporary respite,[21] and when they enter the Salle des Fêtes of the Majestic Hotel in Paris the words of Sarkin Aung Wan promise that peace is possible. The girl who has served as their guide all this long way argues in favor of responding to the inner voice of the humanistic conscience, and her gentle persuasiveness is an argument in itself that it is possible to do so.

> "During the many months it has taken us to reach this table . . . we have traveled some eight thousand American miles. As irony will have it, this number has its exact complement in American lives lost over that same

period. I find no humor in this. I find it sad. But this sadness is neither inevitable nor unending; we might still develop a common vision of happiness, and by our action here we might begin the realization of that vision.

"It is easy, of course, to fear happiness. There is often complacency in the acceptance of misery. We fear parting from our familiar roles. We fear the consequences of such a parting. We fear happiness because we fear failure. But we must overcome these fears. We must be brave. It is one thing to speculate about what might be. It is quite another to act in behalf of our dreams, to treat them as objectives that are achievable and worth achieving. It is one thing to run from unhappiness; it is another to take action to realize those qualities of dignity and well-being that are the true standards of the human spirit." (*GC*, pp. 319–20)

This is a positive call to action. The concern is no longer with answering the accusations of the authoritarian conscience. It is not enough for the man who wants to be good not to do what is wrong. He must do what is right. He cannot just choose not to kill or not to run away. He must choose to live. And this, as Sarkin Aung Wan makes clear with her consideration of the difficulties involved in making the commitment to life that the humanistic conscience requires, is the most difficult thing of all. Sarkin Aung Wan urges Paul Berlin to step boldly into his own dream, to commit himself to love and growth, to be brave, and not to be frightened by ridicule, censure, embarrassment, or name-calling.[22] A new Paul Berlin, grown mature, seems to respond to her plea, but then he turns away to follow the orders of his authoritarian conscience. It is almost dawn. The fantasy must be ended. Paul Berlin is a soldier, a man who recognizes himself not as an individual but as a member of a group.

As daybreak and the end of the fantasy approach, Oscar Johnson, the toughest soldier of the group,[23] requires that each of the survivors of the very bad time in the Lakes region touch Cacciato's rifle in turn. The gesture, I think, can be understood as an expression of a commitment to group survival. Following this, Paul Berlin concentrates on the image of the twinkling silver star, the reward for bravery, i.e., killing. These two things would seem to be part of the narrative of real life events. Then Oscar (this is fantasy) leads Paul Berlin down the hallway in Paris to Cacciato's room, throws the door open, and stands aside.

Then reality takes over, and the only defense is partial loss of memory.[24] The choice that has to be made is still the same—fight-or-flight—but Paul Berlin remembers just enough to know that he did not run from battle. He shot and kept on shooting until all his ammunition was gone, but he remembers it as trying to drop and trying to throw a weapon that kept on shaking him. He proved that he was not the "yo-yo" or "fuck-up" or "dip-stick in the overall slime" that Oscar accused him of being. Whether he was fully conscious of what he was doing or not, he satisfied the demands of the conscience that required him to try to kill other human beings. And the fantasy of escape ends, as all fantasies must, with the coming of day.

Neither the "I" of *Combat Zone* nor O'Brien's further self projection, Paul Berlin, was able to say no to the claims of the authoritarian conscience and follow the counsel of the inner voice of the humanistic conscience; but whether they were able to respond to the inner voice as they might have wished or not, they continued to hear it. Tim O'Brien could not go against the code of his culture, but he judged his course of action in terms of his inner sense of what it is right for a human being to do. Paul Berlin could not choose to be happy, but the fact that Sarkin Aung Wan (who was, after all, a projection of his own longing to live up to his human potential) *urged* him to do so is a sign that he could still hear his inner voice. *Northern Lights,* the third book to be discussed here, gives further attention to the possibility that saying yes to the inner voice can lead to happiness. Like Tim O'Brien and Paul Berlin, Paul Perry, the central character of *Northern Lights,* attempts to evaluate his own behavior in terms of his inner sense of right and wrong; and, as *Northern Lights* approaches its conclusion, he takes a few giant steps toward fuller awareness of himself as a human being.

The central character of *Combat Zone* and *Going After Cacciato* has now split in two. One side of Paul Berlin becomes Harvey Perry, who returns from Vietnam with one eye missing; the other, more dominant side becomes his myopic older brother, Paul Perry. Big-balled Harvey, the bull, the hunter and woodsman, does not know what to do when he gets home again. He wants a house in Nassau, he wants to go on a bike tour through Canada, he is going to live in Montana or Oregon; he thinks of retiring to Tibet; he will take a sailboat trip on the Mediterranean, he will have a house in Alaska—or Boston or Miami or Berlin or Australia; he will go to Africa, My Khe, Asia, Afghanistan, Algiers, Atlantis, Allentown, Aruba, Athens—to one of the A's, at least; he plans to go to New Guinea some day. He persuades his sedentary agricultural agent brother Paul to go on a ski trip that nearly takes both their lives, and, home again, Harvey continues to plan. He will go to Key West, Seattle, Nassau, Italy, and so on. But Paul Perry, an apparent avatar of the Paul Berlin who loved only the land of Vietnam—the red earth, the rice paddies, and the animals—is hard to persuade to go on adventures; and since his is the central consciousness of *Northern Lights,* the whole action of the third book of O'Brien's trilogy takes place in Northern Minnesota.

Going After Cacciato's persistent concern is with demands of the authoritarian conscience that must be satisfied and with guilt for having done what the authoritarian conscience demanded. These are minor concerns in *Northern Lights.* To be sure, the women of *Northern Lights* express interest in what Harvey may have done and felt. Grace, Paul's wife, whose generous nature is fully in keeping with her name, says to Paul:

> "I guess Harvey's war . . . experiences . . . you know, he never talks about them. Yesterday he was talking about his training but he never talked about

the war. I think it would be good for him to just talk about it. . . . Don't you wonder if he killed anyone. . . . I wonder about that. But I'm sure if he did kill somebody then he just had to do it." (*NL*, p. 131)

Addie, the girl Harvey wants to marry, is less kind. She says she'll drag his memories out of him, she's good at that. She'll drag out " 'the whole gruesome story and make him feel all better about it,' " but Harvey tells her nothing about Vietnam and nothing about how he lost his eye. The only person he ever talks to about it is Paul, and then the conversation goes like this:

"Did you know I lost an eye over there? Do you know how it happened?"
"No."
"Me either. Turn the bloody light off. Can't even remember. Cow shit and mildew." (*NL*, p. 141)

If there is a metaphor of vision in *Northern Lights*, it is a metaphor of defective vision. There is no starscope, no microscope of dream to help probe the hidden places of the soul here. The new glasses Paul buys after losing his old ones on the nearly fatal ski journey his restless brother persuades him to take merely give him headaches. In *Northern Lights* the only way to illuminate the darkness of existence is to live tenaciously until the light is seen. And this is the book's central concern: choosing to live, which, in terms of the perspective being employed here, is choosing to respond fully to the inner voice of the humanistic conscience. And learning to do this is a long and arduous task.

Northern Lights meanders. O'Brien said himself that he needed to rewrite the book and take out at least eighty pages. The novel, nevertheless, has great value for its presentation of an individual in the process of coming to an acceptance of himself as a human being. The first part of *Northern Lights*, which deals with the reunion of Paul and Harvey Perry when Harvey returns from war, suggests the difficulties of individuation that both brothers have; the second provides an account of the growth of Paul Perry, which can be understood as a series of responses to the demands of his humanistic conscience. Here, in introducing the two brothers in relation to their father, I will give some attention to the difficulties made apparent by the first part of the novel, but the main purpose will be to show how the main action and the flashbacks of the second relate to the early refusal of Paul Perry to live by his father's values and to his later growth.

Home from Vietnam, Harvey is very strongly identified as his father's, " 'the old man's,' " son. Old Jud Harmor, mayor of Sawmill Landing, whose own identity is conflated with that of the dead father (Paul Perry says he is getting just like the old man was, always yelling about not selling the house), confuses Harvey with his dead father when Paul first tells him that his brother has come home. " 'Thought he [meaning Harvey] just got himself wounded in the eye?' "

(*NL*, p. 28), Jud Harmor asks Paul, who has just told him for perhaps the hundredth time that his *father* is dead; and he confuses son with father again when he delivers a speech at a farcical parade in Harvey's honor.

Harvey identifies himself with his father as his cough worsens on the ill-fated ski journey that comprises most of the second part of the novel. Giving up hope of ever getting back to civilization again, he says his cough is just like his father's was when he had pneumonia. Like his father, and like his grandfather before him, Harvey accepts the apparent inevitability of death, if not with a joy of recognition, at least with equanimity. Pehr Pehri, the first of this line of Perrys, took to preaching death and punishment when he lost an arm; the son and grandson of preachers of fear and death, one eye gone, recognizes death when he sees it as having a certain familiarity. Harvey is very much the son of his authoritarian father.

Paul Perry, on the other hand, tries to become his own person. Having been punished for daring to try on his father's clerical vestments, that is, as he interprets it, for presuming to see himself in the role of a person capable of making moral judgments, Paul Perry refuses ever to go to hear his father preach again. He is, however, called Brother Paul and Reverend in his adulthood, and it seems that he is thus seen, like Harvey, as an extension of his father. Indeed, some of his anger at the long ago disbelief in his seriousness may still show in his mockery of the man who does succeed his father, whom he calls the " '*reverend* Reverend Stenberg' " (*NL*, p. 54) and in his jealous rivalry with Harvey, whom he blames for somehow preventing him from being what he might have been. But the way Paul Perry speaks of what he might have been shows that even if he had entered his father's profession he would not have been like his father.

Pehr Perry and his father before him preached what Fromm calls "authoritarian religion."[25] They preached the apocalypse, the coming of darkness; they preached fear and punishment to a people that wanted to be frightened. But if Paul Perry had done what he regretted never having the chance to do he would have given comfort and love. He would have entered the service of "humanistic religion." And, aside from the question of a choice of profession, if he had followed through on his first halting steps toward individuation, he might have learned to use his own reason to know his own human strengths, he might have developed his powers of love for himself and for others, and he might, at least occasionally, have experienced the joy of being at one with his fellow human beings and felt a sense of solidarity with other living creatures. But he chose neither to be the minister of a humanistic religion nor to follow his own humanistic conscience, and all too often he is conscious of having no more maturity than he had when he used to sit on his tricycle and say " 'Pooooooor me.' "

It is not until he has faced death and confronted it bravely that Paul Perry begins to have the courage to be himself. Part of the reason that he is able to accept himself at this time, of course, is that when his strength is put to the test he finds out that he has the strength to live; but it is also important that he learns that his early self assertion did not result in the loss of his father's love; and, even more important as far as learning to live by the values of his humanistic conscience is concerned, he also learns that insisting on being himself did not mean that he did not love his father or does not love his brother. He learns all this on the ill-fated ski trip.

As the brothers realize that their father's map will not guide them safely home, they exchange their separate memories. Harvey talks about the year he got the gun for Christmas and dreaded having to learn to shoot it, about his resentment when Paul would not help him build the bomb shelter their dying father insisted on having built, and about the year he went to boot camp. He recalls that he thought then that Paul expected him to be killed in the war. The most important thing he tells his brother, however, is that Paul, who may well have exaggerated his father's insistence on obedience, was the one their father most truly loved. This is what Paul, who thinks his oppression by the black biles of melancholy could have begun when his father insisted that he learn to swim in Pliney's pond or when he punished him for trying on his robes, very deeply needs to know. Paul had his father's love. He did not lose it when he rebelled against his rule.

The Reverend Perry, O'Brien says, preached from the Finnish national epic, the Kalevala, as much as he preached from the Old Testament. He could have derived a value system that had a place for defiance from either of the two sources. As Harvey's memory shows, for the Reverend Perry—with his tough, old fashioned set of values—obedience was not the only acceptable response to power. Heroism, old-time self assertion, even if it was just the boy heroism of "I won't," could not only be tolerated, it might even be appreciated. When Paul told his father he would never go to his church again, Harvey tells Paul, the old man smiled and winked. Thus Paul learns that it is possible to assert one's individuality, to sever the primary bonds that bind one to immaturity and dependence, to pit one's will against the person in whom authority is vested—and still not be cast out from the circle of his affection. God did not respond with anger when Abraham challenged Him, Fromm says,[26] and what we see here, in O'Brien's development of a modern moral consciousness, is an individual reaching the point at which authoritarian religion can be superseded by humanistic religion. But the boy, having overestimated the cost of saying "I won't," is unable to go further.

The man learns to say "I will." The blizzard worsens, the brothers' food supply dwindles, and their hopes for survival diminish, but Paul's sense of his own basic capabilities begins to grow. He sleeps in the same foul sleeping bag with Harvey to keep him from freezing, and he emerges from that sleeping bag, image of the womb from which both of them were born, with the knowledge that he is his brother's keeper. As Harvey drifts closer to death he slits him out of his sleeping bag, which is then compared to an animal carcass, and there is a sudden startling image of birth by Caesarean section from a dead womb. He breathes life into his brother's collapsed lungs, thus giving him a second gift of life. He kills to secure food, he at last finds shelter from the storm for Harvey, he goes on alone because he has to, and he sends back help that comes in time.

O'Brien said that *Northern Lights* is a book about courage. This is true in both an obvious and a more subtle way. Paul Perry's survival of a very severe test of the elements proves that he has sufficient courage and strength to take care of his own basic needs and those of his brother, whom he has always considered to be physically stronger than himself. But recognition that he has the capability to survive when he must rely completely on himself is not enough to satisfy the need for self respect of a man with Paul Perry's introspective predilections. His inner voice, which manifests itself as the black biles of melancholy, again impinges upon his awareness; his old sense of failed potentiality—of numbed awareness, of being half alive, unrelated to the people he should love and unable to love himself—returns. The act of courage now required is nothing less than a choice to be reborn.

Near the end of *Northern Lights,* Paul Perry enters the long-dreaded Pliney's Pond; and it becomes an enormous womb of awareness of life in the natural world in which he immerses himself by an act of will. There,

> eyes closed, ears closed, there were no sounds and no lights. He lay still in a bath of secondine, blood and motherwarmth.
>
> There was no wind. The waters were stagnant. There was nothing to carry him in one direction or another, and he floated dead still as a waiting embryo. In an infant's unborn dream, the future was neither certain nor even coming, not even the future, and the past was swimming like so many chemicals around him, his own black bile running like diarrhea into the pool of elements.
>
> He opened his eyes, rolled over, face down, submerged, put his feet into the mud bottom and submerged like a turtle, opened his eyes again, relaxed, calm, warm, suspended, at home. Things moved around him. He pushed toward the bottom and took a handful of slime and squeezed it between his fingers. Then his breath left him.
>
> Coming out, emerging, he saw the great lights. (*NL,* p. 344)

Having chosen to immerse himself in life, Paul Perry is aware of being alive, and of being glad to be alive.

Tim O'Brien, Paul Berlin, Paul-and-Harvey Perry—the complex self of *If I Die in a Combat Zone, Going After Cacciato,* and *Northern Lights*—is alive. He has faced death and the fear of death in all three books, and fear of life in *Northern Lights.* He has experienced the guilt of taking life in *Going After Cacciato* and the shame of being unable to love in *Northern Lights.* He has proved that he can do what his authoritarian conscience says he must do, and he has also shown that he can do what his humanistic conscience says he is able to do. His need for a phantasmagoric complexity of defenses is past, and his need for evasion of a continuous sense of failure to become what he could be is also past. He can never regain the innocence of the boy of *Combat Zone* who played with the silver star his father won for valor in World War II. He is neither clean nor beautiful nor particularly good, but he is human and alive and, at least for the moment, fully aware of his immersion in life and of the life that is in him. And he is aware of his human capacity for goodness. Reality can be endured, and, more than that, love can be shared.

Northern Lights began with Paul Perry mercilessly "ejaculating" a whole can of insecticide (p. 4). It ends with him floating in Pliney's Pond, tolerant even of the mosquitoes who buzz in his ears, and returning, whole at last, to share with his wife the life that is in him. O'Brien's trilogy began with the question of whether a man who wants to be good can follow the demands of his authoritarian conscience. It ends with a demonstration that a man can learn to listen to the inner voice of his humanistic conscience. O'Brien's work shows what some men forced to follow the demands of authoritarian conscience in our time have suffered, and it tells about some of the risks that have to be taken in learning to love oneself.

Tim O'Brien read Fromm, he says in *Combat Zone,* and he says simply that, but I feel certain that he read enough to know that he shared the commitment to life that runs as a continuous thread from *Escape from Freedom,* the first book Fromm published in English, through his last book, *The Anatomy of Human Destructiveness.* Judging from the attention O'Brien gives to the conflict of authoritarian and humanistic consciences in *If I Die in a Combat Zone* and *Going After Cacciato,* he shared Fromm's understanding of our need to reject the conscience so strongly associated in our time with death, and to respond to the conscience that urges us to live—and to live with the fullest possible awareness of what it means to be human and alive.

In his *Anatomy of Human Destructiveness,* Fromm said that he hoped to write in another book about the love of death as it manifests itself in modern literature, and he had already given attention to the conflict of authoritarian and humanistic consciences in Kafka's *The Trial* and to the celebration of life of some of the Hebrew Psalms.[27] I think it is reasonable to believe that Fromm would have read O'Brien's *If I Die in a Combat Zone* with compassion, that he would have understood the proliferation of defenses of *Going After Cacciato,* and that he might have rejoiced at the triumph of the will to live with which *Northern Lights* concludes. In any case, as I hope this paper has demonstrated, Fromm's contributions to our understanding of ourselves as human beings can be helpful to our understanding of the three books in which Tim O'Brien tells the story of a man who survived the Vietnam war.

NOTES

1. Larry McCaffery, "Interview with Tim O'Brien," *Chicago Review* 33 (1982): 129–49.
2. In the McCaffery interview O'Brien refers to *Northern Lights* as his first novel. However,

since *If I Die in a Combat Zone* and *Going After Cacciato* (as far as the real events of *Cacciato* are concerned) cover roughly the same period, Summer 1968 to Spring 1969, and the dates of *Northern Lights* (except for flashbacks) are Summer 1970 to Spring 1971, I will treat *Northern Lights* as a chronological third member of the trilogy.

3. Tim O'Brien, *If I Die in a Combat Zone* (New York: Delacorte Press/Seymour Lawrence, 1969), p. 34. Hereafter cited in the text as *CZ*.

4. Erich Fromm, *The Anatomy of Human Destructiveness* (New York: Holt, Rinehart and Winston, 1973), p. 187.

5. In *You Shall Be as Gods* (New York: Holt, Rinehart and Winston, 1973), pp. 24–25, Fromm speaks of the *right* of living creatures to live guaranteed by God's covenant with Noah.

6. See Erich Fromm's discussion of the authoritarian conscience in *Man for Himself* (New York: Holt, Rinehart and Winston, 1947), pp. 143ff., and his comment on Freud's "punishing" conscience in *Anatomy*, n. 465.

7. See Bernard J. Paris, *A Psychological Approach to Fiction* (Bloomington: Indiana University Press, 1974), p. 47, for Horney's definition of the "intrinsic conscience," and *Man for Himself*, pp. 158ff. and *You Shall Be as Gods*, pp. 55–56, for Fromm's definition of the "humanistic conscience."

8. Michael Maclear, *The Ten Thousand Day War: Vietnam: 1945–1975* (New York: St. Martin's Press, 1981), p. 267.

9. "For my Family" and "With gratitude to the Arrowhead people . . . ," the dedications of *If I Die in a Combat Zone* and *Northern Lights* (New York: Delacorte Press/Seymour Lawrence, 1975), bear witness to O'Brien's regard for family and community, while the dedication of *Going After Cacciato* (New York: Delacorte Press/Seymour Lawrence, 1975) to Erik Hansen apparently relates to the friend's shared concern about the morality of serving in the Vietnam war. *Going After Cacciato* hereafter cited in the text as *GC*, *Northern Lights* as *NL*.

10. O'Brien's experience of aloneness is comparable to the aloneness Fromm discusses in *Escape from Freedom* (New York: Holt, Rinehart and Winston, 1941), pp. 19–21, 29–31.

11. In *Northern Lights*, p. 59, Harvey Perry, who represents the less sensitive and less dominant side of the central character of *Combat Zone* and *Cacciato*, jokes about examining the testicles of another old man after a heat storm from which Harvey has sought protection in a backyard bomb shelter, and Harvey's mockery seems to represent the direct opposite of Paul Berlin's shame.

12. *Perry*, the last name of the central character of *Northern Lights*, is also similar, the initial consonant being the voiceless counterpart of the bilabial voiced stop of *B*erlin and O'*B*rien. Doc *P*eret, if his name is pronounced /p ré:/, one of the selves into which Paul Berlin splits in the narration of the journey to Paris, may be an anticipation of Paul Perry, who, like Doc Peret, has a tendency to theorize, and, of course, Paul Berlin and Paul Perry share a first name. Perhaps this seems to claim more continuity than O'Brien intended, but O'Brien's discussion of name changes in *Northern Lights* seems to direct attention to the sounds of names. The first of the Sawmill Landing line of Perrys was Pehr Pehri. His son's name was Pehr Lindstrom Pehri, and the Lindstrom, perhaps the name of his mother, was dropped when the second Pehr Pehri changed the family name to Perry.

13. For discussion of the narrative structure of *Going After Cacciato* see Arthur M. Saltzman, "The Betrayal of the Imagination: Paul Brodeur's *The Stunt Man* and Tim O'Brien's *Going After Cacciato*," *Critique* 22 (1980): 23–38; Dennis Vannatta, "Theme and Structure in Tim O'Brien's *Going After Cacciato*," *Modern Fiction Studies* 28 (1982): 242–46; Tobey C. Herzog, "*Going After Cacciato:* The Soldier-Author-Character Seeking Control," *Critique* 24 (1983): 88–95; and Michael Raymond, "Imagined Responses to Vietnam: Tim O'Brien's *Going After Cacciato*," *Critique* 24 (1983): 97–104.

14. It is almost twelve o'clock in Chapter 2, the first "Observation Post" chapter, and six o'clock in Chapter 45, the last "Observation Post" chapter.

15. The real life tunnels, for example, become a tunnel that turns into a wide avenue of escape, and the Alice in Wonderland entry is made possible by an explosion. This particular explosion

follows the killing of a water buffalo (both explosions and killing of animals are part of real life) by a soldier named Buff who is himself killed later in an above-ground explosion. The Vietnamese girl who guides the group may be a transformation of the Vietnamese people, with whom Paul Berlin wanted to, but could not, communicate.

16. Erich Fromm, *The Forgotten Language* (New York: Holt, Rinehart and Winston, 1951), p. 167.

17. A more subtle use of the "war story" defense comes with the anticipation that the terrible events of the present can become the war stories of the future, when the men will once more be home and safe.

18. The modern theory of humors recurs in *Northern Lights,* where Paul Perry experiences fear and melancholy as the effects of a punctured sac of black bile.

19. Fromm, *Forgotten Language,* pp. 90–91, says that the naked body can symbolize the real self, while clothes symbolize the social self that thinks in terms of the current cultural pattern.

20. In *Combat Zone* O'Brien said that the blacks fragged their officers. Here Paul Berlin, the central character of a story narrated in the third person, shares the responsibility.

21. The change from "officer" to "Ovissil" requires only a change of the voiceless to the voiced labiodental fricative, and from one liquid, /r/, to another, /l/.

22. Fear of ridicule runs through all three books: the Tim O'Brien of *Combat Zone* speaks of a fear of the opposite of order—chaos, censure, and embarrassment; *Cacciato* has an extensive lexicon of terms of ridicule, most of which involve insult to intelligence or masculinity; and Harvey Perry of *Northern Lights* tells what it was like to always be afraid of doing something stupid.

23. Oscar Johnson may well represent the part of Paul Berlin that enabled him to survive "the very bad time" that he speaks of at the beginning of the novel.

24. On the level of reality, with its intentionally blurred events of a "very bad time" in the Lakes region, Cacciato seems to have died on a grassy hill at the beginning of the novel. Michael Raymond, however, speaks cautiously of Cacciato's "apparent escape," and Dennis Vannata thinks that Cacciato got away "because of Paul Berlin's blunder."

25. Erich Fromm, *Psychoanalysis and Religion* (New Haven: Yale University Press, 1950), pp. 34–38, defines "authoritarian" and "humanistic religion."

26. In *You Shall Be as Gods* Fromm interprets the Old Testament as a revolutionary book that shows man moving from obedience to an authoritarian God to the independence of full humanity, a movement that does not incur the wrath of God.

27. Fromm, *The Forgotten Language,* pp. 249–63, and Fromm, *You Shall Be as Gods,* pp. 220–23.

13

Fiction as Revenge: The Novels of Jerzy Kosinski

Andrew Gordon

The world of Jerzy Kosinski's fiction is a lonely, tortuous landscape of predator and prey, executioner and victim. Life for Kosinski's protagonist is a constant struggle for survival, a combat against the collective antagonists of the Total State and all its institutions and also against other people, whether enemies or lovers. These treacherous others would not only deprive the hero of his life but threaten even to penetrate and extinguish the precarious integrity of his self. "I am always afraid," Kosinski once said to an interviewer, "that some oppressive societal force will go after me, and will try to penetrate not only my apartment—let them do it, there is nothing there—but also my inner life."[1] As a result, the Kosinski hero fights against this multitude of oppressors with all the means at his disposal, with manipulation, subterfuge, disguise and deceit, and, if necessary, brutal force. Determined not to be a victim, the Kosinski hero gains control by becoming a secret agent, a saboteur, an underground man operating through silence, self-imposed exile, and cunning.

But the same thing that applies to his fictional heroes applies equally well to their author. As Barbara Gelb writes: "Kosinski took precocious revenge . . . for what was done to him [as a child during the Holocaust]. In order to survive, he had learned to hurt back. Himself betrayed and abused, he discovered very early in life a talent for duplicity, for concealment, disguise. The need to be someone he was not became a habit. That other someone can be found in the cruel novels he turns out rhythmically every two or three years. All of them are about Kosinski."[2] Paul Lilly agrees: "Those years [of his youth] formed in Kosinski a faith in power—any power that would redeem him from the role of victim. This need for survival to a great extent shaped Kosinski's fiction, and his novels are for him the form of power in which he puts his faith."[3] His novels function in part as a way for Kosinski to turn the tables, to gain revenge. "If I were ever magically to turn into Tarden, the protagonist of *Cockpit,* or George Levanter of *Blind Date,*" says Kosinski, "I would do to the oppressors what my protagonists have done to them."[4]

Kosinski is often criticized for the narrow emotional range and brutality of his subject matter. Nevertheless, this century has exposed the apparently boundless capacity of human beings to commit evil against others, and Kosinski is one of the contemporary novelists who have expanded the boundaries of our fiction by exposing that human perversity. Andrea, the deceptive and vengeful villainess of Kosinski's *Pinball* (1982), cites Artaud's comment as she is about to spring her trap on her victims: " 'Cruelty is an idea put in practice.' "[5] If Artaud posited a "Theatre of Cruelty," then Kosinski has perfected a "Fiction of Cruelty," a literature of violence, perversion, and shock effect designed to make an indelible impact on the reader. Kosinski wars against a cruel world with scenes of brutal cruelty.

Ironically, however, if Kosinski uses fiction in part to gain revenge on the world, he also seems to conceive of it as a revenge on the reader. He says, "Fiction assaults the reader directly, as if saying: It is about you. You are actually creating the situation when you are reading about it; in a way you are staging it in your own life."[6] Referring to his novel *Steps* (1968), Kosinski speaks of the reader being "implicated" as an "accomplice" of the narrator, but he also refers to the narrative "luring the reader deeper into the book" where "he may be trapped."[7] Elsewhere Kosinski has justified this assault on the reader as necessary in "today's atomized societies" in which "literature—above all—triggers imagination, mobilizes emotions, and ultimately arms its readers to face his very own self [sic] and cope with the unknown in his very own existence."[8] These rather martial metaphors ignore the pleasure that Kosinski as literary drill instructor feels in putting his recruits through their paces. Perhaps the fundamental truth of his imagined relationship to his readers is revealed when he refers to the reading of *Steps* as an *agon* "between the book (the predator) and the reader (the victim)."[9]

The strain of vindictiveness that runs throughout Kosinski's fiction—the protagonists' desire for revenge, and, implicitly, the author's wish to revenge himself against the world and against the reader—can perhaps be put in perspective by Marvin Daniels' analysis of "Pathological Vindictiveness and the Vindictive Character."[10] Daniels agrees with the psychoanalyst H. F. Searles that there is a similarity in the etiology of the melancholic and the vindictive character, that "early loss of a loved one, with attendant grief and separation anxiety, is often the basis for chronic vengefulness" (p. 181). Daniels further speculates that vindictiveness, like depression, actually expresses a "desperate cry for love" (p. 181): "vindictiveness functions to effect a reunion with the disappointing beloved one through mutual suffering or, finally, through mutual annihilation" (p. 189). The vindictive type "feels that he had been a good child and lost favored status without good cause. His contention is that he was cheated out of his birthright, and he aims to do something about it. . . . Each loss is a symbolic reenactment of the loss of parental love which once was his and then was suddenly, inexplicably taken away from him" (pp. 175–76).

What distinguishes the pathologically vindictive character is that "time does not heal" his hatred. "He savors his fantasies and carefully plots revenge. For him, vengeance readily becomes a vital, coordinating principle on the basis of which he organizes his life" (pp. 169–70). Although he begins by wishing to get revenge on the parents, he gradually generalizes vindictiveness into his operating principle in relation to the whole world. "People are now surely so many personifications of the forces against which he has to pit himself. . . . The other is experienced as an instrument to be utilized and exploited as he himself has been exploited, and as he still exploits himself as the vehicle of his own willful machinations. . . . Vindictiveness *is* the goal. . . . He is possessed by it" (p. 188). Unlike the sadist, who preys on the weak, the vindictive character usually attacks stronger people (substitutes for the parents) "to make them as miserable as he is in order to alleviate his terrible loneliness" (p. 173). He does not seek power for its own sake, but rather "the power to redeem himself after a real or imagined injury" (p. 175). Finally, the vindictive character is "inclined to be a 'loner' " (p. 175).

Daniels acknowledges a debt to Karen Horney's *Neurosis and Human Growth* for his portrait of the pathologically vindictive character. He finds her depiction of the interpersonal aims of the "arrogant-vindictive" character "admirable," but feels that she "stints on etiology" (p. 178). Whereas Horney is deliberately synchronic in her psychoanalytic theory, emphasizing neurotic behavior as an autotelic system with its own inner logic, Daniels is more Freudian and diachronic, searching for the origins of current behavior in past events. As he writes, "Something remains to be said regarding the specific nature of parental handling which is conducive to the formation of the structural aspects, or 'architectonics,' of vindictive thinking" (p. 183). Despite this shift in emphasis, Daniels' description of the behavior patterns of the vindictive type is compatible with Horney's. The advantage of Daniels' model, for my purposes, is that it corresponds not only to Kosinski's fictional characters but also to what is known about Kosinski's traumatic childhood.

Daniels' analysis provides us with a description of the character and interpersonal relationships of most of Kosinski's protagonists: the boy in *The Painted Bird* (1965; revised 1978), the narrator in *Steps* (1968), Jonathan Whalen in *The Devil Tree* (1973; revised 1981), Tarden in *Cockpit* (1975), Levanter in *Blind Date* (1977), and Fabian in *Passion Play* (1979). There are two apparent exceptions, but even these fit the rule: Chance in *Being There* (1971) is an apparent innocent, an orphan and an idiot. In actuality, he is able to achieve a vindictive triumph over an entire gullible country without even seeming to will it; thus he only *appears* blameless. And the dual heroes of *Pinball* (1982), Domostroy and Goddard, also appear blameless; the vindictiveness is shifted instead to the evil, scheming Andrea and her rock star boyfriend, Chick Mercurio.

If we look for the roots of the vindictiveness in Kosinski's life and fiction, we find that he fits the pattern described by Daniels of the good boy unjustly deprived of his birthright and therefore determined to exact revenge. The central trauma of Kosinski's life was his separation from his parents during the Holocaust. Barbara Gelb writes:

He was six years old—the gently bred, only child of well-off Jewish parents, his father a distinguished classicist and teacher at Lodz University, his mother a pianist trained at the Moscow Conservatory—when the Nazis occupied Poland in 1939. Jerzy Nikodem Kosinski, lovingly nicknamed Jurek, was sent away into the remote countryside by his desperate parents to save his life; they themselves did not expect to survive the war. The friends to whom his parents entrusted him abandoned him, as hundreds of other children were abandoned in that time of terror, and he became a wanderer, forced to beg for food and shelter among the most backward, brutish peasant communities of the inaccessible Polish countryside.[11]

Certainly a child of six would not fully comprehend the reasons for his separation from his parents and would only experience it as an unjust and painful abandonment and loss of their love. Fabian in *Passion Play* was, like Kosinski, a child displaced by the war in an Eastern European country, described as "a refugee from the city where, for the time of yet another war, his parents chose to remain without him."[12] "Chose" could be read as implying resentment of the parents' willful abandonment of the boy.

In any case, Kosinski went from being a favored child to being tortured by brutish peasants. At age nine, he was tossed into a pond of human excrement by a hostile mob and suffered from hysterical mutism for five years thereafter. Miraculously, both he and his parents survived and were reunited after the war. His survival testifies to his strength of will, but it is not surprising that he bears permanent physical and psychic scars from his prolonged childhood ordeal.

These horrendous early experiences were transmuted into his brilliant first novel, *The Painted Bird*, a picaresque narrative of the nightmare world of an Eastern European peasant culture in wartime as viewed by a wandering child. It is impossible to say how much of the work is based on his actual experiences and how much is invented or heightened for the purposes of fiction; in the end, it does not matter, for it is all of a piece, deriving from Kosinski's unflinching confrontation with horror. The novel grips us with its unrelenting power, like the worst kind of bad dream from which we wake up screaming. It is archetypal, touching on primal horror.

The novel is patterned by a progressive series of separations and losses. At first, the boy cries for his parents, expecting them to come for him "any day, any hour."[13] After the old crone who is caring for him dies, he still expects his parents to rescue him: "I believed that now I would meet my parents in the ravine. I believed that, even far away, they must know all that had happened to me. Wasn't I their child? What were parents for if not to be with their child in times of danger?"[14] He calls out to them but to no avail. This first chapter establishes the pattern of continual separation and loss as the boy wanders from one village to the next, always searching for substitute parents to protect and nurture him.

Later in the novel, after he has been abused too often and gone mute, the boy gets a taste for revenge. His first lessons come from a Russian soldier who befriends him, a sharpshooter and ex-sniper named Mitka. The boy assists as Mitka snipes from a tree and slays four peasants at random in retaliation for the murder of four Russian soldiers by a mob from that village. "Human being, he explained, is a proud name. Man carries in himself his own private war, which he has to wage, win or lose, himself—his own justice, which is his alone to administer."[15] This concept of the "private war" and administering personal justice runs throughout Kosinski's fiction, justifying the vindictive code of his heroes. Later, Mitka explains to the boy:

> What would preserve his self-respect and determine his worth was his ability to take revenge on those who wronged him. A person should take revenge for every wrong or humiliation. . . . Only the conviction that one was as strong as the enemy and that one could pay him back double, enabled people to survive, Mitka said. A man should take revenge according to his own nature and the means at his disposal. It was quite simple: if someone was rude to you and it hurt you like a whiplash, you should punish him as though he had lashed you with a whip. If someone slapped you and it felt like a thousand blows, take revenge for a thousand blows.[16]

Karen Horney has beautifully described this behavior pattern.

> The neurotic lives between the two alternatives of pride and self-contempt, so that hurt pride rushes him into the abyss of self-contempt. . . . The aim of the neurotic vindictive revenge is not "getting even" but triumphing by hitting back harder. Nothing short of triumph *can* restore the imaginary grandeur in which pride is invested.[17]

At first, the boy is an apprentice at revenge, a bystander as Mitka avenges his friends or as "the Silent One," a fellow mute in the orphanage, derails a train, killing hundreds to avenge the injury a single peasant did to the boy. Although the boys suffer anguish when they discover that their intended victim was not aboard the train, nevertheless the protagonist does not lose his thirst for revenge; he merely learns that vengeance must be selective. The awareness that he holds the power of life and death over all the passengers on the train elates him "with a sense of great power."[18] He goes on to exact revenge for other injuries and slights done to him, including breaking the arm of a four-year-old boy his parents have adopted and dropping two bricks on the head of a theater attendant. Both acts of revenge seem grossly disproportionate to the minor annoyances the boy has suffered; they make sense only if we see that he is reacting, like Mitka, in response to a psychological injury, a wound to the self.

The power that the boy craves is the power to inflict harm in retaliation for a permanently damaged self-concept. To a child, the parent has the godlike power to bestow or withhold love at random. By withdrawing his love, the parent betrays the child and plunges him into despair. Being bound by love is therefore dangerous to the Kosinski hero since it traps him in dependency and makes him vulnerable. As the narrator of *The Painted Bird* says, "At all times a man risked falling into the snares of those who hated and wanted to persecute him, or into the arms of those who loved and wished to protect him."[19] Jonathan Whalen in *The Devil Tree* expresses similar sentiments when he thinks of his need for his lover Karen: "It was bad enough to be trapped in Times Square by the rain and anonymous pursuers without being reminded that he was also trapped by Karen."[20] Thus when the parents of the boy in *The Painted Bird* come to claim him after the war, he feels "smothered by their love and protection" and likens himself to a caged rabbit. He says, "I would much prefer to be alone again, wandering from one village to the next."[21] Like Daniels' vindictive character, the Kosinski hero is typically a loner, a wanderer, craving intimacy but fearful of it and incapable of maintaining it. He finds an aloof, vindictive stance, control over others, and the power to do harm far safer than the dangers of love.

That the original objects of the hero's vindictive impulses are the parents is suggested in other Kosinski novels. Tarden in *Cockpit,* the most vindictive of Kosinski's protagonists, resents his father's cowardice in acquiescing to the orders of the Party bureaucracy to resettle in conquered territory. The teenager makes telephone calls to numbers selected at random from the directory, using an assumed voice and pretending to be a Party official, and orders people to travel to the Capital. He justifies his trick by saying, "If, like my father, they had abjectly surrendered their rights, they deserved to be punished."[22] Tarden's father is arrested and briefly detained when the plot is uncovered. This subterfuge is the beginning of Tarden's long, malicious career in espionage and deceit to gain revenge. Jonathan Whalen, scion of an American tycoon in *The Devil Tree,* murders a set of substitute parents, the Howmets, who had been close friends of his deceased mother and father and trustees of the estate. Significantly, Whalen destroys them by *abandoning* them in a dangerous situation: he invites them on vacation, takes them on a boat to a small sandbar in the Indian Ocean, and leaves them to be drowned by the incoming tide (Whalen's own father had been found dead along the shoreline of a beach).

According to Daniels, the "vindictive child's willful, seize-by-force orientation is readily converted into a desire to be both judge and executioner" (p. 187). Mitka in *The Painted Bird* was happiest as a sniper choosing his victims, being, as the narrator says, "both judge and executioner."[23] And there is an episode in *Steps* that could have come from *The Painted Bird:* the narrator recalls being abused by a farmer as a child during the war. He takes revenge by enticing the farmer's child to swallow a ball of bread in which he has concealed fishhooks and ground glass. "From then on I gazed boldly into my persecutor's eyes, provoking their assault and mistreatment. I felt no pain. For each lash I received my tormentors were condemned to pain a hundred times greater than mine. Now I was no longer their victim; I had become their judge and executioner."[24]

Moreover, Daniels claims that the vengefulness of the vindictive character is "generalized as an abstract principle of justice" (p. 187). This rationalization is exemplified by Levanter in *Blind Date,* who avenges political prisoners through elaborate, sadistic schemes that he characterizes as impersonal justice. On one occasion, he disposes of the Deputy Minister of "Indostran" (probably Iran), a country that is persecuting its intelligentsia, by planting a bomb in a set of skis and triggering the device by remote control as the Minister is riding at a ski resort in an aerial gondola suspended over a chasm. Levanter is proud of his effort, his technical ingenuity, and the cleanness of the dispatch. He is guiltfree, "inspired and elated" after the act.[25] Later Levanter avenges a friend, a heroic saber fencer who had been tortured and imprisoned in an East European country. Adopting a disguise, Levanter lures to a hotel room the spy who had informed on his friend, and administers the "lex talionis": he impales the informant with a saber thrust up the rectum. Once more he feels no guilt: "Levanter reminded himself that what he was about to carry out was impersonal revenge, as simple as the verdict of a military tribunal."[26] He becomes distanced both from the victim and from himself, an impersonal agent of military justice in the "private war" he constantly wages. Levanter never pauses to consider the personal significance of avenging an injured father figure through an act of homosexual rape and murder. As Daniels suggests, the vindictive character uses and exploits both others and himself in pursuit of his real goal, which is not justice but vindictive triumph, a triumph over the parents and over the world that is short-lived and must be perpetually reenacted.

In *The Art of the Self: Essays A Propos Steps,* Kosinski expounds his ideas concerning revenge. He refers to the killing of the farmer's children by the boy in *Steps* as not a crime but a "ritual murder." Kosinski speculates that "perhaps these murders satisfy the murderer's sense of self and gain for him an increased solidity, a temporary freedom, a previously unreachable equality, and at the same time an absolute superiority." In this regard, he contrasts Othello's hot-blooded murder of Desdemona with the cold-blooded machinations of Iago, which result in a sort of "ritual murder" of Othello's self: "Iago's actions upon Othello . . . make him an equal of the Moor and ultimately his superior. . . . Iago has estranged himself from the relationship; he has projected himself so wholly upon the Moor that, although the play in the early stages is about Iago, the later stages are about Othello, who has adopted Iago's *persona.*"[27] In fact, most of the murders that Kosinski's heroes carry out are plotted as intricately and cold-bloodedly as Iago's destruction of Othello; they take on the aspect of ritual murder. Kosinski is close to the psychological truth about his characters when he recognizes that the aim of their vindictiveness is relief from a damaged sense of self by achieving a temporary superiority over their victims.

Kosinski also speaks of murder as "an act of intimacy, a potent bond between killer and victim," and he equates murder with sex, "the symbolic killing of the other in an intimate relationship."[28] Certainly Kosinski's heroes stalk their victims, spy on them, and penetrate all the secrets of their lives, attaining a kind of intimacy at a distance before they violate them. Daniels too sees the murderous rage to annihilate of the vindictive character as an act of love: "The vengeful tragic hero, his protestations notwithstanding, remains enamored of the object of his venomous passion. His is the fury of the suitor scorned" (p. 191). The original object of that fury is the parent who has deprived the child of love.

A final characteristic that the Kosinski hero shares with Daniels' pathologically vindictive type is the creation of a fortress self. Daniels describes the vindictive character as "a living fortress which walks around. . . . Upon occasion he sallies forth to counterattack. Yet his posture is predominantly defensive. . . . The vindictive character comes to limit, as much as he is able, all intercourse with the rest of the world. He remains watchfully on guard behind the walls. . . . He is imprisoned in his hardening inflexibility, which increasingly precludes the possibility of obtaining intimacy anywhere" (pp. 186–87). The epitome of the fortress self is described in *Cockpit.* Tarden, the ex-spy, rents similar apartments in major cities under different assumed names. He is careful not to stay too long in any one apartment, and each building must have a requisite number of exits for quick escape. Tarden remains unknown to his neighbors in each location. The furnishings of each apartment suggest a tightly concealed inner self equipped with numerous lines of defense.

> I have covered the walls with a layer of cork and hung heavy curtains between the main rooms and foyers to make each apartment soundproof. I have installed locks on every door. Under each darkroom's large work counter, I have cushioned a space large enough to sit up or stretch out in, and covered the front of it with a false wall. I can remain there for hours, unseen, hearing every sound in the apartment. . . . I can monitor incoming and outgoing telephone calls. From my niche, I can also trigger various explosions all over the apartment. Those in the kitchen and bathroom would stun anyone who happened to be in either room and give me ample time to escape unseen.[29]

In real life, writes Barbara Gelb, Kosinski "takes a childlike joy in describing the secret hiding places he has in his various apartments, where he can conceal himself in case the K.G.B. or SAVAK or maybe even SMERSH should knock on his door."[30]

But his fictional hero Tarden recognizes that by these extreme defensive maneuvers he has also walled himself off from others. He fears dying alone, like the lonely man he reads about in the paper whose decomposing corpse was found in his home only after he had been dead for two months. That protective womb can easily turn into a tomb, like the elevator in which he finds himself trapped for hours: "Here, in the solitude of my capsule, I sensed a curious time warp. Encased in a steel and rubber sarcophagus, I was completely cut off from my past: a royal mummy, safely cradled and sealed for the long voyage ahead."[31]

Tarden is the archetypal Kosinski hero: secretive and withdrawn, a loner and a control freak. He resembles the prostitute Veronika, a woman he uses and later kills when she crosses him: "Like an actress who never lets down her guard, her every movement was studied and controlled."[32] Tarden is a master of disguise who seems to have no existence of his own. He always conceals his own identity even as he enjoys intruding into the lives of others, learning their secrets and their weaknesses, and then establishing control through imposture and game playing. Kosinski has some of the same characteristics himself: "He likes to play tricks, to wear disguises and provoke reactions from strangers. . . . Kosinski turns into a wicked little boy, shows you the 23 concealed pockets in his custom-made trench coat, his false identity cards. . . . He is secretive about many things, and often he contradicts himself, possibly by design—another form of trick or test, to catch you out, part of his social experimenting."[33] But Tarden is incapable of intimacy: he is able to relate to women only as whores and mistresses, and he uses sex primarily for power. Deeper than his need for intimacy is his need to defend himself and triumph vindictively by controlling others. At one point, as he spies on his neighbors from the attic of his rented house, he gives us a perfect metaphor of his situation: "I felt like a lookout in a fortress able to observe and be ready to receive any unwanted intruders."[34]

Since Kosinski deals again and again with these lonely, vindictive heroes, he is well aware of their psychological dilemma: they are trapped inside that fortress self. Jonathan Whalen in *The Devil Tree* comes closest to such psychological self-awareness in this plaintive confession to his lover Karen:

> I told her that even in sex I was always trying to conceal both portions of my personality: the manipulative, malevolent adult who deceives and destroys and the child who craves acceptance and love. Now I know that I really tried to conceal the child at the expense of the adult. While my dominant concern all my life has been with not admitting needs, not asking for things, not squandering money, my worst terror has always been that I might seem helpless, and that in appearing helpless or childish I might again be judged in relation to my parents.[35]

But recognition of the dilemma does not imply any solution to it. The Kosinski hero stays holed up in his fortress, like Fabian in *Passion Play,* who cruises the highways endlessly "in his Van Home, in a private chamber of his private fort,"[36] or Patrick Domostroy in *Pinball,* who secludes himself in an abandoned ballroom: "He had gradually succeeded in turning his private universe into a well-guarded fortress."[37]

The most revealing and unforgettable fortress image occurs in *The Painted Bird.* While he is wandering in the woods, the boy comes upon "a deserted military bunker with massive reinforced concrete walls."[38] The bunker is filled with trapped rats eating each other alive. Later, in order to save his own life, the boy lures a carpenter to the bunker and pushes him into the pit to be devoured by the rats. If, as we have seen elsewhere in Kosinski, the fortress represents the guarded self, then those swarming rats may be an image of the savage, consuming violence he fears in his own psyche. Lacking fresh victims to appease that savage hunger, the mind begins to cannibalize itself.

This may be one of the motives behind Kosinski's prolific, apparently compulsive production of fiction: as a way to relieve that all-consuming hunger for revenge and prevent it from turning on himself. Fiction seems to provide Kosinski with a socially rewarding release of his vindictive fantasies, at the same time that it allows him to manipulate the reader the way his protagonists wish to control other people. Fiction is his fortress, his game kingdom where he is at the controls, like the cockpit in which Tarden plays his lethal games.

In Kosinski's work we see not merely fiction *about* revenge but fiction *as* revenge. Perhaps the key concept linking Kosinski as author with his vindictive protagonists is the notion of "plot," with its dual association with narrative and revenge. Kosinski seems to say to the reader what Tarden says in *Cockpit* as he is springing the trap on an editor who has slighted him: " 'Now I'm in charge of the plot. It's my novel.' "[39]

But is the reader really the "victim" of Kosinski's fiction? Can we benefit in any moral or psychological sense from experiencing his works? There seem to be two dangers involved in reading Kosinski: first, that we will be seduced by the detachment of his protagonists and of the narrative style into simply identifying with his heroes and indulging our own power fantasies; and second, that we will be repelled by the cool vindictiveness of the novels and condemn their author. Paul Lilly goes so far as to criticize Kosinski as a writer who offers only a series of powerful moments with no moral vision, each moment "nearly a hollow shell."[40] But Lilly fails to acknowledge the psychological perceptiveness of Kosinski's fictional portraits or to sense beneath his characters' vindictiveness and cool detachment the terrible price they pay in incompleteness and loneliness, a price of which we are constantly made aware. In fact, it is not Kosinski's narrative moments but his *protagonists* who are "hollow shells." His heroes ache with loneliness but are forever trapped in their strategems of manipulation and aloofness. The silent scream in every Kosinski novel is a cry not for revenge but for love. Kosinski's vivid novels allow us access into the inner world of the pathologically vindictive character; in that sense, we are not Kosinski's "victims" but the beneficiaries of his psychological intuition and his fiercely controlled imagination.

NOTES

1. Jerzy Kosinski, *Writers at Work: The Paris Review Interviews*, Fifth Series, ed. George Plimpton (New York: Penguin, 1981), p. 328.

2. Barbara Gelb, "Being Jerzy Kosinski," *The New York Times Magazine*, 21 February 1982, p. 45.

3. Paul Lilly, "Comic Strategies in the Fiction of Barthelme and Kosinski," *Publications of the Missouri Philological Association* 4:32.

4. Kosinski, *Writers at Work* interview, p. 326.
5. Jerzy Kosinski, *Pinball* (New York: Bantam, 1982), p. 274.
6. Kosinski, interview by Joe David Bellamy, in *The New Fiction: Interviews with Innovative American Writers* (Chicago: University of Illinois Press, 1974), p. 149.
7. Kosinski, *Writers at Work* interview, p. 337, and Jerzy Kosinski, *The Art of the Self: Essays A Propos Steps* (New York: Scientia-Factum, 1968), p. 14.
8. Jerzy Kosinski, "Presidential Papers," *American P. E. N. Newsletter* (Summer 1973): 1.
9. Kosinski, *The Art of the Self,* p. 14.
10. Marvin Daniels, "Pathological Vindictiveness and the Vindictive Character," *The Psychoanalytic Review,* 56, no. 2 (1969):169–96. Hereafter this article is cited in the text.
11. Gelb, "Being Kosinski," p. 44.
12. Jerzy Kosinski, *Passion Play* (New York: Bantam, 1980), p. 144.
13. Jerzy Kosinski, *The Painted Bird* (1965; rev. ed., New York: Bantam, 1978), p. 3.
14. Ibid., p. 12.
15. Ibid., p. 217.
16. Ibid., p. 227.
17. Karen Horney, *Neurosis and Human Growth* (New York: Norton, 1950), pp. 102–3.
18. Kosinski, *The Painted Bird,* p. 233.
19. Ibid., p. 241.
20. Jerzy Kosinski, *The Devil Tree* (1973; rev. ed., New York: Bantam, 1981), p. 173.
21. Kosinski, *The Painted Bird,* p. 243.
22. Jerzy Kosinski, *Cockpit* (New York: Bantam, 1976), pp. 124–25.
23. Kosinski, *The Painted Bird,* p. 211.
24. Jerzy Kosinski, *Steps* (New York: Bantam, 1969), p. 36.
25. Jerzy Kosinski, *Blind Date* (New York: Bantam, 1978), p. 41.
26. Ibid., p. 184.
27. Kosinski, *The Art of the Self,* pp. 27–28.
28. Ibid., pp. 28–29.
29. Kosinski, *Cockpit,* pp. 14–15.
30. Gelb, "Being Kosinski," p. 46.
31. Kosinski, *Cockpit,* p. 272.
32. Ibid., p. 237.
33. Gelb, "Being Kosinski," pp. 45–46.
34. Kosinski, *Cockpit,* p. 210.
35. Kosinski, *The Devil Tree,* pp. 173–74.
36. Kosinski, *Passion Play,* p. 131.
37. Kosinski, *Pinball,* p. 131.
38. Kosinski, *The Painted Bird,* p. 60.
39. Kosinski, *Cockpit,* p. 186.
40. Paul Lilly, "Vision and Violence in the Fiction of Jerzy Kosinski," *The Literary Review* 25, no. 3 (Spring 1982): 400.

14

Third Force Analysis and the Literary Experience

Robert de Beaugrande

1. PSYCHOLOGY AND LITERATURE

The relationship between psychology and literary criticism is hard to define. However, it seems plain that a concerted interaction between the two disciplines would be not merely relevant, but urgent. The most decisive events in writing and reading are operations of the mind, operations that are crucial for human capacities to know and understand. In the last ten years, the production and comprehension of discourse have therefore become chief topics of study for psychologists.[1] Since literature is a conspicuous and respected mode of communication, it obviously deserves to be included in these investigations. The special status of literature must be related to certain things that happen during communication; it is not explainable in terms of words printed on a page.

However, research in psychology has traditionally been dominated by two major trends whose application to literary criticism is perplexing. One major trend is behaviorism, construed as the observation of human behavior in tightly controlled laboratory situations. Here, the human being figures as a conditioned organism whose behavior is described in terms of statistical generalities for the whole species, with the lower-order animals (rats, dogs, etc.) serving as the implicit model. Literary studies, on the other hand, is concerned with the interpretation of literary texts in personal, intuitive reading encounters. Here, the human being figures as a creative intellect whose products are described in terms of artistic uniqueness, with the higher-order genius serving as the implicit model. It is far from apparent how these two incompatible disciplines can apply to each other.

The other major trend in psychology is the psychoanalytic approach made popular by Sigmund Freud. This second usage of the term "psychology" is somewhat misleading, because there has been little cooperation between experimental psychology and psychoanalysis. The experimentalist works with large groups of anonymous test-subjects and distills out what is common to all.[2] The psychoanalyst works with the individual patient and distills out what is most personal, intimate, and idiosyncratic for each single case. The test-subjects are not supposed to know what the inquiry intends to find, nor to change their behavior for the occasion. The patient needs to learn as much as possible about his or her own mental state and to change its unhealthy patterns or aspects. Given these diversities of interest and intention, the relative lack of interaction between empirical psychology and psychoanalysis is readily understandable, but none the less unfortunate for both sides. Whereas empiricists tend to lose sight of the individual personality and its intellectual capacities, analysts tend to improvise uncontrolled or peculiar methods of fact-finding.

Because psychoanalysis is focused on symbolic interpretation, it has been used in literary studies considerably more than empirical psychology has. Typically, literary scholars accept Freud's writings as the accredited framework, without considering that important changes have been made in both theory and method. Freud's orientation was heavily pessimistic, because he deduced human nature from immature or neurotic persons, not from healthy ones. He concluded that humans are profoundly alienated by continual conflicts between their instinctive drives and their defensive maneuvers to control or defend against those drives. To describe such conflicts, he devised an elaborate, sometimes fanciful rhetoric of causes and agents, such as "psychic energy," "ego," "superego," and so on.[3] The interpretation of mental problems or case histories tended to assume a mythologizing cast: a small set of hypothetical constructs associated with events in infancy was applied to explain all manner of adult developments. Each case history became a story acted out in the barely accessible domain of the "unconscious," with dreams and symptoms serving as disguised evidence. Childhood was viewed as a locus of obscure causes (such as "castration anxiety") that were postulated in the hindsight of current effects. Problems in later life were traced back to bodily drives emerging at an age when the child is being shaped by repressive cultural standards of conduct. Since an infant neither understands potential conflicts, nor possesses realistic means to resolve them, the chances for a healthy adult life appear dishearteningly remote. Moreover, the adult patient has little direct access to such early stages of life, due to lapse of time and memory, and generally has to accept the analyst's interpretation in order not to seem defensive or uncooperative. Thus, the Freudian approach allows the analyst considerable leeway to interpret people's lives in terms of a gloomy and restrictive mythology.

As might be expected, the use of Freudian psychoanalysis in literary criticism tends to inherit the same difficulties. Art figures as a kind of neurosis, or as a "defense" against infantile drives and fantasies.[4] The interpretation of a literary work is pervaded by a rhetoric of bodily functions (eating, excreting, etc.), desire, anxiety, mutilation, and perversion.[5] In the process, the literary text is metaphorically displaced by another text, a "story" of causes and effects staged in a dark era of infancy. For instance, the "Oedipal stage" postulated by Freud is adopted as grounds to assert that Brutus and Cassius are bad sons murdering their father in Caesar, whereas Antony is the good son avenging the patricidal act;[6] and the interpretation then proceeds from this story. Yet the fact that these personages were not members of the same family is dramatically relevant, the more so in view of Shakespeare's feelings about the special nature of violating ties of blood—as revealed in such dramas as *Hamlet* and *King Lear.* That is, we have suppressed a relevant fact to obtain a story whose relevance is plain only if we subscribe to the Oedipal myth that sons unconsciously and archetypally wish to kill their fathers in order to claim exclusive possession of their mothers. In Shakespeare's play, Cassius is about the same age as Caesar and resents the unequal outcomes of their parallel careers—hardly a motive equivalent to competing for a mother.

This interpretation of literary constructs in terms of unconscious content is a persistent problem for Freudian approaches. Since we stand to lose considerably by reducing the riches of literary content to a small set of infantile fantasies, we deserve to be shown what we stand to gain. For instance, if the Oedipal myth is offered as the "real" story of *Julius Caesar, Hamlet, Macbeth,* and so on, why do these dramatic realizations affect us so differently? In the third part of *Henry VI,* Shakespeare deliberately used parallel father-son slayings as the ultimate emblem of civil war, showing "what strategems, how fell, how butcherly, erroneous, mutinous, and unnatural, this daily deadly quarrel doth beget" (2.5.89–91). From a literary and dramatic point of view, the father-son battle is deployed here as an expressly privileged symbol of an "unnatural" conflict. Such an intention is blurred if we merely suppose that Shakespeare and his audiences are all equally pervaded by the same Oedipal myth that they unconsciously see acted out whenever one man does deadly battle with another.

In effect, the Freudian interpretation of literary works resituates plot, characters, and tropes in an infantile framework that is hardly less reductive than the animal-conditioning model of behaviorist psychology. The "Third Force" method presented by Bernard Paris in this volume suggests an escape from the perplexity of being forced to choose between these two older reductionisms. His interpretations do not displace the text with an infantile reconstruction. Instead, he provides an account of the motives for actions and characters as the author presented them. Conflicts are seen as determined not by early infantile drives, but by current strategies for interacting with the external world. Paris's major theme is that realistic (or "mimetic") characterization is precisely a literary principle that follows the same character patterns observable in human lives. Ultimately, Paris engages the work in an interpretive move that brings it closer to its psychological uniqueness, rather than leveling it by a regression into undifferentiated "libidinal" phases of childhood. I shall try to show that this move is indeed an intriguing extension of the literary encounter, rather than its displacement. Though Paris's results may be disconcerting, I find them enlightening in ways that draw the work closer together, instead of dismantling it along Freudian or behaviorist lines.

Moreover, Paris provides a way to view literary response in terms of the reader's own interactive strategies. Such a step seems to me vital for helping literary criticism to develop an explicit epistemology that includes its own activities as part of an interactive process of discovering and reporting on literary works. This issue is probably the most central one now confronting both the human sciences and the humanities, where human activities are both the object and the substance of every investigation.

2. THIRD FORCE PSYCHOLOGY AND ITS VIEW OF THE HUMAN

"Third Force psychology"—significantly also called "humanistic psychology"—differs from the other two "forces" discussed in section 1 by its emphatic concern for the "evolutionary constructive force" that "urges us to realize our given potentialities" (*INT,* p. 11).[7] The goal is termed "self-actualization," an "episode" in which "the powers of the person come together in a particularly efficient way" (*HM,* p. 35). This notion suggests a "different philosophy of human nature" from those of the two older psychologies, one projecting "greater optimism" and "a more holistic approach to human behavior" (*INT,* p. 11). However, it is a serious mistake to regard Third Force psychology as naively optimistic about human development. On the contrary, the approach deals extensively with the ways that healthy development can be diverted or converted into neurotic counterparts. At best, the optimism lies in the imperative to seek "self-knowledge" as a "means of liberating the forces of spontaneous growth."[8] The "Third Force" is always moving toward realization. Conflicts do occur, but they are not already permanently foreclosed by infantile precedents.

In contrast to Freud, Third Force psychology asserts that our "basic needs are not in conflict with civilization and our higher values" (*HM,* p. 30). A "conflict" between "reason and impulse" only "comes from deprivation." What Carl Rogers calls "a congruent person" is "not self-deceived or torn by unconscious conflicts"; "there is no significant disparity between his conscious and unconscious selves" (*HM,* pp. 38–39). A "transparent person" produces "acts, words, and gestures" that "are an accurate indicator of what is going on inside," so that "honesty" and "genuineness" naturally follow (*HM,* p. 39). Whoever is both congruent and transparent feels no "inhibition" in "experiencing and expressing the real self." This person is "self-actualizing" and "presses toward" "good values," the lists of which seem impressive indeed: "truth, goodness, beauty, wholeness," "uniqueness, perfection," "justice, order, simplicity, richness, effortlessness, playfulness, self-sufficiency," "serenity, kindness, courage, honesty, love, unselfishness" and so on (*HM,* pp. 39, 37). These values, about which Freudian and behaviorist approaches had little to say, are construed as the standards people would choose if "their natures" "were highly enough evolved to give them the opportunity for choice" (*HM*, p. 34). "The pleasures of self-actualization" figure here in place of the striving toward libidinal pleasures and immediate rewards, postulated as the motivating principles in Freudian and behaviorist theories. The hope is to "incorporate what is valid" in Freud's "pleasure principle," yet not to "leave out" the "pleasure and fulfillment found in the encounter with an expanding reality and in the development, exercise, and realization" of "growing capacities, skills, and powers."[9] The new "values" are "conducive to a fuller realization of human potentialities" (*HM*, p. 34).

A utopian tendency might be seen in the precept that "essential human nature" can be defined via the "observation" of "the people in whom this nature has achieved its fullest growth"; and that we can thereby attain "an idea of what would be good" for "all people" (*HM*, p. 34)—a model superego distilled from an elite group.[10] Ostensibly, "an adequate conception of human nature and human values can be derived only from the perspective of the most fully evolved people" (*HM*, p. 28). Paris sees some "difficulties" in this scheme, which in effect sets up absolutes without giving reliable procedures for deciding who will serve as arbiters. As he points out, "all value systems" based on an "essential human nature" entail a "leap of faith"; "there is no one perspective that does not involve some distortion" (*HM*, pp. 34, 28). The problem is then how to define "a universal norm of psychological health" whose values are "generated by the nature of the species," given the potentially "misguided values of individual societies" (*LBC*, p. 93).

The "leap of faith" would become obvious as soon as we tried to infer the essential "nature of the species" from actual observation. "The possibility" of "health" and of being "happy, harmonious, and creative" is allowed for "no more than one percent of the population and perhaps less" (*HM*, pp. 34, 30). "The voice of the real self," which seems to offer the only "chance for a meaningful life," is "faint," typically emerging when an unhealthy development has already occurred: "every time" someone "chooses against the interests of his real self he incurs self-hatred" (*HM*, pp. 30, 44, 52). The prospect here is of an inner reality we might not find in the outer reality we are obliged to observe. What we tend to find are destructive counterparts, so that the positive version would have to be inferred as a converse of the negative version.

Moreover, the select group we are searching for seems to be the only one qualified for conducting the search. Only "self-actualizing persons" are deemed capable of being "objective": the state where "thought" is able to "contemplate its object fully and recognize it in relative independence from the thinker's needs and fears."[11] This viewpoint (termed "allocentric") provides "complete openness and receptivity" toward "the object" "perceived in its suchness" and hence a "clearer perception of what is there," including "seeing other people as they are in and for themselves."[12] "Defensive people," on the other hand, are "subject-centered" ("autocentric") and do not "focus on the object in its own right" (*HM,* p. 40). Thus, essential nature could only be inferred by the same group of "allocentric" people whose standards are the ones in question; there is no additional authority to decide who belongs to the group.

Accordingly, this theory of human potential tends to focus mainly on how and why that potential is so seldom attained. Society is not well designed to foster self-actualization. Instead, most people are obliged to develop "defensive strategies" in order to interact with the world. Paris suggests that the "wide applicability" of Horney's theory may be due in part to its close correlations with the "basic mechanisms of defense" found in all "animal behavior," namely, "fight, flight, and submission" (*HM,* p. 59).[13] But a more important reason might be that defensive behavior is encouraged in virtually every personality or tendency of everyday living. This factor leads to a different pessimism than Freud's. Whereas he supposed that everyone has to be neurotic, Maslow and Horney believe that the possibility of psychic health is never foreclosed, though it cannot be naively taken for granted. In addition, the Freudian focus on "lower needs" has been enlarged by a new focus on "higher needs" no longer simply "reducible to the lower ones" (*HM,* pp. 28–29).

A skeptical stance toward naive optimism is indicated by the effort Horney invests in denouncing the "idealized image" people have of themselves. The image can be beneficial in "providing inner unity and a sense of identity" (*HM,* p. 53). But a person with an exaggerated idea of "what he could be or should be" is likely to pursue the unrealistic "aim of actualizing the ideal self" by "reaching out for greater knowledge, wisdom, virtue, or powers than are given to human beings" (*HM,* pp. 53–54). This "falsification of reality" is contrasted with the way the "healthy individual reaches for the possible" and "works within cosmic and human limitations" (*HM,* p. 54). Of course, a person might not know what is "possible" before "reaching out." Horney suggests that the decisive criterion is whether "pride is the motivating force" behind "the drive for perfection."[14] Since this standard suggests a quasi-theological parallel to the fall of Satan or to the prideful seeking of trans-human knowledge in the garden of Eden, we are not surprised when Horney equates "the search for glory" with "the devil's pact" where "the individual" must "lose his soul—his real self" (*HM,* p. 54).

The implied imperative seems to be moderation and a close orientation toward reality. We should "accept limitations," "give up the search for glory," and not "reach beyond ourselves" (*HM,* p. 57). But "inner salvation" (*HM,* p. 58) is not so easy. Reality is scarcely a helpful guide if most people are "self-alienated" and have a "view of the human situation" that "is not very reliable" (*HM,* p. 32). That view is "characterized by distortion, projection, and externalization." These three defects in turn seem to be imminent in the everyday course of things: "distortion" results from "accounting for all needs in terms of the ones in focus"; "projection" is a natural effect of "choosing those whose personalities and value systems are parallel to one's own"; and "externalization" serves our need not to be aware of our problems (*HM*, pp. 29, 35, 32). In the face of such perils, orienting one's actions according to what one construes as reality is likely to be a difficult and uncertain task. The child would appear to be the least alienated, provided that he or she is "allowed to have his own feelings, tastes, interests, values" and to "make his own choices" (*HM*, p. 38). Frustration presumably begins in childhood, a notion that Freud also entertained. But Third Force psychology defines the child's needs in terms of self-actualization, whereas Freud attributed to the child such gruesome fantasy-wishes as rape and murder—wishes that *had* to be denied.

Just as the devil is capable of endless imitation and mockery, defensive behavior keeps reflecting back the aspects of healthy behavior. A neurotic person may do in a compulsive manner things that resemble what a healthy person does in a free and genuine manner. For instance, the "healthy person" does not remain exclusively expansive, compliant, or detached, but "moves in all three directions" (*HM*, p. 45). But a neurotic "person cannot move in all three directions without feeling confused and divided" (*HM*, p. 46), because of "incompatible value systems and character structures" whose tension may indeed "paralyze" the person (*HM*, p. 46). Neurotic attempts toward combination and compromise are likely to miscarry, though outward appearances may deceptively suggest progress. "The substitution of one defensive strategy for another" can masquerade as "education" (*HM*, p. 46). "Neurotic pride" strives to "reconcile irreconcilables" (*HM*, p. 56), and the "neurotic" "idealized image" may seem like "an artistic creation in which opposites appear reconciled" and in which "submerged trends" are seen as "compatible aspects of a rich personality."[15] The "detached" person is capable of "swinging" from "an extreme appreciation for human goodness" over to a "jungle philosophy of callous self-interest" (*HM*, p. 52). Thus, compulsive strivings toward a balanced personality may lead instead to more elaborate defenses. Yet placing total emphasis on "a value system based on only one or a few needs" is also unhealthy (*HM*, p. 28). No matter how much a person stresses one tendency, the others still "exist quite powerfully" and "manifest themselves in devious and disguised ways" (*HM*, p. 46).

Many apparently positive traits may turn out to be only more side-products of defensive behavior, once "basic needs" are turned into insatiable "neurotic needs" (*HM*, p. 43). The virtues are then no longer "genuine ideals," but merely "necessary" to one's "defense system" (*HM*, p. 47). The "compliant defense" brings with it the "values" of "goodness, sympathy, love, generosity, unselfishness," and the belief in "the goodness of human nature" (*HM*, p. 47). The "values" of the "aggressive" person include "success, prestige," "recognition," "efficiency," "resourcefulness," and a "zest for living" (*HM*, pp. 48–49). The "narcissistic" person attains "charm," "buoyancy," "perennial youthfulness," and "optimism," and wants to be "the benefactor of mankind" (*HM*, p. 49). The "perfectionistic" person works for "high standards, moral and intellectual" (*HM*, p. 49).[16] The "detached" person's vision is capable of "serenity," "imagination," and "superiority," as well as "ironic humor" and "stoical dignity" (*HM*, pp. 51–52). This person may be an "excellent observer of his own inner process" and attain "objective interest" (*HM*, p. 51). He or she has a "high evaluation of freedom" and "cultivates individuality" and "self-reliance" (*HM*, p. 52). Only "arrogant-vindictive" persons have little to recommend them beyond being "competitive" and "self-sufficient" (*HM*, p. 50); but this low estimate could be interpreted as an instance where "ambition" and "power are abhorred," yet "secretly admired because they represent 'strength' "; or a revenge for "despising the Christian ethic" and "traditional morality" (*HM*, pp. 47, 50–51) (e.g., for accepting the "devil's pact").

Such personality descriptions indicate that common social virtues might be attributes of defensive persons who are basically "vulnerable to disappointment" or "disillusionment," or are "ambivalent," "dependent," or "insecure" (*HM*, pp. 47ff.). Persons who are "alienated from their spontaneous desires" pursue unrealistic virtues because they "overrate their capacities," make "exaggerated claims," and "equate standards and actualities" (*HM*, pp. 51, 49). All the same, their actual accomplishments might be quite remarkable. Many major advances in the history of ideas, art, and technology have been the work of people whose unrealistically high opinions of themselves may have acted as the impetus for extraordinary exertions: Julius Caesar, Napoleon, Beethoven, Wagner, Schopenhauer, Nietzsche, Yeats, Shaw, and so on. As we will see in section 3, Paris readily admits the defensive nature of literary authors, even Shakespeare. Conversely, "healthy" people may have gone unrecorded in history because they "gave up the search for glory" and did not "reach beyond themselves." If so, whether people were "self-alienated" may not be relevant for their achievements. Still, creativity is certainly not always neurotic, and neurosis is certainly more often a blocking force than an inspiring one.

The unhealthy person is unlikely to gain useful insight into his or her problems. Since "self-actualization" tends to be "stifled by culture, family, environment, learning," and "existential problems arise out of the disparity between our natural wants" and "the unalterable cosmic and historical conditions of our existence" (*HM*, pp. 38, 31), it is reasonable to blame some of our difficulties on the environment. The neurotic person, however, tends to construe his or her personal problems "as historical or existential in nature" (*HM*, p. 32). Dealing with failure may also be an occasion for devious maneuvers. It is equally "neurotic" when "failures" are "rationalized away" or else taken as reason to "renounce, withdraw, or resign" (*HM*, pp. 55, 57). Or, the "defensive reactions" of "destructiveness and aggression" may set in as a response to the mere threat that basic needs will be frustrated (*HM*, p. 29); the person may not wait to see if failure actually occurs. The mandate might seem to be to escape failure by not trying anything overly ambitious. But that recourse too is perilous: it "can actually cripple a person's life" if "he does not embark on any serious pursuits commensurate with his gifts lest he fail to be a brilliant success."[17] Whereas the healthy person can deal with failures, the neurotic one is prone to misunderstand or overinterpret them in ways that reinforce the neurosis.

In my view, the most crucial point in all this is how a person could interpret such issues as virtues, achievements, problems, and failures in such a way as to help him or her transcend neurotic trends. It would help if the terms "healthy" and "neurotic" were applied not to *people,* but to *episodes in people's lives.* Health would then be a process of ongoing interpretation according to constructive rather than destructive guidelines. Experiences would be taken as occasions to improve the scope and coherence of one's general understanding of the human situation, and not as occasions to draw radical lessons about the insensitivity or perversity of "Fate." Definitive satisfaction should not be expected, since "satisfaction of any one need produces no more than a momentary tranquillity" (*HM,* p. 30). When basic needs are satisfied, it's time to "feel frustrated about the larger personal, social, and intellectual issues."[18] But one's needs can be defined by setting concrete goals whose attainment is feasible from within the given situation.

In this sense, then, Third Force psychology would truly be "humanistic," fostering an understanding of human interests and values and asserting the human capacity for self-realization. Action and interpretation would be closely balanced to work against superficial or compulsive judgments. People would remain aware that "all rubricizing" is "an attempt to freeze the world," to "stop the motion of a moving, changing process world" that is "in perpetual flux";[19] "there can be no closed system of beliefs, no unchanging set of principles."[20] As we shall see in section 3, this enterprise can be significantly supported and enriched with the experiences attainable through literature. In fact, literary authors typically represent more of the human situation than they are able to interpret explicitly. They offer us alternative realities to contemplate, without being able to foreclose for us what those realities can mean. Hence, the literary experience tends essentially toward the allocentric, a perceptive mode Ernest Schachtel depicts as "enriching, refreshing, vitalizing."[21] Literature too can show how "the immediate live contact with the ineffable object of reality is dreadful and wonderful at the same time."

3. A THIRD FORCE FOR CRITICISM

The relation between discourse and human reality is far more complex than is commonly acknowledged. On the one hand, society and its institutions have strong vested interests in privileging one version of "reality" by assigning it the independent status of something given outside and distinct from human understanding. On the other hand, no single version of "reality" can be adequate for all human purposes. If people couldn't imagine other worlds than the one they are experiencing at any moment, they couldn't gain any deeper insights or make progress. In consequence, the structure of each society reflects an uneasy project of controlling (and deciding who can control) the boundary between the "real" and the "imaginary," or the "fact" and the "fiction."

Traditionally, this kind of control is accounted for in theories of discourse by drawing a distinction between *logic* as the truth of a test versus *rhetoric* as the perspective of the author. Yet all language is rhetorical in the sense that rhetoric is a means for substituting (using "tropes") and arranging (using "schemes"); after all, words are not the things they represent, nor is the order of words the same as the order of things, so that to use language means to substitute and arrange. Hence, speaking or writing the truth cannot be done independently of some authorial perspective, whether or not the latter seems conspicuous.

I believe it can be shown that literature is essentially an enterprise that subverts this overly simple distinction between logic and rhetoric. Literature is about alternatives: participants in literary communication are free and willing to use discourse for constituting and contemplating other "worlds" besides the accepted "real world." Whether or not the text is offered or accepted as "realistic," the author has, at least by implication, undertaken to create a world with its own facts. "Realism" becomes another principle for making literary decisions according to certain kinds of constraints but it does not dictate the execution of the work itself, because the literary imagination is characteristically not fixed or committed to a single perspective. Paradoxically, this imagination invents what it wants to understand, yet cannot definitively understand what it has invented. A literary representation stands for the human situation at large and, for that very reason, the author can never fully or finally explain it.

According to this conception, which I have undertaken to justify in detail elsewhere,[22] literature attains truth not by disclaiming, but by radically acknowledging, human interests or perspectives toward reality. By relaxing its reference to a specific reality, literature challenges readers to make sense of the world from a humanistic standpoint. To construct the world of a novel or a play, readers must achieve their understanding without their everyday reliance on experience or multiple eyewitness reports. Thus, mental functions are intensified both for logic (what is true) and for rhetoric (who presents it to whom and why), yet without the conflict or shattering we would expect if the two were indeed opposed. Literature is the domain where reality and invention heighten, rather than disavow, each other.

The motivational issues made accountable by Third Force psychology would seem to fall under rhetoric in the traditional sense: what vested interests people have in interpreting things in certain ways. Paris himself apparently accepts the traditional sense when he cites "rhetoric" as a tool for "glorifying" or "romanticizing" particular "strategies of defense" or "neurotic solutions" (*PAF*, p. 279; *INT*, p. 16; *HAR*, p. 234). An author's vested interests should become plain if "his rhetoric will affirm the values, attitudes, and traits of character which are demanded by his dominant solution, while rejecting those which are forbidden by it" (*LBC*, p. 84; *JA*, p. 169). This view might imply that rhetoric could divert or even conflict with the "inner logic of the work," its mimetic "portrayals of experience" (*LBC*, p. 83; *INT*, p. 20).[23] However, people's personality structures are likely to influence not only how they present their ideas but also how they see the world and what they can make sense of. Hence, each personality type invests in its peculiar rhetoric and logic while imagining them both to be a part of the natural order of things. "Bargains with Fate" are rhetorical, involving a teleological metaphor of a supreme sapient, sentient entity that links actions to values and that insists on a proportion between efforts and rewards, or between concessions and gratifications. Yet the bargains are also logical, because they explain how facts are connected and how causes generate effects in some version of reality. The myth of "Fate" is not questioned because to do so would endanger the human need to see a concatenation of personal circumstances as a coherent individual destiny to which labels such as "just," "unjust," "tragic," "ironic," "memorable," can be meaningfully applied. A certain branch of logic is needed as a basis for a certain brand of rhetoric.

Thus, it is both necessary and unsettling to bring personal motivations into the focus of literary inquiries. Of course, Third Force analysis does not pretend to predict or uncover an exact correlation between personality and the literary formation of texts or character. To do so would be reductive in much the same manner as the other two "forces" reduce human acts either to conditioned behavior or to a defense against repressed fantasies. Like "most behavior," literary writing or reading is "multi-motivated" (*HM*, p. 27). The "hierarchy" of human needs "will determine what we want, but not necessarily how we will act" (*HM*, p. 27). A Third Force analysis can thus relate the actions of writers or readers to certain classes of motives without introjecting symbolic counterparts of the Freudian kind. The analysis leaves the realization of the work not only intact, but looking more coherent than it did before.

Paris has to face the problem that Third Force psychology was not offered as a theory of art or literature. "Maslow includes aesthetic needs" "among our basic requirements, but he does not integrate them into his hierarchy" (*INT*, p. 12). Horney compares art to dreams as a way in which " 'our unconscious imagination can create solutions for an inner conflict.' "[24] In her view, whether these solutions are "constructive or neurotic" has "great relevance" for " 'the value of an artistic creation' " (*PAF*, p. 129). " 'If an artist presents only his particular neurotic solution,' " then the work's " 'general validity' " is " 'diminished,' " no matter how much " 'superb artistic facility and acute psychological understanding' " may be displayed. The proper role of art should be to " 'wake people up to the existence and significance' " of " 'neurotic problems' " and to " 'clarify' " them. Paris infers that Horney is arguing for a "consistent and healthy" "moral norm" that "identifies neurotic solutions as destructive and suggests constructive alternatives." According to the only true norm available in the Third Force approach, the artist should be a self-actualizing person; but in fact, artists are often highly defensive. Paris takes it for granted that "wisdom and health are not essential to great art" (*PAF,* p. 22).

Still, a close reading of Paris's works indicates that he hopes great art will be self-actualizing in spite of the self-alienated tendencies of authors and characters. "Allocentric" perception can, he feels, emerge from "mimetic achievement," even if the author's defensive strategies make him or her unaware of this accomplishment. A correlate for this hope might be seen in Paris's remark that "the aesthetic perspective" calls for "a free, contemplative, nonneeding mode of perception" (*LBC,* p. 66)—an outlook reminiscent of Kant's classical definition of beauty in *The Critique of Aesthetic Judgment.* This "allocentric perception," typical of the self-actualizing person, is deemed "the healthiest component of literature," even though Paris does not concur with Horney's demand for self-actualizing artists. "Allocentric perception," as we saw in section 2, is needed in order to be "objective"; "thought" must be "free from the pressure of urgent needs or fears" if it is to "contemplate its object fully" and to "see other people as they are in and for themselves." Such objectivity does not come readily or immediately, however, to the artist. Significant "mimetic achievements" require both authors and readers to "rise to allocentric perception" (*PAF,* pp. 286–87). Whereas the "rhetoric" of the "great realist" "may be a reflection of his conflicts or a justification of his predominant solution," his "mimetic" achievement is "a triumph of healthy perception" (*HAR,* p. 236).

Hence, Paris's line of argument revises Horney's by uncoupling the literary process as such from the author's ability explicitly to deliver a "healthy moral norm" according to which the work must be interpreted. Paris sees art and literature as persisting in a shifting association with defensive and neurotic perception, but they achieve their greatness by transcending it—a kind of healing process that, like successful therapy, brings back a clearer vision of reality less distorted by personal wishes and fears. It should therefore not be surprising that art might appear in the guise of defensive behavior. Art could be one of "the larger personal, social, and intellectual issues" in respect to which "frustration" sets in when basic needs are satisfied. Art might be a vehicle for the "high intellectual standards" of the "perfectionistic" person. Also, Horney depicts "the detached person looking at himself with a kind of objective interest, as one would look at a work of art."[25] Or, a "self-alienated" person might use literature as a way to disguise neurotic feelings as "existential Angst" or as a "philosophic sense of the absurdity of human existence" (*HM,* p. 32).

The ties between art and defense are in any case firmly established by Paris's assumption that "Horney's theory" of "the defensive strategies that arise in the course of self-alienation" is the "most useful" of the Third Force theories "for the study of literature" (*INT,* p. 12). Paris admits that "fictional characters and their creators are more frequently self-alienated than self-actualizing" (*INT,* p. 12). Indeed, he can discover very few characters, and virtually no authors, not even Shakespeare, who merit being described as self-actualizing. Paris remarks that this "absence" in literature is "accounted for" by the "widespread feeling that health is uninteresting" (*LBC*, p. 62). But then too, the two genres Paris usually selects, the novel and (more recently) the drama, demand conflicts that typically get represented in terms of disparate character types, disproportions, attacks and defenses, aggression and self-effacement, and so forth. It is hard to imagine that a world of exclusively self-actualizing characters would sustain a plot, even if they could be successfully depicted with a mimetic claim. When such a character does appear, such as Sir Thomas More in *A Man for All Seasons*, conflicts soon arise with other characters or with a social order that demands self-alienation. In any event, literary custom, especially in the theatre, has tended to encourage the presentation of characters who "reached beyond themselves" and refused to "give up the search for glory": Tamburlaine, Caesar, Antony, Coriolanus, Faust, Wallenstein, Ottokar, and many more.

Paris introduces an important restriction of his method to "realistic characterization" (*INT*, p. 13). "Not all literary characters are appropriate objects of psychological analysis. Many must be understood primarily in terms of their formal and thematic functions in the artistic whole of which they are a part." Though Paris's work hardly deals with actual instances, the implication might be that aesthetic considerations can stand in tension with the realistic development of character; i.e., that literary form can encourage an author to discount the requirements of plausible characterization. If the "characters" of a "realistic novelist" are "subordinated to their aesthetic" "function, they will be lifeless puppets" (*PAF*, p. 11). Conversely, when such a character as Austen's Fanny Price is "a highly realized mimetic character whose human qualities are not compatible with her aesthetic and thematic roles," the result may be that "readers cannot identify" with her (*JA*, p. 22). The suggestion is made that we should not "go to novels looking for unified aesthetic systems" (*HAR*, p. 212). Yet I would be more inclined to say that we should not go there expecting to find an obvious or harmonic unity; we should rather expect the imposition of unity to be quite complex and arduous, much as it would be in real life if we experienced the latter as literature.

Paris's conception of the "aesthetic" reflects his adoption of the typology of Scholes and Kellogg,[26] who distinguish between "aesthetic, illustrative, and mimetic characterization" (*JA*, p. 18). "Aesthetic types exist mainly to serve technical functions or to create formal patterns and dramatic impact." "Illustrative characters" serve as "'concepts in anthropoid shape'" in "works with a strong allegorical or thematic interest." Mimetic characters are "'highly individualized figures who resist abstraction and generalization,'" so that their "motivation" can be seen in terms of "the ways in which real people are motivated." If so, only these "individualized" characters—Forster called them "round"[27]—can be construed to "have an internal motivational system" (*INT*, p. 13).

This scheme seems to disagree with my own impression that readers routinely interpret any literary character in motivational terms, though those motives may not appear transparent or compelling. As a reader, I may be encouraged to feel that the character is "realistic" or "mimetic" because his or her motives are ones I readily recognize as cogent for myself or for people I know. But the converse does not follow: that unrealistic characters must lack the kind of motivations I see in reality. I can't read even fantastic literature without assuming that gods, wizards, and heroes have cogent motives somebody might share.[28] If the motivation of characters seems totally flimsy or contrived, I will judge the work not as unrealistic or nonmimetic, but as poor literature. However, the motives of complicated or unorthodox characters may well not be transparent, e.g., those of Pierre Bezuhov, Monsieur Teste, Malte, Leopold Bloom, Randle McMurphy, and so on. Still, instead of simply abandoning my attempts to infer or contemplate potential motives, I may indeed regard this opaqueness as a realistic trait for interesting, complex personalities. Psychological intelligibility of motives need not be tied to the verisimilitude of the characters: the motives might well seem realer than the characters who pursue them—and that is why they can engage my interest.

Paris would hardly contest that a reader's definition of "realistic" is tied to his or her conception of "reality." This factor, which I raised in section 1, allows for the possibility that works may seem mimetic to one reader or audience, but not to another. Paris admits this possibility when he avers that "critics" have judged such a character as Heathcliff "unrealistic" because "his behavior has escaped their comprehension" (*HEA*, p. 102). Using motivation as a standard for deciding what is realistic seems more intriguing to me than superficial verisimilitude, which Paris uses as a more commonsense standard when he makes the "realistic" status of *Wuthering Heights* hinge on "the presence of ghosts" (*HEA*, p. 116). A compromise position is indicated when he recognizes an element that is unrealistic in the commonsense way, namely "magic," as means to solve the "problem" of "how to take revenge and remain innocent"; and relates this mode of solution to his classification of the work *(The Tempest)* as "romance" and "fantasy." This is what I think nonmimetic literature presents: not the absence of believable motives, but the pursuit of motives with unbelievable means. It is thus possible (as Paris shows) to perform a motivational analysis on Prospero, a character who is not realistic in the commonsense way, but whose motives are mimetic—i.e., realer than he is—which is why I can identify with him so well.

The compartmentalizing account of Scholes and Kellogg may appear plausible within the context of the critical fashion that Harvey termed " 'the retreat from character' " in modern criticism.[29] Critics would " 'dismiss the subject' " of character in favor of " 'allegedly more important and central subjects—symbolism, narrative techniques, moral vision, and the like.' " For instance, the New Critics devoted their attention to "imagery, symbolism, or structural features that have little to do with characterization."[30] No doubt such concerns appeared to favor a tidy, objective analysis as compared to the untidy, subjective issues raised by character analysis: identification, emotional response, convincingness, and so on. Academic criticism had no accredited theory of characterization comparable to the methods of linguistics and stylistics. Besides, the neglect of character accorded well with the fashionable doctrine "art for art's sake" that offered a welcome defense against the intensifying political and social engagement of art in the later nineteenth and early twentieth centuries.

The ultimate stake may have been the allegiance to an old aesthetics of harmony. Like Ernst Cassirer, critics often assume that "every facet" of an art work "is part of a 'coherent structural whole'."[31] The "aesthetic structure" underlies the "organic whole" of the work. In fact, however, this assumption is exaggerated because critics typically present as being "in" the work the structure they themselves have created. That is, only the final resolution is displayed, while the problematic constructive process of reading and organizing the work gets taken for granted and is barely acknowledged. This practice profoundly abridges the nature of art if we assume, as many aestheticians have, that "beauty" arises from the interaction between "variety" and "order,"[32] or between "variety" and "unity,"[33] or between the "manifold" and the "unitary connection."[34] The aesthetic factor is not a simple noticing of harmony, but rather the dynamics of imposing a structure upon a presentation of considerable functional complexity and diversity.[35] As realism came to dominate fiction, authors felt that a straightforwardly harmonious representation was naive, indeed, unfaithful to reality, the more so as society presented the impression of increasing diffuseness and alienation. In consequence, authors aggressively used characterization to oppose or debunk the traditional aesthetics of harmony; and the academy responded by "retreating from character."

The notion that an "aesthetic character" is distinct from a "mimetic" one might be reinterpreted in view of this state of affairs. An author might be so concerned with conveying a harmonious unity as to adopt the facile expedient of creating characters whose functions and actions do not appear to obey the constraints and pressures of everyday reality. But a more encompassing aesthetics that places reader activities in focus, rather than hiding the critic behind the supposed structure of the work itself, would not encourage this kind of disparity. In such an aesthetics, the "harmony" or "unity" of the work would always be recognized as a provisional and intentional achievement against lesser or greater resistance. Authors would not have to sacrifice their perception of reality in order to offer an easily attainable harmony. Indeed, a "great" work of art resists the definitive imposition of just one resolution, either for the single reader or for the whole reading community. Each reading of the work has to start afresh and may well combat a different resistance and press for a different unification. However, academic critics traditionally want to impose on their reading a unity they can then claim is "in" the work, so that the reading seems authoritative and privileged. Exactly because their task is elusive and precarious, critics want to show how well they have done it and to conceal how much trouble and doubt they encountered along the way.

Accordingly, I feel that a disparity of perspectives in characterization is by no means an external, disturbing factor or an aesthetic flaw, but just one more diversity whose encompassing, however provisional, is an integral part of the aesthetic experience. It is not merely "characterization" that "overflows the strict necessities of form";[36] all literature of any merit does so. When Paris unifies the characterization of a novel as diffuse as *Vanity Fair,* he is extending, rather than discounting, the aesthetic act implied in all reading of literature. He has appropriated a special theory for the purpose. But I suspect that the appeal of Horney's theory itself is partly aesthetic: its ability to encompass in one compact system such a diversity of feelings and actions. The same aspect makes it quite useful for analyzing literary characterization in a variety of works; but that use is precisely a literary one, and its successes are aesthetically satisfying.

In literature, realism is not a decision to report what actually happened at some particular time and place, but a decision to accept a certain orientation as a constitutive artistic principle. One of the consequences is to restrict the extent to which the author can use events and characters as evidence of a teleological structure not easily attributable to everyday experience. However, the representation of reality is itself a goal, so that the selected elements have a teleological structure in terms of the artistic task and intent, e.g., that Balzac's *Human Comedy* should be accepted as representing the human situation at large. In nonrealistic literature, this artistic teleology is typically reinforced with explicit nonhuman teleologies, such as magic or divine intervention, which, as I suggested before, enable motives to be realized with unbelievable means. But these means and their supporting teleologies remain in an uneasy tension with human needs and actions, and the dynamics of the work as literature is to narrate that tension. The plans of gods and wizards do not triumph simply or immediately, and sometimes not at all, being out of step with humans. And if this were not so, nonrealistic works would be of slight human interest at least as literature, though we might read them as theology, cosmogony, and so forth.

In realistic literature, on the other hand, it is the characters' own teleologies that come in conflict with the human scheme. Conflicts are always possible because that scheme itself is so diffuse. Human values often collide with each other, or cannot be realized by two interdependent characters at the same time. One situation may support an interpretation that another situation undermines. A "great" realistic work retraces this shifting of perspectives without insisting on just one that could make sense of or refute all the others. Even if authors and readers sincerely believe that one such privileged perspective exists, or even if they think they know just what it is, they also know (at least unconsciously) that it is something they have to add to their daily experiences; and that other people do not always agree. Hence, a totally coherent teleology for daily life tends to be repeatedly strained and disrupted, though it may not get denounced or discarded. Failures may be rationalized as injustices, exceptions, or perversities engineered by a mythic force called "Fate"—the same myth that some realistic literature projects in place of older theological powers.

Therefore, the disparities we often find in the realistic novel can be a major part of its claim to realism. Paris notes that "there is a conflict of values within realistic fiction itself" (*PAF*, p. 283); "some of its effects are incompatible with others" (*PAF*, p. 284). Therefore, "the writer of realistic fiction is doomed to leave somebody, and perhaps everybody, unsatisfied" (*PAF*, p. 22).

Commonplaces about "poetic license" and similar notions should not blind us to the irreducibly paradoxical nature of authorial freedom. The author can invent facts, but certainly not at will or at random. It is impossible to sustain a plot without allowing for points where different events are possible, and the author has to decide which track to take. Such decisions cannot be separated from comparisons about which track might be better or worse from the standpoint of the characters. Thus, motivation is already implicit in the construction of any plot. The author is readily entrained in a structure of rewards and punishments as the characters do or do not seem to get what they want or deserve. A case in point is the classical, even mythic, structure where a wrong is set right, the outcome being a change of roles. Wronged people who assert themselves act out a shift from compliance to aggression, as Paris has ably shown for numerous characters in *Vanity Fair* (*PAF*, pp. 93ff). In such a case, a shift of perspectives has enforced itself on the author as a consequence of having to navigate the dynamics of the plot. In ways like this, the invention of a literary world controls the exigencies of characterization.

It might be a defensive reassertion of freedom when authors insist on the right to interpret the facts invented under such constraints. Intriguingly, the author's defensive intrusions seldom yield a solution that works very well or very long. Adopting "the classical moralistic perspective"[37] allows the author the privilege of accompanying the "representation" with an explicit "interpretation"—that is, to embroider the work's logic with a conspicuous rhetoric. But given the diversity of the human scheme, we find that "in many realistic novels," "the classical moralistic perspective continues to exist alongside of, and often in disharmony with, the concrete" "representation of life" (*PAF*, p. 7).

The alternative is a defense that acknowledges the problem, namely, to adopt what Auerbach calls the "problematic existential perspective," in the "conviction that the meaning of events cannot be grasped in abstract and general forms of cognition."[38] Instead of "the representation of life in terms of fixed canons of style and of ethical categories which are a priori and static," we find "a stylistically mixed, ethically ambiguous portrayal which probes 'the social forces underlying the facts and conditions' " (*PAF*, 6f).[39] That perspective readily results from the intention to be mimetic, to represent what one experiences in the world, whether or not an author is willing to give up the privilege of interpretation. "The mimetic impulse that dominates most novels often works against total integration and thematic adequacy" (*PAF*, p. 9), thereby increasing the resistance readers need to overcome for an aesthetic resolution. "Mimetic characters" that are "truly alive" "tend to subvert the main scheme of the book," "to escape the categories by which the author tries to understand them, and to undermine his evaluations of their life styles" (*PAF*, p. 11; *INT*, p. 15). This effect is especially likely when "more extensive and socially inferior human groups" become the "subject matter";[40] readers must then encompass within their experience characters for whom conventional types are not readily available, and, in so doing, adopt a broader and more flexible concept of personhood.

Though we can see why authors, readers, and critics might fail to attain a unified interpretation in realistic literature, we can also see why they tend to hope for one. The act of invention needs some motivation to suggest why we can learn any more from it than from some everyday lie; hence, interpretation includes a concern for motivation. Naturally, this interpretation can be simplified by trying to make one perspective do all the work, so that aesthetic unification is more facile. Wayne Booth is a critic with some nostalgia for such accessible harmony; he claims that "a story will be 'unintelligible' " "unless the reader is made clearly 'aware of the value system which gives it its meaning.' "[41] "The author, therefore, must not only make his beliefs known; but he must also 'make us willing to accept that value system, at least temporarily.' " If, for Booth, "the rhetoric of fiction" brings about "a concurrence of beliefs of authors and readers,"[42] then authors have the responsibility to reflect valid or convincing systems of values and beliefs. Such systems could also be enlisted by critics like Booth to be the framework for a valid interpretation. Paris, however, doesn't see literature as a source of "ethical guidance" (*PAF*, p. 20), since he doesn't expect authors to be models of mental health, and his research keeps uncovering the unsoundness of authorial interpretations.

A major achievement in Paris's work, and one that originally cost him considerable time and exertion, was to realize that divergent perspectives are not only found in realistic literature, but are crucial for the latter's intent to be both realistic and literary. In consequence, the author's interpretations of what he or she represents are prone to appear either inconsistent within the whole work or invalid for what has been represented. Only rarely does "the implied author emerge as a deeply integrated and coherent being" (*PAF*, p. 14). More typically, "implied authors" are "no wiser or more consistent" than anybody else; and "as interpreters of experience" they "usually do not know what they are talking about" (*PAF*, p. 20). Paris keeps arriving at the conclusion that "great psychological realists have the capacity to see far more than they can understand" (*PAF*, p. 8; *INT*, p. 15; *HAR*, p. 215).[43] However, we should also acknowledge that representation is in principle less vulnerable than interpretation. For instance, we hardly quarrel with Thackeray if he tells us that Amelia Sedley decided not to marry William Dobbin; but we readily quarrel with him if he tells us that "it is those who injure women who get the most kindness from them" (*Vanity Fair,* chap. 50). We've agreed to let him make up the plot, but we reserve the right to contest what it demonstrates, particularly if his conclusions seem objectionable, both logically (generalization from one example) and rhetorically (vindictive accusation of women, casting doubt on the author's motives).

The outcome of these deliberations would be that the literary encounter with realism includes experiencing a represented world as one whose realness cannot be exhausted by interpretative commentary. Of course, it is easier to detect the author's unreliability when interpretation becomes obtrusive. Yet a critique of the author's perspective can be applied to any work in its entirety, or even to all of an author's works. We may note the author's "recurring preoccupations, the personal element in his fantasies, the kinds of literary characters he habitually creates, and his rhetorical stance" (*LBC,* p. 84). The work can be viewed as the author's effort "to resolve his inner conflicts by showing himself, as well as others, the good and evil consequences of the various trends that are warring within him." It is natural that "the author's attitudes toward his characters are often self-contradictory as a result of his inner conflicts" (*INT,* p. 16). Indeed, these conflicts can lead to an involuntary grasp of reality—the "allocentric" perspective Third Force critics tend to associate with great art, as we saw earlier. For example, Jane Austen's "inner conflicts contribute" to "her remarkable understanding of a wide range of psychological types" (*JA,* p. 198). She "is constantly trying to achieve equilibrium between opposing forces"; "she has a need to criticize each solution from the point of view of the others, and a strong movement in any one direction tends to activate the opposing trends" (*JA,* p. 199). She "longs for aggressive triumph" despite "her insistence on goodness and her criticism of expansive values" (*JA,* p. 181). The upshot of the conflict is a freedom of perspective that lends her novels an "immediacy" even for readers who find her "morality quaint and her themes outdated" (*JA,* p. 21).

This critical movement in which the psychological analysis first deconstructs and then restores literary values is highly characteristic of Paris's work and mirrors the movement in which Third Force psychology implies a recovery of optimism out of pessimism. An analogous trend might be seen in certain practices of the "deconstructionist" critics, though of course many differences remain.[44] Paris's diagnosis of his own "blindness and insight" (*LBC,* p. 88) even uses Paul de Man's motto,[45] though not in precisely the original way: a problem de Man situates in language corresponds to a problem Paris situates in the personality. For de Man, every system of concepts is blinded by the necessity of taking at least some of them for granted; a "deconstructive" reading can call these concepts into question and, consequently, the insights that presuppose them. The blindness is not mere error someone else can set right once and for all; it is a constitutive aspect of being systematic enough to generate insights. For Paris, however, blindness results from the projection or distortion entailed in the natural tendency to identify with and approve discourses that conform to one's own defensive strategies. A really deconstructive reading would have to be allocentrically conceived, and the possibility of this cannot be taken for granted. Moreover, Paris's readings leave the story intact and affirm its readability, whereas the deconstructionists' readings disseminate the story and assert its "unreadability."[46]

Moreover, Paris's method is reassuring, whereas deconstructionism, with its roots in the darker Freudian interpretive frame, is decidedly not. De Man follows Nietzsche's argument that "the human subject as a privileged viewpoint is a mere metaphor by means of which man protects himself from his insignificance by forcing his own interpretation of the world upon the entire universe, substituting a human-centered set of meanings that is reassuring to his vanity for a set of meanings that reduces him to being a mere transitory accident in the cosmic order."[47] Although "this metaphoric substitution is aberrant," "no human self could come into being without this error." Paris believes that the self not only exists, but can be actualized by asserting its peculiar identity. In addition, the encompassing nature of Third Force analysis has the reassuring corollary that human nature is essentially constant unto itself, so that particular insights may always imply general ones—which would mean that, given appropriate conditions, "allocentric" perception could always result from "autocentric" (just the reverse of what deconstructionists would assume). Paris accordingly avers that "manners change and values are debatable, but human needs and conflicts remain much the same, and mimetic truth endures" (*JA*, p. 21). All characters, even bizarre ones like Heathcliff, can "show us some very real potentialities of our own personalities" (*HEA*, p. 116). That the understanding of human nature from skillfully drawn exemplars is the most cogent motive for literature is an insight we repeatedly encounter in the theory and practice of literary criticism. But it is important to appreciate the specific tactics Third Force critics deploy in order to attain this insight.

Somewhat disturbingly, the continuity of human nature entails not a unity, but a diversity of interpretive perspectives and the questionability of one "true" one for rating the others. This prospect may not be easy to live with, though we must do so if we want realism, or indeed, any worthwhile literature. As Paris is well aware, many participants in literary communication are not likely to welcome an endless pluralism that calls in question their own interpretative results. But Paris's account of that pluralism is additionally unsettling because it seems unflattering to authors of literature, regarding whom our culture has accumulated an imposing mythology of adulation. A suggestion that authors are "neurotic" is likely to be taken as sacrilege. "We are disturbed by a critical perspective which frustrates" the "craving to see our great authors" as "sages" or "god-like figures" (*PAF*, p. 280). When an author's "attitudes, judgments, and world views are seen as expressions" of a "defense system," "they lose weight as truths about the human condition and as guides to life" (*PAF*, p. 286).

In recompense, Paris maintains that the mythologizing of authors in fact leads us to *underestimate* their real achievement. If we merely "rationalize their inconsistencies," we tend "to remain unaware of the richness of their personalities" (*PAF,* p. 280). Moreover, "if we judge them as authorities, we are likely to make much of the fact that they so often seem to be wrong," and to "condemn them as false prophets." For instance, Thackeray's silly generalization about women might be adduced as evidence of his poor artistry. But no such condemnation need be implied if we see the author as a "dramatized consciousness whose values can be as subjective and confused" as those of an "ordinary" person (*PAF,* p. 25). As a real person struggling to understand the world, an author can easily offer an "interpretation" that appears "confused, too simple, or just plain wrong" (*PAF,* p. 276). It should not be surprising to find realistic literature displaying a "genius in characterization despite" "deficiencies in analysis" (*INT,* p. 16). On the contrary, it is the "great realist" who "will, without an instant's hesitation, set aside" "his most cherished prejudices or even his most sacred convictions" and "describe what he really sees."[48] Only "the second-raters," Lukács goes on, "nearly always succeed in bringing their own Weltanschauung into harmony with reality." One readily recalls the dreary moralizing that makes much of Victorian literature seem so unpalatable to us.

The diversity of perspective and the vulnerability of single interpretations is not, I feel sure, limited to realistic literature. All the great literature I can think of is not a harmonious demonstration of one single-minded, incontestable philosophy of life. The author might consciously set out to give such a demonstration, as may have been the case with *Paradise Lost* or *The Prelude;* but the result is usually that the work breaks free and subverts or qualifies what it was intended to prove and affirm. Satan's outlook seems more humanly appropriate than God's; Wordsworth's poet must continually distrust the faculties of his own inventive power in confrontation with nature; and so on. More often, the author accepts the diversity, at least implicitly, and delivers the great work as a problem for which the presented solution, if one is openly offered, is obviously not the only one, and perhaps not even a very satisfying one. Chaucer's recantation at the end of the *Canterbury Tales* hardly unifies or supplants the diversities of perspective in the rest of the work. It is difficult to read a plain and valid lesson from *Romeo and Juliet, King Lear, Hamlet,* or *Macbeth,* even though each play ends with the restoration of a comparatively positive order. The apparent happy endings of the comedies are also typically unsatisfying when we try to imagine the future of such characters as we have encountered in *The Tempest, All's Well That Ends Well, Much Ado about Nothing,* or *The Taming of the Shrew.* Their selfish, manipulative nature is not likely to be permanently revoked by a flurry of forgivings and marryings. Even fantastic literature falls down if it announces itself as a parable for a unitary ideology. Compare for instance how impressively *Alice in Wonderland* succeeds where *Sylvie and Bruno* fails: the latter moralizes in ways that fatally intrude upon the integrity of the work.

If this conjecture is correct, then a disparity between representation and interpretation may be related only in complex ways to the opposition between "mimetic" versus "mythic." Paris essentially accepts this opposition drawn by Northrop Frye, for whom mimesis is commonsensically related to "plausible content" (*PAF*, p. 8). If, as Frye asserts, "the realistic writer soon finds that the requirements of literary form and plausible content always fight against each other,"[49] we should assume along with Paris that "form derives from generic conventions and ultimately from mythic patterns, which are inherently unrealistic; realistic content obeys the laws of probability, of cause and effect, and belongs to a different universe of discourse" (*PAF*, p. 8). My own argument would be that myth reconciles representation with interpretation by relaxing the audience's disposition to apply plausibility as a standard of valuation. However, this transaction may not be a conscious or deliberate one. In fact, adherence to one version of reality has a mythical aspect of its own.

Myths are above all culturally shared explanations that function as origins. The culture cannot reach beyond them without setting off a chain of interrogations which, if relentlessly pursued, would call for a large-scale reorganization of the culture's ideology. Hence, myths are not normally questioned, but are simply placed at the most remote beginnings of things, where their authority can be appropriated for a multitude of purposes, further ensuring their centrality and perpetuation. In this way, myths can act as a super-mimesis, a summation of all changing realities. That is, myth is what is believed on a very deep level, whereas mimesis (in the usual sense) is what is believed on the surface level of the fairly explicit representation of people and incidents. If we situate myth and mimesis on the same level, then their opposition can only come into view from another cultural perspective, a process that may appear as insight or as blindness, depending on whose interests are at stake. The authorial interpretations that later seem "antiquated" or "plain wrong," such as generalized attacks upon women,[50] may well have been invisible to the culture whose myths encouraged them. The author may not have seen them as interpretations at all, but as well-known facts that came to mind in view of the events in the novel.

Consider for a moment the well-known problem of ending a literary work. On the one hand, we could argue that life is an open-ended enterprise, so that we enter belatedly or exit prematurely from any story at arbitrary points. But this consequence conflicts with the author's implied claim that the facts of the story were selected in terms of their human significance, and not in terms of random or arbitrary choice. Hence, a long-standing literary convention demanded narrative structures with prominent closures. In consequence, the myth of the closed ending has become so pervasive we do not see it as arbitrary except when we can detach ourselves from the story enough to interrogate its origins. Paris's work offers a framework for one kind of interrogation, such that he can view the well-known "happy ending" as "an aesthetically pleasing resolution" in which "plausibility and realistic detail are sacrificed" (*PAF*, p. 277). In exchange, "endings which try to be faithful to the mimetic impulse by suggesting open-endedness do not satisfy our aesthetic demand for completion." .Yet the "mimetic" awareness being applied here is a product of not accepting the closed-ending myth as a privileged origin (and thus as mimetic on a deeper level). Another culture might favor a myth of open-endedness that would effectively prevent its readers from viewing the closed ending as a realistic representation, e.g., of the end of reading or the transitoriness of all things. But our own cultural tradition still favors the closed-ending myth with its conspicuous submyths, such as living happily ever after (thanks to wealth or marriage), being reunited in heaven, or (on the tragic side) being struck down by envious gods or fates that can endure no truly great mortals.

All the same, contemporary trends in literary fiction toward open-endedness, detached characters, and noninterpretive representation are probably symptoms of a decline among our more traditional myths. Some authors protect the old myths, or avoid a confrontation with them, by relying on irony, "the means by which the implied author negates what he has affirmed and protects himself from the consequences of commitment" (*PAF*, p. 87). Literature can only gradually engender new myths; more often, it borrows from them on a deep level and intertwines them with mimetic appropriations on a surface level. The same element, such as the happy ending, may seem mythical, mimetic, or purely formal, depending on the awareness we bring to bear on it. The author's necessity to close the text is perfectly real and there is nothing peculiarly literary about an optimistic ending. The latter is found even in much scientific and technical writing.[51] Readers must be solicited, and like to feel that they have gained something positive when they are finished. Paris's own works are a case in point; witness his optimistic chapter endings: "mimetic truth endures" (*JA*, p. 21); "Jane Austen seems to be emerging from embeddedness and embracing life" (*JA*, p. 201); the individual must have "'a beginning wish for his real self and a beginning wish for inner salvation'" (*PAF*, p. 70); "no other technique could have produced the same brilliance in social satire and comedy" (*PAF*, p. 132); "this book" "must suggest the potency of Third Force psychology and the promise which it holds" (*PAF*, p. 290). Yet he was certainly not intending to be unrealistic; the more so as this optimism has to be wrested from many pessimistic insights.[52] It would appear that the happy ending is neutral regarding one's mimetic or realistic intents. Yet the standard literary closed-ending is a case where the demands of form and myth happen to coincide. Their alliance seems powerful and attractive to their own culture, and may be used by a different or later culture to explain literary conventions.[53]

Essentially, literature as an institution tends to blur or suspend such categories as mimesis versus myth, realism versus nonrealism, or fact versus fiction, even though each individual work invites readers to classify it in terms of what they believe and understand about the world. These categories reflect the principles whereby creative decisions are made with respect to certain teleologies rather than others. Even palpable myths and fantasies by no means abolish "the laws of probability, of cause and effect"; they only invest them in different ways, such as allowing the pursuit of motives with unbelievable means. A disparity emerges in the hindsight of our later culture, in which theological and magical explanations are officially rejected in favor of physical, social, and psychological explanations. Yet this disparity is in part a gesture of decorum toward the teleological myths we accept but do not designate as such, just as we forget that truth depends on the perspective that sees it.[54] The suspending of disbelief depends on what is believed and on what motives are served by doing or not doing so.[55] Readers appreciate the "mimetic achievement" Paris finds in great realistic literature (and I find in all great literature) by entertaining the author's invented facts in order to attain a higher-order truth about the human condition. Paris's argument is that this attainment is not an action the author can be expected to foreclose for us with interpretive intrusions. The author can no longer control or prescribe what the facts he or she has invented must mean for everyone else. Still, the temptation to try is understandable, since the author wants readers to consider these facts significant.

The historic shifting of myths bears on fiction especially because "the novel came into being in a world in which men were losing their belief in the supernatural and institutional basis of life" (*PAF*, p. 6). Some of the earliest great novelists, such as Rabelais and Cervantes, played thematically on the decline of older mythologies, though not without some nostalgia. Yet the fact that realism could eventually step into the functional gap left by this decline should give us pause in assuming that a genuine reversal had occurred. Instead, the myths may have merely been forced underground because their structure seemed inadequate for literary treatment of an increasingly complex and diverse society and readership. These readers could be better served with what Frye termed the "low mimetic mode in which 'the hero is one of us' and we demand from the author 'the same canons of probability that we find in our own experience.' "[56] Still, the inclination of authors to intrude with privileged interpretations may be sign of continuing nostalgia for some myths that might yet act as authoritative origins—darwinism, evangelism, utilitarianism, the work ethic, and so forth.

The novel put the author into a new version of an old dilemma. The novel was not usually staged or presented orally as the older narrative genres had been; the medium of print became indispensable. The weakening of the performative aspect encouraged a strengthening of the interpretive one. The novel needed a narrator who had somehow come to know the "facts" being narrated. The history of the novel is in part the chronicle of devices adopted to account for this knowledge without openly admitting it had been expressly invented. Such devices were predictably mythologizing and would not bear determined interrogation, since the author kept telling more than he or she could possibly have found out from external sources alone. The author might appear as an actual character in the novel, either as narrator or as someone to whom the narrator told the story. Or the author might pretend to be editing someone else's manuscript, or to be reproducing the letters or diaries the characters wrote. Whether or not the novel was intended to seem realistic, the author was able to delegate (or pretend to delegate) to somebody else the responsibility for having produced the facts. Yet the author still retained the function of convincing readers why these particular facts were worth narrating or reading, and the pressure for interpretation readily followed. The author might simply claim the facts were extraordinary, entertaining, or amusing, borrowing a typical strategy of the older tellers of tales and myths. But as the novel reached steadily larger segments of society, a justification in terms of the prevailing ideology became more commonplace. Since the ideology precedes the novel, yet cannot determine or exhaust it if the novel is to be any good, the fit is often rather uneasy, if we assume that literature is in principle a negotiation of possible realities. The tendency to try telling us what the "facts mean" is an additional step for which the author may not be well qualified, and which can make the novel seem dated or quaint to a later age that still grants the author's basic right to invent facts.

Paris's case now is that "a psychological point of view" is a good tool to help account for the "disparity between interpretation and representation" (*INT*, p. 15) that arose from such historical conditions as these. His method offers an alternative to the more conventional view in literary studies that this disparity is just an incidental weakness of particular authors or works, rather than a constitutive dilemma of realistic literature—and, less obviously, of all literature. Instead of excusing the disparity or rationalizing it away as a product of our own faulty vision, Paris wants to account for it in a systematic way. At some moments, he does not seem to have fully accepted his own premise, in that he is still inclined to equate the signs of the disparity with "aesthetic flaws" (*PAF*, p. 21). This inclination seems tied to a classical view of aesthetic harmony that underestimates the dynamics of imposing unity against resistance. But at other moments, he acknowledges those dynamics and lauds the "marvelously rich portrayal of a particular kind of consciousness making ethical responses to a variety of human situations" (*PAF*, p. 24). This "dramatized consciousness" might be an exercise of allocentric perception transcending the author's more autocentric interpretations.

On another level, to be sure, psychology threatens to claim the status of a privileged system of interpretation. Thus, it must be applied with caution in order not to dismantle or explain away the literary work by imposing the same limitations some authors unsuccessfully attempt with their interpretive intrusions. "The psychologist enables us to grasp certain configurations of experience analytically, categorically, and (if we accept his conceptions of health and neurosis) normatively" (*PAF*, p. 26). However, the psychology Paris applies does not offer correct interpretations we are supposed to insert into the literary text in place of the author's shaky ones; it only hopes to show how the latter's interpretations may have been motivated in much the same way that human actions of all sorts are motivated. Whereas a Freudian interpretation becomes a new story in place of the author's, a Third Force interpretation enters the old story at certain points with explanations that not only leave the story intact, but demonstrate that it is more motivated and coherent than we may have imagined. In consequence, the author can appear more skillful than he or she was judged by conventional criticism. Just where a traditional critic might complain that Heathcliff is "an unsatisfactory composite," or that Becky Sharp is an "unremittingly evil monster," or that Maggie Tulliver is "immature" (*HEA*, p. 101; *PAF*, pp. 83, 165), Paris can show that these characters are significant mimetic achievements of substantial depth and power.

Paris's work is likely to encounter stubborn resistance not because it destroys literary values (this is a crude or willful misreading), but because it relocates and restates them according to norms with which academic criticism is not familiar. As I outlined before, traditional criticism presents a harmonious end product as the correct reading of the work, so that remaining disparate elements have to be disqualified as literary mistakes. The criteria of harmony usually enlisted are rather formal, such as symmetries, balances, reversals, evenness of style, correspondence of tropes, and so on. Third Force criticism also presents a harmonious end product, but one in which disparate elements are read as emblems of mimetic insight. Criteria of harmony are now psychological, grouped under the headings of personality, strategy, defense, and so on. To allow "that a novel's weaknesses and strengths are often complementary, and that it may be impossible to realize all the values of fiction simultaneously" (*PAF*, p. 132) is to allow that the traditional critic's insistence on a rather static formal unity may be falling far short of the work's dynamic unity, which cannot be explicated with the aid of formalizing categories alone.

Thus, Paris's demonstrations of the literary skills of authors may not be reassuring to more traditional critics. He surmises that "Shakespeare's inner conflicts have much to do" "with the richness and ambiguity of his greatest art" (*LBC*, p. 85). The "illumination" that "art supplies" is not "wisdom," but a "phenomenological knowledge of reality," "an immediate knowledge of how the world is experienced by the individual consciousness and an understanding of inner life in its own terms" (*PAF*, p. 23). Thus, "mimetic characters" have "universality and perpetual relevance" and are "endowed with the human interest which real people always have" (*PAF*, p. 281). Academic critics are being asked to learn new values and to own that they were not fully clear about why they really liked literature all along. The huge investment in biographical and adulative criticism seems misplaced when the greatness and insight of the work are systematically uncoupled from a vision of the author as a universal sage and interpreter. It no longer seems productive to "preserve the glory of the author by demonstrating the perfection of his creation"; or to "attribute" to authors a "higher degree of integration," "greater wisdom, and a more coherent set of values than other people have" (*INT*, p. 17). Such an attribution is not entailed in asserting the greatness of the works, and may in fact block an adequate perception of the author as a human being.

All this is still not as disturbing as the prospect that the method works on critics just as well as on authors or characters. The principle of "projection," i.e., "choosing those whose personalities and value systems are parallel to one's own" (*HM*, p. 35), puts the whole issue of critical values in a new light. It would not be hard to rewrite Paris's statements about authors as if he were talking about critics. For instance, his method might explore a critic's "recurring preoccupations" and "the personal element in his fantasies."[57] The critic would "tend to glorify characters whose strategies are similar to his own and to criticize those who embody his repressed solutions."[58] The critic's "rhetoric will affirm the values, attitudes, and traits of character that are demanded by his dominant solution."[59] And so on. Anyone who doubts the aptness of such suppositions might consult the uninhibitedly self-indulgent criticism that has been showered on a work like Rilke's *Duino Elegies.*[60]

For the time being, Paris has discreetly kept the lid on this issue by using himself as the test case. In his early criticism, George Eliot's "self-effacing solution" was given a "full, accurate, and sympathetic exposition" (*LBC*, p. 88). But he failed to see the "destructiveness of the solutions at which her characters arrive" (*LBC*, p. 89). Only later, when he began "trying to exorcise the self-effacing trends" that "get in the way of [his] self-actualization" could he recognize how he failed to "distinguish between her *representation* of a character, which is usually complex, accurate, and enduring, and her *interpretation*, which is often misleading, over-simple, and confused" (*LBC*, pp. 90, 89). His "psychological evolution" reached the point where his evaluation of literary works was reversed. Something similar occurred when he was first "attracted" to the novels of Thomas Hardy and later "disenchanted" by them (*HAR*, p. 203). But these personal stories too have happy endings, because, thanks to Paris's new insights, these novelists' lack of "coherent moral vision" no longer clouds his appreciation of their "great genius in the observation and portrayal of human experience" (*HAR*, pp. 209, 203).

The negative converse of such an evolution might be the case where readers strive to minimize or even eliminate any detachment from the author's interpretative framework. Such immediate influence might represent a deliberate lowering of defenses against the author, though the whole transaction might be a defense against nonliterary experiences. People can and do modify their personalities by imitating the traits of characters they encounter in literature. This tendency might be self-effacing or aggressive, that is, using influence to deemphasize or aggrandize one's own personality; but it might merely result from a hope for variety and enrichment. The prospect here would be that literature or art itself can be an *instigator* of someone's tendency to prefer certain kinds of strategies or defenses. This prospect would reintroduce the authorial responsibility for cogent interpretation that Paris disputed against Horney and Booth. Or, we might resolve the issue by assuming that such a response is not a genuinely literary one, because the work's alternative world is naively introjected in place of the reader's previous one.

A fair amount of my own erratic and bizarre activity in my student days was so directly inspired by literary and artistic sources that it in some sense functioned as quotation, though my contemporaries seldom recognized this. No doubt I hoped that art could provide standards for meaningful action in the alienating scenes of Paris and Berlin at the end of the 1960s. Since, like many students of literature, I worked my way from the classics to the moderns, my conduct and discourse became increasingly less harmonious and attained alarming allegorical propensities when I got to the Expressionists, Surrealists, and Absurdists. The ruinous, nearly suicidal consequences (a mimetic narration of which would seem utterly fantastic) finally forced me to acknowledge the failure of this solution and the neurotic image it was conveying to the people I met, most of whom couldn't recognize the sources in question anyway.

Even so, literary influences remained immanent, whether or not I consciously resisted them. My master's thesis obliged me to read the *Fleurs du mal* over and over, since I had selected the problems of its translation by Stefan George as my topic—a seemingly safe philological inquiry. Yet rereading the poems kept drawing me into Baudelaire's dark world view, his neurotic patterns of repression and release, dejection and exaltation, detachment and engagement, and so on. Later, my doctoral dissertation obliged me to keep reading the *Duino Elegies* by Rilke, another complex and self-conscious neurotic like Baudelaire. This time, I was acting as the translator in order to find out what criteria were involved in such a transaction.[61] The more I read the *Elegies,* the less appealing they seemed as philosophy. I began to suspect that I—and most of their readers—had wrongly revered them as messianic affirmations of existence, though they are more basically self-destructive evasions. Nonetheless, I still had to admit their ideology in order to understand their coherence. The main ideas needed to hold them together thematically and aesthetically are ones I did and do consider patently foolish and destructive: that pain and suffering should be valued over joy; that dying young is a great privilege; that love works best with no recipient; and so on. Since I was acting as a translator with a theoretical focus on what I was doing, I could apply these ideas consciously, and thereby resist their influence. Yet most readers probably accept them unconsciously and thus uncritically. I came to resent Rilke's imposition and the rhetorical ornamentation and circuitousness that disguised it.[62]

The implication might be—though neither Paris nor I would want to go on record as partisans for the claim—that literary authors have a responsibility for the mental health of society, even though they may be neurotic themselves. This conclusion would lend an ominous sense to such statements as "fiction helps us to know what the psychologist is talking about" (*PAF,* p. 27). The demand for a "moral" art, stretching back to Plato or Dr. Johnson, would reappear in psychotherapeutic guise at a time when none of us really believes it could be openly enforced, even in the barely conceivable event that all critics agreed to try. Paris and Horney seem to rest their hopes on the "allocentric" perception that literature can inspire, and on the "self-actualizing" potential that such perception encourages. As we have seen, however, this resolution may require us to expressly discount the authors' explicit interpretations. Paris wants to comfort us by remarking that if "the psychological theories available to them were inadequate to their insights, it was inevitable that their interpretations would be inferior to their representations" (*PAF,* p. 13).[63] But this statement could be misread as an injunction for authors to get a better theory, whereas much of Paris's argument has been against the feasibility of delivering any definitive interpretation of human experience. Or, if "their value judgments were bound to be influenced by their own neuroses" (*PAF,* p. 13), we might call for nonneurotic artists with trustworthy values. But as Paris remarks, the traditional search for eternally valid value systems in literary works has transformed artists from real human beings into nonhuman idols.

My own conclusion would be that psychotherapy applied as criticism will naturally uncover a complex projection of healthy and unhealthy tendencies among the participants. The representation of a neurotic tendency may lead either to imitation (as happened to me with Baudelaire) or to conscious reflection and rejection (as happened to me with Rilke). Seeing the tendency acted out in literature might spare many readers the duress of trying it out in real life. This positive gain, I should think, would be favored by just such analytic methods as Paris advocates. They sharpen our allocentric perception of tendencies we should not take at face value or at the author's own estimation. The therapeutic obligation I sketched for literature might be delegated instead to an allocentric criticism that helps the general reader avoid an exaggerated commitment to a single interpretation.

But this ambitious project may not be urgent, because literature is what it is—and not psychology, philosophy, theology, or criticism,—in order to tell us that human experience always runs beyond interpretation, yet will always seem to need it. To dethrone the authors' own interpretations is a logical consequence of this conclusion, the more so as the Third Force critic does not just throw them out, but suggests motives why they came out as they did and why we might not agree with them. The assertion that this method is "less reductive" than others (*PAF,* p. 26; *INT,* p. 20) can be construed in the sense that the critic explains without explaining away, and that criticism can never conclude because readers and critics have their own personalities. The theory's categories are broad and flexible, but do not lead to stereotyping an author or character if they are applied not "mechanically," but "with empathy and concern for the peculiarities of his or her own situation" (*INT,* p. 20). At the end of the analysis, we should see "highly individualized human beings, with different histories, problems, inner lives, and human qualities" (*PAF,* pp. 285)—diversity in unity, the aesthetic result of this method. Then, we can "go back to the work" for the "immediate experience" no criticism can "replace," but only "enrich."

NOTES

1. Cf. Roy Freedle, ed., *Discourse Production and Comprehension* (Norwood, N.J.: Ablex, 1977); Roy Freedle, ed., *New Directions in Discourse Processing* (Norwood, N.J.: Ablex, 1979);

Robert de Beaugrande, *Text, Discourse, and Process* (Norwood, N.J.: Ablex, 1980); Robert de Beaugrande, "Design Criteria for Process Models of Reading," *Reading Research Quarterly* 16 (1980–81): 261–315; Robert de Beaugrande, *Text Production* (Norwood, N.J.: Ablex, 1984); August Flammer and Walter Kintsch, eds., *Discourse Processing* (Amsterdam: North Holland, 1982); Walter Kintsch and Jean-François le Ny, eds., *Language and Comprehension* (Amsterdam: North Holland, 1982); Teun Adrianus van Dijk and Walter Kintsch, *Strategies of Discourse Comprehension* (New York: Academic Press, 1983).

2. I do not consider here the use of behaviorist psychology as therapy. There too, its methods were inspired by the metaphor of the lower animal as the model for the human being, so that symbolic representations were entirely ignored. See de Beaugrande, *Text Production* and Robert de Beaugrande, "Freudian Psychoanalysis and Information Processing: Notes on a Future Synthesis," *Psychoanalysis and Contemporary Thought* 7, no. 2 (1984): 147–94, for discussion and references.

3. Cf. de Beaugrande, "Freudian Psychoanalysis."

4. E.g., Norman N. Holland, *The Dynamics of Literary Response* (New York: Oxford University Press, 1968).

5. Deconstructionism is one trend much given to the darker Freudian rhetoric. For example, Paul de Man avers: "copulation or murder are the most effective emblems for the moment of literal significance that is part of any system of tropes"; and "writing always includes the moment of dispossession in favor of the arbitrary power play of the signifier and from the point of view of the subject, this can only be experienced as a dismemberment, a beheading or a castration." Paul de Man, *Allegories of Reading* (New Haven: Yale University Press, 1979), pp. 182, 296.

6. Paris uses this case to illustrate that in Freudian analysis, "we are no longer constrained by the text" (Introduction, this volume, p. 14). His own reading of the play is offered in "Brutus, Cassius, and Caesar: An Interdestructive Triangle," to appear in *The Psychoanalytic Study of Literature.*

7. The key to quotations from the works of Bernard Paris is: *HAR:* "Experiences of Thomas Hardy," in Richard Levine, ed., *The Victorian Experience* (Athens: Ohio University Press, 1976), pp. 203–37; *HEA:* "'Hush, hush! He's a human being!': A Psychological Approach to Heathcliff," *Women and Literature,* n.s., 2 (1982): 101–17; *HM:* "Horney, Maslow, and the Third Force," this volume; *INT:* Introduction, this volume; *JA: Character and Conflict in Jane Austen's Novels* (Detroit: Wayne State University Press, 1978); *LBC:* "Third Force Psychology and the Study of Literature, Biography, Criticism, and Culture," this volume; and *PAF: A Psychological Approach to Fiction* (Bloomington: Indiana University Press, 1974). The source of a quotation is omitted if it is identical with that of the immediately preceding quotation.

8. Karen Horney, *Neurosis and Human Growth* (New York: Norton, 1950), p. 15.

9. Ernst Schachtel, *Metamorphosis* (New York: Basic Books, 1959), p. 9; cf. *HM,* p. 42.

10. Paris does not want to associate this "intrinsic conscience" with the "superego" (*HM,* p. 37), presumably because the former animates, whereas the latter restrains. Only as guides with higher values could they be said to be parallel.

11. Schachtel, *Metamorphosis,* p. 273; cf. *HM,* p. 40.

12. Schachtel, *Metamorphosis,* p. 179; Abraham Maslow, *Motivation and Personality* (New York: Harper and Row, 1954), p. 41; cf. *HM,* pp. 40–41.

13. The prospect seems to be to reincorporate behavioral psychology at the risk of repeating the same reductive error from human to animal. The illegitimacy of such a step is indicated when Maslow says that "basic needs" "are not like the instincts of animals" (*PAF,* p. 31).

14. Horney, *Neurosis,* p. 14.

15. Ibid., p. 104; cf. *HM,* p. 53.

16. Intellectualizing could also be a means for disguising one's problems, e.g., when people "confuse neurotic anxiety with existential Angst and neurotic despair with a philosophic sense of the absurdity of human existence" (*HM,* p. 32).

17. Horney, *Neurosis,* p. 107; cf. *HM,* p. 57.

18. Maslow, *Motivation,* p. 70.

19. Ibid., pp. 212–13.

20. Carl Rogers, *On Becoming a Person* (Boston: Houghton Mifflin, 1961), p. 27.

21. Schachtel, *Metamorphosis,* pp. 177, 193.

22. Robert de Beaugrande, "Toward a General Theory of Creativity," *Poetics* 8 (1979): 269–306; Robert de Beaugrande, "Schemas for Literary Communication" (Paper delivered at the Hungarian-American Conference on the Perception of Social Interaction in Literature, Budapest, 1983); de Beaugrande, "Freudian Psychoanalysis;" Robert de Beaugrande, *Critical Discourse: A Survey of Literary Theory,* in preparation.

23. Paris uses the term "logic" here to cover the pattern and themes of the work, rather than the more or less logical (consistent, rational) acts of characters.

24. Horney, *Neurosis,* pp. 330–31; *PAF,* p. 128.

25. Karen Horney, *Our Inner Conflicts* (New York: Norton, 1945), p. 74.

26. Robert Scholes and Robert Kellogg, *The Nature of Narrative* (New York: Oxford, 1966).

27. E. M. Forster, *Aspects of the Novel* (New York: Harcourt, Brace and World, 1927).

28. Robert de Beaugrande and Benjamin Colby, "Narrative Models of Action and Interaction," *Cognitive Science* 3 (1979): 43–66.

29. W. J. Harvey, *Character and the Novel* (Ithaca: Cornell University Press, 1965), p. 192; *PAF,* p. 2.

30. Ibid., p. 200. A similar charge is leveled in Paris's Shakespeare book *Bargains With Fate: A Psychological Approach to Shakespeare* (in preparation) against formalism, structuralism, and deconstructionism, which I think is not quite fair. I would rather say that these movements encouraged different treatments of character from Paris's. The first two worked in terms of narrative structures (cf., for example, Boris Tomaševskij, *Teorija literatury* [Moscow: Gos. Izdatel'stvo, 1925]; Vladimir Propp, *Morfologia skazki* [Leningrad: Akademia, 1928]; Victor Šklovskij, *O teorija prozy* [Moscow: Federatsia, 1929]; Claude Lévi-Strauss, "La structure et la forme," *Cahiers de l'Institut de Science Economique Appliquée* 99 [1960]: 3–36); and it can be readily shown that these structures presuppose and contain characters (Robert de Beaugrande, "The Story of Grammars and the Grammar of Stories," *Journal of Pragmatics* 6 [1982]: 383–422).

31. Ernst Cassirer, *An Essay on Man* (New York: Anchor, 1953), p. 181; *PAF,* p. 71.

32. Gottfried Leibnitz, *Lehrsätze über die Monadologie* (Jena: Myers, 1720).

33. Georg Hegel, *Ästhetik* (Berlin: Duncker and Humblot, 1835).

34. Gustav Fechner, *Vorschule der Ästhetik* (Leipzig: Breitkopf and Härtel, 1876).

35. Cf. Max Bense, *Theorie der Texte* (Cologne: Kiepenheuer and Witsch, 1962); Rul Gunzenhäuser, *Ästhetisches Mass und ästhetische Information* (Quickborn: Schnelle, 1962); Siegfried J. Schmidt, *Ästhetizität* (Munich: Bayrischer Schulbuchverlag, 1971).

36. Harvey, *Character,* p. 188.

37. Cf. Erich Auerbach, *Mimesis: The Representation of Reality in Western Literature* (New York: Anchor, 1957).

38. Ibid., p. 391; cf. *PAF,* p. 7.

39. Cf. Auerbach, *Mimesis,* p. 27.

40. Ibid., pp. 433–34; cf. *PAF,* p. 6.

41. Wayne Booth, *The Rhetoric of Fiction* (Chicago: University of Chicago Press, 1961), p. 112; cf. *PAF,* p. 17.

42. Booth, *Rhetoric,* p. 140.

43. The term "understanding" is being given a special meaning here, i.e., "conceptual" as opposed to "intuitive" understanding (cf. *HEA,* p. 102). To be sure people are not really concepts that mean rather than act.

44. The deconstructionists would not, for instance, allow for mimetic truth or psychological continuity in literary language, no matter what anyone's motives might be. Their notion of "defense" is not conceived in terms of a balance of strategies, but emphasizes just one at a time, e.g. aggressive-vindictive (Harold Bloom, *A Map of Misreading* [New York: Oxford, 1975]), detached (de Man, *Allegories of Reading*), and so on. Also, deconstructionist aesthetics are neither Kantian (pleasure without interest) nor Hegelian (unity in diversity); they enjoy subverting unification.

45. Paul de Man, *Blindness and Insight* (Minneapolis: University of Minnesota Press, 1971).

46. Cf. de Man, *Allegories of Reading.*

47. Ibid., p. 111.

48. Georg Lukács, *Studies in European Realism* (New York: Grosset and Dunlap, 1964), p. 11.

49. Northrop Frye, "Myth, Fiction, and Displacement," in *Fables of Identity* (New York: Harcourt Brace & World, 1963), p. 36.

50. It was not just uneducated or unreflective people who held such views, but some of the most prominent thinkers of the day: "difficult learning or painstaking thought, even if a woman should excel in them, will destroy the good features belonging to her sex" (Kant); "women" "are not made" "for higher science and philosophy" (Hegel); "the mere sight of the female shape shows that the woman is not intended for major intellectual work" (Schopenhauer) (quoted in Ariane Barth, "Mann oder Frau—wählt, was ihr wollt," *Spiegel* 38, no. 9 (1984): 192–206.

51. De Beaugrande, *Text Production*, pp. 302ff., 312–13.

52. Whence the mixed endings we also find in Paris's works, such as: "George Eliot's experiments in life do present enduring truths, but they are not the truths for which she was searching" (*PAF*, p. 189).

53. A case in point is the myth of revenge that offered a radical closed-ending for Elizabethan tragedies, namely, via the deaths of all the main characters. Shakespeare tried to revise this revenge myth, but did not arrive at a realistically coherent, workable alternative, as Paris notes (*LBC*, pp. 84–85).

54. Einstein himself could never resolve the conflict between quantum theory and his own personal teleology of the universe (John Gliedman, "Einstein Against the Odds: The Great Quantum Debate," *Science Digest* 91, no. 6 [1983]: 74–80, 109). Recent studies indicate that a large portion of our society still holds a pre-Newtonian mechanics (Michael McCloskey, "Cartoon Physics," *Psychology Today* 18, no. 4 [1984]: 52–58), to say nothing of a pre-Einsteinian one.

55. The *amount* of belief suspended does not determine the effort of reading, whence the use of fantastic stories in children's readers. Effort depends rather on the proportion between what has to be done and what will be gained from doing it (de Beaugrande, "Creativity").

56. Northrop Frye, *Anatomy of Criticism* (Princeton: Princeton University Press, 1957), pp. 33–34; *JA*, p. 14.

57. Cf. *LBC*, p. 84.

58. Cf. *LBC*, p. 84; *JA*, p. 20.

59. Cf. *LBC*, p. 84.

60. Cf. surveys in Jacob Steiner, *Rilkes Duineser Elegien* (Stockholm: Almqvist and Wiksell, 1962); Robert de Beaugrande, *Factors in a Theory of Poetic Translating* (Amsterdam: Rodopi, 1978).

61. De Beaugrande, *Poetic Translating.*

62. Typically enough, my statements to this effect were construed by my colleagues as evidence that I had *not* understood the work. As de Man *(Allegories of Reading)* points out, Rilke has been the subject of a vast adulative mythology that nearly always proceeds from a distortion of what he said.

63. An intriguing issue is whether Renaissance psychology could be a framework for interpreting literary works of the period. For instance, if an author set about to dramatize the theory of the four temperaments or humours, as Ben Jonson did, can the characters still be assigned a motivational analysis? Paris thinks not and would class them as "illustrative" characters in the sense of Scholes and Kellogg. But for me, this view would suggest that the plays are devoid of human interest, which is how I do tend to respond to them.

Third Force Psychological Theory and Its Applications: A Selective Bibliography

THEORY

"Abraham H. Maslow: A Bibliography." *Journal of Humanistic Psychology* 10, no. 2 (Fall 1970): 98–110. This journal, founded by Maslow, contains many essays relevant to Third Force theories.

Allport, Gordon Willard. *Becoming: Basic Considerations for a Psychology of Personality.* New Haven: Yale University Press, 1955.

Angyal, Andras. "Aesthetic Experiences." *Journal of Humanistic Psychology* 2, no. 2 (Fall 1962): 123–25.

———. *Neurosis and Treatment: A Holistic Theory.* Edited by E. Hanfmann and R. M. Jones. New York: John Wiley, 1965.

Ansbacher, Heinz L. "Alfred Adler and Humanistic Psychology." *Journal of Humanistic Psychology* 11, no. 1 (Spring 1971): 53–63.

Arieti, Silvano. *The Intrapsychic Self: Feeling, Cognition, and Creativity in Health and Mental Illness.* New York: Basic Books, 1967.

Aronoff, Joel. *Psychological Needs and Cultural Systems: A Case Study.* Princeton: Van Nostrand, 1967.

Brés, Yvon. *Freud et la Psychanalyse Américaine Karen Horney.* Paris: J. Vrin, 1970.

Bugental, J. F. T. "The Third Force in Psychology." *Journal of Humanistic Psychology* 4, no. 1 (Spring 1964): 19–26.

Cherry, Rona, and Laurence Cherry. "The Horney Heresy." *New York Times Magazine,* 26 August 1973.

Coles, Robert. "Karen Horney's Flight from Orthodoxy." In *Women and Analysis,* edited by Jean Strouse, pp. 216–21. New York: Dell, 1975.

Daniels, Marvin. "Pathological Vindictiveness and the Vindictive Character." *Psychoanalytic Review* 56 (1969): 169–96.

Dobrenkov, V. I. *Neo-Freudians in Search of "Truth."* Translated by Katharine Judelson. Moscow: Progress Publishers, 1976.

Evans, Richard I. *Dialogue with Erich Fromm.* New York: Harper and Row, 1966.

"Finding the Real Self: A Letter—with a Foreword by Karen Horney." *American Journal of Psychoanalysis* 9 (1949): 3–7. This journal, founded by Horney, contains many essays devoted to the development of her theory.

Freeman, Nathan. "Concepts of Adler and Horney." *American Journal of Psychoanalysis* 10 (1950): 18–26.

Fromm, Erich. *The Anatomy of Human Destructiveness.* New York: Holt, Rinehart and Winston, 1973.

———. *The Art of Loving.* New York: Harper and Row, 1956.

———. *The Dogma of Christ and Other Essays on Religion, Psychology, and Culture.* New York: Holt, Rinehart and Winston, 1963.

———. *Escape from Freedom.* New York: Farrar and Rinehart, 1941.

———. *The Forgotten Language: An Introduction to the Understanding of Dreams, Fairy Tales, and Myths.* New York: Rinehart and Winston, 1951.

———. *The Heart of Man, Its Genius for Good and Evil.* New York: Harper and Row, 1964.

———. *Man for Himself: An Inquiry into the Psychology of Ethics.* New York: Rinehart, 1947.

———. *Psychoanalysis and Religion.* New Haven: Yale University Press, 1950.

———. *The Sane Society.* New York: Holt, Rinehart and Winston, 1955.

———. *To Have or to Be?* New York: Harper and Row, 1976.

———. *You Shall Be as Gods: A Radical Interpretation of the Old Testament and Its Tradition.* New York: Holt, Rinehart and Winston, 1966.

Fromm, Erich, and Ramon Xirau, eds. *The Nature of Man.* New York: Macmillan, 1968.

Garrison, Dee. "Karen Horney and Feminism." *Signs: Journal of Women in Culture and Society* 6 (1981): 672–91.

Goble, Frank G. *The Third Force: The Psychology of Abraham Maslow.* New York: Grossman, 1970.

Goldstein, Kurt. *Human Nature in the Light of Psychopathology.* Cambridge: Harvard University Press, 1940.

———. *The Organism: A Holistic Approach to Biology Derived from Pathological Data in Man.* New York: American Book Co., 1939.

Goodman, Paul. "On a Writer's Block." In *Nature Heals: The Psychological Essays of Paul Goodman*, edited by Taylor Stoehr, pp. 193–201. New York: Free Life Editions, 1977.

———. "The Psychological Revolution and the Writer's Life-View." In *Nature Heals: The Psychological Essays of Paul Goodman*, edited by Taylor Stoehr, pp. 170–78. New York: Free Life Editions, 1977.

Horney, Karen. *Feminine Psychology.* Edited by Harold Kelman. New York: Norton, 1967.

———. *Neurosis and Human Growth: The Struggle Toward Self-Realization.* New York: Norton, 1950.

———. *The Neurotic Personality of Our Time.* New York: Norton, 1937.

———. *New Ways in Psychoanalysis.* New York: Norton, 1939.

———. "On Feeling Abused." *American Journal of Psychoanalysis* 11 (1951): 5–12. (Reprinted in Kelman, 1964, pp. 29–46, and in Rubins, 1972, pp. 81–88.)

———. *Our Inner Conflicts: A Constructive Theory of Neurosis.* New York: Norton, 1945.

———. "The Paucity of Inner Experiences." *American Journal of Psychoanalysis* 12 (1952): 3–9. (Reprinted in Kelman, 1964, pp. 47–64, and in Rubins, 1972, pp. 97–103.)

———. *Self-Analysis.* New York: Norton, 1942.

———. "The Value of Vindictiveness." *American Journal of Psychoanalysis* 8 (1948): 3–12. (Reprinted in Kelman, 1965, pp. 27–51.)

———, ed. *Are You Considering Psychoanalysis?* New York: Norton, 1946.

Kelman, Harold. *Helping People: Karen Horney's Psychoanalytic Approach.* New York: Science House, 1971.

———, ed. *Advances in Psychoanalysis: Contributions to Karen Horney's Holistic Approach.* New York: Norton, 1964.

———, ed. *New Perspectives in Psychoanalysis: Contributions to Karen Horney's Holistic Approach.* New York: Norton, 1965.

Keyishian, Harry. "Karen Horney on 'The Value of Vindictiveness.'" *American Journal of Psychoanalysis* 42 (1982): 21–26.

Laing, R. D. *The Divided Self: An Existential Study in Sanity and Madness.* Baltimore: Penguin, 1965.

———. *The Politics of Experience.* New York: Pantheon, 1967.

———. *Self and Others.* 2d ed. Baltimore: Penguin, 1971.

———. *The Voice of Experience.* New York: Pantheon, 1982.

Leary, Timothy. *Interpersonal Diagnosis of Personality: A Functional Theory and Methodology for Personality Evaluation.* New York: Ronald Press, 1957.

Maddi, Salvatore R., and Paul T. Costa. *Humanism in Personology: Allport, Maslow, and Murray.* Chicago: Aldine-Atherton, 1972.

Maslow, Abraham H. *The Farther Reaches of Human Nature.* New York: Viking, 1971.

———. *Motivation and Personality.* 2d ed. New York: Harper and Row, 1970.

———. *The Psychology of Science: A Reconaissance.* New York: Harper and Row, 1966.

———. *Religions, Values, and Peak Experiences.* Columbus: Ohio State University Press, 1964.

———. *Toward a Psychology of Being.* 2d ed. New York: Van Nostrand, 1968.

———, ed. *New Knowledge in Human Values.* New York: Harper and Row, 1959.

Oates, Joyce Carol. "The Potential of Normality." Review of *The Farther Reaches of Human Nature,* by Abraham H. Maslow. *Saturday Review,* 26 August 1972, p. 53–55.

O'Connell, Agnes N. "Karen Horney: Theorist in Psychoanalytic and Feminine Psychology." *Psychology of Women Quarterly* 5, no. 1 (1980): 81–93.

Perls, Frederick S. "Four Lectures." In *Gestalt Therapy Now: Theory, Techniques, Applications,* edited by Joen Fagan and Irma Lee Shepherd, pp. 14–38. Palo Alto, Calif.: Science and Behavior Books, 1970.

———. *The Gestalt Approach and Eye Witness to Therapy.* Ben Lomond, Calif.: Science and Behavior Books, 1973.

———. *Gestalt Therapy Verbatim.* Edited by John O. Stevens. Lafayette, Calif.: Real People Press, 1969.

———, Ralph F. Hefferline, and Paul Goodman. "Verbalizing and Poetry." In *Gestalt Therapy: Excitement and Growth in the Human Personality,* pp. 320–32. New York: Julian Press, 1951.

Regelski, Thomas A. "Self-Actualization in Creating and Responding to Art." *Journal of Humanistic Psychology* 13, no. 4 (Fall 1973): 57–68.

Rogers, Carl R. *On Becoming a Person: A Therapist's View of Psychotherapy.* Boston: Houghton Mifflin, 1961.

———. "A Theory of Personality." In *Theories of Psychopathology and Personality,* 2d ed., edited by Theodore Millon, pp. 217–23. Philadelphia: W. B. Saunders, 1973.

Rubins, Jack L. "Karen Horney: A Complete Bibliography." In *Developments in Horney Psychoanalysis, 1950 . . . . . 1970,* edited by Jack L. Rubins, pp. 42–45. Huntington, N.Y.: R. E. Krieger, 1972.

———. *Karen Horney: Gentle Rebel of Psychoanalysis.* New York: Dial, 1978.

———, ed. *Developments in Horney Psychoanalysis, 1950 . . . . . 1970.* Huntington, N.Y.: R. E. Krieger, 1972.

Schaar, John. *Escape from Authority: The Perspectives of Erich Fromm.* New York: Basic Books, 1961.

Schachtel, Ernest G. *Metamorphosis: On the Development of Affect, Perception, Attention, and Memory.* New York: Basic Books, 1959.

———. "On Alienated Concepts of Identity." *Journal of Humanistic Psychology* 1, no. 1 (Spring 1961): 110–21.

———. "On Creative Experience." *Journal of Humanistic Psychology* 11, no. 1 (Spring 1971): 26–39.

Sedgwick, Peter. "R. D. Laing: Self, Symptom and Society." In *R. D. Laing and Anti-Psychiatry,* edited by Robert Boyers, pp. 1–50. New York: Octagon, 1974.

Wachtel, Paul L. "Reconsideration: Karen Horney's Ironic Vision." *The New Republic,* 6 January 1979, pp. 25–28.

Wilson, Colin. *New Pathways in Psychology: Maslow and the Post-Freudian Revolution.* New York: Taplinger, 1972.

APPLICATIONS

Breitbart, Sara. "'Hedda Gabler': A Critical Analysis." *American Journal of Psychoanalysis* 8 (1948): 55–58. [Horney]

Butery, Karen Ann. "The Contributions of Horneyan Psychology to the Study of Literature." *American Journal of Psychoanalysis* 42 (1982): 39–50.

———. "The Victorian Heroine: A Psychological Study." Ph.d. diss., Michigan State University, 1980. [Horney]

Curtis, Jane Elizabeth. "Muriel Rukeyser: The Woman Writer Confronts Traditional Mythology and Psychology." Ph.D. diss., University of Wisconsin, Madison, 1981. [Horney]

Eldredge, Patricia Reid. "Karen Horney and *Clarissa:* The Tragedy of Neurotic Pride." *American Journal of Psychoanalysis* 42 (1982): 51–59.

———. "Samuel Richardson's *Clarissa:* A Psychological Study." Ph.d. diss., Michigan State University, 1983. [Guntrip, Horney, Laing, Maslow, Schachtel]

Falk, Doris V. *Eugene O'Neill and the Tragic Tension: An Interpretive Study of the Plays.* New Brunswick, N.J.: Rutgers University Press, 1958. [Horney]

Girgus, Sam B. *The Law of the Heart: Individualism and the Modern Self in American Literature.* Austin: University of Texas Press, 1979. [Laing]

———. "Poe and R. D. Laing: The Transcendent Self." *Studies in Short Fiction* 13 (1976): 299–309.

———. "R. D. Laing and Literature: Readings of Poe, Hawthorne, and Kate Chopin." In *Psychological Perspectives on Literature: Freudian Dissidents and Non-Freudians, A Casebook,* edited by Joseph Natoli, pp. 181–97. Hamden, Conn.: Archon, 1984.

Graeber, George. "Comic, Thematic, and Mimetic Impulses in Jane Austen's *Persuasion.*" Ph.D. diss., Michigan State University, 1977. [Horney]

Greene, Donald. "The Sin of Pride: A Sketch for a Literary Exploration." *New Mexico Quarterly* 34 (1964): 8–30. [Fromm, Horney]

Haselswerdt, Marjorie Burton. "On Their Hind Legs Casting Shadows: A Psychological Approach to Character in Faulkner." Ph.D. diss., Michigan State University, 1981. [Horney, Maslow]

Herring, Henry D. "Madness in *At Heaven's Gate:* A Metaphor of the Self in Warren's Fiction." *Four Quarters* 21, no. 4 (1972): 56–66. [Laing]

———. "The Self and Madness in Marlowe's *Edward II* and Webster's *The Duchess of Malfi.*" *Journal of Medieval and Renaissance Studies* 9 (1979): 307–23. [Laing]

Hirsch, H. N. *The Enigma of Felix Frankfurter.* New York: Basic Books, 1981. [Horney]

Huffman, James R. "A Psychological Critique of American Culture." *American Journal of Psychoanalysis* 42 (1982): 27–37. [Horney]

Knapp, John V. "The Double Life of George Bowling." *Review of Existential Psychology and Psychiatry* 14 (1976): 109–25. [Laing]

Paris, Bernard J. "Bargains with Fate: A Psychological Approach to Shakespeare's Major Tragedies." *The Aligarh Journal of English Studies* 5 (1980): 144–61. [Horney]

———. "Bargains with Fate: The Case of Macbeth." *American Journal of Psychoanalysis* 42 (1982): 7–20. [Horney]

———. *Character and Conflict in Jane Austen's Novels: A Psychological Approach.* Detroit: Wayne State University Press, 1978; Brighton: Harvester Press, 1979. [Horney, Maslow, Schachtel]

———. "Experiences of Thomas Hardy." In *The Victorian Experience: The Novelists,* edited by Richard A. Levine, pp. 203–37. Athens: Ohio University Press, 1976. [Horney]

———. "Hamlet and His Problems: A Horneyan Analysis." *The Centennial Review* 21 (1977): 36–66.

———. "Horney's Theory and the Study of Literature." *American Journal of Psychoanalysis* 38 (1978): 343–53. [*A Doll's House*]

———. " 'Hush, hush! He's a human being': A Psychological Approach to Heathcliff." *Women and Literature,* n.s., 2 (1982): 101–17. [Horney, Laing]

———. "The Inner Conflicts of *Measure for Measure.*" *The Centennial Review* 25 (1981): 266–76. [Horney]

———. *A Psychological Approach to Fiction: Studies in Thackeray, Stendhal, George Eliot, Dostoevsky, and Conrad.* Bloomington: Indiana University Press, 1974. [Horney, Maslow]

———. "Richard III: Shakespeare's First Great Mimetic Character." *The Aligarh Journal of English Studies* 8 (1983): 40–67. [Horney]

———. "Third Force Psychology and the Study of Literature." In *Psychological Perspectives on Literature: Freudian Dissidents and Non-Freudians, A Casebook,* edited by Joseph Natoli, pp. 155–80. Hamden, Conn.: Archon, 1984. [Horney]

———. "The Two Selves of Rodion Raskolnikov." *Gradiva, A Journal of Contemporary Theory and Practice* 1 (1978): 316–28; garbled text on p. 320 corrected in 2 (1979): i–ii. [Horney]

Portnoy, I. " 'The Magic Skin': A Psychoanalytic Interpretation." *American Journal of Psychoanalysis* 9 (1949): 67–74. [Horney]

Rabkin, Leslie Y., and Jeffrey Brown. "Some Monster in His Thought: Sadism and Tragedy in *Othello.*" *Literature and Psychology* 23 (1973): 59–67. [Horney]

Rendon, Mario. "Horney Theory and Literature: A Symposium: Introduction." *American Journal of Psychoanalysis* 42 (1982): 3–5.

———. "Psychoanalysis and Literary Criticism." *The Literary Review* 24 (1981): 178, 180. [Horney]

Rosenberg, Marvin. "In Defense of Iago." In *The Masks of* Othello: *The Search for the Identity of Othello, Iago, and Desdemona by Three Centuries of Actors and Critics,* pp. 166–84. Berkeley: University of California Press, 1961. [Horney]

Rusch, Frederik L. "Approaching Literature Through the Social Psychology of Erich Fromm." In *Psychological Perspectives on Literature: Freudian Dissidents and Non-Freudians, A Casebook,* edited by Joseph Natoli, pp. 79–99. Hamden, Conn.: Archon, 1984.

———. "Marble Men and Maidens, The Necrophilous People of F. Scott Fitzgerald: A Psychoanalytic Approach in Terms of Erich Fromm." *Journal of Evolutionary Psychology III* 1–2 (1982): 28–40.

Showalter, Elaine. "R. D. Laing and the Sixties." *Raritan* 1, no. 2 (1981): 107–27.

Tharaud, Barry. "Dickens and Maslow: The Case History of *Oliver Twist.*" *Journal of Humanistic Psychology* 22, no. 3 (Summer 1982): 68–82.

Thomson, David T., Jr. "Pip: The Divided Self." *Psychocultural Review* 1 (1977), 49–67. [Laing]

Tuch, Ronald. "The Dismantled Self in the Fiction of Nathanael West." *Psychocultural Review* 1 (1977): 43–48. [Laing]

Tucker, Robert C. "The Georges' Wilson Reexamined: An Essay on Psychobiography." *The American Political Science Review* 71 (1977): 606–18. [Horney]

———. "Memoir of a Stalin Biographer." *Princeton Alumni Weekly,* 3 November 1982, pp. 21–26, 31. [Horney]

———. *Stalin as Revolutionary, 1879–1929: A Study in History and Personality.* New York: Norton, 1973. [Horney]

Van Bark, Bella S. "The Alienated Person in Literature." *American Journal of Psychoanalysis* 21 (1961): 183–97. [Horney]

———. " 'The Sudden Guest': A Critical Analysis." *American Journal of Psychoanalysis* 8 (1948): 59–62. [Fromm, Horney]

Vlastos, Marion. "Doris Lessing and R. D. Laing: Psychopolitics and Prophecy." *PMLA* 91 (1976): 245–58.

Vollmerhausen, Joseph W. " 'Pavilion of Women': A Psychoanalytic Interpretation." *American Journal of Psychoanalysis* 10 (1950): 53–60. [Horney]

Yalom, Irvin D., and Marilyn Yalom. "Ernest Hemingway—A Psychiatric View." *Archives of General Psychiatry* 24 (1971): 485–94. [Horney]

Notes on Contributors

ROBERT DE BEAUGRANDE is professor of English at the University of Florida. He has published numerous books and essays. His major works include *Text, Discourse, and Process* (1980); *Introduction to Text Linguistics*, with Wolfgang Dressler (1981); and *Text Production* (1984). He is currently completing a volume entitled *Critical Discourse: A Survey of Literary Theory.*

KAREN A. BUTERY has taught at Michigan State University, Oakland University, and California State University. Her dissertation, *The Victorian Heroine*, uses Horneyan psychology to provide reinterpretations of four major novels. She is currently designing and marketing training programs for Sony Corporation in New York City.

PATRICIA R. ELDREDGE is affiliated scholar at Earlham College and teaches at Earlham and Indiana University East. She is working on a book-length psychological study of Richardson's *Clarissa* (see *American Journal of Psychoanalysis* 42 [1982]).

NORMAN FRIEDMAN is professor of English at Queens College and the Graduate Center, City University of New York. He has published three books on e. e. cummings, a book on theory of fiction, a book of poems, and numerous articles and reviews. He is a certified social worker with a private practice in Gestalt therapy. He is interested in the relations between psychology and literature and is presently at work on a book analyzing experimental lyric forms in Victorian poetry.

ANDREW GORDON is associate professor of English at the University of Florida and associate director of the Institute for Psychological Study of the Arts. He has published many essays and is the author of *An American Dreamer: A Psychoanalytic Study of the Fiction of Norman Mailer* (1980). He is currently at work on a study of the fiction of Saul Bellow.

MARJORIE B. HASELSWERDT has taught at Michigan State University and at Canisius College. Her dissertation, *On Their Hind Legs Casting Shadows*, applies Third Force psychology to four Faulkner novels.

JAMES R. HUFFMAN is professor of English and coordinator of American studies at the State University of New York College at Fredonia. He has published many essays and is currently working on a book to be entitled *In Sickness and in Health: A Psychological Approach to American Culture.*

CATHERINE R. LEWIS has taught at the University of Kentucky, St. Catharine College (Kentucky), and the University of Louisville and is a doctoral candidate at the University of Florida. Her dissertation will apply Third Force psychology to selected poems of Robert Browning.

MARIE NELSON is associate professor of English at the University of Florida. She has published essays on Old and Middle English poetry and on Arthurian fiction. Her current interest is aggression in literature.

BERNARD J. PARIS is professor of English at the University of Florida and director of the Institute for Psychological Study of the Arts. He has published numerous essays, a book on George Eliot, and two books (*A Psychological Approach to Fiction* and *Character and Conflict in Jane Austen's Novels*) that employ Third Force psychology in the study of literature. He is currently at work on a book to be entitled *Bargains with Fate: A Psychological Approach to Shakespeare.*

BARBARA M. SMALLEY is associate professor of English at the University of Illinois. She has published *George Eliot and Flaubert: Pioneers of the Modern Novel* and an edition of George Henry Lewes's *Ranthorpe.* She is currently working on a book-length study of four works of fiction in relation to Third Force psychology.

JOE STRAUB has published short stories, reviews, and newspaper articles and is an editor of *Sundog,* a literary magazine published by Florida State University, where he is finishing a Ph.D. and a novel. He was raised in the Roman Catholic Church and greatly admires Graham Greene's novels.

Index